A Throw of the Dice

Also by Gordan Millan

Pierre Louÿe ou le culte de l'amitié (1979)

A Throw of the Dice
The Life of Stéphane Mallarmé

GORDON MILLAN

FARRAR STRAUS GIROUX
NEW YORK

Library of Congress Cataloging-in-Publication Data
Millan, Gordon.
A Throw of the Dice: The Life of Stéphane Mallarmé/Gordon
Millan.
    p.   cm.
Includes bibliographical references and index.
ISBN 0–374–27707–9
1. Mallarmé. Stéphane, 1842–1898—Bibliography.   2. Poets.
French—19th century—Biography.   I. Title.
PQ2344.Z5M49   1994
841.8—dc20

For Anne Adams

Contents

Illustrations

1. Stéphane Mallarmé at the age of twenty (Bibliothèque Littéraire Jacques Doucet, Paris)
2. André Desmolins, the poet's grandfather (private collection)
3. Anne Mallarmé, the poet's stepmother (private collection)
4. Numa Mallarmé, the poet's father, a year before his death (private collection)
5. Emmanuel Des Essarts (by kind permission of Mme Jean Paysant)
6. Henri Cazalis (by kind permission of Mme Jean Paysant)
7. Marie Mallarmé during the time she and Stéphane lived in Avignon (by kind permission of Mme Jean Paysant)
8. Contemporary photograph of Mallarmé's summer house in Valvins (Musée départementale Stéphane Mallarmé, Vulaines-sur-Seine)
9. The bridge over the Seine at Valvins photographed by Mallarmé's landlord, Abel Houdry (by kind permission of Mme Jean Paysant)
10. Mallarmé on his boat at Valvins (by kind permission of Mme Jean Paysant)
11. Drawing of Mallarmé and a raven by Paul Gauguin, 1891 (Roger-Viollet, Paris)
12. Mallarmé's study at Valvins, decorated by himself in the Japanese style (Roger-Viollet, Paris)
13. Méry Laurent photographed by Nadar and a quatrain

addressed to her by Mallarmé on New Year's Day 1896 (by kind permission of André Rodocanachi)

14. Mallarmé in the garden at Valvins with his wife and daughter and one of their friends, Mme Normant (private collection)

15. Mallarmée *c.* 1890 standing in front of his portrait by Manet in the tiny dining-room of his flat in the rue de Rome (Bibliothèque Nationale, Paris)

16. Mallarmé and Auguste Renoir in the home of Berthe Morisot some time in the early 1890s (Bibliothèque Nationale, Paris)

17. Early draft of the preface written to accompany the publication of *Un coup de dés* in *Cosmopolis* (private collection)

18. Mallarmé towards the end of his life (Roger-Viollet, Paris)

Introduction and Acknowledgements

Stéphane Mallarmé died suddenly and unexpectedly in 1898 at the age of fifty-six. Outside the literary and artistic circles of Paris many of his countrymen had never heard of him, and few had ever read a line of his poetry. For them, his name was inevitably associated with the much derided Symbolist school of poets. It conjured up the image of a dry, bloodless aesthete, a deliberately obscure and impenetrable writer. Yet for a small but steadily growing number of loyal admirers and followers, many of whom had found their way to the regular Tuesday evening gatherings held over the previous twenty years in his modest flat in the Batignolles district of Paris, he had already become a revered and respected figure.

In one respect, little has changed during the century or so since Mallarmé's death. Most people today, including well educated and cultivated Frenchmen, still regard him as the epitome of the obscure and unnecessarily difficult writer. On the other hand, the gradual revelation of his fascinating but incomplete posthumous works, recent trends in critical and literary theory which place a new emphasis on the linguistic nature of human awareness and behaviour and, above all, the exceptional interest shown in his work during the past few decades by influential French critics such as Barthes, Derrida and Kristeva have combined to place Mallarmé at the very centre of the current debate on the nature and function of literature. As a result, his reputation has continued to grow and his pre-eminence is no longer disputed. In his 1984 preface to the re-edition of his collected essays, *Language and Silence*, George Steiner names Mallarmé, along with Joyce, Kafka, Beckett and Borges, as one of the 'master-builders of Modern literature'.

The status which Mallarmé now generally enjoys has been achieved at a price, however. Whilst it is undeniable that Kristeva, Derrida, Barthes and others have brought fresh insights to bear upon parts of Mallarmé's work, their studies have tended to be selective, and not always free of polemic and political bias. There are hazards in such a partisan and narrow approach. By tending to concentrate upon those aspects of its subject's work which are of relevance to the critic's own theories, it has led to several unfortunate and serious distortions. Attention has shifted away from Mallarmé's poetry to focus almost exclusively upon his theoretical writings, his great experimental work *Un coup de dés* and the unfinished project *Igitur*. This excessive emphasis upon the unfinished works, or at any rate on those which he himself felt unable to publish, has in turn meant that in most people's minds Mallarmé is now clearly identified with the notion of failure. Lastly, and most seriously, the man himself has been all but forgotten, eclipsed and overshadowed by his writings. Anyone reading recent Mallarmé criticism could be forgiven for wondering whether he ever had a life.

The main purpose of this book is to correct such distortions by treating Mallarmé's life and work as an organic whole. It is written in the firmly held if nowadays unfashionable belief that a better understanding of an artist's life can lead to a deeper appreciation of his work. It seeks therefore to remind the reader of the human being who existed behind the works themselves and the various myths and legends which Mallarmé allowed to grow up, and sometimes fostered, around himself. It constantly places the life and the work in their mutually illuminating contexts. It examines Mallarmé's relationships with his family and friends, many of whom were the most important writers, musicians, artists and critics of his or any epoch. Above all, it endeavours to illustrate what Mallarmé's real intentions were and to explain how and why, for the better part of twenty years, this small, kindly, unflamboyant man came to occupy such a central position in the literary and artistic life of Paris during one of the most exciting and important periods in its cultural history.

Given the incredibly wide range of Mallarmé's interests and acquaintances this undertaking has proved a time-consuming business. Over the years I have contracted many debts to as many people. All scholars owe an immense obligation to Henri Mondor, Mallarmé's first biographer, who in the 1930s rescued many of his manuscripts from obscurity and oblivion. His numerous books and his manuscript collection, now housed in the Bibliothèque Littéraire Jacques Doucet in Paris, remain an indispensable and rewarding starting-point for any serious biographer. What I owe to the edition of Mallarmé's correspondence now completed and published in eleven volumes by Lloyd James Austin will become only too apparent from the frequent references to that monumental work in the body of the text. Readers will find almost as many references to the *Documents Stéphane Mallarmé* published by my late mentor and friend Carl Paul Barbier. I am particularly grateful to him for having first introduced me to the poetry of Mallarmé when I was an undergraduate of his many years ago.

Other Mallarmé scholars, either through their books or through helpful discussions, have been of great assistance. I would particularly like to single out the works of Robert G. Cohn, whose books I have always found most stimulating, and those of Gardner Davies, who has paid me the compliment of becoming a personal friend. Mallarmé's early years have been exhaustively researched and analysed in exemplary fashion by the late Austin Gill. The difficulty of his poetry has at last been tackled, with consummate skill, by Malcolm Bowie in what must remain one of the most significant contributions to Mallarmé studies for years to come.

Much of the manuscript material which I have used is to be found in the various collections of the Bibliothèque Littéraire Jacques Doucet. I would like to express my thanks to François Chapon and Nicole Prévot and Jacqueline Zacchi of that establishment. At the Bibliothèque Nationale, Florence de Lussy has always been extremely helpful. I would also like to thank Marie-Anne Sarda of the Musée Départemental Stéphane Mallarmé for her kind assistance.

Many other documents still remain in private hands. I would therefore like to express my gratitude to the following scholars, librarians, collectors and friends, some unfortunately no longer with us, but all of whom have made important contributions to the pages which follow: Pierre Bérès, Robert Blacklock, Louis Clayeux, Gardner Davies, Sheelagh Graham, Tetsuo Ihara, John Keiger, Bernard and Marc Loliée, Bernard Malle, Paul Morel, Jacqueline Paysant, Jean Prinet, André Rodocanachi, Dieter Schwartz, Colonel Daniel Sicklès, Agathe-Rouart Valéry. Others, who prefer to remain anonymous, have also been of invaluable help.

I would particularly like to take this opportunity of thanking Marie Barbier, who over the past few years has unfailingly made available to me the enormous amount of documentation accumulated during a lifetime's research by her late husband, Carl Barbier. Finally, and most importantly of all, I am delighted to be able to acknowledge publicly the constant help and encouragement which I have received from my wife Anne and my two children David and Bryony who, for more years than I care to remember, have put up with what, at times, must have seemed to be a rather irascible husband and a harassed and distracted father. Without their help and cooperation this book would never have been completed.

Gordon Millan

Edinburgh, 1 September 1992

★

Author's Note   In order to make the text of this book accessible to as wide an audience as possible the poems of Mallarmé are printed in French but are followed by a fairly literal translation in English. For the same reason, letters and other documents in the body of the text are given in English. The French originals are referenced in the appropriate footnotes. All translations are the work of the present author.

The text of Mallarmé's poems quoted in this work is that of the new popular French edition of his *Poésies* published by NRF Gallimard in 1992, edited by Bertrand Marchal.

Beginnings

Where and when does a destiny begin? How far do we hark back in the history of an individual to understand the intricate interplay of forces which determines and shapes it? What possible connection, for example, exists between the poet Stéphane Mallarmé and someone as apparently remote as François René Auguste Mallarmé, a great-great uncle on his father's side, a particularly bloodthirsty and zealous supporter of the Revolution? What part did he play, compared with those of the poet's more immediate family, his parents and grandparents, a maiden aunt, a sister?

For Stéphane Mallarmé's contemporaries these questions remained not only unanswered but largely unasked. With the exception of the great-great uncle (who until Stéphane himself was the only Mallarmé to achieve anything approaching notoriety), little was known about the family background of this most convivial and gregarious and yet most private and discreet of men. The only public account he gave of himself, in a celebrated letter to Paul Verlaine which the latter went on to use in the first recorded attempt at a biographical portrait, not only failed to address any of these issues but actively sought to obscure them. The following passage is typical of the whole letter:

> As a child of seven I lost my mother and was initially brought up by a doting grandmother. Then I drifted through many a boarding-school and lycée, a romantic Lamartinian soul who secretly wanted

to replace the poet Béranger one day because I had met him at the house of a friend. Apparently all that was far too complicated a dream to be realized, but I spent a lot of time trying to do so in countless little notebooks which were always confiscated, if I remember correctly.[1]

There are some elements of truth in this deceptively casual account of Mallarmé's destiny. Written when he was in his mid-forties and anxious not only to shape the image that posterity would retain of him, but to rewrite and enhance his relationship with his grandmother, these lines, with their not too subtle hint at the possibility of a faulty memory, are a poorly disguised attempt to formulate and perpetuate the romantic myth of the lonely, misunderstood yet predestined poet that Mallarmé felt he had by then become. He was deliberately creating a myth which was to go unchallenged in his lifetime and, for the most part, ever since.

In the past few years, however, mainly thanks to the twin pioneering efforts of Carl Barbier and Austin Gill,[2] a more accurate, if at times patchy, documentary account of Mallarmé's childhood and youth has gradually emerged. The young Mallarmé remains at times a shadowy figure, but he is all the more fascinating for that.

Stéphane, or more exactly Etienne Mallarmé (as his birth certificate named him) was born around seven o'clock on the morning of Friday, 18 March 1842. His birthplace was the second *arrondissement* of Paris, at number 12 rue de la Ferrière, which his parents had shared with his grandparents since their marriage the previous June. Although born in Paris, Mallarmé did not, as he later liked to claim he did, come from Parisian stock. On his father's side his family was decidedly provincial and solidly middle-class. Up to the time of the Revolution, the Mallarmés had been lawyers with successful practices in and around Nancy, the capital of Lorraine. François René Mallarmé (Stéphane's great-great uncle) had been one of the few to break with the family tradition, abandoning the law for politics to become first an agent of the Revolution and later an official under Napoleon.

A more traditional and conservative path had subsequently been chosen by Stéphane's grandfather François Auguste Alexandre Mallarmé, who regained for the family a safe middle-class respectability by following a career in the Registry and Domains (a branch of the civil service set up during the Revolution as a part of the Ministry of Finance). Indeed, François Auguste Alexandre's desire for respectability took him even further. First, he married Anne Posson, the divorced wife of an émigré, thus tenuously linking the family with the aristocracy through the two daughters Herminie and Adèle whom he inherited from his wife's previous marriage. Second, of the six sons he had with Anne, five joined the army and went on to pursue successful careers. One of them (Henry Victor) spent most of his career in Algeria and ended up inspector-general of administration attached to the Governor; another (Martial) became a major; yet another (Jules) was promoted for gallantry and rose to the rank of camp commandant; another (Emile) studied at the Ecole Polytechnique and reached the rank of colonel in the artillery.

Of François Auguste's sons only one followed him into the Registry and Domains. This was Numa, Stéphane's father. It was sometime in 1840, when he was thirty-four years old, that Numa Mallarmé's career brought him from the Chartres to the Paris office of the Registry, where he met and married the only daughter of one of his new superiors, André Desmolins.

If, on Stéphane's father's side, the family was decidedly respectable, his mother's side rivalled or outdid their social status. Here the menfolk had been in the Registry and Domains from its very beginnings at the time of the Revolution. Under the ancien régime Stéphane's maternal great-grandfather Blaise Magnien had been *vérificateur des domaines du roi*. His daughter Louise Etienne Magnien (whose middle name Stéphane was to share and whose life was to be intricately involved with his) had married an ambitious young man. André Desmolins was born in 1789 into a family of highly placed civil servants. Curiously enough, he too had begun as a soldier. He was wounded in Madrid in 1808, then joined the Hussars and saw distinguished service in the Spanish campaign of 1811–14 before leaving the army in 1816 and starting a second career in the Registry. After some years in various minor posts in the provinces, André and his wife returned to settle permanently in Paris in 1825. From that date on, his career was a steady rise. Their only child, Elizabeth Félicie, was twenty-three years old when she gave birth to her first-born, Stéphane.

Clearly then, Stéphane Mallarmé was born into a comfortable, indeed affluent middle-class family. His birth certificate makes impressive reading. The witnesses to the event were his maternal grandfather André Desmolins and his paternal uncle Jules Charles Mallarmé, a lieutenant in the Municipal Guard. Both were already holders of that coveted badge of respectability and success, the *légion d'honneur*. It is not difficult to see why, as he wryly put it later in a letter to Verlaine, our poet felt that from the outset he had been destined to a steady career in the civil service.[3]

Precious little information has survived about the first few years of Mallarmé's life. His parents appear to have continued to live with his grandparents until the birth of a second child, Maria, on 25 March 1844 forced Numa to think of a move. On 22 August that year, he bought a property with a garden in the Hameau de Boulainvilliers in Passy, just outside Paris. The address given in the bill of sale is 44 rue du Ranelagh, which places it just a few doors away from Numa's aristocratic half-sister Herminie, who lived at number 38. The Mallarmés appear to have moved there some time after October 1845, although the exact date remains uncertain.[4]

The family had not been long in Passy when, at the beginning of August 1847, shortly after her return from a trip to Italy, Elizabeth Mallarmé suddenly and rather mysteriously died. The circumstances of the trip are not entirely clear, but an extant letter from Stéphane's grandmother to her daughter suggests that the journey to Rome had been undertaken as a pilgrimage rather than a holiday. Perhaps it was a desperate attempt to prevent the inevitable. In her letter Madame Desmolins addresses Numa and her daughter as 'my poor dear exiled ones!',[5] from which we may surmise that they had not exactly chosen to be there. Another letter makes it clear that a major event during the trip had been a visit to the Vatican where the Pope had been able to bless a cross held in Elizabeth's hands.[6]

What killed Stéphane's mother? Henri Mondor, his earliest biographer and himself a doctor, confesses difficulty here. He says that family tradition had it that she died of the same disease that was to kill her daughter, namely rheumatoid arthritis linked to a weak heart.[7] Certainly, rheumatic conditions were to afflict several of Mallarmé's close family. He himself was a lifelong sufferer, and both his sister and his son Anatole were to die very young of rheumatic complaints. His grandmother Desmolins had a different view. A strait-laced woman, generally suspicious of any kind of nonconformity, she ascribed her daughter's death to her highly strung nature. Years later, writing to her cousin and confidante Mélanie Laurent to announce the birth of Mallarmé's first child Geneviève (who happened to be born on her own dead daughter's Saint's Day, Saint Elizabeth's day), she felt constrained to add a note of caution: 'I just hope the dear little creature inherits the good qualities of her unfortunate ancestor but not that vivid imagination which so undermined her constitution.'[8]

Clearly, Mme Desmolins is expressing a moral, not a medical judgement. A more relevant if tantalizingly ambiguous clue to her daughter's death is provided in another letter written to her grandson some years later. Referring on this occasion to the terrible suffering of a great niece, she pointedly reminds Mallarmé of his mother's frequent and excessive bouts of coughing: 'It is pitiful to constantly hear . . . that terrible cough which reminds me so much of your mother's . . . will she last to the end of the year?'[9] This remark would lend credence to another theory which suggests that Stéphane's mother's death was due to tuberculosis.[10]

What killed Elizabeth Mallarmé at the early age of twenty-eight will probably remain an open question. There is no doubting, however, that her untimely departure had a powerful impact on the destiny of her young children.

A measure of caution is required here. We need to distrust the temptation (which too many critics have found irresistible) of exaggerating the personal impact of his mother's death upon the young Mallarmé. For some, this loss, soon to be followed by his sister Maria's, marks the beginning of a morbid preoccupation with death and absence which has frequently been detected in Mallarmé's work. Clearly these themes exist, and must be dealt with, but we have to remember two things. First, Mallarmé was only five years old when his mother died: the whole event may have seemed somewhat remote to him. Second (and we shall return to this point when considering the death of his sister Maria), in the western Europe of the middle to late nineteenth century death at an early age was very much more commonplace than it is today. We must avoid the temptation of viewing such events with twentieth-century eyes and preconceptions.

Fortunately, we need not limit ourselves to idle speculation, for Mallarmé's own belated account of his reaction to his mother's death has survived. He confided it (some fifty years later) to one of his younger friends, Henri de Régnier, who had the good sense to record it in his diary. It makes interesting reading:

Mallarmé talked about his childhood reminiscences. He can see himself for the first time in 1847, his mother having died on returning from a trip to Italy. He was rather unaffected by her death because of his age and also because he had been put out to nurse. A few days after the event he was called into the drawing-room where his grandmother was entertaining a friend, and as the latter referred to the unfortunate event, the child, who felt embarrassed by his lack of grief which prevented him from reacting as was expected, decided to throw himself on a tiger-skin rug lying on the floor and tear at his long hair which kept getting into his eyes.[11]

Of course we must be careful not simply to swallow whole Mallarmé's own version of events which had occurred such a long time in the past, but this sober recollection squares with the facts as they are known. Further evidence to support the view that Elizabeth Mallarmé's death did not permanently scar the young boy's mind is somewhat ironically provided by his grandmother herself. In a letter to Stéphane of 6 July 1868, recalling the years they had all spent in Passy, she contrasts her own sad memories of the place (now irrevocably linked to the deaths of her daughter and granddaughter) with Stéphane's clearly happier ones as a young boy:

> Yes, my friend; my thoughts often return to those relatively happier times in Passy which stir your childhood memories. But my memories go further back, as far as Boulainvilliers, where two more or less happy seasons spent in family pleasures were followed by others that proved so cruel. What a fatal place to our happiness! I never think of it without real heart-ache, because that is where so much personal anguish came from, anguish which only your grandfather knew about and shared. But I realize that for you who were not aware of all these things, all these memories are pleasant ones.[12]

In fact, for Stéphane, the immediate consequences of his mother's death were of a practical rather than an emotional nature. A family council was held on 28 August, some three weeks later. André Desmolins was appointed subrogate guardian to Stéphane and Maria, to represent on his own and his wife's behalf the interests of their deceased daughter. The children's father Numa remained their legal guardian until they reached their majority, at which time they would inherit between them 20,500 francs from their mother's estate.

For a while it seems that Stéphane and Maria lived with their Desmolins grandparents, who moved to Passy (number 7 Grande rue), probably to be nearer Numa in Boulainvilliers. This cosy arrangement expired when a little more than a year later, on 27 October 1848, with what his former mother-in-law considered to be indecent haste, Numa married the nineteen-year-old daughter of a retired captain in the artillery. At that point the children went to live in their father's house in the rue du Ranelagh in Boulainvilliers.

This new arrangement did not last long. Perhaps the permanent presence of two stepchildren proved too great a dampener on the newly-weds. For whatever reasons, it was soon decided that Maria would live with the Desmolins, staying occasionally at Boulainvilliers, while Stéphane would remain with his father and stepmother but spend the odd weekend or holiday with his grandparents.

So it was at this sensitive and formative point in Mallarmé's life that a key figure, his maternal grandmother, entered the scene. She was to remain ever present in his mind until her death in 1869, and even managed to exert influence from well beyond the grave. Louise Etienne Desmolins (or Fanny as she liked to be known to her intimates, who significantly never really included her grandson, Stéphane) was an exceedingly complex woman who found herself in a very difficult situation. There remains little direct evidence of how she and Stéphane actually got on when he was a child but, if the letters she later wrote to him about his own child Geneviève are anything to go by, her attitude towards children in general was clear enough. She was a woman of quite definite and determined views: children should not be coddled; they must learn to be obedient; they should be seen and not heard, actively discouraged from being too vain or interesting or individual. (Later she fretted that Geneviève's independent and determined nature might have been inherited from what she saw as the 'basic flaw in the family character'.)

As well as being strict, Fanny Desmolins was also implacably and publicly devout – all the more so because she was married to a man who for most of his life did not share her religious fervour. Yet she was a good and sincere woman who took very seriously her responsibilities both to her family and to her God and did not delight in severity. She could chide Stéphane and his sister for meddling or tampering with things, or dawdling in front of shop windows, but she was clearly fond of them both and of Stéphane in particular. At the same time she wished to be liked. She realized she could be abrasive, and she also knew that she had an unattractive manner.[13] In fact, at heart (and certainly by her own lights) she was a caring grandmother who had been placed by harsh circumstances in an extremely awkward situation. She had 'inherited' responsibility for her dead daughter's children primarily because their rather selfish father was inconvenienced by them. That made it difficult for her to feel anything other than hostility towards the young woman who had usurped the place of her own dead daughter in her son-in-law's affections.

The suddenness of the second marriage had upset everyone: Fanny Desmolins herself, her husband André, and of course the children, Stéphane and Maria. A hint of the complex and conflicting pressures Fanny found herself subjected to is manifest in the following extract from a poignant letter she wrote to her young cousin Mélanie Laurent at the time of the birth of Stéphane's first half-sister:

> Since Wednesday morning, our little ones [Stéphane and Maria] have *a sister*. Yes indeed, a real sister, I must convince myself of that no matter how repugnant I find it to accept. Poor innocent little thing she is, belonging as she does to our family! Mr M[allarmé] is over the moon, I can see that. This is the fulfilment of his new life, a closer link with his new family. Seeing that he had no conscience about getting married again, he must have wanted a proof of his current affections, seeing that ours only served to remind him of a past he would rather forget. Here again I can understand his happiness, but it causes me pain to witness it and even greater pain to pretend I can

share in it or even feign an interest which does not exist in my heart. And then I have to encourage the children's affection for the new arrival which does not interest them. The first day, after her father left thinking he'd delighted her by talking about her new sister, Maria said to me: she's not my sister, she's my stepmother's daughter and my stepmother means nothing to me! And I had to explain to her that being her father's daughter, the child really was her sister and that she had to love her *as she does her brother*. That's my duty at the moment, Mélanie, I need God's help to accept it and to fulfil it without protest, no matter how cruel it all is for me![14]

Any reservations that Mme Desmolins may have had about her former son-in-law's new marriage soon became secondary to some other more pressing considerations. Decisions must be taken about Stéphane and Maria's education. It was agreed that Maria's schooling was to remain largely the responsibility of her grandparents. She was to be educated first in their home, later at a convent school. It seems that Stéphane was to stay with his father and stepmother, attending a local day-school, but spending his free Thursdays with his grandmother.

The arrival of a half-sister (the first of three) soon brought that arrangement to an end. Numa's house in the rue du Ranelagh was quite small, so at the end of September 1850 (one month before the birth of the new child) Stéphane, now aged eight and a half, was sent to a boarding-school selected largely, it would appear, on the advice of his father's half-sister, Herminie. She, like Fanny Desmolins, had a keen interest in the boy's education. Indeed, the decision to send Stéphane to this aristocratic establishment seems to have been the outcome of a family struggle. Numa and aunt Herminie quite understandably wanted to limit the Desmolins' influence, particularly in view of the fact that Stéphane's other grandmother had died in September 1849.[15]

That the decision to send Stéphane to this school seemed to suit his aunt Herminie much more than the Desmolins is clear from a letter Fanny Desmolins addressed in some pique to her cousin Mélanie Laurent on 24 September 1850. She was quite determined that in spite of the new arrangements, Stéphane would continue to see her:

> I'm sorry when I think you will no longer find our dear Stéphane here. The poor child is due to go to boarding-school next week. We've only one Thursday left to spend together. Although the poor little dear has been for some time reconciled to the idea and although I try to encourage him as best I can, pointing out only the advantages and the inevitability of this decision, his poor little heart is tearful at the prospect of no longer coming here as before. Even I have to take a good hold of myself not to follow his example. Even so, I intend using all his days off to see him as much as possible even if his father complains about the disruption. It seems to me that I am quite entitled to that at least, seeing that I am standing in for his poor mother. I've been granted a short reprieve. I rejoice in it and thank God, for this change will always come too soon for us, no matter how long it is delayed.[16]

The main excuse for sending Stéphane to this expensive boarding-school for young gentlemen had been to educate him in the social niceties that it was felt he sadly lacked. Letters from Fanny Desmolins to Mélanie Laurent provide some evidence that indeed there was an improvement on that score, although the experience of living away from home appears to have been less successful at first on the academic side. On the whole, then, whereas the two years Mallarmé spent at the school did him little harm, it would seem that the one who benefited most was his maiden aunt Herminie. She used it both as a means of limiting the Desmolins' influence over her nephew and as a convenient venue for gossiping with old aristocratic cronies with whom she had long since lost touch.[17]

Two years later, at the end of the summer term of 1852, despite signs of a modest if somewhat last-minute improvement in his scholastic prowess, Stéphane was transferred to a Jesuit college in Passy. This boarding-school, run by the Christian Brothers, was situated in the rue Basse near his father's home. No doubt it was felt that the proximity of the parental abode would exert a salutary influence on the boy.

His general progress was pretty poor, however. His first term report was not exactly encouraging: 'Religious Study: passable; work: highly unsatisfactory; conduct: leaves a lot to be desired; behaviour in prayers: unsatisfactory; general attitude in class: rather careless: demeanour at playtime, at the table: lacks cleanliness.'[18]

The second term report (for mid-April 1853) was equally critical and pointed out somewhat ominously that Stéphane had become a disruptive element within the class.[19] In fact Fanny Desmolins' letters reveal that his sister Maria was being difficult too. On 26 February she complained that Maria was beginning to be insolent. Both children were probably reacting to the arrival of yet another half-sister (born in January the previous year) and the announcement that yet another child would grace their father's marriage that summer. If this were not enough, a month previously Stéphane's father had announced that he was being promoted to 'conservateur des hypothèques' in the town of Sens some 120 km away from the capital.

Clearly, Stéphane found it hard to settle in such circumstances. Inevitably, in spite of a last-minute improvement, he was asked to repeat the year. During this second year at the college his work gradually improved, but his reports show that he remained persistently hostile to Religious Study and was consistently singled out by his teachers for being something of a loner.[20]

Most of the summer holidays of that year he spent at his grandparents' home, chiefly because his stepmother was once again heavily pregnant. He had one companion in his cousin Anatole Rain, who was destined for the Seminary at Saint-Sulpice. His other constant companion during the vacation was, as usual, his younger sister, Maria.

At the start of the next school year Stéphane was allowed to move up a class, but his work soon deteriorated. Barely a month after term began, Fanny Desmolins was again resigned to the situation. In fact, she was remarkably philosophical about it all. 'I can't get angry with him,' she confided to Mélanie. 'He is so nice really.'[21] By the middle of the second term however, the situation was becoming serious. Madame Desmolins was now actually receiving complaints from Stéphane's teachers. They told her that he was stubborn and insubordinate and would never accept he was in the wrong. Fanny was quite mortified. She wrote an anguished letter to her cousin. The local priest had advised her, she said, that the boy would soon find it in his heart to relent and conform. However, for her part, she felt she had failed with both her daughter's children:

> His father is due here today. What a pathetic welcome! Complaints, always complaints about that son of his who ought to be a consolation to both our families. What emotional and material sacrifices have been made for those children on both sides, with such meagre rewards! Isn't it a shame for us all! Whilst their other children only fill us full of joy those two provide such a sorry example to their little brother and sisters![22]

Although she herself signally failed to realize the true significance of her remarks, Fanny Desmolins had unwittingly pinpointed what was clearly the main problem with Stéphane and Maria – the different status they enjoyed or rather suffered compared to their half-brother and half-sisters. If they were 'difficult' and headstrong, was it not largely because they felt in part rejected by their own father? No doubt they resented being treated unfairly and to their eyes more harshly, compared to a younger brother and sisters who continued to live with their parents in Sens while they were both being educated as boarders away from home and spent most of their holidays and days off school with their grandparents. Constant comparisons with their younger brother and sisters could hardly have helped to improve the situation.

Even if she could not understand why Stéphane was so difficult, Fanny Desmolins was certainly quite right to be alarmed. Indeed, events proved her fears to be only too well justified. By the end of March 1855 Stéphane had been expelled from the school after further complaints from his teachers and a final and inevitably acrimonious confrontation.

No doubt as a direct result of recent events, both Stéphane and Maria were at last allowed to spend the summer holidays of 1855 with their parents in Sens. The atmosphere was far from festive, however. Numa Mallarmé was preoccupied by his father-in-law's poor health and also anxious about other members of the family involved in the Crimean War. The children were left largely to their own devices, and a series of fishing expeditions were both the main source of distraction and the subject of their letters to their distant grandparents.

What happened at the end of that summer is not clear. It appears to have been decided that Stéphane was not to return to school but to study indoors in his grandmother's house. Eventually it was agreed that the following Easter he would be transferred to the lycée in Sens, which allowed him a term to settle in before the start of the full school year. Significantly, however, he was to remain a boarder, despite the fact that his family lived in the town. He entered the Lycée Impérial de Sens on 15 April 1856, and after an initial period of adjustment appears to have settled down and done quite well. Clearly, he now saw more of his father and stepmother than before, but he still remained rather cut off from his sister Maria, who was now being educated at a convent school in Paris. So it was decided that to remedy this Stéphane and Maria should be allowed to spend some time together that particular summer and the following ones. A pact was struck between the Desmolins and the Mallarmés: one half of the holidays was to be spent in Passy, the other half in Sens.

Just before the start of the holidays Stéphane wrote to his sister. His letter clearly illustrates the special bond that existed between the two of them:

Dearest Maria, the holidays will soon be here and we shall see each other soon. Perhaps it is the thought of me coming to Passy where you will be able to say to me just what you like which explains why you have not written to me. I think my father must have sent you by now a letter I wrote you at the beginning of the month and which, forgetting to post, he kept for three weeks. That's one for a start, plus another one that dates from the christening of the Imperial baby. Now that's two unanswered letters you little horror! . . . One of these days you'll have to write back and let me know when your holidays begin, because I really do have to know. It's very important to me. Mine, according to the other boys, begin on the 12th of August. I'll maybe get away on the 13th. If not I'll leave for Paris on the 14th. I'll be travelling alone . . . I know Sens quite well now. I know 8 pretty villages where there are farms where we can go and drink milk. Put 25 sous of your money aside for that. I'll do the same. For 3 sous you get three times the amount you get in grandmother's bowls. As you can see it's pretty cheap. I don't know if stepmother will manage to bring me back my warship from Caen, because it costs 8 francs and according to my father I can't put more than 3 francs towards it. Perhaps if they are careful they'll find me a small one for that price. We could play with it on my aunt's pond. Goodbye dearest sister, I embrace you, your loving brother.[23]

The holidays seem to have worked out to everybody's satisfaction, but Stéphane and Maria were not to see each other as frequently as they would have wished. Later that year Stéphane was forbidden to attend his sister's first communion because he had not been working hard enough, or at least that was his father's excuse.

Then, the following year, at the end of the summer term of Stéphane's first full year at the lycée, as he was looking forward to spending the summer with his sister, tragedy struck. He arrived at the Desmolins' home on 11 August 1857 to spend the first half of the summer holidays with them and Maria, as agreed. Everything seemed fine. At last he had begun to do quite well at school. The previous day he had picked up two minor prizes (third runner-up in French composition; runner-up in Greek translation), which to his great relief had delighted his grandmother and his father. These triumphs were short-lived. A few days after she arrived at Passy, Maria fell seriously ill with a recurrence of the rheumatic complaint which had temporarily paralysed her hands a few years earlier. This attack was much more serious. A mere fortnight later, on 31 August 1857, she died.

It is extremely difficult to assess the impact of Maria's death upon her brother. First we have little contemporary evidence upon which to base a reasoned judgement. Most of the surviving letters between Stéphane and his sister are limited to conventional exchanges at the time of Maria's first communion, and as such were written as much to conform to parents' or grandparents' expectations as anything else. Furthermore, as has been observed about the death of Elizabeth Mallarmé, there is a real danger of exaggerating the impact of such an event if it is considered from the perspective of twentieth-century Britain where child mortality is far lower. In the France of the 1850s and later, infant mortality was not unusual. Mallarmé's own son Anatole would die young, as would several of the children of his friends.

Nonetheless – and the letter quoted earlier substantiates this – what can be said for certain is that Maria held a special place in Stéphane's affections and her death deprived him of someone to whom he felt especially close. After all, Stéphane and Maria were aware that they were different from their half-brother and half-sisters. They were the children of the same deceased mother, and as such had been encouraged to see themselves as special by Fanny Desmolins herself. A letter written later to one of Mallarmé's earliest literary friends, Henri Cazalis, makes the point most tellingly. Referring to Cazilis' sweetheart Ettie, whose photograph he had just received, Mallarmé writes:

> There is a touching expression which illuminates the whole of your letter: it is this: 'Here, my dear Mallarmé, accept the portrait of *our sister.*' It is that simple because we are brothers and yet it is so nice! Yes I'll store her in my dreams next to all the Chimènes, Beatrices, Juliettes and Reginas. What is more I'll put her in my heart next to

that poor young ghost who for thirteen years was my sister and the only person I ever adored, before I met you all.[24]

It is obvious from this letter written at a highly emotional point in Mallarmé's life (when he once again discovered what it was to have true friends of his own age) that his young sister Maria had occupied a special place in his affections. At the same time, there is nothing in these remarks (or any others for that matter) that invites us to exaggerate the effect of his sister's death, or to tie it to his mother's as the springboard or hidden source of much of Mallarmé's work, as some critics have been tempted to do. Indeed, the rare comments he made about Maria's death all point the other way. Witness the remarks made much later in a letter to his wife Marie, which show that far from being forever traumatized by the event, Mallarmé had learned to come to terms with it in a mature and responsible way: 'Did you remind Geneviève that it was on a 31 August in 1857, 16 years ago my dear, that we had the misfortune to lose poor Maria, who would have been thirty-one today? My God what a misfortune. What a fine woman, what a mother she would have made. And you Geneviève would have played with her children, your boy or girl cousins.'[25]

In fact, rather paradoxically, the immediate effect of Maria's death was if anything beneficial to Stéphane. His father's attitude towards him seems to have mellowed quite a lot, as did those of his grandmother and stepmother, although all the evidence suggests that the latter was kind-hearted in any case. Indeed, both families seem to have grown closer together, united in a common sense of loss. Henceforth Stéphane was treated more indulgently by his father, who in any event could not fail to be encouraged by an improved performance at school. At the prizegiving at the end of his second year at the lycée Stéphane won second prizes for French composition and Latin translation, the class prize in English and fourth place for Latin verse.

In September he began the two-year preparation for the baccalauréat. At first his work went well and his father could write with relief and indeed some pride to André Desmolins commenting upon his success in Greek translation. A few weeks later, however, at the end of February 1859, Stéphane fell seriously ill with violent rheumatic pains and a fever. The symptoms were alarmingly familiar, and his grandmother was in distress. Two doctors were consulted. They ascribed the attack to a chill, and ruled out any infection of the joints (which had led to the demise of his mother and sister). After a week of agonizing suspense, the pains failed to spread above the knees and the worst was over.

The first repercussion of this crisis was to the benefit of Stéphane's stepmother, Anne Mallarmé. The kindness and consideration she had shown in keeping Mme Desmolins informed of developments with daily or even twice daily bulletins seems to have convinced Fanny that she had been rather unfair to her in the past. The second repercussion was quite different in nature. It was during the subsequent enforced convalescence and absence from school that Stéphane was able to given rein to his recently discovered passion for poetry. Unaware as yet that his son's interest in this new world was no mere passing whim, Numa Mallarmé wrote somewhat naïvely and dismissively to André Desmolins at Easter 1859: 'You'll find our lad dreaming of poetry and only admiring Victor Hugo, who has nothing to do with the Classics. All that is not very helpful for his education. All those people who have his interests at heart chide him for it and I have had to forbid him from reading the Romantics except for pleasure and to exhort him to read Corneille, Racine and Molière, which he has got to know in order to finish his studies.'

Already his father was thinking about Stéphane's future. 'All things considered,' he continued, 'I lean towards our jobs in the administration, which put bread on the table and give you something to hand on to future generations. Strengthen his resolve, I beseech you, in this notion.'[26]

In fact, unknown to his father, who clearly seems already to have suspected that his son had no taste for a vocation in the Registry, not only was Stéphane devouring poetry, he had also begun to write some himself, both during the evening study periods and sometimes during classes, on the evidence of the schoolboy verse he collected and copied out under the heading *Entre quatre murs* (*Within these four walls*), a title suitably borrowed from a Hugo poem.[27] Indeed, if we accept the dates given in his own anthology (and there is no reason not to do so) the earliest poems date from the beginning of that year of 1859.

Ironically, this passion for poetry, so utterly alien to his grandparents' tastes, seems to have positively flourished during the summer he spent in Passy in 1859. There, to Fanny Desmolins' consternation, because she had to attend to her ailing husband, Stéphane was to be left largely to his own devices. Shortly before his arrival, she had confided to Mélanie the contradictory feelings his arrival provoked:

> The pleasure of welcoming him is tinged with anxiety as how to pleasantly fill his holiday. We've nothing left here to amuse him: Poor old aunt Desaussey is no longer here, another uncle living in Passy is due to leave in several days, the English and American families have left. Finally his cousins the Chérons are off to Brittany. The poor child will be dreadfully alone. Especially as his grandfather and I are feeling very old. We'll just have to allow him a little more freedom, and that's what really bothers me! Pray God with me that he uses his enforced freedom profitably![28]

'His enforced freedom'. A wonderful expression. It says a lot about Fanny Desmolins and the world in which she lived.

Little is known of what Stéphane did that summer. The death of his aunt Herminie which had occurred the previous Christmas, and the absence of the young people with whom he had amused himself the previous summer, must have condemned him to a fair amount of solitude. To judge by the evidence of *Entre quatre murs*, much of that time was spent writing poetry, some of it inspired by memories of those who were now absent. We also know that during one of his 'escapes' to Paris he went to the Père Lachaise cemetery to visit the tomb of the only poet he had ever met, writing a plaintive, histrionic (and mercifully uncompleted) elegy 'Sur la tombe de Béranger, fragment' ('Fragment: On Béranger's Tomb') to mark the occasion. This trip and the commemorative poem were, as much as anything else, a gesture of solidarity and homage to the figure whose bust, frequently admired and commented upon at the neighbouring house of the Dubois-Davesnes in Passy, had now come to symbolize the path he had already chosen for himself.[29]

For the moment such thoughts, like the gesture itself, were to remain purely private ones, consigned like so many of his hopes, fears and aspirations to the secrecy of a school note-book. As far as his parents and grandparents were concerned, after a successful year at the lycée the boy seemed well placed to pass his baccalauréat. That would enable him to enter the career which it was assumed on both sides of the family that he would follow.

In fact, things did not go so smoothly. In February of Stéphane's final year at school, his father, who had already been quite ill the previous November, suffered a serious stroke. At one point his life was feared for, and it was felt necessary to administer the last rites. He survived, but was left seriously paralysed and a mere shadow of his former self. André Desmolins too was ill that year. To crown it all, despite the fact that in its account of the annual prizegiving ceremony at the lycée the local paper had pointed him out as one of the academic stars of the school, Stéphane, to his own private humiliation and to the utter consternation of all around him, failed the August diet of the baccalauréat. It was a serious blow for the family. His father had only been able to work in the office with the aid of an amanuensis, and it was clear that he would be forced at some point to take early retirement. The prospect of paying Stéphane's school fees for yet another year was very worrying, as was the possibility of a delay in his starting a career.

Inevitably, the boy's failure cast a shadow over the holidays. The three weeks he spent with his grandparents that summer were dismal ones. The Desmolins themselves were still recovering from the cost and disruption of the move to Versailles earlier that year, upon André's retirement from the Registry in March. Both of them were beginning to feel their age, especially André, who was now quite befuddled and beginning to suffer from occasional dizzy spells. Besides, they were both more than ever conscious that they had little to offer in the way of distraction for their daughter's son.

Still, Stéphane was even less welcome at Sens. Fanny Desmolins wrote to her cousin Mélanie:

> Our existence is not very enlivened by the presence of Stéphane, who arrived here three days ago. His lack of success has saddened everybody, and besides I'm sorry to see that he tires his grandfather and is not enjoying himself here at all, with his tastes being so different from ours. Our extremely monotonous routine which so suits our age is not at all exciting for a young man, I realize that. Seeing that we have made no acquaintances other than those ladies I mentioned, we cannot, since they are away at the moment, procure any other distraction for the boy. I just don't know how the holidays will turn out. On the other hand, I know that they find him an embarrassing burden in Sens because of the state of his father's health, which is still poor and weakening.[30]

In the event, the three weeks Stéphane spent at Versailles served their purpose very well. They afforded him some rest from his studies, even if the only distraction seems to have come in the unwelcome form of taking walks.

In November, he took the resits, and to his and everybody's relief, this time he passed. Now it was time to think about the future. Fanny Desmolins had no doubts as to this. As far as she was concerned, the only impediment to her preferred career for Stéphane had now been removed. (The baccalauréat was obligatory for entry into the Registry and some of the higher offices of the civil service.) Less than a week after the results, she wrote to announce the good news and to thank her cousin for her prayers, which had obviously had the desired effect, even if, to her annoyance, she had only been informed of the date of the exam at the very last minute:

> Anyhow, it's a great step forward towards a position in society. Very soon now he'll start as an unpaid apprentice to a Receiver. What I find most advantageous in this outcome is that he'll remain in his father's house, with the family, for at least two or three years before assuming any responsibilities. In this way he will be exposed to fewer dangers than he would be in Paris, for example, if he had gone on to study Law, or any other place for that matter where he would have been left to himself, without any guide or mentor. We are very concerned about him being able to shoulder the responsibility that goes with being an accountant in the future. We must just hope that his years as an apprentice will mature him somewhat and teach him to acquire the habits of order and regularity in his life which are signally lacking.[31]

As if such criticism was not harsh and unfeeling enough, she then went on to complain bitterly about the young man's lack of social grace. 'The poor child also has a long way to go to become sociable and convivial. At the moment things are very difficult for him and I have little inclination to exhibit him in company, so far removed is he from what I had hoped for him, and so cruelly have my hopes been dashed.'[32]

Fanny Desmolins' confidence that Stéphane would blindly agree to follow the career she had thus mapped out for him would have been diminished had she taken the time to scan some of the poems he had written during the last year. In these she would have found some explanation of the sullen moods and antisocial behaviour which so puzzled her.

Clearly, it would be dangerous to read too much into the adolescent verse which Mallarmé wrote during his seventeenth and eighteenth years. Like most apprentice poets, he began by reading and studying other poets, and much of *Entre quatre murs* is highly derivative. It is a motley collection of both trivial and serious verse which tells us a lot about the voracious extracurricular reading habits of its author. The Romantics, Lamartine, Musset, Chénier and particularly Victor Hugo had been closely studied and assimilated, indeed the discovery of Hugo was possibly the driving force behind Mallarmé's passion for poetry. It was an admiration that he was to share with many of his later friends, and was to endure long after other enthusiasms had evaporated, throughout his life. By the following year he had acquired the recently published two-volume edition of *La Légende des siècles* and had copied out extracts from the banned *Les Châtiments*.[33]

On one level, the poems illustrate quite an impressive technical competence, despite occasional awkwardnesses and some inelegant attempts at rhythmic experimentation. But the technical achievement hardly announces the great poet that Mallarmé was to become, and it does not interest us here. The forty or so poems collected in this school jotter can tell us something about their author. They complement and indeed compensate for our somewhat sketchy knowledge of the boy at this crucial moment in his life. Many of the themes are those traditionally associated with youthful exuberance and revolt. Most have obvious literary antecedents. Echoing Musset and Hugo, both obligatory role-models for budding poets of the time, a whole range of poems project the image of the Bohemian and the Revolutionary, who is challenging the authority of teachers and parents. There is plenty of posturing and bravado, and the several allusions to the local taverns and other dens of iniquity which the older boys (including the poet) now haunted may owe more to wishful thinking than to life. Certainly, the lurid yet naïve accounts of nights of debauchery smack more of literary echoes or plain erotic fantasy than actual physical experience.

Indeed, the reader is entitled to be sceptical about the significance of an enigmatic set of notes later added to the back cover of *Entre quatre murs*. There, in the circumstances which we shall later describe, the young man purports to divulge some of the momentous events in his life. If we are to believe him, he had taken advantage both of his greater privileges as an older pupil and of his father's less than watchful eye to lose his sexual innocence. Next to the date 'April 1859' he scribbles: 'I passed a night with Emily'. Next to '5 July 1860' (a mere month before his baccalauréat, when his family thought him preoccupied with his studies) he notes: 'The first time I was alone with JF – '[34]

Not all the poems of *Entre quatre murs* deal with such distractions. Many others reveal that heightened awareness of death and the destruction of Beauty which is not uncommon in sensitive adolescents. In some of these poems, however, the traditional Romantic revolt against the injustice of a world in which people die gives way to a deeper questioning born of personal experience. Two young girls whom Stéphane had fleetingly known but who had died in their early teens – Harriet Smythe and Emma Sullivan, and indeed Maria, his own sister – haunt a whole series of poems.[35] Here we begin to see that the hostility to the religious teachings of his family and school so consistently recorded in Stéphane's school term reports was turning into something much more important. He was beginning to seriously question some of the basic teachings with which he had been brought up. Fanny Desmolins would have been horrified to read a poem like 'Hier: aujourd'hui: demain' ('Yesterday, Today and Tomorrow'), inspired by and dedicated to Maria and written after a visit to her grave. Here there is no vague sentimentality, just the quiet acceptance that she is dead and forever beyond his reach. The final lines, spoken by the dead girl's spirit, allow no possibility of their ever being reunited:

Hier! c'était le noir cercueil!
Hier! Les pleurs! hier, le deuil!
Mais un bel ange sous la plume
De son aile me fit un nid,
Et prit son essor vers un monde
Où l'encens sur la tête blonde
Vole en nuage: où l'on dit:
'Père!' à Jéhovah quand il gronde!
'Mon frère!' à l'ange Gabriel! –
Aujourd'hui, c'est le ciel! Demain . . . sera le ciel!

[Yesterday! It was the dark coffin!
Yesterday! Tears! yesterday, mourning!
But a beautiful angel with the feathers
Of its wing made a nest for me,
And flew away towards a world
Where incense on the blond head
Flies in a cloud: where people say:
'Father' to Jehovah when he chides them!
'My brother!' to the angel Gabriel! –
Today, it is heaven! Tomorrow . . . it will be heaven!]

A more open criticism of Christian values is to be found in the poem 'Sa fosse est creusée' ('Her grave is dug'), inspired by the memory of Harriet Smythe, who had died of consumption. The poem takes the form of a rebuke addressed directly to God himself. The first half of the poem recounts the standard clichés and banal explanations by which the Christian community explains away to the bereaved both the importance of Eternal Life and the necessity of the death of their loved ones. The second half revolts against such platitudes and, in the final stanzas, calls God himself to account. Harriet's brothers will ask where she is and deserve an honest answer. The young Mallarmé can stomach platitudes no longer. The closing lines do little credit to his poetical talents but the emotion is clearly heartfelt:

Où donc est votre soeur – elle est où l'a ravie
Dieu que vous bénissez et qui brise les coeurs
Et c'est pour vous apprendre à pleurer dans la vie.[36]

Et les pauvres diront: Voici l'hiver qui glace!
Sous la brise les fleurs chanteront: Dies irae! . . .
Jour de colère . . . eh! non, pour Dieu sans pleurs il passe
   – Et moi, je maudirai!

Dieu, ton plaisir jaloux est de briser les coeurs!
Tu bats de tes autans le flot où tu te mires!
   – Oh! pour faire, seigneur, un seul de tes sourires,
     Combien faut-il donc de nos pleurs?

[Where is your sister – she is where she has been taken
By God whom you continue to bless and who breaks hearts
And the purpose of this is to teach you to cry in this life.

And the wretches will say: Here comes the glacial winter!
Blowing in the wind the flowers will chant: Dies irae!
Day of Wrath . . . what! No, for God passes by without a tear
But I'll be there to curse him!

Envious God, you take such pleasure in breaking our hearts!
Your past deeds muddy the waters in which you are reflected!
Oh! to bring about, O Lord one of your smiles
Just how many of our tears will it take?]

The most direct challenge to Christianity is to be found in the most ambitious poem of the collection, 'Pan', which in some respects prefigures later poems. Many of the themes to which Mallarmé will return again and again in his mature works are already present, in particular the solar and flower imagery that will later become so central. Well before 'Toast funèbre', which will elaborate some of these same themes and images, Mallarmé is questioning the role of religion in the human condition, although in this early poem the scope is more limited, the targets more clearly defined. They are quite simply the abstraction of the Catholic ritual and dogma.

Composed in July 1859, significantly only a short time before Stéphane was due to undertake his annual pilgrimage to the house of that most pious of women, Fanny Desmolins, 'Pan' is dedicated to an older pupil at the lycée, Emile Roquier, then greatly admired for his verse. The poem offers a momentous gesture of defiance that rejects Christianity and in particular the Catholic ritual in favour of a more acceptable pantheism, as the title implies. Importantly, it is not God or the notion of a Deity which is abandoned, just the rituals of the Catholic Church. The poem recounts how, one evening in May as the natural world is ablaze with living flowers, a young man feels he can no longer tolerate the artificial claustrophobic world of the Church which denies and mocks Nature. Alluding specifically to the habit of strewing rose petals during the Corpus Christi procession in honour of the Eucharist, he undertakes a gesture of defiance:

Or, ce soir-là, j'entrai dans leur temple poudreux
Pour voir leur Christ béni par leurs hymnes moroses.
J'eus des pleurs dans les yeux: ils effeuillaient les fleurs!
Les fleurs! . . . à peine ouvrant leurs feuilles à la vie,
Leur sein aux papillons, au jeune amour leurs coeurs!
(. . . . .)
Et devant un soleil d'argent, toutes ces têtes
Se courbaient . . . Seul, debout, j'étais là frémissant,
Comme sure l'Océan, quand l'aile des tempêtes
A refoulé les flots d'un souffle mugissant,
Se dresse, inébranlable, un roc que bat l'écume.

[That evening, I entered their crumbling temple
To see their Christ blessed by their dismal hymns.
I had tears in my eyes: they were removing the petals from the flowers!
The flowers! . . . hardly had they opened up their petals to Life,
Their breast to the butterfly's, to young love their hearts!
(. . . . .)
And before a silver sun all those heads
Were bowed . . . Alone, erect, I stood there shivering,
Just as in the Ocean, when the tempest's wing
Drives back the waves in a thundering roar,
There emerges an immovable rock battered by the foam.]

The over-melodramatic gesture, and the clear borrowing of Hugolian marine metaphors to highlight the majesty of the solitary rebel, do not require the conclusion that everything in these verses is derivative or insincere. The concluding lines in particular, with their exhortation to contemplate and worship the rising sun as a symbol of the human condition more accessible and more meaningful than the sacrament of the Eucharist, are an early, almost instinctive expression of what will become a major preoccupation of Mallarmé's mature works: a quest for something modern to replace the currently outmoded myths and rituals of the past.

Mallarmé's contempt and loathing for the ceremony of High Mass were genuine enough, and the thoughts expressed here are strangely reminiscent of remarks made to Henri de Régnier much later. Recollecting his visits to church, and how the excessive piety of his family (most probably of his grandmother) had put him off religion, Mallarmé cites an instance which goes a long way to explain the opening section of 'Pan': 'Mallarmé tells me that when he was taken to High Mass every Sunday as a boy, he was always so forcibly reminded to lower his gaze during the Monstrance that he always had the idea that just then "something that wasn't nice" was being exhibited.'[37]

For the moment, these rebellious and blasphemous thoughts remained absolutely private, consigned to poems that no teacher nor any member of the family was expected to read. But clearly a crisis was looming. It would not take long to surface. Once he had left school Stéphane felt even less inclined to hide his true feelings. Incensed by a last-minute conversion to the faith by his grandfather André Desmolins, whose failing health caused him to succumb after some forty-three years of resistance, Stéphane chose, much to the chagrin of his grandmother, to openly parade his disobedience, thus opening between himself and Fanny Desmolins a wound that would never be healed.

The growing confrontation between Stéphane and his family, so clearly announced in many of the poems of *Entre quatre murs*, was not to be limited to matters of religion, however. There remained the matter of his career. Although the exam had been passed at the beginning of November, there followed a delay, probably due to his father's health, before any decision was taken. Inevitably, the Desmolins, now virtually legally responsible for Stéphane given his father's condition, had their way. It was on his Saint's Day, the day after Christmas, that he was articled as an unpaid clerk to the Receiver in his father's office in Sens.

The young man who thus dutifully entered the Registry Office on 26 December 1860 was not without allies in the struggle ahead. Since leaving school that summer he had continued to remain friendly with the English master, a Monsieur Motheret, and through him had kept up his contacts with the other former pupils who had some literary pretensions. Now that he had passed his baccalauréat, his headmaster, Monsieur Clément, looked less critically than before on his passion for poetry, and was to prove a useful friend.

Paradoxically, one of the most important sources of support had been unwittingly provided by André Desmolins himself. Some time after his move to Versailles, no doubt in an effort to dissuade Stéphane from attempting a literary career, he had shown some of his grandson's poems to a former colleague at the Ministry of Finance who now lived in retirement in Versailles and whose literary opinion he respected. He had hoped, of course, that Emile Deschamps would not be impressed by what he saw. The very opposite was true. Deschamps, a former comrade in arms and friend of Victor Hugo, an admirer of Baudelaire and a translator of Shakespeare, liked nothing better than to encourage budding talents. Mallarmé was soon invited to his home, which had become a Mecca for young poets.

It was probably Deschamps, or even the English master, or both of them who encouraged Mallarmé to read more widely and introduced him to the works of Poe and Baudelaire. It was certainly around this time, summer to autumn 1860, that Mallarmé began to copy out over 8,000 lines of verse by poets whose works he did not himself possess. This Herculean task, confided in neat writing to three school notebooks, would explain why he wrote little poetry himself during this period, although he began to translate several poems by Edgar Allan Poe. Another, simpler explanation is that he was undertaking an entirely different and more meaningful apprenticeship than the one which had met so easily with his grandmother's approval. It is perhaps in the context of his recent discovery of Baudelaire and Poe, of the approval, the encouragement and the friendship of Deschamps and the other poets of his acquaintance, that we can best understand the notes he appended in pencil to the inside back cover of his fair copy of his juvenile verse:

> 18 June 1854 – 1st comm[union]
> 31 August 1857 – Maria's death
> April 1859 – I passed a night with Emily
> 5 July 1860 The first time I was alone with JF –
> 8 November 1860 obtained baccalauréat
> 26 December 1860 first steps into a brutish existence[38]

There is no reason to suppose that these lines were composed or even added at the time of the last entry in the list. But even if we allow that they were added at a later date, it is obvious that on that feast-day of 1860 which ought to have been a celebration, the young man must have been aware, as never before, that he had left his childhood far behind and faced a serious confrontation. Fortunately, when that moment came he would not face it alone. He would be able to count on the support and encouragement of a man who had a crucial part to play in fulfilling his literary dreams. A young schoolmaster named Emmanuel des Essarts was about to enter the lycée at Sens and the life of Stéphane Mallarmé.

2

Rebellion

Late in December 1860, or more probably at the start of 1861, now that the hurdle of the baccalauréat was safely behind him, Stéphane Mallarmé bowed to the inevitable and started work as an unpaid apprentice clerk under the watchful eye of one of his father's colleagues in the Registry Office at Sens. There had been some brief talk about the possibility of him going on to university to study Law, but Fanny Desmolins had dismissed the suggestion as wholly unsuitable for someone as immature and unreliable as her wayward grandson.[1] As far as she and the rest of the family were concerned, it was much more sensible for the boy to enter the Registry. There he could study for the professional exams which would allow him, at the end of a five-year probationary period, to find a permanent post with the attendant security that mattered so much to his father and grandfather.

Mme Desmolins would have been less confident about these long-term prospects had she chanced to read the petulant and defiant remarks inscribed by her grandson in the inside cover of his little notebook of adolescent verse. They make it only too clear that Stéphane loathed the prospect of the career which had been singled out for him, and it comes as no surprise to find that he very soon came to hate the Registry and everything associated with it. Later, when he learned that one of his friends had started work as an articled clerk, he bitterly recalled the unforgettable smell of official documents and the mindless, endless, copying. 'I feel sorry for you,' he wrote with genuine

sympathy. 'I've been through all that. I know what it's like!'[2]
In spite of all the valiant efforts of his supervisor, he made
very little progress in the Registry and did not do well in his
professional exams.[3]

Despite his aversion for the job, he persevered as long as he
could, and it was almost a year before he requested permission
to leave. During those first few months in the Registry, he
could do little else except resign himself to his fate. He was
still a minor, totally dependent on a family whose wishes he
could not easily oppose. Moreover, there were other influences
at work. His father's continued poor health cast its shadow
over everything. Numa Mallarmé may have improved sufficiently in April 1861 for the family to be able to move in to
Les Gaillons, a villa which he had purchased and comfortably
furnished on the outskirts of Sens near the old town gates, but
the reprieve was to prove only temporary. By the end of the
year he had suffered another relapse and was once more on sick-
leave. Enforced retirement was now only a matter of time.

With Numa Mallarmé in no position to act as the head of
his family, this responsibility fell to Stéphane's official guardian, André Desmolins. But he himself was no longer a young
man. He could not keep as close an eye on his grandson as he
would have liked. Besides, his health too was beginning to
fail. In March of Stéphane's first year at the Registry André
Desmolins fell seriously ill with a seizure that caused him to
choke and spit blood in a protracted bout that alarmed his wife
and provided serious cause for concern. For the moment at
least, Stéphane therefore felt compelled to persevere in the
Registry. If he remained privately quite determined to become
a writer, his only outward display of dissent took the form of
a refusal to attend church which only too easily achieved its
objective of upsetting his grandmother.[4]

One positive advantage of the condition of his father and
grandfather was that during his months at the Registry,
Mallarmé enjoyed what was in those days an unusual amount

of freedom for someone his age. He did not exploit the situation. On the contrary, he appears to have lived largely within his family circle, generally avoiding the other inhabitants of Sens, with whom he was convinced he had little in common and for most of whom he felt nothing except utter contempt.

In his defence it has to be admitted that a small provincial town like Sens had little to offer a young man with serious literary ambitions. Culturally, there was not much to do, except to visit the local theatre when a travelling repertory company passed through, or to attend the regular Saturday-night dances held in the basement of the establishment which seems to have been the main meeting place for the young people of the town. As we shall see, Mallarmé made several visits to the theatre, but a reticent temperament still kept him ill at ease in the company of people whom he did not know, and he steered clear of the Saturday-night dances.[5]

Those friends Mallarmé did cultivate were few in number and carefully chosen. He kept in touch with one or two former school acquaintances, and especially with Emile Roquier, himself a budding poet and whose verses, like Mallarmé's own, had been chosen to grace the school's *Cahier d'Honneur*. He also seems to have remained quite friendly with one of his former teachers, Monsieur Motheret, a young English master only a few years older than himself. As with Roquier, the basis of the friendship was a common interest in literature. Motheret himself had modest literary ambitions and took a special interest in any pupil who had shown either interest or talent during his school career.

Basically however – and it seems clear that this was quite a deliberate decision on his part – Mallarmé chose to avoid Sens and its townsfolk, living what amounted to a kind of self-imposed exile. He divided his time between his home and the Registry Office, escaping from the numbing drudgery of the latter by indulging his twin passions of reading and writing poetry.

This largely solitary existence was brought to a wonderful and quite unexpected end in October of that year when a newcomer arrived in Sens to take up what was his first teaching post at the local lycée. Emmanuel des Essarts had studied in Paris at the Lycée Napoléon (now known as the Lycée Henri IV) before going on to the prestigious Ecole Normale. A mere three years older than young Stéphane (who was not yet twenty), he was destined to become not only a good friend and companion but above all an important source of encouragement and advice.

Des Essarts came preceded by quite a reputation. Whilst still at school he had won first prize in the national poetry competition organized by the Société des Gens de Lettres. *Le Gaulois*, an established and respected Parisian newspaper, had published some of his verse and *L'Artiste*, an important literary magazine which included among its regular collaborators all the major writers of the day, had hailed him as a promising new literary talent. Furthermore, as he arrived in Sens to take up his post, his first book of collected verse, boldly entitled *Poésies parisiennes*, had been accepted by none other than Poulet-Malassis, the publisher of Charles Baudelaire and Théodore de Banville. In any case, Des Essarts was himself already quite familiar with and known to the literary circles of Paris. As a child he had become accustomed to seeing personalities such as Victor Hugo and Banville at the literary gatherings regularly held in their family home by his father, Alfred des Essarts, himself a practising poet and novelist. Whilst at the Ecole Normale, Emmanuel had begun to frequent the literary cafés and salons of Paris, making contacts which would later serve not only himself but his friends very well.

Physically, Emmanuel des Essarts was not impressive. Short in stature, chubby and rather awkward in manner, by all accounts he read his own poetry very badly. This is how a contemporary, Maurice Dreyfous, remembers him at about the time he entered Mallarmé's life:

He didn't look very impressive, our old friend Emmanuel. He was small, too fat for his height and especially for his age. He stammered when he spoke. He was beginning to get a reputation as a poet and would gladly read or recite his poems which unfortunately he completely ruined by exaggerating their cadences and by rolling his eyes in an imploring and lugubrious manner, flailing his arms about and gesticulating theatrically with hands that were too large for his stumpy arms. His excessive short-sightedness would have made him a figure of fun had we not all known what a valiant spirit, what a reliable and kind fellow we had before us![6]

Emmanuel des Essarts had not been long in Sens when some of his new colleagues at the lycée mentioned Mallarmé to him. The two young men met and quickly became good friends. For Mallarmé, the friendship could not have been better timed. Des Essarts' genuine warmth and understanding, above all his bubbling enthusiasm, provided a vivacity that his earlier life had singularly lacked. Suddenly, in what he had seen as a hopeless cultural backwater, he encountered a kindred spirit upon whom he could rely, a fellow traveller, a real published poet who did not dismiss or make fun of his literary ambitions.

In addition to this moral support and genuine companionship, invaluable in themselves alone, Des Essarts provided Mallarmé with something he could only have dreamed of in the past, namely direct contact with Paris and its artistic circles. Yet the rapidly growing friendship between the two young men was not as one-sided as it might appear. Their need was mutual. Exiled from his beloved, his indispensable Paris ('that Parisian *par excellence*' was how Mallarmé referred to him),[7] for all his apparent confidence, Emmanuel des Essarts needed someone to confide in, and with whom he could share his own dreams and aspirations.[8] Nonetheless, at the beginning of their friendship it was clearly Mallarmé who benefited the more. Des Essarts generously put his Parisian contacts at his young friend's disposal, and it was no doubt on his recommendation and certainly with his encouragement that, barely a few weeks after their first meeting, Mallarmé sent some of his poems to a

41

little avant-garde Parisian review, *La Revue fantaisiste*, edited by Catulle Mendès, a very good friend of Des Essarts. Although on this occasion the poems were rejected, the contact would prove useful and Catulle Mendès would later become one of Mallarmé's closest friends.

Other contacts bore more immediate fruit. Within a month or two of Des Essarts' arrival in Sens, as that first and, for Mallarmé, largely wasted year in the Registry Office drew to a close, he could at least draw comfort from the knowledge that his name would soon appear on the covers of a Parisian literary magazine. Thanks to his new friend, Mallarmé was at last to become a published poet. First the little review *Le Papillon* (co-edited by Charles Coligny, another useful acquaintance of Des Essarts) then the highly respected *L'Artiste* itself (again temporarily edited by Coligny) opened their columns to the unknown young man from Sens.[9]

It was probably again at the suggestion of Des Essarts (although we cannot be sure of this) that Mallarmé was invited to deputize for the temporarily indisposed drama critic of the local newspaper.[10] On 7 December 1861 there appeared in *Le Sénonais* the first of a series of three unsigned theatrical reviews now known to be his work.[11]

In theory, the three articles, or rather one long article in three quite uneven parts, had as their subject the performances of a troupe of travelling players who had paid several visits to Sens. As dramatic reviews, admittedly the three pieces are singular failures. There is little here to suggest the exquisite pages which Mallarmé would later write on the subject of the theatre for *La Revue indépendante* and *La Revue blanche* before assembling them under the deliberately casual heading 'Crayonné au théâtre' ('Theatre jottings') in his important volume of collected prose, *Divagations* (*Some Musings*). The following brief extract from the opening piece is typical of the heavy-handed irony directed at the unsuspecting regular readers of *Le Sénonais*:

We have in Sens a company of actors which offers us the unheard-of peculiarity of being precisely that, a company, and a director who affords us the strange spectacle of being . . . a director. Until now – at least for many years now – our stage has witnessed a few Chinese shadows clustered around the odd talented individual, himself hopelessly lost and completely out of place. These shadowy figures have vanished, replaced by *real* actors, conjured up by the clever magic of Mr Besombes. I have named the person I can call a director and not a travelling salesman in theatrical wares! His vigilance does him praise! . . .

It was a feast where the menu was chosen with exquisite tact, a *literary* feast. Let us pronounce that word very quietly. Shouting it out too loud in Sens might do the reputation of Monsieur Besombes irreparable harm . . .

I mentioned the name César de Bazan a moment ago. We shall see him on Thursday – 'In a play by Dennery?' – 'No, you are not with me at all!' 'In a play by whom then . . . ?' – 'Hugo, of course.'

The following week, flushed with his rather facile initial success, Mallarmé was determined to combine his genuine admiration for the theatrical achievements of Victor Hugo with yet another merciless attack on the ignorance of his fellow citizens. The result was that he clearly overreached himself, resorting to a complicated charade that involved a far too protracted imaginary conversation between a drama critic and an outraged but naïve member of the local populace. In Mallarmé's inexperienced hands the device was so absurdly complicated in its intention and so poor in its execution that it was a total failure. What he imagined he had written in the most transparent irony was interpreted literally by his readers, and he was forced to devote the major part of his third and final article to a clumsy attempt to justify and explain his elaborate manoeuvre.

As Mallarmé's first attempt at literary criticism, these pieces are probably best forgotten. From the purely biographical point of view, however, they provide a rare insight into his thoughts and feelings at a crucial stage of his development. These rushed and mostly bungled pieces of bravura tell us much about the impatience and frustration of the young man who felt compelled to write them. First of all, some rare but moving and totally unexpected lyrical passages emerge from the general harshness of his tone to show that Mallarmé now wholeheartedly identified himself with the creative artist whom he pictured (in images coloured by his recent reading of Baudelaire and Edgar Allan Poe) as a lonely individual shunned and despised by the masses and wholly misunderstood by a hostile and indifferent society whose main preoccupation was money and power. Similar views are found in a satirical poem entitled 'A un poète immoral' ('Ode to an immoral poet') written the week the first of the three *Sénonais* articles appeared. Here too, alluding as much to himself as to any actual or identifiable poet, Mallarmé defends the outrageous Bohemian life-style of those who are interested in love and poetry against the hypocrisy of the townsfolk with their 'wrinkled virtue' who claim to be incensed by such immoral behaviour whilst indulging their own lust for money, power and politics. Another poem entitled 'Galanterie macabre' ('A macabre act of gallantry'), probably written only a few months later in homage to and in the style of Baudelaire's *Tableaux parisiens*, expresses solidarity with the poor who, even in death, are treated with contempt by the more fortunate.[12]

What is most remarkable about the prose and verse composition of this period is the depth of emotion and pent-up frustration they reveal. The cruel irony which Mallarmé directed at the inhabitants of Sens was clearly aimed first and foremost at those members of his immediate family, most obviously his grandmother Fanny Desmolins and his uncles – 'a bunch of pot-bellied egos', he later called them[13] – who could see no value whatsoever in his literary activities. The extended diatribe against the philistinism of his fellow citizens (for that in essence is what these newspaper articles are) shows just how constricted Mallarmé felt himself to be in

Sens, and equally how determined he had by now become to follow his own chosen path rather than the one his elders had prescribed.

Finally, what is most significant in these articles is their extraordinarily assured tone. They exude a confidence, indeed an arrogance, which says much about the impact which Emmanuel des Essarts had had upon his young friend. Such a virulent and open[14] attack upon his fellow citizens would have been inconceivable only a few months earlier. This new intensity is to be found in an important poem, 'Le Guignon' ('The Curse'), the most original he had so far written, which dates from this period. When Des Essarts arrived in Sens the poetry Mallarmé was writing, whilst it displayed a growing technical mastery, consisted either of light-hearted trivial conceits reflecting his continued interest in the poets of the late seventeenth century, or experimental poems in the manner of writers he was currently reading: Baudelaire, Gautier, Banville. Indeed it was one of these frivolous conceits, 'Placet', a clever pastiche of baroque preciosity and a finely turned compliment to the blonde editor of the review to which it was sent, which had just been accepted for publication by *Le Papillon*.

'Le Guignon', however, deals with a more important subject and one extremely close to Mallarmé's heart: the relationship between the writer and society. It contains genuine anger and reflects many of the conflicting emotions raging within Mallarmé at this time as he was making his difficult but irrevocable decision to become a writer. Dark and brooding, occasionally dense and elliptical, perhaps the poem suffers from being too close to Mallarmé's inner contradictions. It is nonetheless a powerful piece of writing. The opening section, depicting a new breed of uncompromising rebels prepared (like Mallarmé himself) in their fanatical attachment to their ideals to confront the wrath of God and deny the existence of Paradise, has a

45

new energy and strong visual impact. The text that follows is an early version of the poem, similar to the one reproduced in the Gallimard *Poésies* edition of 1992.

> Au-dessus du bétail écoeurant des humains
> Bondissaient par instants les sauvages crinières
> Des mendieurs d'azur perdus dans nos chemins.
>
> Un vent mêlé de cendre effarait leurs bannières
> Où passe le divin gonflement de la mer,
> Et creusait autour d'eux de sanglantes ornières.
>
> La tête dans l'orage, ils défiaient l'Enfer:
> Ils voyageaient sans pain, sans bâton et sans urnes,
> Mordant au citron d'or de l'Idéal amer.
>
> [High above the hideous herd of Humanity
> Could be glimpsed the wildly tossing manes
> Of the azure beggars lost in our paths.
>
> Their banners were straightened in a wind tinged with ash
> In which passed the divine swell of the sea
> And which hollowed around them ruts filled with blood.
>
> Headlong into the storm, they defied Hell,
> Travelling without bread, without staffs and without drinking water,
> And biting into the golden lemon of the bitter Ideal.]

Prior to Des Essarts' arrival, Mallarmé had a strong sense of being isolated and vulnerable. Now, however, fired by the presence of his new companion in arms, his youthful idealism and enthusiasm for Art overflowed. The rest of the poem can only fully be understood if we imagine the sense of outrage Mallarmé must have felt on discovering what he regarded as a double act of treachery by his great hero Baudelaire. The first was the latter's savage criticism of the new generation of poets in his preface to Léon Cladel's *Les Martyres ridicules*. The second was his highly publicized decision to seek election to that pillar of the Establishment, the Académie Française. Alluding both to the title of Cladel's book and to Baudelaire's scornful dismissal of those who succumb (which was thrown into sharper relief by the tragic suicide some years previously of Baudelaire's former friend and fellow poet Gerard de Nerval), Mallarmé's poem ends bitterly, defending to the last the integrity of all martyred poets:

> Quand chacun a sur eux craché tous ses dédains,
> Nus, assoiffés de grand et priant le tonnerre,
> Ces Hamlets abreuvés de malaises badins
>
> Vont ridiculement se pendre au réverbère.
>
> [When every one has vented upon them all their bile,
> Naked, thirsting for greatness and invoking the thunder,
> These Hamlet figures assailed by playful disquiet
>
> Ridiculously go and hang themselves from a lamp-post.]

Reading such lines, so full of scorn for a fallen idol, so unforgiving in their adolescent idealism and so full of genuine anger,[15] we are not surprised to learn that the arrival of Emmanuel des Essarts had another important consequence for Mallarmé. Encouraged by their growing friendship, emboldened also by the knowledge that he was soon to become a published poet, Stéphane now felt ready for the confrontation which had been inevitable from the very first day he had been forced to enter a professional world so little to his liking. Now, largely thanks to Des Essarts, the battle could be put off no longer.

By December 1862, as he finished the first of his three articles for *Le Sénonais*, Mallarmé had privately made a decision. He would follow the example of Des Essarts and Motheret (with whom he seems to have had several discussions at this time) and quit the Registry to become a schoolteacher, thus providing himself, as he saw it, with a career which would bring some financial security yet allow him to pursue his real objective of becoming a writer. That Christmas therefore, as the first year of his apprenticeship drew to a close and the prospect of a second loomed on the horizon, he raised the whole issue of his career with his stepmother.

During the next fortnight, unknown to Numa Mallarmé (who was to be kept in the dark until matters were fully resolved), a series of hasty meetings and discussions took place in Sens. Anne Mallarmé, an intelligent and sensible woman and herself something of an amateur water-colourist, readily understood and accepted as genuine her stepson's distaste for the world of bureaucracy and his desire to follow a career more in keeping with his temperament. She talked the matter over with her brothers (who happened to be in town on a family visit), and she also spoke to Emmanuel des Essarts. Everyone was in agreement. Stéphane was wasting his time at the Registry and nothing would be achieved by forcing him to stay. The problem was that as he was still a minor, he could not change career without the express permission of his legal guardian, his grandfather, André Desmolins. In mid-January 1862, therefore, no doubt greatly encouraged by the knowledge that he could now count on the support of his stepmother and his friend Des Essarts, Stéphane wrote to André Desmolins bringing matters to a head:

Dear Grandfather,
   I was quite sincere in everything I said to you on your Saint's Day [30 November], on Boxing Day and on New Year's Day. I really did want to cheer up and try to persevere in the Registry. But truly, I am quite unhappy there.
   When I left school, I expressed the desire to go on to University. That is what suited my character best. Unless you really like it, the Registry not only takes up a lot of time, it takes over your personality as well. At University, however, the more a teacher works and studies, the greater his intellectual stature.[16]

It was not an auspicious opening, and these less than diplomatic remarks to a man who had spent much of his working life as a career civil servant were followed by a highly optimistic and unrealistically rosy picture of the new career Mallarmé intended for himself.

48

Modern Languages must be considered among the University chairs that can take you furthest. There is an annual exam in Paris. I could sit it this year just to see what it is like and present myself as a serious candidate next year in English. If you pass you become a teacher with a basic salary of 2,000 francs not including extra classes and private lessons. In the Registry I would only get 1,600 francs, and that at the end of five years and as long as I agree to earn them in some Godforsaken village. My father is due to retire. Five years is a long time to wait with expenses and no income.

Once I am a teacher I'll study for my degree solely in order to submit my doctoral thesis. For me a thesis on a foreign writer would be a diversion as much as work. After the doctorate, a whole bright future opens up. With a few rudiments of Italian and Spanish you can become a University professor of foreign literature.

As you can see there is the possibility of just as brilliant a future there as in the higher echelons in the Administration. Even if you don't reach those at least you have some security which is also one of the attractions, indeed the only attraction of the Registry for me.

To back up what he clearly imagined to be an irrefutable case, after a further paragraph describing the allegedly handsome salary earned by one of his former masters and pointing out (rather naïvely, as his own career would demonstrate) that promotion chances for people like himself were exceptionally good, Mallarmé fired what he surely considered to be his best shot. First, almost casually, he let slip that Anne Mallarmé approved of his decision. Second, and most cleverly of all, he pointed out the financial benefits arising out of his proposed change of career.

I have been thinking about this for a week to ten days now. Perhaps you have already received a letter from my mother on this subject (if not you soon will do so). We have had a serious family discussion about it. Above all just carefully consider this: as our income is going to be severely reduced because of my father's imminent retirement, I would only be a burden on the family for eighteen months instead of four or five years.

As much as the unexpected and wholly unwelcome tidings which it conveyed, it was probably the tone of this letter, with its irritating confidence bordering on impudence, that most upset André Desmolins. He was quite taken by surprise and was therefore careful not to reply immediately. Instead, he sought to ascertain through Anne Mallarmé whether Stéphane was really serious in what he had written. The enquiry came in the form of a letter from Fanny Desmolins to Anne Mallarmé which has not survived. Anne Mallarmé's extant reply was polite, firm and very carefully worded. It began almost casually in an attempt to defuse the situation:

> Yes indeed, my dear madame, we have had a family discussion about Stéphane's future, which seems to us to be totally compromised as far as the Registry is concerned.
>
> Since that career is not at all to his liking – judging by some remarks I understand him to have made to others, he would have given up sooner or later anyhow in order to follow his own inclinations – I am beginning to wonder whether his coldness and reserve are not perhaps provoked by the anguish he is suffering in an employment for which he has no liking. I cannot get him to spend extra hours at the office. He never goes there willingly and is making no effort at all to learn anything. We would all have some anxious moments if there was to be another exam. I fully understand the pain that his letter must have caused you. This latest of his decisions does not leave me without some anxiety, but if he really can succeed, as is clearly his intention, in becoming a professor of foreign literature in a University, then it is a very good situation for him and his apprenticeship as a teacher of English would only be a means towards making a start down that road. I believe he intends studying here in Sens for an exam which would allow him to qualify as a teacher within two years, with more than a good chance of passing and a salary of 2,000 francs which he is very pleased about.[17]

In an attempt to forestall any criticism that she might appear to be giving in rather too easily and siding too quickly with Stéphane, she cleverly ended her letter by requesting additional time to assess the whole situation:

> In any event, allow me a few days to obtain the details I intend requesting from the headmaster of the lycée, who has always taken

such a keen interest in Stéphane. He is a serious man and a responsible father. I think his opinion might carry some weight in your eyes. I have also talked all this over with that young teacher Monsieur Des Essarts. He knows just how repugnant Stéphane finds his work and how much he wants to change his career. Stéphane has also had serious talks about this with my brothers, who would be sorry to see him carry on vegetating as he has done for a whole year.

In the struggle thus engaged between an impatient and determined young man and equally unbending and determined grandparents, Anne Mallarmé was to play a vital role. Genuinely sympathetic to the needs and anxieties of her stepson, whose artistic leanings she both understood and in part shared, yet equally sensitive to the views of grandparents convinced that they were conscientiously discharging a trust which had been imposed upon them, she sought from the very start to act as a buffer, cooling tempers and avoiding open conflict.

Her task was not an easy one. When it eventually arrived, the reply from André Desmolins was not entirely unexpected. He was seriously alarmed that his grandson was contemplating giving up a career which had such a secure future for one which appeared so uncertain. He had clearly been hurt by Stéphane's intemperate and disrespectful remarks about the Registry and said so. Furthermore, despite the fact that both Stéphane and his stepmother had studiously sought to avoid the subject, he made it very clear that he was in no doubt as to what really lay behind his grandson's latest manoeuvre. He wrote more in sadness and genuine dismay than in anger:

To be sure we have no intention of making you unhappy by *forcing* upon you an occupation for which you have no liking. But you will allow me to point out that the Registry where you have such good chances of succeeding with the support of all our good friends is not to be so easily dismissed as you imagine. To begin with those 15 or 16 hundred francs which seem such a paltry sum to you are not unreasonable as a commencing salary and would rise within a few years to 3 or 4 thousand, which is something you ought to take into account. Besides the work is not so demanding that it would not be possible, with a bit of willpower, to find time to pursue literary interests since, unfortunately, in your case that is what outweighs everything else including common sense! Finally, at least you are assured of food in your later years, which is worth some consideration. As for the profound disdain you display for a profession which has honourably sustained your entire family and where you had an assured place, you must allow me to point out that you are still a novice and are in no position to judge the relative merits required to exercise such a profession or to rightly claim that it takes over the individual who can very easily, *if he so chooses*, retain his integrity. Besides it is not absolutely essential to *like* a career in order to succeed in it. Common sense and individual circumstances have to be taken into account. I myself after some ten years of very active military service also had to sacrifice some of my likes and habits. Yet through willpower, hard work and determination I managed to create for myself a position which you could have obtained for yourself in due course. It is therefore not without the gravest misgivings that I would see you give it up. You are aware of all this already, and had your poor father retained all his faculties, he most certainly would not have allowed you to throw away your future in this manner.[18]

As is clear from the rather desperate emotional blackmail in the last few lines of his letter, André Desmolins already sensed that his advice would fall on deaf ears. Indeed, even before these objections had been formulated and confined to paper, he had been outmanoeuvred. The day before this letter was sent Stéphane, accompanied by his stepmother, had been to see the local headmaster, who not only approved of the young man's decision but stated his willingness to do all in his power to ensure that an opening was created for him in the teaching profession, if necessary within his own school. He also recommended that Stéphane begin English lessons immediately, prior to spending a full year in England in order to perfect his oral proficiency.

Again, at this critical moment, Anne Mallarmé came to Stéphane's aid when he wrote to his grandfather a letter he could hardly wait to send, giving an account of their visit to the headmaster. Suspecting, quite correctly, that Fanny Desmolins was, of the two, the one who most objected to Stéphane's proposed change of career, Anne took care to enclose a letter of her own addressed to Fanny Desmolins. 'My dear Madame,' it began:

> I've just read Stéphane's letter telling you about what happened when we saw the headmaster. I have nothing or virtually nothing to add to the details he has given you save to say that they are absolutely accurate. He sees in this outcome both a guaranteed future for Stéphane and an occupation totally suited to his inclinations. Stéphane is merely awaiting your agreement and that of his grandpapa in order to set to work and begin his English lessons. The headmaster is very impressed with the teacher who is going to provide them for him.[19]

Anne Mallarmé's stratagem of seeking counsel from the local headmaster was a masterly stroke. Neither Fanny Desmolins nor her husband could refuse for long a proposal which enjoyed the active support and full approval of a figure so respected in the local community. Somewhat grudgingly, therefore, towards the end of the month André Desmolins made some concessions. He did not, as yet, feel able to formally approve Stéphane's decision, but neither would he stand in his way. He had other reservations. He was quite sceptical of the prospects offered by a teaching career. He too had made some enquiries which had not, he insisted, corroborated Stéphane's rather optimistic view of things. He was also concerned about the expense both of immediate private tuition and above all of a trip to England. Finally, in a rather feeble and desperate attempt to restore his authority, he felt it necessary to comment on his grandson's bad spelling and poor handwriting.

There were several more letters exchanged between Sens and Versailles, but already the main outcome was no longer in doubt. Stéphane and his stepmother had won. He would, after all, be allowed to leave the Registry. In order to appease his grandfather, he made a minor concession and agreed not to formally do so until the month of June, when he would normally have sat his exams. Delighted at the outcome of the confrontation, Mallarmé accepted full responsibility for his future and gave his grandparents hasty assurances which would come back to haunt him more than once in the years ahead. 'I can promise you,' he wrote, 'that my work and, some day, my success will make you change your mind about the reservations you currently have when you think, as my mother whom you are replacing would have done, about my future. You will never, I assure you, have cause to regret my decision.'[20]

This letter, conciliatory in tone and dutifully signed 'Your loving grandson', was written when Stéphane was serenely confident that he had won the day and was about to begin his daily English lessons. Such niceties were quickly forgotten, however, as attention now focused on his proposed trip to England. His grandfather was mainly concerned about the expense of the whole enterprise, but this objection was easily dealt with. We can imagine the pleasure it must have given Mallarmé to point out to his grandfather that if he had learnt anything at all in the Registry, it was that since he was over the age of eighteen he was legally entitled to the interest earned on the capital he would fully inherit from his mother at the age of twenty-one.

A second objection was not so easily dismissed, stemming as it did from Fanny Desmolins' deepest convictions. She was greatly concerned at the moral risks involved in allowing someone as immature and irresponsible as she felt her grandson to be to live unsupervised in London. André Desmolins, who shared some of his wife's anxieties, insisted therefore that in order to protect him from what he referred to as 'the dangers of all sorts to which that country exposes gullible young people' he spent the year in England in a Catholic college or boarding-school. The final lines of his letter were totally uncompromising:

So if you really are sincere in what you say about your work and you really are *seriously* thinking about making a future for yourself, you will understand our anxieties and gracefully accept the only conditions which will guarantee you some safety. If however you try to resist, all you will do is prove that your secret design is *merely to be free* and to rid yourself of any form of control. In that case it will be our *duty* to prevent you, using all the means at our disposal, from committing further stupidities. I am sorry to have to use such stern language but I am compelled to by your lack of sincerity. You really must realize, despite your having studied your so-called rights, that families have their rights too, which are always backed up by the Law, especially when it is a matter of removing their children from situations which would mean their ruin. If you think a little more seriously about your duties, my young man, you will understand our motives. If you really do love us you will not increase our worries by pointless resistance and you will prevent us having to resort to even more painful measures. I await your *formal* consent.[21]

Stéphane was taken aback both by the tone and by the content of this letter. Nonetheless he stood his ground. The reply he sent to his grandmother, whom he rightly suspected of being the real force behind this last letter, was equally uncompromising. It shows just how much he valued the independence he had acquired since leaving school (and equally, by implication, just how much he had hated his own schooldays):

If you mean that I have to be locked up unhappy and alone for a whole year within the four walls of a college; that I have to start all over again eating in a refectory, going to bed at eight o'clock in a dormitory and getting up at six in the morning; walking about playgrounds under the watchful eye of supervisors and with children (I say children because in England classes in colleges end in fifth year, higher classes are followed as students at University). If you want to see me deprived of the right to read any newspaper, without my books and unable to write to my friends or receive a letter without having it read first, endlessly chanting useless things instead of learning English, hating such a prison and living in despair. If all of that is what you mean by a Catholic boarding-school, quite obviously I cannot submit to that, having enjoyed two years of freedom.[22]

Once again it was Anne Mallarmé who broke the deadlock. Backing Stéphane at this most crucial moment, she pointed out to Fanny Desmolins that absolutely no one, not even the local headmaster, could get him to submit to such a rigorous discipline or to agree to attend religious services which were, as she put it, 'despite his upbringing, so alien to his tastes'. Above all, she regretted the time that was being wasted in endless letter-writing and suggested that a meeting might be more helpful. We do not know whether or not a meeting took place. What we do know for certain, however, is that the flurry of letters dramatically stopped. It was apparently agreed that Stéphane would go to England the following January as a young man of independent means in order to study English prior to embarking on a teaching career. The question of his continuing in the Registry would not, it was agreed, be raised again.

In the event, Mallarmé was to leave for London several months earlier than everyone expected. What is more, he would not be travelling alone, although for reasons which will become apparent he found it preferable to conceal this particular fact from his stepmother and grandparents. For the moment, however, released from the boring routine of the Registry Office (to which it seems that he never returned), he began to enjoy what, for a young man of the time, was a quite remarkable amount of freedom.

As had been agreed, he took English lessons for one hour each morning with a teacher from the lycée at a cost of 50 francs a month to his father. This, as he had hoped and planned, left him plenty of time for other, more literary pursuits. He spent much of his time reading, devouring the works of some of the newer poets: Leconte de Lisle, Théophile Gautier and Théodore de Banville. That he continued to read Shakespeare is manifest from the frequent references to the plays which pepper his correspondence of the time. He did not however desert his earlier idols Hugo and Baudelaire, his interest in the latter now extending beyond the poems to the critical writings on Art and fellow artists, and in particular to Baudelaire's essays on Victor Hugo and Théophile Gautier. Most important of all, through Baudelaire's translations Mallarmé became more familiar with the works and ideas of Edgar Allan Poe, whose poems he decided to translate and whose writings in general became a major focus of his attention.

He was also writing himself, and some of his work was now beginning to be published. Two more reviews for the local press now proudly bore the signature 'SM'. In July 1862, thanks to the continued support of Emmanuel des Essarts' friend Charles Coligny, some of the poems he had written the previous year made their appearance in what was admittedly a rather lightweight seasonal magazine, *Le Journal des baigneurs de Dieppe* (*The Dieppe Bathers' Journal*). In September (again thanks to Coligny) an energetically combative (if largely derivative) article, 'Hérésies artistiques', appeared in *L'Artiste*. Other literary projects entertained by Mallarmé that summer included a volume of *Contes étranges* (*Strange Tales*) which was clearly inspired by his passion for the writings of Edgar Allan Poe, and which was to have been written in collaboration with Emmanuel des Essarts.[23]

Not all of Mallarmé's time was spent reading or writing, and he used his new freedom to enjoy himself and to make friends. He saw Emmanuel des Essarts almost daily, and continued to keep in touch with Emile Roquier, but now that he considered himself to be a man of letters, he clearly felt that the time had come to expand his circle of acquaintances. He cultivated Léon Marc, the older poet-actor whose acting talent and devotion to his art he had praised in his very first article, and whose new three-act play he enthusiastically reviewed for the local press. Marc's busy schedule and travelling commitments did not allow him to spend much time in the company of his new young friend, but, largely due to Mallarmé's absolute determination to sustain their relationship by his letters, an episodic but durable friendship survived for the next several years.

Mallarmé also decided to contact a former classmate of Emile Roquier's called Eugène Lefébure. Three classes ahead of Mallarmé at the Sens lycée, Lefébure had enjoyed a considerable reputation as a poet amongst his schoolfellows. Despite a brilliant scholastic record, he was now working as a humble clerk in the Post Office in Auxerre, some thirty-five miles to the south of Sens. When Mallarmé learned (either through Roquier or even perhaps through his teacher friend Motheret, who was a native of Auxerre) that Lefébure had continued to write poetry and actually owned an edition of the poems of Edgar Allan Poe, he wrote to him some time in February 1862 asking to borrow it for the translations which he himself was now planning.

Lefébure could hardly have expected a letter from a former schoolmate to whom he had not paid much attention. He was certainly quite unaware of how eagerly Mallarmé awaited his response, and did not reply to the first letter he received. Undeterred, Mallarmé tried again two months later, pressing his initial request. This time his persistence was rewarded. 'I've just received your letter,' Lefébure replied, 'and as I can see that you are very keen to have the poems of E. Poe, let me quickly tell you that they are no longer in my possession. In fact last night I gave them to Courtois [a friend] who is due to leave this morning and will bring them to you. I'm writing to let you know this because I know that he is at least as lazy as I am and that, like me, he could keep you waiting for two months, and that would mean four months altogether.'[24]

Himself a great admirer of Poe, Lefébure approved of Mallarmé's projected translations and transcribed the first stanza of a poem which he himself was working on. As for arranging a meeting, he made a vague promise to come to Sens whenever he could manage it, but claimed (either genuinely, or possibly as an excuse) that it was extremely difficult for him to escape his duties at the Post Office, and suggested that it might be more practical for Mallarmé to visit him in Auxerre. Indeed, it is clear from the next part of his letter that he was mildly bemused to have been contacted by someone whom he did not know all that well. 'Since I turn out the odd line or two,' he continued, 'I suppose you must write lots of them. A poet must be more prolific than a Post Office employee! From time to time I see articles of yours in *Le Sénonais*, but seeing that I have neither *Le Papillon* nor *L'Artiste*, I have not read any of your poems. Anyhow, up till now, I haven't read all that much of your verse.'[25]

All the same, there was genuine warmth in Lefébure's letter. Sensing this, Mallarmé wrote him at least two more letters, sending hand-written copies of his poems along with some photographs of himself. After another interminable delay, he eventually received a long detailed reply full of apologies and bubbling with enthusiasm. 'The more I think about it,' Lefébure concluded, 'the more annoyed I am with myself for having taken so long to reply to your charming letters. I hope you will not think too badly of me when you learn how hard I have been working. I'll tell you all about that soon.'[26]

Needless to say, despite these remarks, Lefébure did not keep his promise, and so deferred a friendship which two years later developed into one of the most important which Mallarmé ever formed, destined to play a crucial part in sustaining him through one of the most difficult periods of his life. This delay was largely due to Lefébure's legendary laziness, but there were other reasons too. By the time Mallarmé decided to give up on Lefébure, other important people had already entered his life and had begun to transform it.

Mallarmé owed most of these new relationships to the generosity of Emmanuel des Essarts, who gradually introduced him to his circle of Parisian friends. Des Essarts had often spoken of the charming but impoverished poet-actor Albert Glatigny, whom Mallarmé eventually met in September of that year, during a long-awaited visit to Versailles.[27] He had also frequently mentioned Henri Cazalis, a former classmate at the Lycée Napoléon, who had just finished a Law degree and begun work as an articled clerk in Paris. Des Essarts had clearly spoken to Cazalis of Mallarmé's enthusiasm for Baudelaire and Hugo, for when, after the Easter break, he returned from one of his regular trips to the capital, he brought for Mallarmé as a present from Cazalis a copy of *Le Boulevard* magazine that contained an article by Baudelaire on the first part of Victor Hugo's new novel *Les Misérables*. It was an elegant gesture. The letter of thanks which Mallarmé dispatched a fortnight later shows just how pretentious his language could be at this time, and how desperate he was to create the right impression:

My dear . . . friend,
I ought to have thanked you ages ago for the exquisite delicacy with which you intended for me, as soon as it was published, the prose of one of my most revered masters. But I have only now barely emerged from a series of misty sterile days, and my first smile is directed towards you.

That exclamation by Mr Prud'homme, 'This sabre is the best day of my life!', had always appeared exceptionally grotesque to me. But for a fortnight now I have found it quite natural, if not more than that, because if it wasn't the first thing I said when I saw Emmanuel take from his suitcase the newspaper I had hoped for, it was my first genuine thought: 'This *Boulevard* is one of the finest days of my life!'

It is a precious gift indeed, precious in three ways. First because it shows that you thought of me; second because it is a visiting card announcing a short trip to Sens; finally because just as you have been yourself in sending it to me, in it Baudelaire is Baudelaire.

You cannot imagine how impatiently I am waiting for next month, which will bring you to Sens along with the excellent Monsieur Des Essarts – Emmanuel has promised me that, don't make him break his word. I don't think the prisoner in Béranger's poem sighed more longingly for his swallows.

However, I am being selfish in saying that because I know in advance that the one who will be less pleased with the encounter will be you. Emmanuel, who exaggerates out of genuine feeling and whose feelings are rather exaggerated, must have depicted me, if I am to judge by the warm welcome you gave my name every time he mentioned it, in colours whose brilliance was intensified by friendship. How disappointed you will be when you meet a morose individual who spends entire days leaning his head against the marble of the fireplace incapable of any thought: a ridiculous Hamlet figure who cannot explain his lack of energy.[28]

This letter is quoted at length not just because it marks the beginning of an important friendship but because it offers us a glimpse of what Mallarmé really was like at this time. Until now – relying principally on secondary evidence, letters from third parties and recollections frequently penned long after the events which they purport to describe, or drawing inferences from Mallarmé's as yet limited literary output – we have painted a rather fragmentary portrait. Once he begins to correspond with Henri Cazalis, Mallarmé ceases to be a shadowy figure and at last acquires some substance. As both men decide to pursue a relationship which, because of the distance which separates them, can be sustained in no other way, their regular exchange of letters provides a privileged and valuable insight into their respective personalities.

We must never forget, of course, that both correspondents are highly conscious of the image they wish to project. This is especially true of Mallarmé. As a young provincial writing to a Parisian older than himself, he feels that he is at a disadvantage. Trying too hard to impress, he frequently cuts a somewhat precious and at times ridiculous figure, with his embossed monogrammed notepaper, deliberate name-dropping, and constant references to his various literary projects. A wonderfully posed photograph of him taken around this time captures his striving for effect. It shows him seated at a table with the index finger of his right hand resting gently against his cheek – the artist wrapped in thought.[29] Nonetheless, it is clear that in their letters both men soon felt free to confide things which would otherwise have stayed unsaid, even between such close friends as Mallarmé and Des Essarts, who talked endlessly about all kinds of subjects.

In the case of Mallarmé, this first letter to Cazalis confirms much that could already be suspected. It is written by a young provincial keenly aware of his youth and inexperience, yet eager to impress a Parisian two years his elder whom he fears to be somewhat more sophisticated. Obviously that fact goes a long way to explain the hesitant tone, the awkwardness and deliberate self-deprecation in which it frequently indulges. The repeated and occasionally clumsy recourse to convoluted literary references and clichés reveals Mallarmé as a bookish and fairly pretentious young man who finds it difficult to strike the right tone when dealing with strangers. Moreover, he emerges as someone who has so thoroughly absorbed the characters and atmosphere of Poe's tales that he has created for himself a rather exaggeratedly melancholic persona behind which he is able to hide his own vulnerability.

Even so, what emerges from beneath the rhetoric and the posturing is a clear desire to become friends. At times the letter betrays an almost desperate need for friendship, particularly obvious in the clumsy and sententious final lines:

> Life brings its moments of happiness and adversity. And so we can say, quoting that delightful proverb *The friends of our friends* . . . that friends never come along alone. It was already a great pleasure for me to know that rich store of affection and talent called Emmanuel, of whom I have not spoken at enough length in this letter. I could not have dared to hope that that particular friendship would reveal to me another as genuine as the one which will unite you and me. Allow me, my dear friend, as I await your happy arrival in Sens, to shake you by the hand, your devoted
>
> Stéphane Mallarmé

In fact, either because of this letter or more likely in spite of it, Mallarmé was to see Cazalis sooner than he had anticipated. The following Sunday Emmanuel des Essarts invited him on an outing to the forest of Fontainebleau on the outskirts of Paris, where he was introduced to several other Parisian friends. Present on that day was the painter Henri Regnault, a former classmate of Des Essarts and Cazalis who would go on to obtain the Prix de Rome in 1866 before being tragically killed in the Franco-Prussian war of 1871.

There were young ladies too, carefully chaperoned by their mothers. First there was Anne-Marie or rather 'Nina' Gaillard, a year older than Mallarmé, daughter of a rich advocate from Lyon. She was a bubbling, spontaneous young woman, a poet, painter and amateur actress, rather plump, full of energy and vitality. Soon she was to marry Hector de Callias, a journalist and minor writer. He was a drunkard and they separated in 1867. Nina then took her mother's name but kept the *particule* and was known as Nina de Villars. She loved entertaining, and in the 70s her Paris salon became famous for its relaxed if not Bohemian atmosphere. It was frequented by many artists of the day, including Manet, who used her as a model for his *Lady with Fan*. Then there were the Yapp girls, Harriet known as 'Ettie', and her younger sister Isabelle, both daughters of Edward Yapp, an English journalist who divided his year between London and Paris.

The weather was not particularly kind that Sunday, but none of the participants seems to have noticed it, and especially not Mallarmé, for whom to mingle in such exotic and slightly Bohemian company was an exhilarating and unforgettable experience. The outing to the forest of Fontainebleau was to remain indelibly etched upon his memory. 'That magic name,' he wrote jokingly to Cazalis some few months later.[30] As often with Mallarmé's apparently flippant remarks, the jest contained a grain of truth. The forest of Fontainebleau was to remain a privileged location in his psychological as well as his physical geography. It was there in the romantic Franchard Gorge that he would later propose to his future wife. As chance would have it, it was also in the shadow of this same forest that, once he settled in Paris, he would spend many of his happiest hours. Understandably, therefore, a fortnight after the outing and still clearly under its spell, he agreed with Cazalis that the whole experience had been quite extraordinary:

> Oh! what a charming recollection I also have of our wonderful outing! It all seems so distant now, alas, so dreamlike. If Henri [Regnault] had not crushed them under his heels, the strawberries and those lips would be merging now in a pink and purple haze. It is all becoming confused and fading into half tints already. Sens is such a depressing town. Everything fades into a nondescript grey here! But oh those mad dashes over the rocks and the ten of us in that carriage! Those oak trees and periwinkles! That sun in our eyes and in our hearts, even if it was absent from the skies![31]

It hardly seems possible that this letter was penned by the same person who had written so stiffly and selfconsciously to the same correspondent barely a fortnight earlier. Yet the sudden transformation is not hard to explain. For the first time since the death of his sister Maria, Mallarmé had met a group of people with whom he felt a special bond. On that day he caught a tantalizing glimpse of the kind of life he longed for and which henceforth for him would be associated, inevitably, with Paris and its surroundings.[32] Most of all, there in the forest of Fontainebleau he experienced, albeit briefly, the sense of belonging to a privileged community of people with similar tastes and interests. At long last here were people to whom he could relate; to whom he could read and send his poetry; upon whom, above all, he could lavish his love and affection. He admitted as much a short time later when he wrote to Cazalis to thank him for the photograph of Ettie Yapp which the latter had sent him.[33]

Unfortunately, one thing prevented Mallarmé from sharing in these Sunday outings as often as he would have liked. If Cazalis, Des Essarts and the others were all affluent enough to allow themselves regular picnics and outings to the woods of Meudon or Fontainebleau, or dinners and dances in the Bois de Boulogne, Mallarmé could not afford such pleasures. In June his father Numa had been forced by his rapidly deteriorating health to take early retirement, and the family budget was now severely restricted. The whole family – Anne Mallarmé, four children and Numa himself – had to live off less money than Stéphane would have as an allowance during his year in London.[34] At first he tried to make light of his financial position, claiming that he did not wish to trouble his father with money matters and pointedly commenting upon the curious reputation he enjoyed in Sens, where his own family considered him to be a waster, while some of the younger people in the town envied his apparently Bohemian life-style and treated him as if he had several mistresses. The truth, he ruefully quipped, was somewhat different: 'My pockets are nearly always empty and I don't even sleep with the maid!'[35]

As the weeks went by, he found it harder to joke about the matter. His mood darkened as he grew more and more impatient to leave what he now considered to be a prison. In his frustration, he unfairly sought to place all the blame on his stepmother because it was she who held the purse-strings:

> To tell the truth, if it wasn't that I don't want to leave Emmanuel all alone in this desert of Sens, or that I want to see you during the coming holidays. If it wasn't for you both, whom I love, I'd be off to England today. I'd be really very sorry to leave behind my poor father who is ill. But I find this house so repugnant to me, I feel so ill at ease during every one of my silent and brooding mealtimes, I can no longer bear such unseemly efforts at making economies when I have a few thousand francs to my name. I am being stifled here! The worst of it all is that everybody here would accuse me of ingratitude if they could hear me.
>
> Everybody thinks my stepmother is an angel, especially when we have visitors in the drawing-room. Yes, but she is a tight-fisted angel . . . Everything eventually comes down to a matter of money here, so I can't say anything. I'm sure that if I mentioned the Alcazar in Toledo or the Alhambra in Seville, she would say: oh yes, but they must have cost a lot of money to build.[36]

These last remarks were incredibly unfeeling and quite undeserved, given the difficult situation in which Anne Mallarmé found herself. But Stéphane was too steeped in self-pity, too obsessed with his own problems, to contemplate or accept the truth of the situation. He had also conveniently forgotten that it was largely due to the determined and courageous efforts of Anne Mallarmé that he owed the considerable freedom which he now enjoyed.

What was quite understandable in the circumstances was Mallarmé's growing impatience to be free of Sens. Before that, however, another important person was to enter his life, someone who would remain with him not only during the year he was about to spend in London, but for many years to come.

Poetry and Art were not the only subjects frequently discussed by Cazalis, Mallarmé and Des Essarts as their friendship rapidly blossomed. Cazalis soon admitted to his two friends that he had fallen hopelessly in love with Ettie Yapp. Des Essarts, who considered himself a man of the world, just raised an eyebrow in disbelief and sent Cazalis a pompous letter advising caution. Mallarmé sought to conceal his limited (in reality nonexistent) experience of women, whilst passing, with breathtaking male chauvinism, for something of an expert in the matter. He chose to congratulate his friend for selecting as the object of his advances a flower of English womanhood. 'The simple fact of the matter' he began somewhat pompously, 'is that English women are adorable creatures! That soft blondness, those clear drops of the waters of Lake Geneva set in a sea of whiteness which they are pleased to call their eyes, as all women do. Those perfect Greek waists, not a pretentious wasp's waist but the waist of an angel who would unfold her wings from beneath her corsage!'[37]

Cazalis' pursuit of Ettie had for some time been a regular topic of conversation between Mallarmé and Des Essarts when, towards the end of June, Stéphane's own eyes alighted on an intriguing foreign lady who every afternoon collected the children of the local judge at the gates of the lycée. Believing quite significantly (and in fact quite erroneously) that she too was English, and that by securing her affections he could emulate his rich and elegant Parisian friend, Mallarmé took advantage of the fact that his grandparents were away visiting relations to set about an assiduous courtship. We can imagine therefore the pleasure he took some ten days later as he announced his conquest, teasing Cazalis, who was momentarily rather despondent because Ettie had returned to London:

> I am delighted, really delighted that you both like me. Your thoughts, like wood-pigeons, will perhaps bring a twig or two of love into my nest.
>
> O what a funny thing life is! When I realize that at the very moment you were mingling your tears of despair, I was scooping drops of water out of my bowl to sprinkle over a love-letter, pretending they were tears!
>
> I am not going to tell you about my nice little German girl whom I am determined to have. You, the sublimely disconsolate one, the martyr, would be extremely interested, would you not, to learn that a letter of mine was refused this morning but nonetheless that someone wants to speak to me tonight! If only I could be caught in my trap, and, as of course she will love me, love her just a little! That would bring a ray of sunshine and a smile into my life.[38]

Only three letters have survived of those that Mallarmé wrote at this time to the woman who would eventually become his wife.[39] They are fascinating documents which reveal that while he was much more vulnerable and much less calculating and masterful than he would have Cazalis believe, to begin with, at least, the love he expressed for Marie Gerhard had literary sources and was inspired as much by conscious and unconscious borrowings from Baudelaire's poems as by the rather obvious and facile exploitation of Hugo's novel *Les Misérables* which he was reading at the time.[40] Indeed, a highly complex nexus of elements, of which Mallarmé himself was not necessarily entirely aware, was at play here, including the fact that his own dead sister, one of Baudelaire's mistresses, and now the woman upon whom he had fixed his affections, all bore the same Christian name, Marie.[41]

Soon, what had begun in part as a game, in part as a distraction from the prospect of a lonely and boring summer vacation, in part as an attempt to keep pace with older friends, became something quite different. By the end of the first week in August, Mallarmé no longer spoke dismissively of the 'nice German girl'. The game had become very serious indeed. The posturing disappeared, as he confessed to Cazalis that the person who had been caught in his own trap was none other than himself:

> You know how clumsy I am and that I've got myself caught in a swallow trap that I had stretched over Love's bushy knoll. What I mean is this. I had noticed a quite pretty young woman, who was quite striking and sad-looking. She is German and the governess of a rich family from around here. That was six weeks ago. She attracted me for some reason or other and I began to court her assiduously . . . Like all governesses and primary schoolteachers who belong to no class, she exudes a wistful charm which was not without its effect upon me, so much so in fact that I became a little in love with her.[42]

He had tried to resist, he insisted, foreseeing all kinds of difficulties for them both in such a small community. Resistance had been useless, however, and had only made it all the more difficult to forget her. 'She is sad here and she is bored,' he concluded. 'I am sad and I am bored. Out of our combined sadness we perhaps will be able to create some happiness.' These remarks were made half in jest, in an attempt to portray as relatively trivial something which by now was very far from that. As was frequently to be the case, this apparently casual remark contained more than a grain of truth. Marie and he had been drawn together out of a common sense of loneliness.

Stéphane and his 'gentle Marie' were separated for three weeks in September. While Cazalis disappeared off to London to visit Ettie Yapp, only to return more smitten than ever before, Mallarmé spent the first fortnight with his grandparents in Versailles, and most of the third week tracing on the map and following station by station on the railway timetable Marie Gerhard's itinerary as she travelled to and from Germany to visit her father.

When Marie returned to France, Mallarmé consulted a gypsy woman who told him 'the most extraordinary things'.[43] At the end of the same week they spent an unforgettable day in the Franchard Gorge in the heart of the Forest of Fontainebleau. Not only was this beauty spot famous for the night which Georges Sand spent there with Alfred de Musset and which the latter had described in his *Confessions d'un enfant du siècle*, but, much more significantly from Mallarmé's point of view, it was near to the site of that memorable picnic with Des Essarts and his Parisian friends. As a souvenir of that day when he first asked Marie to come to London with him, letting it be understood, without his actually saying so, that he would marry her, he kept some dried wild flowers in a white envelope tied with purple string on which he carefully recorded the place, 'Fontainebleau Franchard', and the date, '29 September 1862'.

When they learned that Mallarmé was quite serious in his intention of getting married to this rather plain-looking governess, both Des Essarts and Cazalis expressed serious doubts. For him to have her as a mistress was one thing, but as a wife – that was quite another matter. Some of their objections were typical of the male chauvinism of the period. She was too old for him, they argued.[44] She was not pretty. She had no culture to speak of and little education. The main objection, however, was of a different order. It concerned her inferior social position. Marie was not a part of the upper middle class to which they all belonged. Her father was a primary school-teacher and she herself was a servant, albeit a governess.

Mallarmé knew full well that this last objection, which was based on prejudice and snobbery, would be shared by his family if they found out whom he was courting. In their reduced circumstances, they had a social position to keep up, and therefore expected him to marry for money. This last point particularly irritated Mallarmé. He was scathing about such a preoccupation with money. 'Why was Marie not rich?' he asked Cazalis.

> Because her father was not a thief. After all, what does being rich mean? It is having something in your pocket with which your neighbour would have bought an overcoat had he not had the stupidity to let it be taken from him. Her father is a primary-school teacher in Camberg. That is a noble occupation. Besides, will I be anything more? He explains German to his pupils. I'll explain English to mine. The only difference is that the children he teaches are twelve years old and mine will be fifteen. That is the difference between primary and secondary schools.
>
> There is one thing I am proud of, and I am very proud of it. My children, if God gives me any, will not have the blood of shopkeepers in their veins. One morning their grandfather will not have placed a piece of sealing-wax under his scales so that they weigh a hundredth of a gram more and deliver a hundredth of a gram less, which hundredth of a gram repeated twenty times a day makes a fifth of a gram, and after five days a whole gram so that after a month, during which time you have deserved six hundred times to go to prison, you make one sou's profit – six grams of molasses being worth one sou. That's business for you.
>
> Before getting married to a rich woman, every honest man should ask: 'Was your money earned producing books, teaching people, living by the pen, out in the open air? I don't want any coins which have echoed on counters!'
>
> The very thought of feeling in my hair a hand which has rolled wafers! of trying to drink the infinite in eyes which for ten years watched for the moment when a customer's back was turned to remove a pinch of powdered sugar! How ghastly! For if she had not done it herself, her father would have. And if not him, his grand-father. If not him the grandfather before that.
>
> My motto is *Nothing suspect*, and all business is suspect. I despise the veuve Clicquot as much as Madame Grégoire. It is theft on a large scale, that's all.[45]

Reading these lines, one suspects that it was in part to flout his family's blatant materialism and conventional middle-class values that Mallarmé persisted in his relationship with Marie.

But there were other reasons, and to begin with the simple fact that he had discovered the joy of love and companionship. The final lines of his letter were entirely to the point:

> I admit that in other people's eyes she is not very pretty and that she has no great artistic soul – although her face exudes a pleasing charm and subtle intelligence and sincerity instead of wit – I admit to all that. But that is not what I sought in her. I wanted to be loved and I am more than anyone can be.
>
> What attracts me to her is some magnetic force which has no apparent cause. She has a particular look which has at some point penetrated my soul and which could not be removed without causing a mortal wound. It is as simple as that.

Of course, in his heart of hearts Mallarmé knew it was not quite as simple as that. He and Marie could avoid the issue by escaping from Sens and hiding in the London fog, but things would not necessarily be any easier on the other side of the Channel. In order to be accepted in polite London society, and in particular by the Yapp family whom he had promised he would visit in order to advance Cazalis' courtship of Ettie, he would have either to be perceived as married to Marie, or to resort to the subterfuge of simply concealing her existence. Anxious not to compromise his friend's matrimonial prospects, Mallarmé seems to have suggested to Cazalis that he and Marie go through a marriage ceremony as soon as they landed in England, secure in the knowledge that the marriage would not be valid in France and that they could decide at leisure whether or not to legalize it. Cazalis, who rightly felt that he was being drawn into a situation which was not of his making and which was highly suspect both legally and morally, advised against such a dangerous course of action. Instead he suggested that the whole question of marriage be put off for a full year. In the meantime the couple could get to know each other better. By implication, he was inviting Stéphane to live with Marie in a kind of trial marriage.

It was a far from ideal solution which left too many

questions open and undermined from the very outset the year the young couple spent in London. In his impatience to be off, however, Mallarmé chose to ignore the serious consequences of his action. He decided to take Cazalis' advice and to live with Marie for a year. They would have left immediately had a sudden recurrence of his grandfather's ill-health in the second half of October not delayed their departure for almost a month. At the beginning of November, unknown to Stéphane's family, who – like her own father in Germany – appear to have had no idea whatsoever of what was going on, Marie Gerhard left for Paris, where she spent a few days with her sister and met Cazalis before travelling on to Boulogne. A few days later Mallarmé left Sens, breaking his journey in Versailles to say goodbye to his grandparents. Fanny Desmolins could not wait to give an account of his visit to her cousin Mélanie:

> We had the poor child here with us for a few days before he left. He set off with our most pressing entreaties as to how he should behave himself ringing in his ears and provided with many letters of introduction for the most respectable echelons of London society, most notably several parish priests (Catholic ones, of course) and Cardinal Wiseman the Archbishop of London itself. We have reason to hope that these connections will be of some use to him, if he is sensible enough to cultivate them . . . He did not fail to make us all kinds of fine promises, let us just hope that he keeps them.[46]

Totally unaware of the circumstances in which her grandson was travelling to England, Mme Desmolins did not realize that there was no question of him attempting to use such letters of introduction. Dismayed at his later unwillingness to do so, she was to accuse him of deliberate and spiteful neglect on this matter.[47] In the meantime, unknown to everyone except Cazalis, he had joined Marie Gerhard in Boulogne, and on 8 November 1862 the couple set sail for England.

They crossed the Channel in perfect weather, moved into a hotel and set about the task of finding accommodation. As far as Mallarmé's family was concerned, the charade of the lonely

bachelor looking for humble lodgings and in search of private
pupils had to be maintained. Mallarmé therefore penned a
suitably woeful and contrite missive to his grandmother, who
reported its contents, not without a hint of smugness and
complacency, to her faithful confidante Mélanie Laurent:

> The poor boy left a fortnight ago, in streaming sunlight which
> abandoned him in London, to be replaced by a foggy atmosphere
> which disillusioned him from the very outset and made him reflect
> sadly, already, upon the solitude and voluntary exile in which he
> finds himself. Seeing that the thick fog affected his throat, as well as
> his mind, he had to keep indoors the first few days to take care of a
> very bad sore throat. He took the opportunity to write us a long
> detailed letter informing us of how he has organized himself. He
> thinks he will be able to cope.[48]

By contrast, the first impressions of London which Mallarmé sent Cazalis were quite different. He admitted that he
had had a bad cough for the first couple of days, blaming the
coal fire in his hotel bedroom and the thick fog outside, both
of which, he wrote, had almost asphyxiated him. Despite the
fact that his poor command of English and his inexperience
had allowed him to be swindled out of the considerable sum
of forty francs within a week of his arrival, he did not conceal
from his old friend the delight he experienced in being in the
English capital. He liked the chocolate-coloured omnibuses,
the leafy squares, the hustle and bustle and sheer joy of the
barrel-organs with the obligatory monkeys in red caps, the
brass bands and the Punch and Judy shows. He and Marie had
by now rented accommodation on the second floor of a four-
storey terraced house at 9 Panton Square, more or less midway
between Leicester Square and Piccadilly Circus. The picture he
painted of their little nest conjured up blissful domesticity:

> I spend my time reading and writing. She does embroidery or some
> knitting. She is forever leaving what she is doing to come over and
> kiss me, embrace me and say the most delightful things. Just add tea
> pots and beer mugs and a big double bed on the second floor of this
> paradise and you can picture our bedroom.[49]

In short, to begin with London was just as Mallarmé had imagined it. It offered a haven, a welcome release from the closed community back home in Sens where everyone knew everyone else's business and where strangers were viewed with suspicion. Everyone was a stranger in London. It was all wonderfully anonymous. 'I love this perpetually grey sky,' he told Cazalis in the same letter. 'You don't need to think. The bright blue sky and the stars are really frightening things. You can feel at home here, and God cannot see you. His spy, the sun, does not dare crawl out of the shadows.' It was an interesting remark, to which we shall return.[50]

Marie Gerhard did not share this cosy, romantic view. She felt rather trapped and vulnerable, living in a foreign country whose language she did not speak, and totally dependent upon Mallarmé for company. Because of the need to keep up appearances, she could neither accompany him on his regular visits to the Yapps, nor risk receiving visitors in their own home. Her growing unease prompted her to add three pages of her own to the next letter which Mallarmé sent to Cazalis. They provide a more sober and indeed more realistic assessment of their situation which is in stark contrast to the idyllic picture conjured up by Mallarmé. Significantly, she wrote in German, which she knew Cazalis understood. This action was rather more than the nostalgia for her native language that she tried to suggest. She clearly did not want Mallarmé to learn of her sense of foreboding:

> Here we are at last in London, the city we have longed for for so long. It remains to be seen if we can live here happy and contented. We often go for long walks in the little village that is London and every day we discover something new and interesting. But frankly I have to confess, Monsieur Cazalis, that I shall never become accustomed to these dark and brooding clouds and this terrible fog. Last Monday the fog was once again so thick that it remained dark the entire day and we had to keep the lamp lit. The fog even comes into all the rooms through the windows and is quite suffocating. Sometimes our days are sad. However on days like these we are even more

impatient for the evenings which we spend relaxing in front of the fire, drinking tea and chatting. We speak of you often and our fondest desire would be that our dear good friend was with us. Oh! if only you could come and spend some hours with us now and then, what wonderful evenings we would have together![51]

Marie's main problem, as her letter confirmed, was that she felt very lonely. She was frequently left to her own devices as Mallarmé paid his duty calls to the Yapps. More than this, she was terrified that she would become pregnant. She was literally quite sick with worry and anxiety, not to mention her feelings of guilt. Invited to add a postscript to her note, Mallarmé tried to make light of the fact that she would not translate what she had written, but his awkward attempt at a male joke shows that, privately, he shared Marie's anxieties. 'You know how impressionable she is,' he told Cazalis. 'Her stomach pains, which are nothing more than indigestion, make her think she is pregnant. And so she cries. It is all very depressing for me, as you can imagine. This last week has been very difficult for me.'

These typically egocentric and rather dismissive remarks must hardly have reassured Cazalis. Despite Mallarmé's attempts, in his subsequent letters, to paint a rosy picture of their life together, it is clear that the initial honeymoon mood quickly evaporated. This was hardly surprising, and to a large extent it was due to Mallarmé's own insensitivity. His visits to the Yapps were not only very frequent, but often quite lengthy. Significantly, it was on his return from one of these, less than a month after their arrival in London, that Marie informed him that she felt it would be better if she returned to France.

Despite the tearful and rather unconvincing letter expressing shock and dismay which he sent to Cazalis, Mallarmé's first instinct was not to resist a decision which could bring to an end the unbearable tension under which they both were living. It would relieve him all the more because he had discovered that his stepmother was aware of his involvement with Marie, although fortunately she did not know about her presence in London with him. In the event, though, he could not bring himself to allow Marie to leave. Unable to resolve the matter by themselves, both of them wrote independently to Cazalis, but he was preoccupied with a crisis in his own relationship with Ettie Yapp, and in no position to offer advice. In the end Marie stayed on, and in the third week of December the couple left their rooms in Panton Square and moved into a flat at 16 Albert Terrace, in the more salubrious (and no doubt more expensive) surroundings of Knightsbridge.[52]

This move, clearly intended to provide a fresh start, only granted them a temporary reprieve. On 9 January 1863, almost three months to the day after they had first crossed the Channel, Stéphane and Marie crossed it again in the opposite direction, and in much less happy circumstances. As if to highlight the point, the crossing on this occasion was extremely rough. Due to thick fog at the mouth of the Thames and then incredibly strong winds in the Channel itself, the boat docked thirteen hours later. They spent a last weekend together in Boulogne then parted. Marie travelled on by train to Paris, where she was met by her sister and Cazalis. Stéphane returned alone to London.

It was the first of two long separations. After barely a fortnight on his own, Mallarmé made a lightning one-day visit to Paris to see Cazalis, who advised him against any thoughts of marriage. He returned to London without seeing Marie and having given his friend a formal promise that he would not change his mind. But his resolve soon weakened once he was on his own, and by 10 February – in the face of his repeated entreaties and against the advice of Cazalis, who found himself in the unenviable position of acting as messenger and counsellor to both of them – Marie returned to the flat at Albert Terrace. In the circumstances, Cazalis felt that decency dictated marriage. Marie probably shared this feeling, but it is clear that she did not press her lover, hoping no doubt that he would come round to this view himself. In typical fashion, he continued to dither, presumably concerned that, as he was still a minor, he would be disowned by his family with disastrous financial consequences. Eventually, after a month, Marie felt she had no choice but to leave him again, this time for Brussels.

Marie left London on 4 March. Late that month, after several weeks of unrelieved loneliness and much soul-searching, Mallarmé was forced to return to France, to attend the army review board in Paris where he was declared exempt from military service.[53] On the way to Paris, secure in the knowledge that he was now twenty-one and thus no longer ran any risk of being disowned by his family, he made a brief but significant detour to Brussels to see Marie and to ask her to marry him.

Once the legal formalities of his inheritance had been completed in Sens, where he had gone for this express purpose, he broached the subject of his marriage with his stepmother. Anne Mallarmé was understanding and extremely supportive, willing to do what she could to prepare his grandmother for the unwelcome news. She even suggested that the couple have a quiet wedding which she would pretend to learn about later in a letter. The gesture, which was typical of her kindness and generosity, surprised Mallarmé, who was forced to concede that in the past he had totally misjudged her. 'In all of this, the poor dear woman has shown incredible tact and great friendship for me,' he wrote to Cazalis. 'I have often been ungrateful to her and have misunderstood her.'[54] The apology was well deserved and long overdue.

On 10 April, with all the legal formalities out of the way but his marriage plans still unknown to his family, Mallarmé said goodbye to his father and returned to Paris on the way to London. The following day, he was about to leave the capital when an urgent telegram arrived from his stepmother announcing that his father had suffered a serious stroke.

Mallarmé dashed back to Sens, but by then his father was in a coma. He died the following day without regaining consciousness.

We have little information about how Mallarmé reacted to his father's death. The only reference to it in his correspondence reveals that he was not entirely unaffected. Writing to Cazalis a fortnight after the event, he refers to it rather briefly, commenting: 'To be sure, my poor father had been dying for four or five years – but there is quite a difference between someone who is dying and someone who has actually died!'[55] It would be unwise, however, to overstate the impact which this loss had upon him. His remarks to Cazalis refer more to the event itself than to the individual who has just passed away. Their relationship was not, nor had it ever been, a particularly close one. At the time of his father's death, Mallarmé rejected virtually everything he stood for. In part because of Numa's unfortunate paralysis during the last few years of his life, in part because of the fact that his son was living abroad and, for all intents and purposes, had been brought up by his stepmother and his grandparents, communication between the two had for some time been minimal. Mallarmé would be much more greatly affected by the death of his grandmother, Fanny Desmolins. It was particularly after she died that he felt a sense of being orphaned.

After the funeral a family council was held at Les Gaillons. One of Mallarmé's uncles, a colonel in the artillery, was appointed guardian of his younger half-brother and half-sisters. Mallarmé himself would return to London as a man of independent and not inconsiderable means.[56]

He stayed on in Sens for another ten days to help Anne Mallarmé sort out his father's affairs, before making another detour to Brussels to collect Marie. By the last week of April they were both back in London and moving from their Knightsbridge address to 6 Brompton Square, near Kensington Oratory, where they were to be married.

Now that he had made his decision to marry Marie, Mallarmé felt the need to justify it to Cazalis:

If I were marrying Marie to ensure my own happiness, I would be quite mad. Besides is happiness obtainable on this earth? And seriously, ought we to seek it anywhere else than in the world of the Imagination? Happiness is not the real goal of existence. The real goal is Duty. Duty, call it Art, the Struggle or whatever you will . . . No I am marrying Marie solely because I know that without me she will not be able to live and because I shall have poisoned her pure existence . . . No, Henri I am not doing this for me but for her alone. Only you in the whole world will know the sacrifice I am making. As for my other friends, I shall pretend to believe that I am using this union to ensure my own happiness, so that Marie is raised in their esteem.[57]

There was of course an element of truth in what Mallarmé was claiming. He was in part marrying Marie out of a genuine sense of duty. But if they were meant to be taken seriously, these arrogant remarks were not only unfeeling but completely unfair to someone who, from the very beginning, had shown herself to be selflessly honest, loyal and steadfast. Of the two, it was Marie who had demonstrated the greater maturity, Marie who had made the greater sacrifice and taken the greater risks. By agreeing to go to London with Mallarmé as his mistress, she had risked everything: her reputation, her close relationship with her own father in Germany, any hope of a future career as a governess, and above all her independence.

Fortunately, this unconvincing attempt to pass himself off as a heroic martyr was not to be taken seriously by someone like Cazalis who, as the principal and at times only confidant to both Stéphane and Marie, had followed in detail the vicissitudes of their tortured relationship. He was better placed than most to know the genuine ties of affection which bound them together. Furthermore, through a previous letter written by Mallarmé from Versailles, Cazalis knew full well that there were several other aspects of the marriage which bothered him considerably. He feared, quite rightly as it turned out, that out of prejudice and snobbery his aunts and uncles would not approve of someone whom they judged of inferior stock. Besides, he had genuinely ambiguous feelings towards the act of marriage himself. As someone who prided himself on being something of a free spirit, he saw that he risked appearing to conform to the conventions of a social class for whose materialistic values he had hitherto demonstrated nothing but open contempt. Writing from the house of Fanny Desmolins as he anxiously awaited the arrival of his stepmother, he had given vent to his sense of frustration:

> I shall ask her [Anne Mallarmé] to say very little about it all to my grandmother this morning. I can just imagine the latter's shrieks and the indignation of those pot-faced aunts when she tells them. I don't want them to talk about this in my family. Because even if they were to take it the right way – which is not possible – I would be hurt. I would not like to have to seek either by letter or in person the approval of a bunch of pot-bellied egos which is what my uncles are. I would even hate them to have an inkling about it all. As I am not getting married for the sake of getting married, but merely to legalize our two hearts beating as one, I don't want this action to be considered more important from the outside than it is for our twin souls. I do not want there to be a lot of talk about this, even well intentioned discussion.[58]

It would be wrong therefore to suggest, as some critics have argued, that Mallarmé entered into a passionless marriage with a woman he did not love. Indeed, there is plenty of evidence to show that he had nothing but the greatest affection for Marie Gerhard, and that as his wife and the mother of his children she would remain extremely important to him.[59] This does not mean, however, that there was no calculation in his decision to marry at a time when, legally, nothing compelled him to do so. On the contrary, he had given his future much thought. Now that he was no longer dependent on his family, he was determined more than ever to organize his life for the sake of his Art. Significantly, when he came to sign his marriage certificate he gave his profession as 'Artist' (whereas on the legal documents he had recently signed after his father's death, he had been referred to as a 'student'). He was equally determined to pursue his goal in the best possible conditions. Remembering what had brought him to London in the first place, he saw no reason to change his initial plans: 'A secondary schoolteacher's life is simple, modest and uneventful,' he reassured Cazalis. 'We shall be quite secure. That is what I am after.'[60]

When he wrote this, Mallarmé had already begun to prepare not only for the marriage itself but – fairly late in the day – for the exams he needed to pass in order to obtain the certificate of proficiency that would enable him to teach English in a secondary school in France. The marriage could not take place for several weeks to allow time for the banns to be posted. As soon as the formalities were complere Stéphane and Marie were quietly married on 10 August 1863 in the Kensington Oratory (today Brompton Oratory).[61] The honeymoon, if indeed there was one, must have been exceptionally brief. Mallarmé had to be in Paris by the 17th of the month in order to sit the first part of his exam.

By mid-September he was informed that he had passed and was now qualified to teach in a lycée. In fact he had only just scraped a pass, in ninth place out of the eleven successful candidates. This was hardly surprising. The ten months or so which he had spent in London had hardly been conducive to study. Nor had they allowed him much opportunity to make contact with the English or even to practise their language. 'All the English look the same to me,' he once wrote to Cazalis, 'just like the rooms in the Grand Hotel.'[62] His social life had been largely restricted either to the company of the Yapps, who lived part of the year in Paris and in whose house French was talked as much as English, or to that of Marie herself, with whom he always spoke French. The only other person whom we can identify for certain as a friend (and not until his return to London after his father's death) was another Frenchman, the elderly and somewhat eccentric Jean-Baptiste

81

François Ernest Le Chatelain, who liked to be known as 'Le Chevalier de Chatelain'.[63]

A few days after receiving his results, Mallarmé officially applied for a teaching post. He requested the school at Saint-Quentin, some ninety miles from Paris, to which his old friend and former headmaster Monsieur Clément had been appointed. The Ministry of Education were not to be rushed, however, and Mallarmé and his bride had to wait to learn their fate. They seem to have spent the second half of September in Sens with Anne Mallarmé, who did her best to get the young couple accepted by the community. At the beginning of October, seeking greater privacy, they moved into Paris itself, to a hotel room in the rue des Saints-Pères, behind Saint Germain des Prés.

As he waited to be assigned to a school, Mallarmé also tackled the thorny problem of having his English marriage legalized in France and transferred to the Registry in Sens. This was necessary because he had failed to meet the requirements of French law, having neither obtained official permission to be married from his grandparents nor published any banns in France. Several tedious formalities had to be completed. He needed copies of the original marriage certificate, and a certificate from the French Consulate in London stating that he had been married in accordance with English practice and custom. Both of these certificates had to be translated by a registered translator. Moreover, he required a written statement from his grandparents saying that they were prepared to overlook the previous irregularities and give his marriage their blessing.

As usual Anne Mallarmé did her best to smooth Fanny Desmolins' ruffled feathers. When Fanny complained about the interminable delay in obtaining the required certificates, which she automatically and unfairly blamed on her grandson, Anne Mallarmé explained that both Marie and Stéphane had been quite ill, he with tonsillitis and she with jaundice. Her wise counsel seems to have prevailed, because on 19 November the Desmolins signed a document recognizing the legality of the London ceremony and agreeing that, once all the due formalities were completed, the marriage of their grandson and his foreign wife could be officially entered in the Registry of the town of Sens.[64]

In the event, largely due to the incompetence of Mallarmé and his friends, the procedure took months to complete. In the meantime, the Ministry of Education had found a post for him. By a ministerial decree of 3 November 1863 he was appointed temporary assistant English master in the imperial lycée of Tournon on the banks of the Rhône, replacing someone who had been granted a year's leave of absence. Confined to his bed with a severe bout of tonsillitis, Mallarmé did not hear of the decision for several days. When he did, he must have been bitterly disappointed. If he had originally requested Saint-Quentin, it was not just because Monsieur Clément was its headmaster. Although the town was further away from Paris than Sens, it was nonetheless within fairly easy striking distance of the capital. Tournon lay some 350 miles to the south, almost as far away from Paris as it was possible to be.

In fact, ever since his return from London that summer, Mallarmé had been acting on what now turned out to be the completely false assumption that for the next few years he would be spending plenty of time in Paris. For that reason he had spent a large part of September and October contacting old friends and making new ones. He had managed, not without difficulty, to retrace Albert Glatigny and had ensured that Des Essarts met Marie (whom he quickly came to like and respect). He had seen quite a lot of Armand Renaud, a minor poet who worked as a civil servant in the Hôtel de Ville and whom he had probably met earlier through Emile Deschamps. But he had sought out new friends too. Glatigny seems to have introduced him to Albert Collignon, a young lawyer who was then gathering a team of young writers for the new literary review which he was about to launch called *La Revue nouvelle*. Mallarmé was particularly enthusiastic about this project, which seems to have taken up a lot of his time during the last few weeks he spent in Paris. In fact, when he had to make a brief return to London at the beginning of December to obtain some additional documents required for the legalization of his marriage, he sought the help of the Chevalier de Chatelain in obtaining some advance publicity for Collignon's magazine in the London press.

It was likewise sometime during September and October of 1863 that Mallarmé at last managed to meet in person Catulle Mendès to whom, some two years earlier with the blessing of Des Essarts, he had sent some of his earlier poems. Mendès, who along with Villiers de l'Isle-Adam and Edouard Manet was to become one of Mallarmé's closest and most important friends, was then a young man of twenty-two. Of a dashing and handsome appearance, he had already acquired something of a reputation as a womanizer. A few years earlier he had arrived from Toulouse, and using money provided by his father had founded the short-lived but highly respected *Revue fantaisiste*, in which poems and articles by himself and Villiers had appeared alongside the works of older writers such as Baudelaire, Banville and Gautier. Mendès had actually obtained a promise of collaboration from Wagner, but although this was announced on the cover of the first number, the German composer never actually contributed anything – he felt Mendès was too young to run a serious review.

Well practised in self-promotion and gregarious by nature, Mendès was a stimulating companion who, after the demise of his own review, had remained closely involved in the literary life of the capital. By the time Mallarmé returned to Paris from London, he had surrounded himself by a host of exciting young writers who, like Mendès himself, had begun to gravitate around another figure. The regular Saturday evening gatherings held by Leconte de Lisle in his modest apartment on the fifth floor of a block of flats in the boulevard des Invalides had already begun to bring together the nucleus of what would soon be known as the Parnassian group of poets.

Mallarmé visited Mendès in a little house on the Seine at Choisy-le-Roi which he was sharing that summer with his friend Villiers de l'Isle-Adam. The meeting was recalled by Mendès many years later. His account of it provides us with a striking portrait of Mallarmé at that time:

> At Choisy-le-Roi, in my father's house, we received the visit of a very young man who had been sent to us by my excellent friend Emmanuel des Essarts. After dinner, Villiers de l'Isle-Adam retired to his room – he was writing *Elen* at the time – and I went for a walk along the banks of the Seine with Stéphane Mallarmé (for such was the young man's name). He was not very tall and rather sickly-looking with a solemn and melancholy face, conveying a slight bitterness upon which were already etched the ravages of anxiety and disappointment. He had tiny little delicate hands like those of a young girl and his gestures of a rather affected nature were awkward and faintly annoying. But his eyes were bright and clear like those of a very young child, with a distant, transparent look, and his voice, which was fluent and accentuated in rather a deliberate way, was very warm and caressing. Apparently indifferent to the sad things he said, he told me that for quite some time he had lived very unhappily in London as a poor French teacher; that he had suffered greatly in that huge uncaring city from solitude and poverty and from a kind of creeping paralysis which for a time had rendered him incapable of any intellectual effort and literary output.[65]

The friend to whom Mendès introduced Mallarmé in the course of that visit was himself a striking figure. Four years older than Mallarmé, Villiers de l'Isle-Adam, the flamboyant youngest son of one of the most ancient if rather impoverished noble houses of Brittany, was already regarded by his peers as the most outstanding man of his generation, even if somewhat eccentric and unpredictable. He knew Baudelaire, had met Flaubert and Banville and was liked by Leconte de Lisle. In his biography of Villiers, Alan Raitt claims that at the time of their meeting the more powerful personality of Villiers totally overwhelmed Mallarmé. 'Mallarmé,' he writes, 'was a shy and sensitive young man of twenty-two, who had still not developed his poetic manner, and was at once subjugated by the effulgence of Villiers' genius, the prestige of his name, and the brilliance of his conversation. Thenceforward, Villiers symbolized for him the absolute figure of the Poet . . . It is no exaggeration to say that Villiers changed the whole course of Mallarmé's existence, both as a man and a poet.'[66]

There is little evidence to support this view. It is true that in the fullness of time, and along with other key figures, Villiers would come to stand in Mallarmé's mind as a particularly striking example of the man of genius totally misunderstood and reviled by the masses. But that was to be much, much later, once the two men had known each other for many years. For the moment, like so many of Mallarmé's Parisian acquaintances, Villiers was destined to remain a figure on the distant horizon. Mallarmé's impending departure to Tournon would see to that.

And indeed, how did Mallarmé and his bride relish this prospect? How equipped were they for the challenge which lay ahead? If the description of the diffident, depressed and rather strained-looking young man who strolled with Mendès along the banks of the Seine that late summer evening is anything to go by, then Mallarmé must have contemplated his future with some trepidation. We must remember, of course, that at that meeting, the desire to impress slightly older and more experienced men may well have encouraged him to strike a deliberately tragic pose. Faced with people who, in their own right, were already well established literary figures, he no doubt also may have felt the need to excuse or justify the absence of any major work of his own. Certainly, when placed alongside the facts as we know them, the account which Mallarmé appears to have given Mendès of his London experience seems an excessively depressing, and in some respects, quite deliberately misleading one. (He was for example by no stretch of the imagination a penniless young man.)

There were elements of truth, of course, in the sombre picture Mallarmé painted for Mendès. For the larger part, the ten months or so which he had spent in London had been dark and depressing ones filled with anxiety and uncertainty. From the literary point of view, they had certainly not been very productive months. His troubled relationship with Marie had left him little time for anything else. Yet London had also been an enriching experience. The relatively small number of poems which were either actually written during the London experience or later inspired by it, poems like 'Le Château de l'espérance' (The Castle of Hope), 'A une putain' ('To a Prostitute'), or 'Le Pitre châtié' ('A Clown Is Punished'), and especially 'Les Fenêtres' ('Windows'), have a greater maturity than his earlier verse. Ironic, bitter and full of self-doubt, these poems express genuine anguish and have a new sense of urgency about them.

Artistically, London was a formative experience for Mallarmé. Its images were to haunt his imagination and permeate his consciousness for some considerable time to come. Several of the prose poems which he wrote the following year in Tournon are the product of this slow process of maturation. In these, a mysterious world is created as various elements – distant memories and feelings related to the early loss of his mother and sister, more recent emotions clustered around his relationship with Marie, incidental details from the London setting – are woven together to create haunting, elusive, impressionistic texts which conjure up a nightmarish landscape of the mind. A dark, brooding piece like 'Plainte d'automne' ('Autumn Lament'), for example, may have some obvious models in the tales of Poe and the prose poems of Baudelaire, but the mental landscape it depicts truly belongs to Mallarmé.

The mood of these deceptively anecdotal but in fact quite disturbing pieces is elegiac. The themes are few in number and obsessive: loneliness, anxiety and despair. They constantly move between the shifting perspectives of the external physical world and the strange inner world of the mind, as the carefully measured and perfectly controlled poem 'La Pipe' ('The Pipe') demonstrates:

> Hier, j'ai trouvé ma pipe en rêvant une longue soirée de travail, de beau travail d'hiver. Jetées les cigarettes avec toutes les joies enfantines de l'été dans le passé qu'illuminent les feuilles bleues de soleil, les mousselines et reprise ma grave pipe par un homme sérieux qui veut fumer longtemps sans se déranger, afin de mieux travailler: mais je ne m'attendais pas à la surprise que préparait cette délaissée, à peine eus-je tiré la première bouffée, j'oubliai mes grands livres à faire, émerveillé, attendri, je respirai l'hiver dernier qui revenait. Je n'avais pas touché à la fidèle amie depuis ma rentrée en France, et tout Londres, Londres tel que je le vécus en entier à moi seul, il y a un an, est apparu; d'abord les chers brouillards qui emmitouflent nos cervelles et ont, là-bas, une odeur à eux, quand ils pénètrent sous la croisée. Mon tabac sentait une chambre sombre aux meubles de cuir saupoudrés par la poussière du charbon sur lesquels se roulait le maigre chat noir; les grands feux! et la bonne aux bras rouges versant les charbons, et le bruit de ces charbons tombant du seau de tôle dans la corbeille de fer, le matin – alors que le facteur frappait le double coup solennel, qui me faisait vivre! J'ai revu par les fenêtres ces arbres malades du square désert – j'ai vu le large, si souvent traversé cet hiver-là, grelottant sur le pont du steamer mouillé de bruine et noirci de fumée – avec ma pauvre bien-aimée errante, en habits de voyageuse, une longue robe terne couleur de la poussière des routes, un manteau qui collait humide à ses épaules froides, un de ces chapeaux de paille sans plume et presque sans rubans, que les riches dames jettent en arrivant, tant ils sont déchiquetés par l'air de la mer et que les pauvres bien-aimées regarnissent pour bien des saisons encore. Autour de son cou s'enroulait le terrible mouchoir qu'on agite en se disant adieu pour toujours.

[Yesterday I found my pipe as I was dreaming of a long evening of work, of fine winter work. Cigarettes were therefore discarded (along with all the childish joys of the summer) into the past illuminated by leaves turned blue in the sun and muslins, and my grave pipe was taken up by a serious person wanting to smoke undisturbed for a long time so as to be able to work better. But I was not prepared for the surprise which my forsaken one had in store. Barely had I drawn a first puff than I forgot about the great books to be written; instead, amazed and strangely moved, I inhaled last winter which began to come back. I had not laid my hands on that faithful old friend since I had returned to France and suddenly the whole of London, London as I had experienced it on my own for a year, reappeared. First of all those dear fogs which muffle up our brains and have over there a special smell when they seep under the window. My tobacco smelt of a dark room with leather furniture finely covered with coal dust on which the skinny black cat curled up. And, oh! those huge fires! and the maid with red arms emptying the coal, and the noise of the lumps of coal as they cascaded out of the iron bucket into the iron basket every morning – just as the postman gave his solemn double rap on the door – which brought me alive! Through the windows I could see the sickly trees of the empty square. I could see the wide open sea that I crossed so often that winter, shivering on the deck of the steamer soaked from the drizzle and filthy with smoke – with my wandering sweetheart clad in travelling clothes – a long faded dress the colour of road dust, an overcoat damply clinging to her frozen shoulders; one of those straw bonnets that have no feathers and hardly any ribbons which rich lady travellers throw away when they reach their destination, so ruined are they by the salt sea air but which poor sweethearts refurbish for many another season. Around her neck was wound the terrible kerchief which people wave when they say goodbye for ever.]

This text moves simultaneously and subtly *through* a series of related images (pipe / smoke / fog / smoke/ coal / fog / steamer / travellers / journey / departure / absence) and *from* the light-hearted, self-mocking and insouciant atmosphere of the opening lines to the mood of foreboding at the end, with its poignant and pathetic lonely figure suggesting separation and even death. As it unfolds, the text not only perfectly captures the almost unbearable sadness and sense of the void which characterized Mallarmé's experience of London but, with a remarkable economy of means (a few chosen images already typically drawn from the world of the senses – here the sights, sounds and smells of London), it conjures up the essence of life in the English capital.

We must also remember that the sickly-looking young man

whose extreme youth and listlessness so impressed themselves upon Catulle Mendès had, by the time he left London, made two crucial and difficult decisions. The first had been to marry Marie Gerhard, against the advice of all his friends and most certainly against the better judgement of his family. The second had been no less significant. The poem 'Les Fenêtres' ('Windows'), the most important that Mallarmé wrote during his sojourn in London, reminds us that marriage was not the only subject which had exercised his mind during that long lonely winter. True, for the greater part of the year thoughts about marriage had tended to obliterate everything else. But once he had undertaken this first act of rebellion, a second revolt had pressed its claims.

Significantly, 'Les Fenêtres' was begun just after Mallarmé's return from his father's funeral in Sens, where a fresh encounter with his family had determined him more than ever to follow his chosen path and become a writer. Simultaneously a proud statement of the importance of Art (which was already beginning to replace a diminishing religious belief) and an attempt to portray the intensely complex and contrasting emotions which such an act of faith released within himself, the poem describes a similar pattern to that of 'La Pipe' as it moves from certainty and almost ecstatic exaltation into that nightmare world of indecision, doubt and anxiety which is so characteristic of Mallarmé's writings of this period.

The first part of the poem consists of a dramatic narrative which tells how a dying old man surrounded by images of hopelessness and defeat nonetheless leaves his hospital bed and goes to the window where, in a defiant and dramatic gesture recalling his childhood innocence, he plants a feverish kiss on the icy-cold glass of the window-pane. For his efforts he is rewarded by a momentary glimpse of the paradise which he has so long dreamed of, in the form of a magnificent sunset. Although the metaphor of this narrative is quite implicit, in the second part of the poem Mallarmé makes an overt comparison with his own situation. Mindful that, although surrounded by squalor and decay and close to death himself, the old man did not give up his dream but simply chose to ignore his unsympathetic surroundings, Mallarmé accepts the implied challenge of the hostile forces he perceives around him and proudly announces his faith in his new religion of Art, which he now embraces with exemplary fervour.

In the last two stanzas, however, his confidence falters as he begins to wonder if he will be able to emulate the unshakeable faith of the old man. In the highly complex and deliberately ambiguous window metaphor of the last few lines, he brings together thoughts of imprisonment, flight and suicidal despair as he wonders if, like the old man, he will remain true to his own dreams, ignoring all the distractions and responsibilities which Life with its varied demands will throw in his path. Having been so recently and so emphatically reminded of the power of these forces, in the form of the pot-bellied uncles at his father's funeral, Mallarmé is left wondering if the fragile barrier of the glass can both contain and protect him. He suddenly feels very vulnerable indeed:

> Mais, hélas! Ici-bas est maître: sa hantise
> Vient m'écoeurer parfois jusqu'en cet abri sûr,
> Et le vomissement impur de la Bêtise
> Me force à boucher le nez devant l'azur.

> [But alas, Life is the Master: its haunting obsession
> Pursues me and sickens me even in this safe place.
> And the foul vomit of crass Stupidity
> Forces me to block my nose before the clear blue sky.

Looking out of the window, as he must have done many a time during his lonely London vigils, and contemplating, not without trepidation, the enormity of the step which he has taken, he wonders if he will ever reach his Eden or whether, like so many other hopefuls, he will plunge without trace into the void:

Est-il moyen, mon Dieu qui voyez l'amertume,
D'enfoncer le crystal par ce monstre insulté
Et de m'enfuir, avec mes deux ailes sans plume,
– Au risque de tomber pendant l'Eternité?

[Is there any way, O God who sees my bitter tears,
For me to break the glass insulted by the Monster
And to fly off on my two featherless wings
– Even at the risk of falling until the end of Time?]

Less than two months after he wrote these anguished lines, Mallarmé left the Kensington Oratory with his German wife by his side. Marriage certificate number 44 of register number 6 of the Registry of Marriage of the District of Kensington in the county of Middlesex records that on 10 August 1863 Etienne Mallarmé, Bachelor, residing at the time at 6 Brompton Square and giving his rank or profession as 'Artist', married Christina Marie Gerhard. In its own way this document provides an eloquent and moving testimony of the two acts of defiance upon which Mallarmé had chosen to gamble his entire future. As he journeyed anxiously southwards to yet another unknown destination, he must have felt that two equally important and irrevocable steps had been taken. There was no longer any question of his turning back.

3

Tournon

By the time Mallarmé left Paris early in December 1863, he had convinced himself that his banishment from the capital was merely a temporary setback. 'Inevitably,' he announced somewhat airily to Cazalis six months after his arrival in Tournon, 'one day or another, you make it back to Paris, either through the University or thanks to the reputation you have made for yourself through works composed in isolation.'[1] This was largely wishful thinking on Mallarmé's part. His typically over-optimistic assessment of the situation was but the first in the long series of unrealistic predictions he would continue to make during the next few years about his career prospects, the possibility of further academic study and, more importantly, many literary projects. It would be almost eight years before he and his wife managed to return to settle in Paris in the summer of 1871, and even when they eventually did so, it was hardly in the triumphant manner which Mallarmé had imagined.

These years of enforced exile, spent first in Tournon, then in Besançon and finally in Avignon, were critical for Mallarmé. During this era, he experienced moments of dark despair and great personal anguish. There were times when, as he much later admitted to Henri de Régnier, he felt that he was truly going insane.[2] In the final analysis, however, these testing years proved to be absolutely decisive in Mallarmé's development both as an individual and as a writer. The dramatically new direction which his whole work eventually took was a direct outcome of his experience in the provinces, and can only be fully understood in its context. The following two chapters will therefore dwell at some length on a crucial period which has not always received the close attention that it merits.

To Mallarmé himself, it must have seemed at the time that this long exile was filled with an unending series of crises. Some were the inevitable outcome of an almost permanent sense of isolation and abandonment, others stemmed from his totally hopeless inability to manage his financial affairs, or from his frequently less than satisfactory performance as a schoolteacher. The most important of these crises, however, those whose darkest moments drove him to the very edge of despair, generally derived from a combination of causes and often followed periods of intense self-doubt and uncertainty to which he was undeniably predisposed.

In the long term, the cumulative effect of these continued and repeated bouts of anxiety and depression was to place an intolerable strain on Mallarmé's mind and body. For much of this time he was too busy to cope with events which increasingly threatened to overwhelm him to appreciate that what he was experiencing, albeit in a quite extreme and in his case belated form, was that difficult and universal transition from adolescence to adulthood. In this sense, his experience in the provinces constitutes an extremely protracted and at times frightening journey of self-exploration at the end of which he succeeded in coming to terms with himself and with the world, to emerge at last with a mature, entirely personal and quite original artistic vision. After a quite remarkable and truly heroic struggle conducted largely – but not entirely – in the splendid isolation that he tended to display to his friends and family, he exorcised his own daemons and discovered that inner serenity and strength which later astounded so many of those who came into contact with him. This long, painful, yet essential transformation began with his arrival in the sleepy little town of Tournon, nestling in a bend of the Rhône valley some 350 miles south of Paris.

The Lycée Impérial de Tournon to which Mallarmé had been appointed by ministerial decree in November 1863 was in fact one of the oldest and most prestigious educational establishments in France, founded as a college by Cardinal de Tournon during the reign of François I in the year 1586. Largely thanks to the presence of the college, Tournon became a recognized centre of culture during the Renaissance. Honoré d'Urfé, the author of *L'Astrée*, the first picaresque novel written in French, was a pupil of the college in 1583. Such splendid and heroic times had long since been forgotten by the time Mallarmé arrived to take up his duties, but important families from the region and elsewhere still sent their sons to be educated at the Lycée Impérial (today the Lycée Gabriel Faure). Its imposing Renaissance buildings stood proudly on the edge of the Rhône looking across the river to its smaller twin-town Tain l'Hermitage, with its celebrated vineyards, its town square and, most important from Mallarmé's point of view, its railway station, which could be reached across one of the oldest iron suspension bridges linking the two communities. Looking towards Tournon itself, the lycée dominated one end of a single main street behind which extended the old quarter of the town: a sprawling labyrinth of narrow, dingy, winding alleyways lined with closely packed houses some of which dated back to the sixteenth century. Their sloping roofs, at times almost touching from opposite sides of the street, excluded most of the daylight and pointed up towards the ancient castle whose ramparts were clearly visible from the bend in the river. Within its walls the eldest son of François Ier had died on the very day in 1536 that another great poet, much admired by Mallarmé, but then a mere twelve-year-old called Pierre de Ronsard, had arrived to take up duties as a page.

Such picturesque details meant little to someone who, from

the very outset, was absolutely determined not to like the place. Thus, when describing Tournon and its surrounding area in his letters to his friends, Mallarmé deliberately chose not to mention the fact that the nearest large town, Valence, a mere twelve miles or so further down the valley, had once boasted a university founded in 1452 and had numbered François Rabelais amongst its students. As far as he was concerned, only one thing mattered. Some anonymous bureaucrat in the Ministry of Education had assigned him to a small, dull country town, hundreds of miles from where he really wanted to be. Less than a week after he had arrived there, he sent his first impressions to Albert Collignon:

> I regret to say that I do not find myself in surroundings in which I can be of more use to you. But I just don't want to get to know anybody here. The inhabitants of this dismal village in which I am exiled live in too great an intimacy with their pigs for me to find them anything other than disgusting. The pig encapsulates the spirit of the household here just as the cat does elsewhere. I haven't even managed to find accommodation which does not remind me of a stable.[3]

These bitter and caustic remarks which smelt so obviously of sour grapes can in part be explained by Mallarmé's having just received from Collignon a copy of the first number of the new review which the latter had just published. On its front cover it proudly sported the names of Catulle Mendès, Villiers de l'Isle-Adam and Albert Glatigny, that is to say the very friends whose stimulating company he had been forced to leave behind. It also happens that both Mallarmé and his wife were quite unwell when he wrote. Marie had not yet fully recovered from the attack of jaundice she had suffered just before their hasty departure from Paris. Mallarmé himself was coming home in the evening utterly exhausted by fruitless efforts to impose his authority upon rebellious pupils – he had the wholly unenviable task of starting his first teaching appointment in the middle of the school year.

To make things considerably worse, the weather in Tournon was at its most inhospitable. A region of extreme seasonal temperatures, the Rhône valley is as bitterly cold and wet in the winter as it is hot, dry and dusty in the summer. When Mallarmé arrived, at the beginning of December, the winter was beginning to take hold. The Mistral, an icy cold wind from the north which at certain times of the year howls its way down the Rhône valley, was already blowing incessantly. Its fraying effect upon the pupils' tempers was well known to Mallarmé's colleagues. Its effect upon Mallarmé himself was equally dramatic. The combination of wind and rain triggered a recurrence of the rheumatic condition of his childhood. Within days of his arrival, the joints of his hands and feet had swollen severely, causing him intense pain.

The plain truth is, however, that Mallarmé's less than flattering first impression of Tournon and its inhabitants was due less to his painful joints than to the blind prejudice and downright snobbery which in those days flawed his personality. As a young Parisian writer already distinguished by publication, he considered himself to be vastly superior to his provincial neighbours, displaying once more that arrogant streak which had earlier brought him into such conflict with his family and schoolmasters.[4] He had simply convinced himself that nobody interesting could possibly inhabit such a 'dismal hole', as he chose to label Tournon in his letters to his friends.

Similar unfavourable first impressions were dispatched to Henri Cazalis and Albert Glatigny. More than capable of recognizing a clear case of self-pity when they encountered it, neither was at all sympathetic. Cazalis tried to joke Mallarmé out of his exaggerated despondency. Albert Glatigny was not so diplomatic. 'You are quite wrong to deplore your exile,' he replied immediately. 'Just think about it. You are in the provinces. In other words you are on your own and are regarded with suspicion by your neighbours. But as they are suspicious of you they do not impose themselves upon you and you can thank the Gods for that! You are free to remain with your books and your charming young wife who ought to be enough for you.'[5]

Mercifully, by the time such friendly and wise advice reached Tournon, Mallarmé's initial bout of petulant self-indulgence had given way to a more positive attitude. Reconciled, at least provisionally, to his fate and determined to make the best of an unwelcome situation, he began by making a modest home for himself and Marie in a tiny rented property situated at number 19 rue de Bourbon, just across the street from the lycée. During the all too short Christmas break he sent hastily scribbled letters to his family and to his Parisian friends whenever he had a moment's respite from the endless chores which moving into a new home entailed. By the beginning of the New Year he was in much better spirits. Unable to venture out to explore the local countryside because of the extremely cold weather and the biting winds, he had taken advantage of his enforced imprisonment to start writing once again.

During that first Christmas in Tournon Mallarmé began a new poem, 'L'Azur' ('The Bright Blue Sky'), which took as its subject the frustrations and anxieties he felt at this time. Once again, as he had done in London, he took his inspiration from what he could observe from the window of his new home. In this case, it was the clear Tournon winter sky with its haunting, unsullied perfection which, mirroring the purity of an empty, unwritten page, fascinated, taunted and disturbed him just as much as the swirling London fog of the previous year had seemed to offer comfort and protection. In some respects, however, 'L'Azur' was an extremely ambitious poem. It was Mallarmé's first serious attempt to put into practice the exciting and challenging literary theories of Edgar Allan Poe which he had recently been rereading in the translations of Baudelaire. He had been particularly struck by Poe's reader-response theory as outlined in an article describing the composition of 'The Raven' as a series of deliberate and carefully calculated attempts to create within the reader's mind a range of totally predetermined effects. Mallarmé's main aim in writing 'L'Azur' was to try to manipulate the response of his reader in a similar way, as he made clear in the unusually lengthy commentary which he enclosed for Cazalis when he sent him the finished poem:

> I swear to you that there is not a single word in the poem which did not cost me several hours of research and that the first word of the poem which contains the first indication of the subject not only contributes to the overall effect, but has as an additional function to prepare the ground for the final word. The *effect produced*, that's what I'm after . . . Oh! Henri what a gulf separates these theories of literary composition from the way in which our glorious Emmanuel [des Essarts] snatches a handful of stars from the Milky Way and scatters them on the page allowing them to form themselves by chance into unplanned constellations! How his soul, so given to his enthusiasms, so besotted with inspiration, would recoil in horror at my way of working! He is truly the lyric poet at his most admirably effusive. However, from now on, every step of the way I shall be faithful to these more exacting notions of poetry which my great master Edgar Poe has bequeathed to me.[6]

In fact, despite constant references in his letters of the time to his inability to write anything, and notwithstanding the rather morbid subject matter of the poem 'L'Azur' (itself a possible tribute to his recent reading of Poe), as the upbeat mood of this letter to Cazalis suggests, those first few months in Tournon were far from unproductive ones for Mallarmé. Not only did he complete 'L'Azur' (and send it for comment to Armand Renaud in the first week of January), but he painstakingly copied out a small selection of his poems for some of his chosen friends (no doubt in part as a subtle reminder of his continued existence). By mid-April he was able to dispatch to Albert Collignon three lengthy prose poems celebrating, under the general title 'Symphonie littéraire', three poets whose work he particularly admired, Charles Baudelaire, Théophile Gautier and Théodore de Banville. By the end of the winter he had finished two more prose poems capturing the atmosphere of the months he had spent in London the previous year. By June he had also completed the first of a series of prose poems inspired by the move to Tournon.[7] In that same month of June he also began review articles on a collection of poems by Albert Glatigny and a play by Catulle Mendès. Although duly completed, neither of these articles was published and both have now been lost.

All in all, it was quite an impressive record of literary activity, especially if we compare it with the relatively small amount of work that Mallarmé had managed to produce during his year in London. Even so, there were clearly many moments of discouragement and despondency during that first cold winter which Mallarmé spent so far away from his family and friends. Needless to say, given the contempt he had shown for most of their new fellow citizens, neither Mallarmé nor his wife made any serious attempt in the first few months to integrate themselves into the local community. The women-folk of the town fared no better than the men. Complaining that, with one notable exception, Marie had found no one to make friends with, Mallarmé described the local female population as 'a hideous herd of cows whose only femininity consists in not having what you need to have to be considered a man.'[8]

One of the main problems for them both was loneliness and a growing sense of isolation. In Mallarmé's case this feeling was compounded by the fact that he seemed to have been totally forgotten by Albert Collignon, who failed to send him the copies of *La Revue nouvelle* which he had promised. Nor, more importantly, was he helped by the fact that Henri Cazalis was now engaged in a tortuous and ill-fated courtship of Ettie Yapp and had provisionally stopped writing to him. Indeed, the rare letters which Mallarmé did receive from Cazalis that winter were not exactly comforting, since for the most part they contained annoyingly enthusiastic accounts of the latter's growing circle of friends in the capital. By the end of the winter, the strain was beginning to tell and Mallarmé's mood was sombre. 'Ah my friend,' he lamented to Cazalis, 'you have to understand that down here you can allow yourself to become totally discouraged. Nothing ever happens. We plod around our weary way in the same restricted little circle like those stupid fairground horses at the circus, and my God, if you could just hear the accompanying music!'[9]

Once again it was the unfortunate citizens of Tournon who were held responsible for his plight. 'If there were no such things as judges' benches,' Mallarmé continued in the same self-pitying vein:

> I would set fire to the wretched, stupid and ugly houses which I cannot avoid seeing from my window every hour of the day. There are times when I would lodge a bullet in the stupid skulls of those wretched neighbours who do the same thing every day and whose petty little lives all merge in my tear-stained eyes into a horrible spectacle of yawn-inducing immobility. If only it was the sun which was immobile. Ah yes! I can feel it. Every day I retreat further within myself. Every day I am quite overcome by discouragement. I am dying of apathy.

Such terrible despondency must hardly have been alleviated by a growing suspicion, only too quickly confirmed, that Marie was now expecting their first child. Fortunately, even if somewhat belatedly, on 8 February of that year their London marriage had at last been legally accepted in France and transferred to the Register in Sens, so there was no risk of the child being illegitimate. This distinct possibility had been a further weight on Mallarmé's mind during his first few months in Tournon.

Announcing his wife's condition to Cazalis, Mallarmé greeted the prospect of fatherhood with less than total enthusiasm. His reaction, in fact, was refreshingly honest. 'You can imagine how all this is helping my recovery!' he noted ironically. 'I tremble at the very idea that I might become a father – what if my life were to be burdened with an idiot or an ugly child? What a horrible thought.'[10]

Despite the doleful note struck in these letters, which in any event expressed as much as anything else Mallarmé's jaundiced reaction to his friend's rather tactless, detailed and highly coloured accounts of his recent encounter with the alluring, gifted and extremely beautiful female musician and poet Augusta Holmès,[11] it would be wrong to imagine that for Mallarmé and his wife life in Tournon was unrelieved gloom. Barely a week after this last depressing letter, thanks first to the arrival of warmer spring weather and second to an unexpected visit by his old friend Albert Glatigny, who stayed for a whole month, Mallarmé's mood brightened considerably. Besides, it ought to be pointed out that he was never quite as isolated as he would have his correspondents believe. In February of that same year, Emmanuel des Essarts had been transferred from Sens to the lycée in Avignon. Admittedly, this was some distance from Tournon, much further, in fact, than Mallarmé had at first imagined and certainly quite far enough to make regular meetings impracticable.[12] Nonetheless, the fact that his old friend and ally was now within physical reach and had indeed suffered a similar fate to his own was clearly of some consolation to Mallarmé.[13]

Furthermore, towards the end of March, in an attempt to reactivate an earlier relationship with Eugène Lefébure which had previously foundered because of the latter's notorious apathy, Mallarmé had sent him one of his hand-copied selections of his poems. This time he had been rewarded with a quick and enthusiastic response. A regular exchange of letters had followed, so much so that already Lefébure was showing every sign of becoming for Mallarmé the literary and intellectual confidant that he needed – a role till then the exclusive province of Emmanuel des Essarts.

The latter of course still remained important to Mallarmé as a vital link with the literary circles of Paris. Indeed, as Mallarmé and Albert Glatigny took advantage of the Easter holidays to explore the local Ardèche countryside, Emmanuel des Essarts was once again up in Paris acting as Mallarmé's literary agent, showing his poems to no less a figure than Charles Baudelaire himself, amongst others.[14] Exceedingly gregarious by nature and exceptionally good at making friends, Des Essarts had not wasted the few months he had already spent in Avignon. As the school year ended, thanks to his old friend's efforts Mallarmé found himself invited to Avignon to meet the Félibriges, a group of local poets and craftsmen who had united around the Provençal poet Frédéric Mistral. Proud of their traditions, the Félibriges were determined to protect the Provençal language, its culture and its history. Two of this little group in particular quickly became good friends of Mallarmé and his wife. Jean Brunet was a skilled decorator and glassblower to whose wife, Cécile, Mallarmé would later dedicate one of his most exquisite sonnets. Théodore Aubanel was a poet and printer whose family printing house proudly stood, as it does today, in the shadow of the impressive walls of the cathedral of St Pierre.

In short, contrary to the dismal picture which Mallarmé rather perversely continued to paint in his letters to his Parisian friends, there is ample evidence to suggest that, as the summer approached, both he and his wife had at last begun to make several good friends within the local community. When the regional inspector of schools made his annual visit to the lycée, he may have found Mallarmé a little too lenient with his pupils, but he also noted that on the whole he was well liked by his colleagues and superiors.[15] The arrangements which Mallarmé and his wife made for the summer holidays that year confirm this judgement. On the Saturday before the annual prizegiving, Mallarmé slipped away to Avignon to meet Mistral (whom unfortunately he had missed on the previous occasion). On the following Tuesday, as the summer holidays officially began, he was able to spend a week in Vichy with Albert Glatigny because Marie had been invited by the German wife of one of his colleagues to visit their farmhouse near Vienne, just south of Lyon. Both returned to Tournon in time for Marie's *jour de fête* on 15 August before setting off by boat to Avignon for a few days as the guests of Jean Brunet and his wife Cécile. At the beginning of September, Mallarmé spent a week with his stepmother and her family up in Sens then a second week with Lefébure, secure in the knowledge that Marie was the guest of her by now good friend Madame Seignobos, the mother of one of his pupils with whom they had both become friendly. When he was later elected a deputy, her husband, Charles Seignobos, proved to be an extremely useful ally of Mallarmé's in his contant battles with the Ministry of Education.

Thus, by the end of that first summer, even though he had just spent ten hectic and invigorating days in the capital, Mallarmé no longer thought of Tournon as the God-forsaken 'hole' of his earlier letters. It was now very much his home. 'I have now got back into my routine and I am not feeling bored yet,' he wrote to Cazalis a few days after returning from the capital. 'For a start there was the thrill of seeing Marie again. And besides, if you could just see how delightfully settled we are with our wonderful birds, the goldfish and our white cat. And my sweet German girl in the middle of all these things, dashing from one to another. She was quite dazzled by the pretty things I had brought from so far and she cannot stop looking at the little Saxony clock.' He was reasonably optimistic about the future too. 'I was quite encouraged by it all,' he concluded. 'Thanks to my surroundings I hope I will not quickly lapse into the dark depths in which I languished for so long.'[16]

A letter from Fanny Desmolins around this time recalling the many conversations she had had with Mallarmé during his

recent visit to Versailles also confirms that by now he genuinely felt that he belonged to a community. 'I have the distinct
impression,' she remarked with the sententiousness and mor-
alizing tone which she felt obliged to adopt when writing to
her grandson, 'that you were much less irritated by these poor
people and that the way they had welcomed you had softened
the severity of some of your earlier opinions. I hope that this
may remain the case. I hope so for your happiness, my friend.
It truly is a boon to know how to be happy with one's lot and
to appreciate the little consolations which God scatters in our
path, which, of course, for none of us on this earth is ever
totally free of thorns.'[17]

Thorns and all, to the relief of his friends and family and no
doubt to his own surprise, Mallarmé had survived the first
year in Tournon.

Mallarmé may now have felt slightly more favourably dis-
posed towards Tournon and its citizens, but the major work
with which he still hoped to engineer his triumphant return to
the capital had not, as yet, been written. With 'Les Fenêtres'
and 'L'Azur' he had already extended his range beyond the
sonnet, but for some time he had felt the need to stretch
himself further by working on a larger canvas. During his
recent trip to Paris, he had announced that he was contemplating a large-scale work, an ambitious theatrical project whose
heroine was a purely imaginary figure called Hérodiade, so
chosen not for the historic or biblical allusions but primarily
because of the sensuous, sonorous tone of the name itself.[18]

Envisaged initially as a short dramatic piece of some 800
lines in the Racinian manner comprising a series of monologues
and dialogues between the heroine and her confidante (in this
case an aged nurse), *Hérodiade* began as yet another attempt to
put into practice the theories of Edgar Allan Poe, for whom
originality had been defined as essentially the pursuit of
extreme sensations. Above all, Poe had put great emphasis on

the organization, hard work and intellectual discipline required if the true work of art were to produce in the reader the specific effects intended by the author. Mallarmé was careful not to mention the name of Poe, preferring to portray these ideas as a discovery of his own in a letter to Cazalis towards the end of October 1864, a fortnight or so after he had returned to Tournon. 'As for me,' he wrote, 'I am hard at work. I have at last begun my *Hérodiade*. I am terrified because I have to invent a language which will inevitably result from a very new poetics which I could best describe in these words: "Paint not the thing itself, but the effect which it produces." '[19]

It was, he admitted, a daunting task, yet one which filled him with excitement. 'As a consequence of all this,' he continued, 'the poetic line is not made up of words but of intentions and all the words are secondary to the creating of a sensation. I do not know if you can follow what I am saying but I hope you will approve of what I am doing when I have succeeded. Because, for the very first time in my life, I really do *want to succeed*.'

From the very outset, however, the *Hérodiade* project caused Mallarmé nothing but problems. To begin with, it was an extremely ambitious concept upon which, as he reminded Cazalis and his other friends, he had chosen to rest his whole future credibility as an artist. Understandably therefore, with so much at stake, he was initially overcome by so intense a fear of failure that it all but paralysed him and certainly made it extremely difficult for him to settle to the task. To make matters worse, he was trying to write in far from ideal circumstances. The cold, grey, dismal October days had already replaced the clear blue skies of summer, announcing that winter was approaching with its bitter winds and frequent rain, both so unhelpful to Mallarmé's rheumatic condition. Furthermore, his initial efforts suffered a whole series of disruptions. First, he now had a heavier teaching load at the lycée, which in itself constantly interrupted his train of thought and made any concerted effort virtually impossible. Second, he had barely made a start upon the first draft when, much to his irritation, his wife's new friend Madame Seignobos came to spend a few days with them to be with Marie as she anxiously awaited the imminent birth of their first child.

Like most inexperienced fathers, Mallarmé totally underestimated the disruptive effect which the arrival of a young baby would have on his own work. A fortnight later, at around eight o'clock on the evening of 19 November (by a strange coincidence, his own dead mother's Saint's Day), the 'great destroyer' (as Mallarmé soon came to call her) arrived in the form of a female child, Stéphanie Françoise Geneviève, to be known by the last of these three names.[20] Weakened by what appears to have been a fairly exhausting labour, Marie was in no position to run the household, and the burden now fell on Mallarmé himself, as they could not afford a maid. In these circumstances, any serious attempt at *Hérodiade* was doomed to failure. On Boxing Day of that year, a dejected Mallarmé wrote to Cazalis:

> My dear Henri, I am extremely late in writing to you. But for some days now the dust has been accumulating on my inkstand. It is so cold, so miserably cold that I remain huddled up by the fireplace in Marie's room where the child's presence requires a fire which is constantly ablaze. I arrive there exhausted from my classes which this year have *robbed* me of nearly all my free hours, and Geneviève continues to shatter my thoughts with her shrieking. I have only one hour of release, the hour before I bury myself for the night in my freezing blankets. Before that, neither my best friend in the world nor the most amazing thought would decide me to spend a moment scribbling at my table.[21]

Once the festivities were over, however, around the second week of January 1865, Mallarmé cleared his writing table and made a second, determined attempt at *Hérodiade*. Again, in spite of all his efforts, progress was painfully slow. Not only did he have lessons to prepare and a noisy child to contend with at home, but at the lycée itself he was now beginning to encounter some serious discipline problems. 'It is terrible not to be able to be exclusively a man of letters!' he complained. 'At every moment my most beautiful flights of imagination, or my rare moments of inspiration which I can never recapture, are interrupted by the hideous occupation of being a school-teacher. When I return home, with pieces of paper stuck to the seat of my trousers and with paper figures pinned to my coat, I am so tired that all I can do is rest.'[22]

There were other reasons why progress with *Hérodiade* was so dreadfully slow. First there were the technical problems of the work itself. As Mallarmé freely admitted to Cazalis, he was finding it extremely difficult to capture and orchestrate the fleet-ing, shifting moods which constituted the subject of the piece. Second, although he himself would only realize this much later, the subject matter of the tragedy was as yet too ill-defined in his own mind and too closely associated with preoccupations he did not fully understand himself for him to be able to give them objective expression. Finally, the intellectual discipline involved, with endless reworkings and painstaking composi-tion, was somewhat alien to his temperament and ran counter to an instinctive tendency towards exuberance and lyricism. He had run into this problem during the composition of the poem 'L'Azur'. On that occasion, as he admitted to Cazalis, he had struggled to banish what he called the 'thousand enticing lyrical thoughts and verses incessantly haunting my imagination'.[23]

During those early months of 1865, as he strove to make some headway, it was primarily with his own fundamentally lyrical nature that Mallarmé had to contend. Indeed, it was precisely because he himself was experiencing such difficulties that he launched a severe and unsparing attack on the latest collection of poems to be published by his old friend Des Essarts. Writing to Lefébure, Mallarmé was scathing about *Les Elévations*:

> The content is loosely expressed and degenerates into clichés and, as far as the form is concerned, all I see is words, words which are frequently chosen haphazardly, 'sinister' which could be replaced by

'lugubrious' and 'lugubrious' by 'tragic' without the meaning of the line being altered. You do not get any new sensation when you read these verses. The rhythm is very cleverly handled and that compensates for so much mediocrity and gossip, but so what? You will tell me that I am being unkind to a friend? No, not at all. Des Essarts is one of those rare people whom I love very much. However, and it is most unfortunate, I cannot stand his poetry, which goes against everything that Art stands for as far as I am concerned.[24]

He then went on to make some interesting comments on the critic Hippolyte Taine, whom Lefébure had advised him to read. His remarks take us to the heart of his own dilemma. One point in particular about Taine's theory of literature seems to have annoyed him:

What I do not like in Taine is his claim that the artist is merely a man extended to his full potential whereas I believe that it is perfectly possible for people to have temperaments as human beings which are very different from their literary temperament. So my judgement on him is the exact opposite of yours. I find that Taine sees impressions as the sole source of works and that he does not place sufficient importance on the thought process. The artist *becomes himself* in front of the blank sheet of paper. For example he does not believe that a writer can totally change his manner, which is quite wrong. I have observed it in myself. When I was young and at school I used to write twenty-page essays and I was renowned for not knowing when to stop. But since then haven't I rather tended to exaggerate on the contrary my love of condensation? I had a tremendous facility and a gushing exuberance, writing everything in a single burst, of course, and believing that emotion was style. Can anything be more removed from that schoolboy of the old days who was brimming with confidence than the writer of today who is horrified by anything that is said without being *pre-arranged*?

Despite the bravura of such remarks (which were probably intended to convince himself as much as Lefébure of the transformation which he liked to think he had already performed within himself), Mallarmé found it virtually impossible for the moment to practise what he preached. Besides, it was not only this conflict within himself (important as it was) which paralysed him. He was subject to other pressures. For all the faults he took pleasure in detailing in Des Essarts' poetry, the fact still remained that the latter had already succeeded in getting two books of verse into print.

Furthermore, Mallarmé had spent a large part of the month of February reading *Elen*, a prose drama recently published by Villiers de l'Isle-Adam, the mysterious yet charismatic companion whom Catulle Mendès had introduced to him shortly before his departure for Tournon. To the modern reader the play appears what it is, a small-scale rather overblown work, quite ill equipped to sustain its heavy philosophical and metaphysical message. To Mallarmé however, struggling as he was to draft the first scene of his own tragedy, the obvious mastery of language demonstrated by Villiers and the clearly metaphysical overtones of his work were hugely impressive. Such was his genuine enthusiasm for the play that he had no hesitation in comparing its final scenes with the cemetery scene in Shakespeare's *Hamlet*. 'Each of the words,' he wrote approvingly to Lefébure, 'produces a different sensation, as when you read Baudelaire. There is not one single syllable which has not been carefully measured during a whole night of reflection. Besides, Villiers has been preparing this work for three years.'[25] The implication concerning his own inadequacy was quite clear.

Towards the end of February 1865 therefore, Mallarmé felt it necessary to revise the timetable of his own work. He informed his friends that *Hérodiade* would not be finished for some time yet. In other words, adopting a tactic which he would later employ with great effect in other, more dramatic circumstances, he decided for the moment to lower his sights and to return to smaller canvases. The poem entitled 'Le Poème nocturne' ('Night Poem'), later retitled 'Don du poème' ('A Poetic Offering'), was probably begun around this time. Its poignant and highly appropriate subject of a still-born poem/child which even the milk from a new mother's breast cannot revive depicts the feelings of anxiety, frustration and guilt that Mallarmé clearly felt at the time for neglecting his wife and child for a project that constantly eluded him:

Je t'apporte l'enfant d'une nuit d'Idumée!
Noire, à l'aile saignante et pâle, déplumée,
Par le verre brûlé d'aromates et d'or,
Par les carreaux glacés, hélas! mornes encore,
L'aurore se jeta sur la lampe angélique.
Palmes! et quand elle a montré cette relique
A ce père essayant un sourire ennemi,
La solitude bleue et stérile a frémi.
O la berceuse, avec ta fille et l'innocence
De vos pieds froids, accueille une horrible naissance:
Et ta voix rappelant viole et clavecin,
Avec le doigt fané presseras-tu le sein
Par qui coule en blancheur sibylline la femme
Pour des lèvres que l'air du vierge azur affame?

[I bring you the child of a night of Idumea!
Black, with pale, bleeding, featherless wing,
Through the glass burned with aromatics and gold,
Through the icy window panes, alas! still dreary,
The dawn threw itself on the angelic lamp.
Palmes! and when it revealed this relic
To this father attempting a hostile smile,
The blue and sterile solitude shivered.
O cradling woman, with your daughter and the innocence
Of your cold feet, accept this horrible birth:
And with your voice recalling viola and harpsichord,
With your fading finger will you press the breast
Through which in sibylline whiteness woman flows
For these lips which the air of the virgin azure famishes?]

The poem was completed in October of that year and sent to Aubanel in Avignon. The little experimental prose poem 'Le Phénomène futur' ('A Phenomenon of the Future') was also begun around this time. Something of a hybrid, which owes much of its atmosphere to some of Poe's more Gothic tales, it is nonetheless an accomplished piece, affirming once again Mallarmé's undying faith in the power and importance of the artist.

Pressure continued to mount, however. Early in March Mallarmé learned through Des Essarts that the three prose poems he had written celebrating the talents of Baudelaire, Banville and Gautier were at last to be published by *L'Artiste*. Des Essarts also announced that Théodore de Banville himself had been sufficiently impressed to offer to seek other publishers for Mallarmé's work. By the end of the same month, once he had learnt of the *Hérodiade* project, Banville himself wrote to Mallarmé proposing a possible venue for the finished work: 'I just cannot congratulate you enough my dear young friend', he commented, 'upon the excellent idea you have of creating a version of *Hérodiade*, because the Théâtre Français has just the décor you require to stage it and that might be a very good reason why they would accept it.'[26]

Thus, during his second winter in Tournon Mallarmé came under increasing pressure from all directions. Most important of all, however, the sheer scale and wider canvas of the project was helping to gather and focus within himself the many contradictions and tensions of which, until then, he had not been fully aware. In the fullness of time, some eighteen months after he had begun *Hérodiade*, these pressures would crystallize into the full-blown metaphysical crisis which we shall examine in due course. For the moment, however, of all the difficulties with which Mallarmé had to contend there was one source of tension which continued to preoccupy him more than any other. It was the fundamental conflict of loyalties which he had foreseen only too clearly in the final section of his earlier London poem 'Les Fenêtres'. What he had then envisaged as a somewhat abstract hypothesis was now a reality however, as he felt more and more torn between the conflicting claims exerted by his poetry on the one hand and his own growing family on the other. Once the first flush of parenthood was over, there were times when he saw his daughter in purely negative terms as nothing more than an annoying disruptive force, an obstacle to his writing. At such moments she became 'the destroyer'. Writing to Henri Cazalis on Boxing Day 1864 about his long and inexcusable silence, he was remarkably candid on the subject of his family:

> So no letters, no poetry. And do not imagine that these duties are replaced by charming domestic bliss. No. I suffer too much when I feel unable to write to be able to enjoy anything and in fact I am determined not to take any pleasure in things so as to avoid believing that such pleasures are the ones I prefer and the very source of my guilt and sterility.[27]

He expressed similar ideas a fortnight later to the same correspondent:

> I am too much of a poet and too much in love with Poetry alone to be able to enjoy, when I cannot work, any inner happiness which to me seems to usurp the place of that other, greater happiness which is provided by the Muse.[28]

Mallarmé's real dilemma, however, was that despite the apparent severity of such remarks he was in fact extremely fond of his family. He was, and would always remain, a loving father and a loyal and devoted husband. A few paragraphs later in the same Boxing Day letter to Cazalis he could not hide his genuine pride as a father. 'I would like you to see our baby,' he wrote. 'She is so beautiful and her skin resembles the skin of a flower. Unfortunately she will have very dark brown hair and will look like me. I would so much have wished to see a miniature version of her mother, a German with two blonde tresses down her back. Her eyes are still almost blue, but they will change, unfortunately.'

Six months later, the congratulations he offered Théodore Aubanel on the birth of his son underline Mallarmé's true feelings for his wife and child:

> A thought which makes me happy when I think of your happiness is that I know that you are going to enjoy a taste of all the charming

sentiments I have experienced in these last few months. – Yes, what a delightful summer you are going to spend – not working of course because in the first months one has eyes for nothing else except the star which has come to a halt over the new crib.[29]

Mallarmé's Avignon friends such as the Brunets, Aubanel and especially his old friend Des Essarts, who all had occasion to see him with his wife and child, could also see that his love for them was deep and genuine, as the poignant anguish of 'Le Poème nocturne' quickly confirms. Thus when, towards the middle of March 1865, Des Essarts felt that Mallarmé was beginning to neglect his duties, he felt compelled to intervene. He conceded that he, of all people, could sympathize with Mallarmé's desire to be in Paris but insisted that he must not allow himself to become so despondent:

> You must be strong, my friend, that is what is required. That is how you can produce those two poems which are your Life and your Work. Otherwise you leave merely the outline of a work and an incompleted destiny. I am more and more convinced of this *each day*. The more you resist, the more you affirm your own existence. Discouragement and splenetic languor are slippery slopes. You need to step back from the edge to avoid falling down to the bottom of the precipice . . . So despite the deadly boredom of Tournon, I say to you: react and resist. I am not saying that to moralize in any bourgeois fashion but I am thinking here, all of us here are thinking with tender concern of your happiness as a husband and lover, of your duty as a father, of all those other fine, noble and important duties which are part of your life. When we do, Théodore [Aubanel] and Madame Cécile and Brunet and I all say to each other as we sadly reflect: as long as Stéphane does not ruin his health and ruin his soul by seeking out and coveting as it were depression and desolation . . . Such are our banal thoughts but they are so sincere, so tender, so full of love for you.
>
> Of course we often have these alarms when we see you frequently discouraged. But, no matter what you say, and your actions contradict your theories, one cannot live uniquely for oneself and you have a duty to your wife and to your daughter to live much more for them than for yourself. It is for them, to whom your smile is so necessary, that you need to take an interest in life again and get rid of this accursed spleen. You will be a better poet for it.[30]

114

The final lines of this letter contained a fraternal, yet forceful reprimand. Mallarmé himself, of course, hardly needed such exhortation. No one knew better than he that torn between his love for his wife and daughter, for whose well-being, as Des Essarts had pointedly reminded him, he genuinely cared, and his desperate desire to prove himself as a writer, he was unable to give to either the time which each deserved, with the result that both suffered equally badly. It was an impossible situation, as Mallarmé himself pointed out to Mistral in his New Year greeting:

> I am in a cruel position. The mundane things of this life seem too vague to me for me to take any pleasure in them and I only feel alive when I am writing poetry. Therefore I am depressed because I am not working. On the other hand, I am not working because I am depressed. How can I escape from all this?[31]

Despite the wise and sympathetic counsel of Emmanuel des Essarts, and similar exhortations from Théodore de Banville, whose help Des Essarts had clearly enlisted, Mallarmé's mood darkened considerably as the winter drew to a close and he sensed that he would have no *Hérodiade* to show his friends in the summer. He was by now beginning to suffer from frequent and severe migraines, brought on by stress and pure physical exhaustion, since in his desperation he had taken to working late at night so as to be able to show at least part of the dramatic dialogue to Banville when he made his by now traditional pilgrimage to the capital. There had also been other cruel disappointments. An unexpected possibility of exchanging his post in Tournon for one in a more favourable environment close to Paris had loomed on the horizon only to vanish as quickly as it had materialized.[32]

On top of all this, there was Geneviève's forthcoming christening to contend with. The arrangements had quickly turned into something of a nightmare, bringing Mallarmé once again into direct conflict with his grandmother, Fanny Desmolins. Prevented by her husband André's rapidly deteriorating health from making the journey south to act as godmother, Fanny was greatly upset when she learned that for the ceremony she was to be replaced by Cécile Brunet, who to her mind was totally unacceptable because she was not a Catholic. This led to a flurry of letters in which Mallarmé tried simultaneously to smooth his grandmother's ruffled feathers and counter her sectarian views. The bitter exchanges and bickering continued right up to the christening itself, which then had to be postponed at the very last minute. Originally planned for 19 March, it did not take place until the end of April because icy conditions prevented the Brunets from coming up from Avignon.

By the beginning of April, convinced (with some justification) that everything was conspiring against him, Mallarmé painted a bleak picture to Cazalis. He felt that he was at the end of his tether:

> I am depressed. A glacial dark wind has prevented me from going out for a walk and I do not know what to do with myself in the house when my feeble brain will not allow me to undertake any work. Besides, I am disgusted with myself. I recoil in front of the mirror when I see a face which is degenerating and emptying of life. I burst into tears when I feel a total void within myself and when I am unable to place a single word on my implacably white sheet of paper. Imagine being a washed-up old man at the age of twenty-three when all the others whom we love live amid the sunlight and the flowers and are ready to write their masterpieces! And I do not even have the resource of my death which might have convinced you all that I was of some worth and that if nothing remains of me, only Fate itself, which had carried me off, should be held responsible.[33]

Once more he blamed Tournon for his failure. What he needed, he thought, was a change of scene. If only he lived somewhere exciting and stimulating like Paris, where he had friends to encourage him and museums to visit. What he hated most was the loneliness and isolation of provincial life. 'When for a fortnight at a time I cannot get out,' he complained, 'my life is spent at the college, which is across the street, and in our house, which I know in every depressing detail. I never open my mouth to speak to another person. Do you understand what I am saying? You will tell me that I have Marie. But Marie is myself and I see myself reflected in her German eyes. Besides, she herself is vegetating here as I am. My Geneviève is charming to embrace for ten minutes, but after that?'

Like similar letters written at moments of great stress, this note to Cazalis was couched in exaggerated, histrionic language and steeped in self-pity. Even so, the profound anguish it expressed, an anguish bordering at times on paranoia, was genuine enough. Mallarmé felt guilty towards his wife and daughter, whom he knew he was neglecting, and towards his literary friends, whose expectations he knew he was about to disappoint. He was convinced therefore that he was letting down the very people whom he loved and who mattered most to him. He ended on a particularly sombre and rather ominous note: 'All of this is poisoning my life. After such humiliations I do not have sufficient inner peace to be able to look on Marie and Geneviève with a happy heart. I am even afraid of my friends. I am afraid of you all as if somehow you are judging me.'

Once again, as he had done so many times before, Cazalis accused Mallarmé of exaggerating his situation and advised him to be patient. 'I just cannot believe everything you are telling me,' he replied, mixing fraternal affection with paternal concern. 'Last year you wrote me similar things, and when I saw you I recognized you straight away, you were quite unchanged, a spell of Paris air had soon put you back on your feet.'[34]

In the circumstances, an unexpected letter from Mallarmé's old school friend Emile Roquier, who had not written for several years, could hardly have been more poorly timed.

> What has become of you in that Tournon which you were so afraid of and where, I am convinced, you are much less bored than you at first feared and imagined? Besides, my dear Stéphane, it would be ungrate-

ful of you to miss anything whatsoever of the abominable and feverish lives we lead in Paris. Down there you have everything anyone could dream of to be happy: your charming and so gentle wife, who is so good and so loving and who so quickly won over the hearts of those of my friends who met her and to whom I hasten to ask to be remembered; your love of poetry which you can indulge and satisfy down there; the tranquillity of a settled and happy existence, far from the petty scandals and the enormous betrayals of the Paris literary world. You have a position which is safe, respected and quite secure.[35]

As he read these lines, Mallarmé must surely have felt that everyone was conspiring against him in their refusal to understand his plight. His response to this last letter and to those which Cazalis, Des Essarts and his grandmother Fanny Desmolins had all written to him over the recent months is perhaps to be found in the poem 'Brise marine' ('Sea wind'), which was composed only a few weeks later as the winter receded and the first blue skies of spring reappeared:

La chair est triste, hélas! et j'ai lu tous les livres.
Fuir! là-bas fuir! Je sens que des oiseaux sont ivres
D'être parmi l'écume inconnue et les cieux!
Rien, ni les vieux jardins reflétés par les yeux
Ne retiendra ce coeur qui dans la mer se trempe
O nuits! ni la clarté déserte de ma lampe
Sur le vide papier que la blancheur défend
Et ni la jeune femme allaitant son enfant.
Je partirai! Steamer balançant ta mâture,
Lève l'ancre pour une exotique nature!

Un Ennui, désolé par les cruels espoirs,
Croit encore à l'adieu suprême des mouchoirs!
Et, peut-être, les mâts, invitant les orages
Sont-ils de ceux qu'un vent penche sur les naufrages
Perdus, sans mâts, sans mâts, ni fertiles ilôts . . .
Mais, o mon coeur, entends le chant des matelots!

[Alas! the flesh is jaded and I have read every book!
I long to flee! To flee elsewhere! I sense the birds are drunk
To be among the unknown foam and the skies!
Nothing, neither the old gardens reflected in eyes
Will retain this heart which dips in the sea

Such nights! Nor the abandoned brightness of my lamp
Above the empty paper which its whiteness defends
Not even the young woman suckling her child.
I will be off! Steamer bobbing your masts
Raise your anchor for an exotic nature!

Despair itself, desolated by cruel hopes,
Still believes in the final handkerchief's goodbye
And, perhaps, the masts which beckon the storms
Are those which a wind will bend over shipwrecks
That were lost, mastless, mastless and no fertile isles . . .
But, my heart, just listen to the sailors' song!]

The traditional view has been to see in 'Brise marine' a basic reworking of some well-known Baudelairean themes. Certainly, there is little doubt that the 'exotic' nature which Mallarmé ascribes to himself in the poem is a borrowing from the title of Baudelaire's poem, 'Parfum exotique'. Likewise, the central image of the sea journey with its association of boats and birds in flight clearly owes much to Mallarmé's reading of other poems in *Les Fleurs du mal*. But once 'Brise marine' is set in its true context, that is to say placed against the letters exchanged between Mallarmé and his friends during the winter of 1864–5, the poem acquires a much greater significance and poignancy. Its subject can be seen to be the terrible months which he has just endured, with their horrendous pressures and impossible choices. It is a poem written by someone who, as the celebrated and much quoted first line indicates, is utterly exhausted, both mentally and physically, but who nonetheless makes a heroic decision to persevere against all the odds and in the certain knowledge that he will require the courage to risk the love of those he holds most dear. As such it is a very intimate confession, which captures in the most dramatic and moving way the private battle which had raged within Mallarmé and almost destroyed him during that second painful winter in Tournon. In this light, it is much more than a tribute to an older master. It is a magnificent lyrical outpouring which celebrates the heroic and total commitment which is ultimately required of the artist.

By the time Des Essarts arrived in Tournon for Geneviève's postponed christening on 30 April, Mallarmé had returned to work and completed a first draft of a scene of *Hérodiade*.[36] He was not yet satisfied with it, however, and by the middle of June, realizing that there was little hope of finishing the piece in time to bring it to Paris at the end of the summer, he wisely abandoned it for the moment and undertook instead another theatrical project whose central character was no longer an ice-cold virginal princess but, as he announced to Lefébure, an amorous and sensuous faun:

> My dear friend, I have some hesitation in deciding to jot down a few words to you on a sheet of writing paper because this will turn into a letter and I had forbidden myself any correspondence this month as much so as not to disrupt my train of thought as because I hate any activity which is alien to what really interests me. I have been in full dramatic composition for the last fortnight and shall be for quite some time to come. I bet that surprises you! I, who was almost a shadow, now showing signs of life! Yes I am! I even think that my research has allowed me to invent a new dramatic verse in so far as the line-breaks are quite slavishly calculated to follow the gestures of the actor without abandoning poetry aimed at mass effects, which is quite rare itself. My subject is an ancient one. It is a symbol. You are reeling from one surprise to another? Oh how I would like to show it to you when you come. Provided I have finished it! It is no more than 400 verses long but you know what that means for me! I intend offering it to the Comédie Française. . . . *Hérodiade*, a solitary work, had sterilized me. I shall keep it for the cruel winters. In my *Faun* (because that is what my hero is) I am enjoying a summertime expansive mood which I did not know I was capable of while carefully exhausting the possibilities of the verse form, which is very difficult because of the action.[37]

The decision to change to a more overtly lyrical subject (in fact the change of subject is more apparent than real) seems to have worked, unleashing in Mallarmé an extraordinary burst of creativity. Despite the blistering heat and his teaching duties which continued right up till the end of the first week in August, he worked every available moment of the day and well into the night, devouring cups of coffee and completing by the end of that month a first version of what would later become known as *L'Après-midi d'un Faune* but which for the moment bore the provisional title *Le Faune, intermède héroïque* (*The Faun, a Heroic Intermezzo*).[38]

The following month, Mallarmé showed his manuscript to Coquelin, the director of the Comédie Française to whom Théodore de Banville had kindly introduced him. Coquelin and Banville both read the text and, to Mallarmé's great disappointment, rejected it out of hand on the grounds that the story-line was not strong enough to sustain the interest of a theatrical audience.

Mallarmé's hopes had been dashed, and he suffered a further, equally galling affront when the photograph of his daughter which he had asked Marie to send up from Tournon to show their Parisian friends turned out to be out of focus and extremely unflattering. After these twin humiliations, Tournon seemed to beckon as an oasis of sanity. 'Oh! my dear child,' he wrote to Marie from his grandmother's house in Versailles, 'how happy I am to be leaving!'

> I long for you and Geneviève – and for the silence of our little nest. I promise that I shall deliciously arrange the new one by the river. Oh Marie, I turned *red* all alone in my room when I received the photograph of Geneviève, it looks so hideous and ridiculous. I wanted to tear it up straight away but I made the mistake of showing it to Cazalis and my grandmother who laughed in my face when they remembered how beautiful I had said she was! I was mortified because like all fathers I seemed to be boasting about an ugly child. How could they turn my Geneviève who is so adorable, into a toad, because that is the first word which came to everyone's lips. Fortunately I am going to see her and to forget, when I contemplate her, that caricature which has ruined her for me.[39]

As the letter indicates, Mallarmé and his family were about to move house as soon as he returned from Paris. Now that both his theatrical projects had come to nothing, in his mind the little house in the rue de Bourbon seemed irrevocably associated with failure. As he journeyed south, he may well have reflected on the letter which his grandmother Fanny Desmolins had sent him at the beginning of that summer. Needless to say she had disapproved of the way he intended to spend his holidays and had reprimanded him in her customary fashion, not seeking to hide her feelings:

> In truth, my dear child, I thought you were wise enough to take advantage of your free time going out into the fresh air with your family or among the flowers of your garden instead of going pale for days on end in front of a blank sheet of paper in search of a rhyme. And why oh why, my dear friend have you aimed your sights at the Comédie Française? Have you really thought about it? Without ever experimenting on a less ambitious stage? Allow me to point out that it is an act of madness! So I have been careful not to mention this to your grandfather, who would have been quite upset. We understand that you might want to have poetry as a distraction even as an interest for your leisure time since you have a taste for it. But to give yourself over to it frenetically to the extent that you are absorbed by it as you put it, and to raise your sights higher than can be reached, unless one is one of the chosen few, like those very few among the modern writers, well, you have to admit that it is far too pretentious an ambition![40]

As his train pulled into the station at Tain, across the river from Tournon, Mallarmé had much to think about. He no doubt hoped that a change of address would also bring a change of fortune.

4

The Crossroads

Around the middle of October 1865 Mallarmé and his family moved out of the rather cramped accommodation in the rue de Bourbon where they had lived for almost two years into a larger and generally much more comfortable house which he had managed to find for them at number 2, allée du Château. Mallarmé himself was only too pleased to leave behind the congested, narrow streets of the lower part of the town where the imposing and majestic façade of the lycée, located rather too close for comfort just across the other side of the main street, had cast its permanent shadow over his existence. It was no coincidence therefore that the new home he had rented for his rapidly expanding family, which now included not only a growing child but a white cat called Snowy, a goldfish and two canaries, was situated well away from the Imperial Lycée.

Perched high up on the steep Tournon hillside and nestling just below the old medieval castle, the house commanded a magnificent view across the valley over the patchwork of tiny red tiled roofs below. From the small window of his bedroom, which, with a typical lack of concern for the actual cost, he set about furnishing with expensive trappings well beyond the modest means of a junior schoolteacher, Mallarmé had a superb and totally uninterrupted view of a wide bend in the River Rhône. He was to spend many an hour at that window, delighting in the constantly changing play of sunlight on the water. Above all, it was with the move to this new and privileged vantage point that he became fascinated with the spectacular sunrises and sunsets which soon began to feature so prominently in his poems. He was quite delighted with his new home and could not wait to tell his friends about it. 'I now have a room worthy of you and I am impatient to offer you its hospitality,' he wrote enthusiastically to Théodore Aubanel, providing the following detailed description of the bedroom which also served as his study:

> It is austere with a large chest in it, some Henri III chairs upholstered in Cordoba leather and some Louis XIII chairs done in tapestry; there is a modern pendulum clock and an old lacework cover on the bed, and quite simply, besides a portrait of Hugo hanging on the wall, the portraits of friends who deserve to be there, especially yourself. But what I really like is that when you pull back the curtains of the only window in the room you can see the Rhône coming towards you, calm and serene like a huge wide lake. I am living amidst nature here and can watch both the sunrise and the sunset. And I can observe the autumn, not the yellow and red autumn with its leaves but the autumn of mists and melancholy waters. In short, I can imagine that I am no longer in Tournon.[1]

In such a charming setting, Mallarmé was soon keen to get back to work. During his recent visit to Paris Catulle Mendès had mentioned the possibility of placing some of his poems in a little review called *L'Art*. At the beginning of November, he suddenly wrote to Mallarmé exhorting him, as a matter of extreme urgency, to send him as many poems as he could muster for a new anthology of contemporary poets to be called *Le Parnasse contemporain* which he had managed to persuade his publisher friend Alphonse Lemerre to produce in weekly instalments.

In other circumstances, Mallarmé would have been pleased and flattered to receive such a request. On this occasion, however, it came as rather a nuisance, as he had already begun to think about reworking the first sketches of *Hérodiade* which he had been forced to abandon in order to complete the *Faun* for Coquelin and the Théâtre Français. In view of the critical comments which Banville and Coquelin had levelled against the *Faun*, Mallarmé was no longer thinking in terms of a piece intended for performance on the stage, but rather of a dramatic poem arranged in loose thematic blocks welded together into a musical structure. This change of perspective is underlined by the working title *L'Ouverture d'Hérodiade* (*Overture to Hérodiade*) which he provisionally gave to the new version and which deliberately stresses the musical nature of the work.[2]

Despite a genuine impatience to get started on this new version of *Hérodiade* with which he hoped to redeem himself in the eyes of his Parisian friends for the humiliating failure of the *Faun*, Mallarmé soon found circumstances conspiring against him once again. To begin with, his wife's sister Anna had time on her hands following her dismissal from her post as a governess. So she decided to take up an invitation to visit them in Tournon which Mallarmé himself had politely (and as it now turned out, somewhat rashly) extended when he had visited her in Paris earlier that summer. She arrived some time towards the end of October and stayed for a whole month. As it happens, Mallarmé was rather fond of his sister-in-law, whose 'doleful and serious demeanour'[3] he found quite pleasing. All the same, her presence was a distraction, and the noise of the sisters' conversations made serious writing quite impossible.

Yet Anna was only part of the problem. Even after she left at the end of November, Mallarmé found it increasingly difficult to settle down to any work. Although in total he was teaching roughly the same number of hours a week, his new timetable at the lycée was not nearly as accommodating as it had been the previous year. In particular, he had lost the two free mornings he had come to rely on. Furthermore, many of his classes were now early ones, which meant that it was not really practical for him to work late into the night. These important changes in his teaching timetable may very well have had something to do with the relatively poor showing he had made during the annual school inspection in June of that year. In his confidential report to the authorities, whilst admitting that Mallarmé got on very well with his other colleagues, that he kept to himself and worked hard, the headmaster had made it clear that he was extremely disappointed with his teaching. He complained that Mallarmé was too preoccupied with Romantic poetry, that he talked too much about literary theory to the older classes, and that he was not respected enough by his younger pupils.[4]

There were other difficulties as well. Once again the arrival of the cold weather took its inevitable toll upon Mallarmé's health. In the first week of December he succumbed to a severe bout of neuralgia which caused him blinding headaches and intense toothache as the nerves of his jaw and teeth became affected. During the rare moments of the week when he was free of pain, he tried desperately to get to work, hurling himself at his poem like 'a desperate lunatic', as he informed both Cazalis and Aubanel.[5] Finally, as if all these complications were not enough in themselves, Mallarmé now found himself in some considerable financial difficulty as the bills flocked in for the expensive furnishings which he had rather rashly acquired for their new home.

Thanks mainly to a generous loan from Théodore Aubanel, who enabled him to pay off at least the most pressing of his creditors, Mallarmé was at last able to make a serious start on the *Overture* some time during the second week of December. He had barely settled to the task, however, when two quite different and equally unexpected events forced him once again to shelve the project until well into the New Year. Firstly, Eugène Lefébure, who following the sudden and tragically early death of his young wife the previous summer had been advised by his doctor to winter in a warm climate, stopped off in Tournon on his way down to the South of France.[6] Secondly, within a day or so of Lefébure's arrival, Mallarmé found himself urgently summoned to Versailles by a telegram announcing the death of his grandfather, André Desmolins.

Mallarmé's finances were so stretched that he could not afford the cost of a railway ticket to Paris to attend his grandfather's funeral. In the end he was only able to make the journey because Fanny Desmolins agreed to make good his expenses. When he arrived in Versailles, Mallarmé spent much of his time seeing to the formalities of the funeral itself and winding up his grandfather's estate. Fanny Desmolins herself was too distraught to be of much practical help. Nonetheless, he did manage to visit Henri Cazalis and Catulle Mendès in Paris. He even contrived to find an excuse to extend his stay in the capital, claiming to Marie, who had fully expected him back in Tournon for Christmas, that a temporary indisposition made it quite impossible for him to travel:

> For a whole day now, I have had a very painful boil located precisely where you whip Geneviève when she has misbehaved. I am in pain, even when sitting on comfortable easy-chairs. It would be a terrible torture for me and in fact quite impossible to spend twenty hours sitting on the wooden seats or even the rough fabric covers of a railway carriage. I shall just have to wait until this annoying indisposition has passed.[7]

The truth of the matter, as he freely admitted later, was that he wanted to stay on in Paris because he had been invited to a special Christmas Eve gathering of writers at the home of the by then acknowledged leader of the up-and-coming Parnassian group of poets, Leconte de Lisle. Thanks to this quite transparent ploy, Mallarmé not only made the acquaintance of the older poet, but that same evening was introduced to younger men such as François Coppée and José-Maria de Heredia, both of whom were destined to rank among his closest friends. Heredia gave Mallarmé a copy of his collection of sonnets and, upon learning of the *Hérodiade* project, a fine print of Titian's *Salome*.

Needless to say, the warmth with which he was received by

such a community of poets was a source of great personal satisfaction to Mallarmé. It went a long way towards compensating for the embarrassment and humiliation which he had experienced during his visit to the capital earlier that summer. Above all, these new friends provided him with both the inspiration and the incentive which he desperately needed in order to persevere with his own work in his total isolation. 'The marvellous mood which I was in for working has been lost,' he wrote with more than a little exaggeration to Heredia upon his return to Tournon, 'and my New Year's greetings only keep me from it further. However, I do believe that, with the help of the pleasing rhythms which rocked me this evening as I read your sonnets, I shall easily be able to get back to work, after a few days of retrospective meditation.'[8]

This was not just a finely turned compliment to a fellow poet. Mallarmé had returned to Tournon quite determined to prove through a finished work that he was worthy of the interest which his new friends had shown in him. So strong in fact was his desire to complete the *Overture* that he went to considerable lengths to avoid any further delays and unwelcome distractions. At the risk of upsetting the very person whose generosity had enabled him to start on the project, and who kept inviting him to stay in Avignon, he informed Théodore Aubanel that such a trip would not be possible until after Easter. He likewise pleaded with Cazalis not to visit him in Tournon until after the *Overture* had been successfully completed. Finally – and most significantly of all for someone whose uppermost fear was of being forgotten in the provinces – for the next three months Mallarmé deliberately broke off all communication with his friends, entreating them to do likewise.

It was an extreme measure, but it achieved its purpose. In the following weeks, working mainly at night and well into the small hours of the morning, Mallarmé managed both to revise a collection of his poems for *Le Parnasse contemporain* and to finish a first version of the *Overture*. When, at the beginning of April 1866, an impatient and by then slightly anxious Cazalis broke his enforced silence to enquire what Mallarmé had been up to, the latter replied with some satisfaction:

> So it appears that I have to give you an account of the past three months! Well it can only be in the most general of terms. It is all rather frightening, really! – I have spent them toiling over *Hérodiade*. My lamp could certainly vouch for that! I have written the musical overture, which is still more or less a draft, but I can say without being too presumptuous that it has some stunning effects and that the dramatic scene which you have seen bears as much relationship to these new verses as a vulgar reproduction in a picture book does to a canvas by Leonardo da Vinci. I need three or four more winters to finish this work, but at the end of it all I shall have at last written what I imagine a Poem to be – something worthy of Poe, which even his admirers will not surpass.[9]

Mallarmé had every right to be proud of the *Overture*. It was by far his most ambitious work to date. The excitement and sense of exhilaration which the rest of his letter expressed owed more however to the week or so which he had recently spent in the company of Eugène Lefébure. By the end of March, physically and mentally exhausted by the work on the *Overture*, he had eagerly accepted an invitation from Lefébure to spend a week down on the Riviera. Absenting himself from his Friday classes at the lycée, Mallarmé left Tournon on the afternoon of 29 March and travelled to Avignon where, unable to find Aubanel, he spent the evening with the Brunets before catching the overnight train to Cannes. For the next week he rested and relaxed in Lefébure's company. The two men spent the first two days exploring Cannes and its immediate sur-roundings. They then visited Nice and Monaco, where Mallarmé won some money at roulette and bought a present for Marie. Towards the end of the week they took a boat ride and spent a wonderful day sightseeing on the nearby Lérins islands, where they were particularly impressed by the ruined cloisters of an abandoned monastery from which the ever vigilant monks had kept a wary eye out for the sails of the Saracen invaders.

From Lefébure's letters to Mallarmé it is clear that he greatly enjoyed the latter's company. 'If you just knew how much I miss you,' he wrote a few weeks later, 'and how much for me you are absent from the blue sky, the sea and the disappearing mountains, vanishing one after another in the blue distance, and from the little corner of spring which has decided to bloom behind my villa . . . I just wish we could wander there together and sit down, as we did at Easter, on the little bench surrounded by huge clumps of tall grass.'[10]

Mallarmé had even more reason not to forget the time which he had spent in Lefébure's company. Later, with the benefit of hindsight, he came to see the 'magical journey' as he described it in a letter of the time[11] as an important watershed in his life.

There were two main reasons why this trip to Cannes at the beginning of April 1866 came to assume such an extraordinary importance in Mallarmé's eyes. First of all, there was the impact which the breathtaking beauty of the landscape had upon him. He had never before travelled further south than Avignon, and had never seen the Mediterranean. Understandably therefore, after weeks of confinement in his study, his senses were literally overwhelmed by the lushness of the vegetation and the intensity of the colours. He was particularly struck by the clear blue sky and the limpidity of the water. 'I am really besotted with the Mediterranean. Oh yes, my dear friend, how splendid that terrestrial sky is!' he wrote to Cazalis. 'My dear child,' he announced to Marie the day after he arrived, 'you are forever with me and I am forever reaching for your hand in empty space to show you yet another example of the unexpected beauty of the scenery.'[12] He was so captivated that he was tempted to ask Marie to join him and to request sick-leave from the lycée so that the whole family could spend the entire summer there.

Second, and at least as important, there was the company
of Lefébure himself. His jovial good humour and endless
curiosity provided a welcome release, a necessary tonic after
the excessive solitude and introspection of the previous
months. Above all, there had been the endless conversations
which he had been able to enjoy with this older and respected
friend. In the weeks and months which followed his return to
Tournon, Mallarmé came to realize that the countless hours
he had spent that Easter discussing anything and everything,
from mutual friends and literary heroes to poetry and Art,
philosophy and religion, had had an extraordinary and profound impact upon him. Writing to Lefébure some two years
later, he had no hesitation in describing that week as an
important, indeed a vital turning-point in his life, the start
of a period that 'will mark me in a way that I want to
commemorate.'[13]

Many years later, long after Lefébure and he had ceased to
communicate with each other, Mallarmé kept his solemn
promise, recording this important moment in his intellectual
and artistic development in the magnificent opening section of
one of the most beautiful and most difficult of his poems,
perversely entitled 'Prose', which takes as its starting-point
a desire to conjure up from the past the memory of an
unforgettable journey to a privileged place with an exceptional
companion:

> Hyperbole! de ma mémoire
> Triomphalement ne sais-tu
> Te lever, aujourd'hui, grimoire
> Dans un livre de fer vêtu!
>
> Car j'installe, par la science,
> L'hymne des coeurs spirituels
> En l'oeuvre de ma patience,
> Atlas, herbiers, et rituels.
>
> Nous promenions notre visage
> (Nous fûmes deux, je le maintiens)

Sur maints charmes de paysage,
O soeur, y comparant les tiens.

L'ère d'autorité se trouble
Lorsque, sans nul motif, on dit
De ce midi que notre double
Inconscience approfondit

Que, sol des cent iris, son site,
Ils savent s'il a bien été,
Ne porte pas de nom que cite
L'or de la trompette d'Eté.

Oui, dans une île que l'air charge
De vue et non de visions
Toute fleur s'étalait plus large
Sans que nous en devisions.

Telles, immenses, que chacune
Ordinairement se para
D'un lucide contour, lacune,
Qui des jardins la sépara.

Gloire du long désir, Idées
Tout en moi s'exaltait de voir
La famille des iridées
Surgir à ce nouveau devoir . . .

[Hyperbole! from my memory
Triumphantly can you
Arise, today but a gramarye
In an iron-clasped book!

For I install through science
The hymn of spiritual hearts
In my patiently elaborated *oeuvre*,
Atlas, herbal or ritual.

We were casting our gaze
(We were two, I insist)
Over the countless charms of the landscape
Comparing its charms to yours, my sister.

The age of Authority is upset
When, without any reason, one says
Of that Southland which our twin
Unconsciousnesses explored

That its site, with a hundred irises
(They know fine if it really existed)
Does not bear a name heralded
By the golden summer's trumpet.

Oh yes! on an island which the air fills
With actual sights and no mere visions
Each flower unfolded greater than the one before
Without our saying anything.

So immense were they that each one
Was naturally adorned
With a luminous contour, a lacuna
Which separated it from the other gardens.

Glory of prolonged desire, Ideas
Everything within me exalted to see
The Iris and its family
Rise to this new duty . . .]

Of course, in common with all true poems, 'Prose' transposes and crystallizes many separate experiences, weaving them into a greater whole, in this case into a wider interrogation about the function of Art itself and the ability of the artist to rescue from oblivion and express in adequate terms the beauty of a fleeting revelation. Nonetheless the journey to a magical island with a special companion (now remembered as a woman not a man), the spectacular landscape, and the discovery of breathtakingly beautiful flowers (symbolizing the first ecstatic glimpse of a new artistic vision), these are all part of Mallarmé's faithful homage to an important turning-point in his life and to the figure (now unnamed) who played a special part in it.

Why then did Mallarmé feel the need for such a solemn commemoration? Why did the Mediterranean with its sensual delights, vibrant colours, luxuriant flowers and sheer exuberance, have such an effect upon him? Why did he later attach such importance to the conversations he had had with Lefébure?

To answer these important questions we need to place the whole experience in its proper context. Mallarmé had arrived in Cannes in a state of considerable anxiety. Not only had he pushed himself to the limits of his physical and mental endurance in his desperation to complete the *Overture*, but during its composition he had made two particularly devastating discoveries which had brought him to the edge of despair. The first of these concerned the very nature of language itself, and was a direct outcome of his work on the *Overture*. One of Mallarmé's principal aims in the latter had been to condense as many layers of meaning as possible into a single line whilst seeking to establish as close a relationship as possible between the sound patterns of his verses and the meanings they conveyed. A few months earlier, writing about the *Faun*, he had referred to this activity as combining 'the sound and the colour of words, the music and painting through which our thoughts, no matter how beautiful, have to pass in order to become poetic.'[14]

Pursuing this tactic even further in the *Overture*, he had painstakingly subjected every word and phrase of the poem to the most intense scrutiny. By delving so deeply into the mysteries of poetic expression, he had come to an inescapable and, for him, terrifying conclusion. He realized that in practice the kind of harmony or correlation between sound and sense which he desperately sought was extremely rare. What was even more disturbing, he discovered that in the French language at least, these two elements which he specifically sought to unite were frequently in direct and total contradiction to each other. It was a fundamental defect in the language which he commented upon much later, and with some humour, in one of his critical essays:

> Compared to *ombre* [*shadow*], which is opaque, the word *ténèbres* [*darkness*] has little density, and how disappointing it is when one is faced with the perversity which, in total contradiction, confers in the

case of *jour* [*day*] and *nuit* [*night*], a tone of dark upon the former, of light upon the latter.[15]

But this was not all. The more he had studied individual words, repeating them out loud again and again to himself, the more they had gradually seemed to lose their form and meaning, until through the very act of endless repetition he had come to see them for what they essentially were, namely rhythmic vibrations in the air totally devoid of any intrinsic meaning. In short, through this experience, Mallarmé had come to realize that language, upon which he and everyone else depended and by which, as a poet, he himself had set such store, was in reality nothing more than a collection of mean-ingless conventional signs. It was a devastating discovery which had completely unnerved him. 'Unfortunately,' he now commented to Cazalis with masterly understatement, 'in dig-ging so deep into poetic expression, I encountered two abysses which have led me to despair. The first is Nothingness itself, which I arrived at without any knowledge of Buddhism. I am still too upset even to believe in my own verse and to get back to the work which this shattering thought caused me to abandon.'[16]

The second discovery (or 'abyss' as he liked to call it) had been no less disturbing. It concerned the precarious nature of life itself, 'the unbearable lightness of being', as Milan Kundera's novel would call it a century later. This disquieting subject had recently been brought into focus for Mallarmé for several reasons. The first was a growing anxiety about the state of his own health. As mentioned earlier, his already weak constitution had been seriously undermined by his exhausting late-night sessions on the *Overture*. Intermittent colds and bouts of flu had developed into a persistent cough which he had found alarming enough for him to consult a homeopathic doctor in Avignon. The latter had assured him that he was suffering from nervous exhaustion and that his life was not in any danger, a view incidentally shared by Fanny Desmolins, who when she heard, somewhat belatedly, that her grandson was not well, affected great surprise and recommended a strong dose of cod-liver oil. 'You were not ill and you were not coughing during your last visit!' she replied somewhat pointedly.[17]

Mallarmé, however, did not share the scepticism of his doctor, or his grandmother. Brooding on his weakened condition, and only too susceptible, in his extreme isolation, to the anxieties produced by his fertile imagination, he had convinced himself that he was seriously ill. This unwelcome reminder of his own mortality had led to an unhealthy and morbid preoccupation with death which the recent loss of his own grandfather and, more significantly still, some well publicized but confused newspaper reports of a stroke which had seriously endangered the life of Charles Baudelaire, had only reinforced. A whole month after his return from Cannes, Mallarmé was still brooding on that particular subject. 'Do not be alarmed by the sadness of my letter, which perhaps stems from the pain which Baudelaire's health is causing me,' he told Cazalis. 'For two days I thought that he was dead. Oh, what a terrible couple of days! I am still devastated by his current plight.'[18]

This sudden and unhealthy preoccupation with the utter vanity of the human condition, exacerbated by what he took to be his own imminent death and that of others whom he held most dear or respected, had led Mallarmé to attribute to everything the sense of void or total emptiness which he had discovered at the heart of language. Through this combination of circumstances, he had become acutely aware of the fundamentally absurd and totally irrational nature of existence and of the extremely fine line separating absence and presence, being and nothingness, life and death, which later, once he had truly come to terms with this essential truth, he would place at the very centre of his work and make the cornerstone of his personal philosophy and his mature poetics.

However, as he journeyed south to Cannes towards the end of March 1866, Mallarmé was still finding it desperately difficult to cope with the enormity of his discoveries. Physically exhausted and on the verge of nervous collapse, he needed help. Above all, having struggled with these terrifying metaphysical questions entirely on his own, he now needed the reassurance that he was not going insane. It was fortunate for him, and indeed for posterity, that it was to Eugène Lefébure that he chose to unburden himself. A more experienced and wiser man who had already survived the tragic loss of a young wife, Lefébure was able to inform his younger friend that he was not the first person to have contemplated what he, himself, with his typical lack of sentimentality, liked to call the 'logical constitution of the universe'.[19] Without being a trained philosopher, Lefébure was extremely well read and had a remarkable grasp and extensive knowledge of both Eastern and Western philosophy. A convinced atheist but a keen student of comparative religions and mythologies (he had for some time been making a detailed study of Egyptian theories of the immortality of the soul), he reminded Mallarmé that speculative minds throughout the ages and in all kinds of cultures had had similar confrontations with the basic absurdity of existence and the terror of cosmic loneliness.

By reminding him of such things at this crucial point in his existence, Lefébure was able to provide Mallarmé with a sense of perspective which had been lacking at the height of his solitary crisis. In so doing, he not only rendered Mallarmé an immense and invaluable service as a friend, but more importantly made a vital contribution to his intellectual and artistic development. Mallarmé returned to Tournon not only physically restored after a relaxing week in the sunshine but above all intellectually invigorated. In the weeks and months which followed his trip to Cannes he underwent a dramatic transformation akin to the experience recounted metaphorically in the poem 'Prose' as the impact of the Mediterranean and above all the reassuring and informative discussions he had had with Lefébure brought into focus many of the questions which had unsettled him of late.

The whole experience acted as a catalyst, unleashing in Mallarmé a period of great lucidity during which many thoughts which until then had seemed random, confused and frequently contradictory started to crystallize in his mind and make sense. It was a period of intense creative energy during which he began to question both the nature and the direction of his work. In the light of recent events, not the least of which was a new heightened awareness of the sheer beauty of this planet as revealed to him by Nature itself in the form of the Mediterranean landscape, he realized how extremely narrow in scope and how exclusively centred upon himself as an individual his work so far had been. Dismissing the selection of poems which he had just dispatched to the *Parnasse contemporain* as 'nothing more than so many intuitive revelations of my own personality',[20] he now realized that the true nature of Art and the artist lay in their ability to express universal truths. The role of the poet, as he now saw it, was not to indulge in a primarily subjective account of his own experience, but to adopt an objective, impersonal viewpoint, speaking not of or for himself but rather on behalf of his fellow men. He consequently concluded that the challenge which he principally faced as an artist and indeed the only legitimate subject for Art itself was to attempt to express, in all its complexity, the basic unresolved and unresolvable paradox of the human condition such as he had discovered it to be, perpetually hovering between absence and presence.

In the excited and, at times, quite densely argued letters which he now began to send his friends, Mallarmé would refer to this subject somewhat elliptically as 'Beauty'.[21] Much much later, with the serenity which comes with absolute certainty, he would define it more appropriately as 'the quintessential but totally elusive quality of Life itself'.[22] Furthermore – and this was in no small measure due to his recent discussions with Lefébure on religion and philosophy – Mallarmé now believed that in pursuing such an ambition, he could legitimize the role of Art and make of it what he had always, instinctively, wanted it to be, namely an alternative to and substitute for the traditional religious beliefs to which, in view of his absolute certainty of the void which he now knew to lie at the heart of everything, he felt he could no longer personally subscribe.

Barely a month after returning from Cannes, Mallarmé had already sufficiently formulated his new theory of literature to be able to describe it in its basic outline to Cazalis. In a remarkably dense passage of a letter he wrote to the latter towards the end of April 1866, he defined the underlying principles of his future work. Adopting an atheistic perspective, he would remain a lyric poet, celebrating not himself or the Glory of God, as previous ages had done, but rather the Glory of the potential and the inventiveness of the human spirit which, with total lucidity, was forever aware of its own limitations in the immensity of the cosmos, and all the more admirable for that. Furthermore, in order to do justice to such a difficult and important subject, he would have to undertake a preliminary study of the various ways in which, throughout its history, mankind had responded to the discovery of the essentially absurd nature of the universe. It was an astonishing outburst:

> Ah yes! I *know*, we are but mere forms of matter – but very sublime ones for having invented God and our souls. So sublime, my friend that I propose to offer myself the spectacle of matter, which, aware of what it is, nonetheless frenetically hurls itself up into the Dream which it knows does not exist, singing of the Soul and all the similar impressions of Divinity which have accumulated within us from the earliest ages and proclaiming, before the Nothingness which is the Truth, these glorious lies! Such is the outline of my volume of lyrical poetry, and such will probably be its title: *La Gloire du mensonge* [*The*

Glory of the Lie] or *Le Glorieux mensonge* [*The Glorious Lie*]. I shall
sing as a man without Hope.[23]

Of course, the fully developed and highly original literary
philosophy or poetics which was eventually to emerge as a
consequence of the convictions and intuitions expressed here
for the first time with the fervour that is typical of a neophyte,
and later solemnly commemorated in the lapidary verses of
'Prose', took a great many years to find its definitive
expression. It was, as we shall see, a protracted, painful and
quite uneven process, with moments of spectacular insight
undermined by recurring doubts and anxieties. There were
times, over the next few years, when Mallarmé's dogged
pursuit of his 'Dream', as he liked to call it, plunged him into
great depression and brought him to the edge of despair. The
months which immediately followed his trip to Cannes,
however, were among the happiest and most exhilarating in
his life. Lefébure, who spent some time with him in Tournon
that summer, found him in extremely high spirits. 'Have you
finished your beautiful great poem?' he enquired a few weeks
later. 'Are you still juggling with the Absolute and Being and
Nothingness, those serpents which you carry around in your
pockets? Do you remember our walks along the edge of the
Rhône on those glorious red evenings and our expeditions to
Iserand or to Caesar's Bridge where it rained so heavily and
you ran pushing Vève [Mallarmé's daughter], our astonished
young queen, in her pram?'[24]

The late spring and early summer of 1866 were an exceptionally productive period for Mallarmé. He began to sketch the
first tentative outlines of what was to become his ambitious
life's work, dispatching hurried and at times quite unintelligi-
ble accounts of his activities to his frequently uncomprehending and bemused friends. Towards the end of May he informed
Cazalis that he was busy laying the foundations for a book on
Beauty and that he had begun three short poems and three

prose poems, each in its own way dealing with the same subject. (It may well be that at this point he made some early drafts of a group of three sonnets later reworked and published together for the first time some twenty years later, although since, as is frequently the case with Mallarmé's later sonnets, there are no surviving manuscript versions of these poems which pre-date their publication, their exact date of composition must always remain conjectural.)[25]

As the summer heat reached its height in mid-July, for once he did not envy those of his friends who could afford to take a holiday. 'I am travelling too,' he insisted, 'but in unknown lands, and if, in order to escape the torrid reality of the summer, I prefer to use arctic imagery, I would say that for a month now I have been amid the coldest glaciers of Aesthetics – that having discovered the Void, I have discovered Beauty – and that you cannot imagine the lucid depths which I am exploring.'[26] That same month, he announced that it would take twenty years to complete the great work which he now envisaged, attempting through a remarkable series of metaphors, many of them still decidedly Christian in origin, to explain to Théodore Aubanel in Avignon the dramatic transformation which his thought had recently undergone:

> As for me, I have worked more this summer than in my entire life. I have laid the foundations of a magnificent work. Every man has a secret within him, many die without ever finding it . . . I am dead and resurrected with the jewelled key of the ultimate treasure chest of my mind. It is now up to me to open it in the absence of any impression borrowed from elsewhere, and its mystery will spread out into a most beautiful heaven. I need twenty years during which I am going to retreat within myself, avoiding any publicity except for some readings to my friends. I am working on everything simultaneously, or rather I mean that everything is so well organized within myself that now, whenever a sensation reaches me, it is transfigured and is automatically lodged in a particular book or poem. When a poem has matured, it will fall. I am imitating the laws of Nature, as you can see.[27]

When Aubanel read this letter he confessed himself quite unable to understand what it meant. Mallarmé tried to make himself clearer by resorting to an analogy with the sacred spider of Indian thought (a choice of metaphor which probably owed more than a little to his recent discussions with Lefébure):

> I simply wanted to tell you that I have drawn up the plan of my entire work after finding the key to myself – linchpin or centre if you like so as not to mix metaphors – whereby I sit poised like a sacred spider on the main threads which have already emanated from my mind and with the help of which I will weave *at the points where they intersect* the most marvellous lacework, which I can imagine and which already exists in the bosom of Beauty.[28]

Significantly, Mallarmé decided not to undertake his annual pilgrimage to Paris that summer. In part, this was for purely financial reasons. He fully expected to be transferred to another lycée at the end of the holidays. In April he had admitted to Cazalis that he was having serious discipline problems with his pupils. A month later he had gone as far as to make an official request for a transfer to Sens on the grounds that he wished 'to be nearer his family'. The main reason why Paris did not attract him that summer, however, was that he wanted to work. After a fortnight spent relaxing in the company of his Avignon friends, he made a start on preliminary research for his great project.

It was at this point in August 1866, and not before, as has been frequently suggested, that Mallarmé began to take a serious interest in scientific and philosophic theories of all kinds (including Hegel's), devouring the limited number of books which he could lay his hands on in Tournon and Avignon. These included cabbalistic works and works on alchemy, for he wished to study as many unifying systems as possible as part of his research into the various ways in which, at different times in their cultural history, speculative minds had tackled the complex relationship between religious ritual, mythology, art and magic, which from now on would remain at the very centre of his own preoccupations.

Mallarmé's major difficulty, however, was that he was neither a trained philosopher nor a scientist. Like most of his contemporaries, he had a basic understanding of Platonic philosophy, which he had briefly studied at school (hence his frequent, if somewhat inconsistent borrowing of the Platonic *Idea* in some of his later critical writings). But two facts have been too frequently ignored by those who seek to exaggerate the impact of external influences upon Mallarmé's thought. First, it is clear that he derived little pleasure from reading works of pure philosophy. Second, he was, if nothing else, a fiercely independent spirit who wished to discover things for himself. Mallarmé made both of these important points quite forcefully himself when, at the end of August, he provided Aubanel with a rather depressing account of his progress so far:

> My befuddled mind refuses to return to its former lucidity and I am just having to endure it, on my divan amongst a pile of books which I peer at and dip into without being able to finish them. It is true that they are books of science and philosophy and that I wish to *experience* through myself each new idea and not to learn it from someone else.[29]

Left to his own devices, Mallarmé would have no doubt spent the rest of the summer pursuing the research which now so completely fascinated him. But it was not to be. Life intervened with its usual inescapable demands. The major serious distraction during the summer of 1866 was his growing alarm at his position in the lycée now that his problems with discipline had compelled him to request a transfer. The results of his latest annual inspection were not exactly encouraging. One observer noted that he did not know how to handle his pupils, commenting that he lacked method and that his pupils were obviously not being stimulated. A second inspector was scathing:

Despite his intelligence and knowledge, which I do not wish to contest, M. Mallarmé has until now only produced poor results from his teaching. All his pupils pronounce English very badly and do not know the most common words. In his first year Special Education class, fourteen pupils all working together could not translate for me 'Give me some bread and water.' Of his entire third form, not one pupil deserves to move on to the fourth form. In the senior classes the teacher has them translate *King Lear* from the text. Inevitably, the pupils understand nothing. I tried to discover the source of the problem and think I detected it in the coldness of the teacher and in the speed with which he intervenes without ever allowing his pupils time to think. The teacher says the words, his pupils repeat them mechanically but they retain nothing whatsoever.[30]

For his part, the headmaster of the lycée tried to be fair but he could not conceal his disappointment with someone who, as the inspector's comments demonstrate, was quite obviously a poor teacher. 'A cultivated, if pretentious mind,' he wrote. 'Talks a lot about poetry and the ideal, but professes only a modest esteem for his fellow men. Yet his conduct is beyond reproach and he has good manners.' As for Mallarmé's request for a transfer to Sens, he had no objection: 'I think that if it is possible, it would be desirable to grant his request,' he added. Clearly, he would not be sad to see Mallarmé leave.

The months of June and July brought growing pressure to remove Mallarmé from the school. It came initially from a small group of parents who had learned that he had published some poems in *Le Parnasse contemporain* and who were outraged by this. The local *sous-préfet*, that is to say a man of considerable influence in the region, went as far as to threaten to remove his son from a school which employed an English master who had the audacity to publish poetry in such an avant-garde collection.

To expedite his transfer, Mallarmé enlisted the help of both his family and his old friend from Versailles, Armand Renaud. During the summer they did what they could to bring pressure to bear on the authorities. But the publication of the poems in the *Parnasse* proved quite a stumbling block. Fanny Desmolins warned her grandson to act with extreme caution. 'Do I need to tell you, my dear boy,' she thundered, 'that it would be wise not to send to the men at the Ministry a certain volume which they have mentioned to me and whose effect upon serious-minded and non-artistic people could only be harmful and not helpful to your interests. It might allow them to imagine that these literary activities take up time which they think ought to be devoted to other duties. This was mentioned to me as a piece of friendly advice but I managed to gather that activities of this sort are not appreciated by bureaucrats.'[31]

Emile Deschamps and Emmanuel des Essarts were also press-ganged into service, but at the start of the new academic year, in early September, Mallarmé was still in Tournon and completely at loggerheads with the administration. To make matters worse, he found himself once more in some financial difficulty. In July and in August he had already been forced to ask his grandmother to advance him the September interest due to him on the remaining 4,000 francs of his mother's estate for which, since her husband's death, she was now solely responsible. By September he asked if he could be allowed to eat into the remaining capital itself. Fanny Desmolins wrote a genuinely shocked reply:

> Truly my dear boy, your request causes me real sadness in several ways. First of all it will make me break the vow I had made myself to follow the *express* and frequently repeated wish of your poor grandfather which was that this sum of money be kept *intact* for the future well-being of your family, as he saw only too clearly that at some point it might be your ultimate resource. In my moments of greatest financial difficulty, faced with the enormous expenses which I incurred in the painful months which I have had to endure, I preferred to resort to the purse strings of all my friends around me rather than to break into that store of money which is doubly sacred to me, even if I intended making good any borrowing. Despite my horror of debts, I still prefer to be crippled by them, in the hope that I shall free myself from them in time, rather than to have been tempted, even for a moment, not to respect a dear wish. You will

understand therefore all the pain that was caused by a letter which I was so far from expecting since I knew you had funds in hand and as I was already saddened by the thought that they had probably dwindled.

In his reply Mallarmé claimed that he had lent money to one of his friends (no doubt to conceal from Fanny Desmolins that the real source of his debts was his own basic inability to live within his means). His grandmother was indignant, and admonished him in no uncertain terms:

> But what, you will surely agree, is unforgivable in the head of a household, is the extreme irresponsibility with which you have handed over all these funds without even thinking about any eventuality which might mean that you needed them yourself. It is all very fine, no doubt, to help one's friends, as far as we can; but to act so generously when you have hardly enough for yourselves, when your family is there which you have to think about above all else, well, that is quite unforgivable![32]

Having made her point, she relented however, and agreed to release 1,000 francs of the capital, a considerable sum of money (the equivalent of almost half of Mallarmé's annual salary). This was a generous gesture, especially because since her husband's death the previous year, unknown to her grandson, Fanny Desmolins had been living in much reduced circumstances, surviving on her widow's pension and the rent from a tobacconist's shop which she owned. In fact, in the first week of October, fearing that the family might not have enough money to survive the month, she took the precaution of sending a 400-franc advance on the promised 1,000. But that was not all. Not the kind of person to be fobbed off by bureaucratic double-talk when her grandson's livelihood was at stake, she battled her way into the Ministry of Education, where one of the deputies, a M. Lebourgeois, who had already heard of Mallarmé's predicament through Armand Renaud, informed her that there were only two free posts currently available. One of them had just been filled. The other, it turned out, was in Algiers!

At the end of the first week of October, unable to tolerate his situation at the lycée any longer, Mallarmé himself wrote to the Ministry of Education stating that unless he was transferred immediately, thus avoiding, as he put it, 'the close proximity of the Rhône and the violent winds', both of which, he claimed, seriously endangered his health, he would be forced to ask for sick leave. He also requested a personal interview in order to be able to put his case. Unknown to him, however, the following day and completely independently the Rector of the Grenoble Academy (in whose province the lycée of Tournon lay) also wrote to the Ministry backing the headmaster's repeated requests:

> Dear Minister, the headmaster of the imperial lycée of Tournon has once again expressed his desire that M. Mallarmé, an English teacher in that establishment, be sent elsewhere. Apart from the inadequacy of this teacher, the headmaster points out the unfortunate effect caused by the publication of some pieces of poetry in the enclosed number of the *Parnasse contemporain*. 'Some parents,' the headmaster writes, 'including the *Sous-préfet*, have stated that they will not send their children to the English class, although such a class is compulsory, and that they propose, if necessary, to write to the Minister to explain their reasons.' I think, Minister, that we ought to avoid this eventuality and I urgently entreat you to exhort his Excellency to move M. Mallarmé.[33]

The Minister had little choice. In 'the interest of the service,' he agreed to the request. A fortnight later, to his grandmother's relief,[34] Mallarmé was transferred to the lycée in Besançon as a *chargé de cours* (course instructor or assistant master) in the English department. In reality, it was a demotion and a form of official disgrace. What was more, in practical terms the move posed a whole series of problems for Mallarmé and his family, as by now they were several weeks into the new school year. They had already paid out a full term's rent on their accommodation in Tournon, which in spite of the recent events it now genuinely pained Mallarmé to leave. Ever sympathetic, Lefébure understood what was going through Mallarmé's mind: 'How many unfinished or forgotten lines of poetry you must have left in the corner of your little house by the Rhône, lost among the cobwebs. How many sunsets you will no longer see which would have found their way into your poems!'[35]

5

Besançon and Avignon

Mallarmé took up his new position early in November 1866. Situated on the north-eastern side of the country, quite close to the Swiss border, Besançon was renowned for the watch-makers who had practised their crafts there for two centuries. This bustling commercial and administrative centre also enjoyed elegant architecture, much adorned with intricate wrought-iron grille-work dating back to the late seventeenth century, when the city had replaced Dole as the provincial capital.

Despite the obvious physical attractions of Besançon and the fact that his personal literary hero Victor Hugo had been born there, Mallarmé did not take to the place. Its bitterly cold and damp climate were unlikely to endear it to him, of course, but what he most disliked was the general air of complacency, the pretentiousness and smugness of its predominantly middle-class citizens. Writing to Emmanuel des Essarts a few weeks after he had arrived in the city, Mallarmé complained that he was surrounded by what he described with utter contempt as 'semi-dilettantes'.[1] To make matters worse, given the less than glorious circumstances in which he had left the lycée at Tournon, he was only too well aware that he had to be extremely careful not to offend his new colleagues and superiors. It was for this reason, more than any other, that he found the first few weeks in Besançon particularly trying, as a large part of his time was taken up with the obligatory and seemingly endless social round to meet people who were little to his liking. He found the whole business quite infuriating and totally demeaning, as he pointed out to François Coppée:

> I am no longer in Tournon, but in Besançon, former city of wars of religion, a sombre prison-like place. I have been here a month. Perhaps I ought to be pleased? So far I am not very well and have barely recovered from the disruption of being forced to move such a distance, from the move itself and from the numerous *visits* which I have had to make to idiots so as not to alienate from the very start my superiors who keep a wary eye on me as if I were a criminal.[2]

There were other reasons why these first few months in Besançon were difficult for Mallarmé and his family. The only accommodation he had been able to find for them at such an awkward time of the year was a far cry from the charming little house which they had been forced to leave behind in Tournon. Furthermore, for several weeks, for reasons which are not at all clear, they only had access to part of the property they had rented in the rue de Poithune. It was fully two and a half months before Mallarmé had a workroom of his own.

As if these annoying delays and disruptions were not enough, he once again found himself in serious financial difficulty. If we are to believe what he wrote to his grandmother (but he may well have been exaggerating the figures in order to gain her sympathy), the rent which he now had to find in Besançon was double what he had been paying in Tournon. What was certainly true, however, was that he was genuinely and seriously out of pocket because of the rent he had paid in advance on the Tournon house. In December he informed his grandmother that he was penniless and pleaded with her to allow him to eat further into his mother's estate. This time Mme Desmolins refused to release what little capital was left but – and once again this was greatly to her credit – she undertook to sell some of her own shares in order to raise 500 francs. In the meantime Mallarmé had already asked his old friend Armand Renaud to enquire through his contacts in

1. Stéphane Mallarmé at the age of twenty

2. André Desmolins,
the poet's grandfather

3. Anne Mallarmé,
the poet's stepmother

4. Numa Mallarmé, the poet's father,
a year before his death

5. Emmanuel Des Essarts

6. Henri Cazalis

7. Marie Mallarmé during the time
she and Stéphane lived in Avignon

8. Contemporary photograph of
Mallarmé's summer home in Valvins

9. The bridge over the Seine at Valvins
photographed by Mallarmé's landlord, Abel Houdry

10. Mallarmé on his boat at Valvins

the Ministry of Education whether it was possible for him to be reimbursed for his removal expenses, which had been considerable. Towards the end of January 1867, Renaud replied saying that there was little chance of any additional money since the Ministry had informed him that their funds for the previous year were already exhausted. He also tried to warn Mallarmé that he was not at all popular with the authorities.

Any illusions which Mallarmé may have still entertained on this subject must surely have been dispelled by the official reply to his request for removal expenses which he received from the Ministry of Education a few days later. The tone was cool and unsympathetic. Its message was quite clear and must have made disquieting reading:

> Dear Sir, you sent me a request for the reimbursement of your removal expenses. Reimbursements of this sort are reserved for employees who have been moved in the interests of the service. Now, if you were moved, it was because at the lycée of Tournon your publications offended a certain number of families and your removal was urgently requested. You will understand, my dear sir, that in these circumstances it is impossible for me to repay removal expenses which you alone occasioned. May I take this opportunity of requiring you to be more careful in the future. If any fresh complaints were to be addressed to me in connection with the poems which you published, I would find it extremely difficult to retain your services as a teacher.[3]

It was a serious blow. The higher cost of living in Besançon had not been offset by any increase in Mallarmé's salary, which remained more or less what it had been in Tournon. To make matters worse, with his typical profligacy and total disregard for the economic realities of life, he had once again used the removal as an excuse for ordering expensive carpets and brand-new mirrors. When she learned of these latest purchases, Fanny Desmolins was quick to point out that she and her husband had had to wait twenty years for any such luxuries. Nonetheless, she immediately dispatched warm clothes for Geneviève and also arranged for some of her old furniture to be sent to them. Even so, money worries continued to preoccupy Mallarmé for the rest of the winter, as the private pupils he had counted upon to supplement his income just did not materialize. The first casualty was the maid he had engaged, for the sake of appearances, to help out Marie. Only a week or two after starting work, she was summarily dismissed.

The winter which Mallarmé spent in Besançon from January to March 1867 was without doubt one of the coldest in all his life. The intensely bitter winds and thick ice which enveloped everything caused his rheumatic condition to flare up, inflicting severe and unremitting discomfort. Above all else, it was an extremely lonely winter. Apart from his obligatory journeys to and from the lycée, he made little contact with the local community. He likewise cut himself off from his distant friends, retreating somewhat self-indulgently into the private world of his own thoughts and his dream of the Great Work. 'Time passes at an amazing speed when you are possessed by an *idée fixe*, and now that I am working harder than ever, I find myself in that situation,' he informed Heredia in one of the rare letters which he wrote from Besançon that winter to congratulate the latter on his marriage.[4]

Typically, it was only after he had survived the winter that Mallarmé felt inclined or indeed able to give any account of it to his friends. In May 1867, however, he wrote two quite extraordinary letters which shed some light on these important months during which he had once again fallen alarmingly silent. These show that quite unknown to his pupils and his colleagues at the lycée a dramatic and terrible personal struggle had taken place behind the modest shutters of Mallarmé's house in the rue de Poithune. The first of these two letters, addressed to Henri Cazalis, began with an astonishing announcement:

> I have just survived a frightening year. My thought has re-thought itself and has reached a Pure Concept. Everything which my being has suffered during this protracted agony is unrelatable, but fortu-

nately, I am perfectly dead and the most impure region into which my Mind can venture is Eternity. My Mind, that hermit accustomed to living in his own Purity, which can no longer be dimmed even by the reflection of Time itself.[5]

The extremely condensed thoughts expressed in these opening lines and the elliptical metaphors through which they are communicated themselves provide ample confirmation of the period of intense self-scrutiny through which Mallarmé had just passed. Once the euphoria of the previous summer had faded, he had seriously begun to question his ability to produce the Great Work which he had announced to all his friends. Physical exhaustion, isolation and continued anxiety over his health, his deteriorating financial position and his teaching career, had plunged him into a sombre mood which the unexpected severity of the winter had done little to dispel. Such had been his loss of confidence in himself and such his despair that at one critical point he had seriously contemplated turning to the faith which, until then, he had steadfastly rejected. It had been, he now admitted to Cazalis, a terrible struggle and a temptation to which he had almost succumbed. He now felt totally exhausted:

> After a final synthesis, I am now slowly rebuilding my strength and I cannot be distracted from the task, as you can see. But oh! how much more easily I could have been several months ago, first of all in my dreadful battle with that wily old bird, God, whom fortunately I managed to bring down. But as the struggle took place on his bony wing which carried me off into the Darkness and caused me more intense agony than I had imagined him to be capable of, I fell, victorious, but seemingly endlessly and without any direction until one day I saw my reflection once more in my Venetian mirror just as I used to be before I forgot who I was several months earlier.

Mallarmé's decision to totally reject the Christian faith into which he had been baptized was an extremely courageous act of defiance and independence. In nineteenth-century France, where religious conformity still ruled, it henceforth set him apart not only from the majority of his contemporaries but above all from the rest of his own family, including his wife. More significantly still, it transformed his view of Art and the role which he ascribed to himself as a writer. Now that he had taken this crucial and irrevocable step, he was free to make of Art an alternative vehicle for spiritual needs which he could no longer direct into the traditional religious beliefs of the day. This renewed and unshakeable faith in literature would sustain him for the rest of his life and provide him with an inner strength and serenity which would only deepen with time. He announced it to Cazalis in the following terms:

> I have descended deep enough into the Void to be able to speak with certainty. Beauty alone exists and it has only one perfect expression, Poetry. Everything else is a lie – except, in the case of those who live the life of the body, for love, and, for that love of the mind, friendship.

Poetry, love and friendship. It was a remarkably prophetic programme which Mallarmé would endeavour to follow for the rest of his life. Above all else, he was articulating for the first time one of his most cherished beliefs. From this point onwards he saw the function of poetry as being primarily sacred and solemn. This fundamental conviction is the key to many of his later pronouncements. It explains the dense, moving, yet quite astonishingly comprehensive definition which he provided many years later for Léo d'Orfer when he stated: 'Poetry is the expression, through human language reduced to its essential rhythm, of the mysterious meaning of the various aspects of existence. In this way it authenticates our sojourn on this planet and constitutes our sole intellectual challenge.'[6] It likewise explains the apparently simple yet absolutely crucial question: 'Qu'est-ce, ô Toi, que la Terre?' ('Tell me, will you, what is the Earth?') which the cosmos asks the shade of one representative of Mankind in the commemorative poem 'Toast funèbre' ('A Funeral Toast') written in 1873 to honour the life and work of a fellow poet and friend, Théophile Gautier. Above all, it explains why Mallarmé can later define his projected Great Work as 'The Orphic explanation of the Earth which is the sole duty of the poet and the supreme literary game.'[7]

The quasi-religious function which Mallarmé now attributed to Art in general and to poetry in particular reinforced some of the conclusions which he had tentatively reached the previous summer concerning the necessary objectivity of the artist. In order to fulfil his mission as a vehicle for expressing the collective experience of his fellow human beings, the individual poet had of necessity to suppress his own personality. In other words, in order to become a true artist, he had to 'die' as a person. Mallarmé had expressed this idea somewhat obliquely at the very beginning of his letter to Cazalis where, working a deliberate change on the Christian notion of Death and Resurrection, he had declared himself to be 'perfectly dead', before adding, not without humour, that there was absolutely no possibility of him going to Eternity! Later in the same letter he returned to the theme, describing himself and his new purpose in Hegelian terms:

> I have to let you know that I am now impersonal and no longer the Stéphane whom you used to know. I am instead an aptitude of the Spiritual Universe which permits the latter to become visible and develop itself through the person who I used to be.
>
> Fragile as my terrestrial appearance is, I can do nothing other than undergo the developments which are absolutely essential if the Universe is going to find, through me, its identity.

As a result of the key decisions which he had made that winter, Mallarmé had modified his earlier plans for 'the Work, the Great Work as our ancestors the Alchemists call it'. He now estimated that this would take him ten years to complete (rather than the twenty he had envisaged the previous year). He also announced that the Work itself would now consist of three poems in verse, one of which would be the as yet unfinished *Hérodiade*, and four poems in prose. This new configuration around seven key works (instead of the six of the previous year) was not fortuitous. It was a deliberate attempt on Mallarmé's part to mirror in the grand design of the Great Work the structure of the constellation of the Great Bear, which seems to have become one of his obsessions at around this time. Like many other speculative thinkers before him, during that crucial winter in Besançon he had spent many a night marvelling at the glittering, star-filled sky. He was literally fascinated by the stars and the essential paradoxes which they seemed to illustrate. On the one hand, their mysterious beauty delighted him, yet at the same time he believed that the light which so dazzled him came from stars which were already dead. As such, of course, they were a perfect analogy for the presence/absence paradox which had so preoccupied him during the last two winters.

Similarly, if, through the patterns which they appeared to impose upon the sky, certain groups of stars had fired the imagination of men through the ages, giving rise to the myths of the constellations, as a total sceptic Mallarmé knew that these were merely meaningless points of light scattered at random throughout the Universe. As such, of course, these constellations furnished a marvellous analogy for the creative power of the human imagination, and indeed for poetry itself. For, just as the human imagination could create meaningful shapes out of totally meaningless points of light, so also, through poetic expression, it could create meaningful patterns of sound and sense out of fundamentally meaningless frag-ments of language. That is what Mallarmé meant when, writing to Villiers de l'Isle-Adam later that summer, he claimed to have discovered what he called 'the ultimate corre-lation between Poetry and the Universe.'[8]

It is no coincidence that from this point onwards the constellations become a major and constant theme in Mal-larmé's work. They figure prominently in two quite magnifi-cent sonnets which, although only finally completed and revised many years later (by which time they had been reworked several times), owe their immediate origins to the crucial winter which he had just spent in Besançon. The first of these sonnets, originally bearing the title 'Cette nuit' ('Night'), which he subsequently dropped, is very close in atmosphere and subject matter to the letter which Mallarmé sent Cazalis in May 1867 describing the death of his old faith and the emergence of a new one.

In its final form the sonnet offers much more than a personal celebration of Mallarmé's new-found faith in himself and his work. Through the magnificent extended hyperbole of the last three lines, which suggest that the light emanating from our planet will eclipse the tawdry and showy tinsel of the galaxies writhing in their death throes, Mallarmé proudly celebrates the great potential of Mankind which, through the power of the human mind as expressed in language, can confront the immensity of the cosmos. In so doing, in a striking parallel with the recent evolution of Mallarmé's own thought, the protagonist of the sonnet ceases to exist as an individual, becoming the spokesman of his fellow men. One of the last of his more readily accessible sonnets, it remains one of his finest poetic achievements. A solitary proud figure observes through his window the onset of night (stanza one) and, contemplating the stars and their paradoxical beauty (stanza two), reflects upon the position of man in the scheme of things (the two final tercets). The journey towards the ultimate, sublime revelation of the final line that celebrates the true greatness of Man is mirrored in the gradual movement from the one to the all and from darkness into radiant light:

> Quand l'ombre menaça de la fatale loi
> Tel vieux Rêve, désir et mal de mes vertèbres,
> Affligé de périr sous les plafonds funèbres
> Il a ployé son aile indubitable en moi.
>
> Luxe, ô salle d'ébène où, pour séduire un roi
> Se tordent dans leur mort des guirlandes célèbres,

Vous n'êtes qu'un orgueil menti par les ténèbres
Aux yeux du solitaire ébloui de sa foi.

Oui, je sais qu'au lointain de cette nuit, la Terre
Jette d'un grand éclat l'insolite mystère,
Sous les siècles hideux qui l'obscurcissent moins.

L'espace à soi pareil qu'il s'accroisse ou se nie
Roule dans cet ennui des feux vils pour témoins
Que s'est d'un astre en fête allumé le génie.

[When the shadow threatened with its fatal law
That old dream, desire and ache of my spine,
Saddened to perish under the funeral ceilings
It folded its indubitable wing within me.

Such luxury, O ebony hall where, to seduce a king,
Celebrated garlands writhe in their deaths,
You are nothing but vainglory belied by the darkness
In the eyes of this solitary man dazzled by his faith.

Yes, I know that far out in the night sky, this Earth
Projects its unusual mystery in a great blaze of light
Across the hideous centuries which darken it even less.

True to itself whether it expands or disappears, Space
Rolls in this boring expanse of vile lights as witnesses
That what burns so bright is the genius of a festive planet.]

A fortnight or so after he had written to Cazalis, Mallarmé sent Lefébure a second equally detailed letter which provides valuable information concerning the historical and cultural context in which the Great Work should be placed. What he envisaged, he informed Lefébure, was something modern which could stand comparison with the masterpieces of the Classical Age and the Renaissance. Referring to a recent article in the *Revue des Deux Mondes* which had caught his attention,[9] he claimed that Western civilization had so far produced two great artistic achievements. The first, the Venus de Milo, he argued, was the product of classical or pre-Christian times and expressed an essentially pagan innocence. The second, the Mona Lisa, was the product of the Christian era, and expressed the loss of innocence. What was required now was something which expressed the values of a modern, scientifically informed and fundamentally post-Christian culture:

> Yesterday I finished my first outline of the Work, clearly delineated and totally endurable, if I myself endure. I contemplated it quite calmly and without any horror and, closing my eyes, *I saw that it existed.* The *Venus de Milo* – which I like to attribute to Phidias, so generic has the name of that artist become to me – and the *Mona Lisa* seem to me to be and *are* the two great shimmerings of Beauty on this Earth and my Work, such as it is imagined, is the third. Absolute and unconscious Beauty, which is unique and inalterable in Phidias's *Venus*; Beauty whose heart, with the arrival of Christianity, received the venomous bite of the Monster, painfully resurrected with a strangely mysterious smile, but a smile of forced mystery which she *senses* to be the condition of her being. Finally, Beauty which, through the knowledge of Man, has rediscovered in the universe *the relative stages of its development*, remembering the secret horror which forced her to smile in Da Vinci's time, and to smile in a mysterious manner – smiling mysteriously now, but happily and with the eternal inner serenity of the *Venus de Milo* which has been recovered, having understood the mystery of which the *Mona Lisa* could only know the fatal sensation.[10]

Mallarmé was convinced, he informed Lefébure, that given enough time he could produce such a work of art. His mind, he felt, was more than equal to the task. What did cause him some anxiety, however, was his health. 'It is my body which is *totally* exhausted,' he lamented. 'After several days of intellectual activity in my flat, I freeze completely and am absorbed by my reflection in the diamond of this mirror – until I suffer agonies. Then, when I wish to revive myself in the warm sun, I dissolve under its effect and it reveals to me the utter disintegration of my physical being. I feel that I am *completely* exhausted.'

This paradox of an agile mind ready to soar to new heights but prevented from so doing by the physical limitations of a weak body forms the central core of another sonnet, 'Le vierge, le vivace et le bel aujourd'hui . . .', which commemorates in part at least the winter which Mallarmé had just spent in Besançon. This terrible agony, all the more terrible in having been a private one which had gone unnoticed by other people, is conveyed by the extended metaphor of a magnificent swan trapped in the ice. Its long neck and proud head reach for the sky but its wings and body cannot free themselves from the frozen ice that holds them fast. Other related and parallel themes have been grafted on to this basic image. The sonnet suggests the dangers of excessive introspection and absorption in one's self and the shock which the mind receives when it returns to the real world and senses that time has passed. The poem also depicts the horrible realization that one is ageing and losing one's strength; the frightening nightmare that comes with the impression or the actual sensation of having temporarily disappeared; the fear of being a mere reflection which, if contemplated too long, eventually vanishes; and the overwhelming sense of being a living ghost, that serves to remind us of the absurdity of the human condition, of the stage upon which we are but passers-by.

Many of these disturbing and uncomfortable ideas (not to mention the bird image itself) are present in the ironic, bantering and typically self-mocking opening paragraph of the letter which Mallarmé sent to Lefébure in May 1867, confirming once again the relationship between the sonnet and his own experience in Besançon:

> How are you? Does your soul, that melancholy stork standing amid motionless lakes, not see itself reflected in their mirror rather too much to your annoyance – which, disturbing with its murky twilight the pure magical enchantment, reminds you that it is your body which is standing abandoned on one leg (the other, injured, is folded up in your feathers)? Now that you have been brought back to a sense of reality, listen to the guttural friendly voice of another old bird, both a heron and a raven, who flutters down beside you. I just hope that this whole picture does not disappear for you amid the shivers and terrible wrinkles of your suffering! Before we allow ourselves our mutterings, a genuine chatter of birds who resemble the reeds

and who share their vague amazement when we return to life from staring fixedly at the pool of our dreams – the pool of our dream where the only thing we ever catch is our own reflection, without thinking of the silver scales of the fish! – let us ask ourselves for a moment just how we are doing in this life!

Such ironic remarks, gently parodying the metaphysical arguments of Pascal (not to mention Mallarmé's own recent speculations), remind us of the serious problem of being which lies at the very centre of the sonnet of the Swan. Both the poem itself and Mallarmé's comments provide a necessary counterbalance to the excessive optimism of his letter to Cazalis and to the idealism of the earlier sonnet. The two poems, like the letters themselves, are inextricably linked. The soaring ambition which in the first sonnet had folded its 'indubitable wing' within the poet becomes in the second the noble bird which is no longer sure if it can fly. Both poems play variations on the same theme, but from different angles. They highlight different aspects of a common drama: a terrible agony that is total, that is to say both physical and mental, and which arises from the complex relationship between these two interconnected levels of being – 'Desire and ache of my spine' is how Man's ambition is referred to in 'Quand l'ombre menaça . . .'

The tone in the second sonnet is much more muted, however. The poem undergoes a subtle shift of mood. The overall movement is almost the exact opposite of the first sonnet, which moves from darkness into bright light. Here we move from light to darkness, from hope to despair, as a resurgence of optimism and hope that comes with every new day (stanza one) gives way to caution that comes of world-weary experience (stanzas two and three). Yet the final mood is not one of utter failure, total darkness. It is deliciously ambiguous as, in the dark night sky, a distant galaxy glitters. In this way, from behind the apparent failure there emerges a glimmer and a potential triumph. The self-mocking irony of the 'pointless exile' of the final line gives way to the final capitalized word of the sonnet with its suggestion that something heroic has nonetheless been accomplished as the Swan, frozen and fixed in the glistening ice, disappears and is imperceptibly transformed into the twinkling constellation of Cygnus.

A parallel and totally compatible interpretation of this line (and indeed of the sonnet itself) is that in his heroic struggle merely to exist and to carry on resisting, despite the certain knowledge that he is ultimately doomed to fail, the Swan assumes his own identity. He has become himself, he has become the Swan. Through this final image the Swan remains fixed in the reader's mind as a constellation: he is Cygnus too. Another unknown individual accepts his tragic human fate. This in itself is a truly heroic act, one that deserves the process of apotheosis whereby in Greek and Roman mythology heroic mortals were transformed into Gods:

> Le vierge, le vivace et le bel aujourd'hui
> Va-t-il nous déchirer avec un coup d'aile ivre
> Ce lac dur oublié que hante sous le givre
> Le transparent glacier des vols qui n'ont pas fui!
>
> Un cygne d'autrefois se souvient que c'est lui
> Magnifique mais qui sans espoir se délivre
> Pour n'avoir pas chanté la région où vivre
> Quand du stérile hiver a resplendi l'ennui.
>
> Tout son col secouera cette blanche agonie
> Par l'espace infligée à l'oiseau qui le nie,
> Mais non l'horreur du sol où le plumage est pris.
>
> Fantôme qu'à ce lieu son pur éclat assigne,
> Il s'immobilise au songe froid de mépris
> Que vêt parmi l'exil inutile le Cygne.
>
> [Will the virgin, vital and beautiful new day
> Tear us free with a drunken wing-beat
> From the hard forgotten lake haunted under the ice
> By the transparent glacier of flights which have not flown!

A swan of days gone by remembers that it is he
Who, magnificently but without hope tries to be free
For he has not sung of the region in which to live
When the monotony of sterile winter shone once more.

His whole neck will shake off that white agony
Inflicted by space on the bird which refuses it,
But not the horror of the ground where his feathers are caught.

A ghost assigned to this place by his pure radiant glow
He moves no more, caught in the cold dream of contempt
Which, in its pointless exile, clothes Cygnus itself.]

The tension between the demands of mind and body was a subject which particularly exercised and fascinated Mallarmé at that time. He had come to realize the contradictions engendered in himself by these two opposing forces, these two warring factions of his being. It was his visit to Cannes the previous year that had first highlighted this inner conflict. His senses had responded to the breathtaking beauty of the Mediterranean, which he had never seen before. Yet at the same time his intellect constantly reminded him that fabulous Nature was, like everything else in the physical world, totally ephemeral. It was nothing but a magnificent deception, a 'glorious lie' as he had described it to Cazalis. Unknown to Mallarmé at the time, this tension, this vibration between presence and absence, a presence which conceals an absence and an absence which is never quite total, had been the real subject of the two major lyrical works which he had earlier attempted and which, for precisely that reason, he had found so difficult to write. The same duality links the apparently ice-cold, aloof and virginal heroine of *Hérodiade*, who within the depths of her being seethes with pent-up physical desire and who hesitates to commit herself to life, and the amorous, sensuous *Faun* who wants to possess all women, but who is held back by the subtleties of his own mind, which wonders if he is perhaps merely the victim of an illusion – 'Aimai-je un rêve?' ('Did I love a dream?') is, after all, the initial question which triggers the rest of the poem.

This absence/presence dialect (and the other related conflicts which mirror it, namely between life and Art, imagination and reality, the intellect and the emotions, death and life, all of which themselves stem from the original conflict of Being and Nothingness) had now become and was to remain the focus of Mallarmé's creative writing, until the very moment of his death. He realized of course that such tensions and conflicts were fundamental to the human condition and could only fully be resolved in death.[11] Nonetheless, from his own recent experience he had become acutely aware of the dangers of getting the balance wrong. He had come to realize that excessive intellectual activity to the exclusion of everything else was extremely harmful. He enclosed with the letter to Lefébure several pages of pencilled notes which make this precise point and which every student of his work and especially those who insist upon describing him as primarily a cerebral poet would do well to read:

> I think that in order to be truly human, that is to say Nature reflecting upon itself, you have to think with your entire body. That provides rounded, harmonious thoughts like the strings of a violin vibrating directly on the hollow sound box. Thoughts which emanate from the brain alone (I made abusive use of this last summer and during a part of this last winter) now seem to me to be like a tune which is played on the upper end of the string with the highest notes producing a sound with which the box is not comfortable – which come and go without 'becoming anything', without leaving any trace. In fact I cannot remember any of the ideas I suddenly had last summer.[12]

The purpose of Art, as Mallarmé now saw it, was to reconcile these conflicting forces and to provide a lasting monument to human existence as experienced through the twin filters of the body and the mind.[13]

In his own particular case, however, there still remained the practical problem of achieving this desirable balance. As he had pointed out to both Cazalis and Lefébure, it was his physical health which was his immediate concern. In the annual report which he submitted that May, the School Inspector noted that Mallarmé was convinced that he was ill. In fact, Mallarmé himself had already decided that he could not survive a second winter in Besançon and had asked his grandmother to see whether Armand Renaud could pull strings to arrange a transfer to a more hospitable climate.[14] This proved difficult to arrange. Mallarmé had been in Besançon less than a year, and in any case he was not exactly popular at the Ministry of Education. Despite the continued efforts of his family and friends the whole summer went by without any real progress being made. Eventually, however, the diplomatic skills of Renaud's friend M. Lebourgeois brought results. At the beginning of October Mallarmé was informed that he was being transferred to Avignon. He took up his new post around the middle of the month, and was joined by his wife and daughter a fortnight later.

The move was most welcome. It cost less to live in Avignon than in Besançon, and besides, Mallarmé had a ready-made circle of friends there. 'I have been resuscitated,' he wrote to one of them upon hearing of the transfer. 'If all of you and the sun were to do the rest with your combined friendly warmth, you would save from oblivion quite a number of divine works which are very upset to have been more or less put off to a future date.'[15]

In the event, such optimism was not justified. Mallarmé certainly appreciated the warm and genuine welcome extended to him by Aubanel and the other members of the Félibrige, but it soon turned out that the more he got to know them the less he realized he had in common with them. 'I see almost no one here, being not entirely made of the same stuff as those Félibres,' he confided to Lefébure.[16] Besides, he was once more back in the Rhône valley. The climate of Avignon with its strong gusty winds and the Mistral itself, although admittedly less harsh than in Besançon, was very similar to what he had endured in Tournon. Inevitably, the winter took its toll. Whilst waiting for a friend at the railway station in the first week of December, he caught a bad cold which quickly developed into congestion of the lungs and kept him bedridden for the greater part of the month.

When spring eventually came, Mallarmé took stock of his situation. His physical constitution had been severely undermined by three difficult winters in succession. It was now two years since he had first conceived his masterwork, but so far there was little to show for it. Because of his illness he had not done much writing during his first winter in Avignon. Indeed, when in April of that year the remains of his sister (along with those of his mother) had been transferred to the Desmolins family plot in Versailles, he had not even felt well enough to compose the little commemorative poem which he felt was called for. Fanny Desmolins, who around Christmas had been so alarmed at her grandson's deteriorating health that she travelled down to Avignon for three weeks to help Marie look after him, tried to allay any guilt he might be feeling. 'Do not tire your brain, my dear child,' she entreated him, 'working on verses which are not necessary to prove to me the tender regret your heart feels for the dear companion of your childhood. I would enjoy reading them of course, but my satisfaction would be tainted with the thought of the pain your poor head had suffered, and that would destroy part of their worth in my eyes.'[17] The seriousness of his recent illness had not been lost on Mallarmé himself. It forced him to pause and reflect upon the risks he was taking with both his physical and mental health. Continuing to suffer from persistent migraines and sleepless nights, he painted an alarming picture to Lefébure:

> I'll just touch briefly on the subject of my health, not wishing to disturb that disquieting cesspit on those rare moments when it allows the pure waters of my mind to rest. Besides, I don't know what to tell you, for I can just as quickly shift from moments where I am

close to madness which I can actually imagine to others when I experience equally intense feelings of ecstasy. The only thing I do know is that I am in a state of crisis which cannot last, and that consoles me somewhat! Either I shall get worse or I shall be cured, I shall die or I shall survive. I don't really care as long as I do not continue to endure these abnormal bouts of anxiety which are weighing me down. To be sure, I am descending earthwards from the Absolute . . . but the two years which I have spent there (do you remember? ever since I stayed with you in Cannes) will mark me in a way that I want to commemorate.[18]

Clearly, something had to be done. Alarmed by his unstable mental state, Mallarmé therefore wisely decided not to abandon his dream of a masterwork but to provisionally restrict the scale of his activities. 'After all,' he concluded, 'poems which have even a hint of the Absolute about them are already something very beautiful – and there are not many of these, besides there is always the possibility that reading them in the future will resurrect the poet I had dreamed of becoming.'

It is obvious from these remarks that Mallarmé felt that he nonetheless had to make some attempt to give poetic expression to the vision which had haunted him for the past two years. In fact he had already begun to think about just such a poem. Almost casually, at the end of this same letter to Lefébure he made an oblique allusion to the possibility of a sonnet with an unusual rhyme scheme using '-ix' sounds. Two months later the poem was finished, and Mallarmé sent it to Cazalis for a collection of sonnets which was to be illustrated by various water–colourists.[19] In the letter which accompanied the finished poem, he seemed remarkably offhand about it:

> I have extracted this sonnet, which occurred to me this summer, from a study I intend making of *La Parole* [*Language*]. It is quite a contrary piece. What I mean is that its meaning if it has one (but I would be quite consoled if this were not the case, thanks to the large dose of poetry which to me it seems to contain) is conveyed through a hidden mirage suggested by the words themselves. If you allow yourself to murmur it several times, it has a cabbalistic feel about it. I have to admit that it is not very 'plastic' as you requested, but it is as 'black

and white' as possible and it would do for a water-colour evoking Dreaming and the Void. For example, an open window at night with both shutters fastened back. A bedroom with nobody in it despite the atmosphere of solidity generated by the shutters . . . In a dark night made up of absence and interrogation – there is no furniture, except perhaps the hint of a vague commode or two – there is the warlike but agonizing frame of a mirror hanging at the back of the room bearing the mysterious starry reflection of the Great Bear which connects this abandoned dwelling place, alone, in all the world, with the sky.[20]

All of this, of course, was deliberately misleading. The humorous banter was an attempt to hide the fact that Mallarmé took this particular sonnet very seriously indeed. He was rather proud of it, so much so in fact that he took the unusual step of bringing it to the attention of his grandmother, Mme Desmolins.[21] It was a first, if small-scale attempt to encapsulate within the confines of a sonnet his absurdist vision of the world as a glorious and tantalizing mirage. Its theme is the absence/presence paradox which lies at the very centre of his poetic universe. Bringing together some of his favoured images – a room, a window, a mirror, the night sky and the emblematic Great Bear – it seeks to depict existence as a series of reflected images, at one and the same time both empty and yet hauntingly beautiful. (In the original French, which it is impossible to replicate in the translation, the idea of a shimmering mirage is constantly suggested by the haunting echoes of the exceptionally rich and intricate sound patterns of the lines.) The cosmic and the domestic are thus reflected in and by each other as, by implication, the fate of both is shown to be identical.

Once again, just as at the end of the Swan sonnet and through the use of similar stellar imagery, there is the merest suggestion that a heroic victory has somehow been snatched from the very jaws of defeat. This is Mallarmé's first truly hermetic poem, stretching language itself and the reader's imagination to their very limits. It is above all else, however, a poem about the fleeting nature of Life itself, whose constant mystery is repeatedly suggested by the unusual rhyme, impossible to render in English, but which in the original French suggests the emblematic letter 'X' (pronounced *eeks*), the unknown.

> Ses purs ongles très haut dédiant leur onyx,
> L'Angoisse, ce minuit, soutient, lampadophore,
> Maint rêve vespéral brûlé par le Phénix
> Que ne recueille pas de cinéraire amphore
>
> Sur les crédences, au salon vide: nul ptyx,
> Aboli bibelot d'inanité sonore,
> (Car le maître est allé puiser des pleurs au Styx
> Avec ce seul object dont le Néant s'honore).
>
> Mais proche la croisée au nord vacante, un or
> Agonise selon peut-être le décor
> Des licornes ruant du feu contre une nixe,
>
> Elle, défunte nue en le miroir, encor
> Que, dans l'oubli fermé par le cadre se fixe
> De scintillations sitôt le septuor.[22]

> [Her pure fingernails high up dedicating their onyx,
> Anguish, this midnight, holds up, in the lamps it bears
> Many an evening dream burnt by the Phoenix
> Which is not collected by any funeral jar
>
> On the sideboards of the empty room: no ptyx,
> Abolished knick-knack of sonorous stupidity
> (For the Master has gone to draw tears from the Styx
> With this sole object by which Nothingness is honoured)
>
> But by the window empty to the North, some gold
> Agonizes in keeping perhaps with the motif
> Of unicorns kicking fire at a nymph,
>
> She, dead cloud in the mirror, whilst
> In the oblivion bounded by the frame, is fixed
> A sudden septet of scintillations.]

With the summer holidays in view, Mallarmé's spirits improved considerably. He was looking forward to a reunion with Cazalis, who had promised to stop off in Avignon on his way south to visit an aunt on the Riviera. He himself was relishing the thought of renewing his acquaintance with the Mediterranean landscape, far away from the lycée and the blistering heat of Avignon, which that summer was playing host to a large contingent of Spanish poets attending the festival of poetry organized by Aubanel and the other Félibres.

A few days after the school holidays began, together with Cazalis, who by then had already spent a week in their company, Mallarmé and his family boarded the train for Marseille. He had managed to find a fairly inexpensive *pension* in Bandol. The only drawback was that it was over an hour away from the wooded hills in which he liked to walk and picnic, and some distance from the sea itself. His budget was very restricted, however, and when the fees from a private pupil failed to materialize, he was obliged to borrow funds from Cazalis so that he could stay on an extra fortnight after Marie and Geneviève had left and avoid attending the poetry festival in Avignon, which was not at all to his taste.

After the summer holidays, a by now familiar pattern repeated itself. The onset of winter brought on depression, undoing all the good work of the summer break. On top of that, Mallarmé was once again in serious financial difficulty. Not only had he incurred additional debts by unwisely and unnecessarily having their Avignon flat redecorated, but there was still money owing for the removal expenses from Besançon. He had also lent some money to Lefébure, who was finding it increasingly difficult to live on the allowance which he received from his grandmother. By December Mallarmé was already beginning to fall behind with his rent when, for the second time in as many months, his salary was reduced. In October, a new headmaster had arrived at the lycée, and by removing several classes from Mallarmé's timetable had caused him to lose 100 francs from his annual salary. Now, in an attempt to reverse an earlier injustice, a ministerial circular regraded the salaries of foreign language teachers, putting them on the same scale as teachers of French. In Mallarmé's case this meant a further loss of 300 francs, as well as additional hours, bringing his weekly total to 25 hours.

By the middle of December Mallarmé had accumulated debts of over 1,000 francs – the equivalent of half his annual income. Thanks to the generosity of Cazalis, who lent him 400 francs, and Lefébure, who returned 100 francs of the money which he had borrowed, he managed to pay off his most pressing creditors. The rest of the money proved much harder to find, however, especially as his grandmother had already sold her remaining shares to help him out earlier and could offer him no more financial assistance. Eventually, unknown to the latter, he borrowed 500 francs from an aunt against the collateral of his future inheritance.

By that time the pressure of these constant financial worries had taken its toll. In early December an alarming bout of hysteria had forced Mallarmé to take to his bed for a couple of days. In February 1869, after weeks of anxiety, uncertainty and recurrent bouts of insomnia, he was totally exhausted and close to a nervous breakdown. His doctor advised him to avoid any form of intellectual stimulation, and went as far as to forbid him to touch a pen. For the next few months he was forced to dictate all his letters to Marie (whose command of French was less than perfect). When an incredulous Cazalis asked Mallarmé to write in person to prove that he was getting better, he dictated the following reply:

> I have to say: 'No Satan, you will not tempt me'. I have made a vow, *in extremis*, not to touch a pen until Easter. All I can say is – didn't I warn you of this in my last letter? – that the simple act of writing causes hysteria in my head, which is precisely what I want to avoid most for all my friends to whom I owe a Book and many years. I am not entirely free of the crisis because, even dictating to my kind secretary, the thought of a pen writing through my will, even if it is by the hand of another, brings back my palpitations.[23]

A few years earlier Mallarmé would probably have ignored such danger signs, but he had learned from the experience of the last two winters. A wiser man now, he informed his friends that he was going to concentrate for the moment not on the Great Work itself, but on the preliminary studies which he knew were absolutely essential if he was to find a way of giving full expression to his complex and paradoxical vision of the world. Nothing less than an exhaustive historical, anthropological and scientific study of Mankind, its religions and its rituals through the Ages was what was required. Or, as he put it rather cryptically in this same letter to Cazalis:

> It will take me a few years, during which time I have to relive the life of the Human Race from its infancy and from the moment when it became aware of itself. To get myself started I will assign to these years of study a practical objective which will be my 'Egyptology' [an allusion to the studies of Lefébure]. But I'll only tell you all about that when I am sure I am totally free from the claws of the Monster.

For the next two months Mallarmé took great care not to over-exert himself, listening to a little music to exercise his memory and studying some German. He also began to reread the New Testament as part of his background studies for his future work. Ironically, this renewed interest in religion led him into a final confrontation with his grandmother. At the height of his most recent crisis (to which she had thus, in her own way, contributed) Fanny Desmolins had reminded him that she had never stopped praying for him. She went on to exhort him in the name of his dead sister and mother to seek refuge in the Catholic Church as her husband, André Desmolins, had eventually done, and to infer that his stubborn refusal had much to do with the predicament he now confronted.[24] Aware, after a recent heart attack, that she herself was now terminally ill, she had spent the next few weeks waging a desperate and protracted campaign to bring her recalcitrant grandson back into the fold. By the end of April, Mallarmé felt that it was time to resolve the matter once and for all:

And now, dear grandmother, it is not without having given much time and thought to what I would say to you that I come to the serious issue which you have raised. You tell me that you are writing to me about it for the last time and I am almost afraid to deny that what you say is true, despite the sadness which these words cause me, a sadness which echoes your own, for I am afraid that if we constantly return to this subject, the entirely different feelings which it arouses in us both will only end up causing us pain. But you will at least allow me will you not to continue to describe our petty existence to which my renewed efforts to change are inextricably linked and to inform you of any small progress which I make? Truly, when I think about all the letters which we have written to each other over the last few months on those evenings when you and I have been reunited again, was it not that desire for an improvement which came from my concentrating on myself instead of directing my mind to other external things, which was the only good news which I announced during your illness, hoping that that in itself would be a source of joy for you? Should I regret having said that? I know that I could easily have said nothing about the New Testament which, read in the context of my new requirements, provided me with more spiritual fulfilment than I can say. But I thought that that would be another source of consolation for you. In my own heart I have nothing to reproach myself with therefore for having unwisely offered you a hope which I now seem to deny you. Your heart (and I sympathize as it grieves me to write this, but is it not better to do so?) sought from me more than I could give, at least up until now.[25]

Sadly, it was the last letter that he ever wrote to his grandmother. A week after she received it, Fanny Desmolins died on 6 May from the serious heart condition from which she had been suffering for the past year. Mallarmé himself was still not well enough to attend the funeral, and any sense of guilt he must have felt on that account could hardly have been diminished when he learned from his wife, who had gone to Versailles in his place, that ever since the death of her husband Fanny Desmolins had been living in far more straitened circumstances than she had ever acknowledged. It now became clear that, while she had been regularly lending him small amounts of money over the past few years, she had been forced to pawn her silverware and jewellery to make ends meet and had died leaving a large number of debts.

From the purely financial point of view it was a bitter blow for Mallarmé, who had been hoping for some form of inheritance to improve his own situation. But the loss of Fanny Desmolins affected him in other, deeper, ways. With her death he had lost the last remaining link with his early childhood and his parents. He had above all lost someone whose genuine love for him he no longer questioned, despite the fact that she had disapproved of his literary activity and despaired when he had renounced his faith. The feelings which now welled up within him were understandably complex and somewhat contradictory. Guilt and regrets on the one hand, yet on the other an acute awareness of the immense debt that he owed his grandmother and her husband. There was also the growing sense of a duty which he felt towards her and towards himself to prove his worth as a writer.

These troubled thoughts preoccupied Mallarmé during the following months as he gradually recovered his physical and mental strength. It is not surprising therefore that when, in July, his doctor found him well enough to begin writing again, he decided to make them the focus of a short story, *Igitur*, in which a young man of that name, the last descendant of his race, is paralysed and driven to the edge of madness by a not too dissimilar set of fears and anxieties.

Mallarmé mentioned his *Igitur* project to Armand Renaud when the latter stopped off briefly in Avignon at the beginning of the summer. He even jotted down some initial outline sketches for it during the walking holiday which he spent in Provence from the middle of August to the middle of September. He continued working on it when he returned to Avignon, but what little progress he made was soon interrupted by the start of the new school year at the beginning of October. Initially, he tried to solve the problem of getting up early in the morning to work for a few hours before setting off to his classes, but he soon found himself unable to sustain such a demanding routine for any length of time. By the end of November, he realized that a more dramatic solution was called for.

Earlier that summer he had discussed with Armand Renaud the possibility of taking time off from the lycée. In the first week of December therefore, having first taken the precaution of writing to Renaud to enlist the support of the latter's good friend at the Ministry, M. Lebourgeois, Mallarmé officially requested an immediate leave of absence from his teaching duties from the beginning of the second term until the end of the school year. His intention, he informed the Minister of Education, was to fully recover his health and to use the time to good effect by returning to his studies in order to further his teaching career. With no private means at his disposal, he asked to retain at least part of his salary during his period of absence. In support of his request he provided a medical certificate from the school doctor confirming his poor health.[26]

Just over a month later, on 19 January 1870, to his utter astonishment and delight, Mallarmé received notification from the Ministry that he had been granted leave of absence from the beginning of the second term until the end of the summer vacation – in other words for a longer period than he had in fact requested. What was more, he was to retain virtually half his normal salary. Such generosity on the part of the Ministry was due, not, as Mallarmé himself believed, to the influence of Armand Renaud's friend Lebourgeois (who in any case was a fairly lowly official) but largely to the direct intervention of the Rector of the Academy himself, who was keen to replace him with an 'efficient' teacher. It was at the latter's particular insistence that he was allowed to retain such a large portion of his annual salary.

Mallarmé was convinced that he and his family could survive financially if he added to his reduced salary the money he could make by giving private lessons and the small sum his wife received as the annual rent from a tobacconist's shop which she owned in Arles. In the following months, therefore, he began to study for an Arts degree prior to tackling a doctoral dissertation. In order to combine these official studies, which were designed primarily to enhance his career prospects, with his own personal interests, he decided to specialize in Linguistics. This choice of subject, he informed Lefébure, would provide a scientific basis for the important work that was from now on his major preoccupation and at the same time would bring him valuable insights into the hidden workings of language itself, which he now quite rightly diagnosed as one of the principal sources of his nervous illness.[27]

As a consequence of all this, for the next nine months or so Mallarmé was at last able to lead the kind of existence which, until then, had been no more than an impossible dream. The initial product of this unexpected freedom was a tremendous burst of creative energy. Poems virtually exploded into his mind, constantly distracting him from his studies.[28] One thing soon became very clear, however: having tasted such freedom for a few months, he was determined, if he could contrive it, not to return to schoolteaching. 'I will not return to the lycée,' he told Lefébure. 'If I have to choose between the means of my own destruction, I prefer to succumb to my own thoughts. I can always escape from these, but not from the other.'[29]

Mallarmé came to another important decision at about this time. Towards the end of May Catulle Mendès, to whom he had earlier sent a part of *Hérodiade* for the second number of *Le Parnasse contemporain*, wrote to him with the following interesting proposal:

> Will you soon be back among us? I would like to make you an offer. I live in Neuilly in the heart of the Bois de Boulogne and am surrounded by pathways which are rarely frequented. My house, which has two storeys and a small garden, is too large for my wife and myself. Would you and your family like to have half of it? The house is designed in such a way that each of its two halves are quite

separate. Your wife and daughter would each have her own bedroom. There are two studies, one for you and the other for me. It is completely and rather pleasantly furnished. The windows look out to the west. The only things which the two families would have to share are the drawing-room, the piano and the dining-room. A few yards beyond the garden gate (yes, there is a garden gate!) there is a huge wood where you can go to think and to work. Our two wives would get on well, because you and I like each other. We live cheaply. You would not need much money to share our existence. What do you say? Answer 'yes' and you will make me happy. See you soon, your brother, Catulle Mendès.[30]

It was, as Mallarmé was quick to admit, an extremely tempting offer. For months now he had been complaining to friends that he had been unable to find in the provinces the books and other materials which he required for his researches. The kind of libraries, museums and art galleries to which he now desperately needed access were only to be found in Paris. Besides, there was little to detain him in Avignon, or in the South of France for that matter. Emmanuel des Essarts had long since left Avignon, and more recently Eugène Lefébure had abandoned Cannes for the security of a post-office job in Saint-Germain-en-Laye, a mere dozen miles or so from the capital. Mallarmé replied enthusiastically, therefore, announcing that he could come to Paris for a few days in the middle of July to discuss the offer in more detail.

Unfortunately, it was not from Paris but from Weimar, where he had gone with his wife Judith Gautier and Villiers de l'Isle-Adam to hear Wagner's new operas, that Mendès wrote back explaining that everything would have to be delayed until September as he had rented out his Neuilly house in order to cover the travel expenses of the trip to Germany. Undeterred by this temporary setback, Mallarmé seems to have nonetheless repeated his acceptance of the offer in a letter to Mendès which has been lost, for, from the poste restante in Munich where he had now gone to hear *Das Rheingold* and *Die Walküre*, the latter wrote back yet again, qualifying some of his earlier enthusiasm and spelling out what, in realistic terms, living in Paris actually entailed:

> Yes, oh yes! But let us be clear about this. Do you have an income of 3,000 francs upon which you can *depend*? 3,000 francs which no one can deprive you of? If so, life in Paris will be a possibility and you will manage to earn what little extra is required to exist. But if you have nothing, nothing that is except hopes of earning 3,000 by your own work, then take care! In the main, to live by your pen is to die! Take myself for example. Alas have you any idea, my friend, how many articles I have had to write during the twenty-nine days that I have been travelling? Twenty-six, each of three hundred lines! I, who own nothing, find it an uphill struggle to survive. Well written articles do not get published. Poetical plays do not get performed. Confidentially I can tell you that *Le Passant* and *Les Deux Douleurs* are two exceptions explained by the novelistic talents of Coppée, and *La Révolte* [a recent play of their mutual friend Villiers de l'Isle-Adam's] only made thirty francs. 'But you get by' you will tell me. My dear friend, don't be forced to put up with what I have to endure! In order to support my wife, I am killing myself! I am lucky if, once every three months, I can find time to write a sonnet. Oh what a wretched state of affairs. Is a poet who would kill someone in order to get some work truly a criminal? No, I dare not invite you to share this hell. There have been days when I have had no food and the bailiffs at the door. I assure you.[31]

Sobering words. It is obvious why, after such a letter, Mallarmé decided that he needed to secure some permanent source of income before attempting to live permanently in Paris – for that was now his determined goal. But there were other reasons why it was prudent to wait a little longer before returning to the capital. On 15 July, whilst Catulle Mendès had been staying with Richard Wagner in Lucerne, the Franco-Prussian war had broken out. Ten days after that event, deciding to remain in Avignon for the moment, Mallarmé wisely applied to extend his leave of absence for a further year.

As he awaited a decision from the Ministry of Education, Mallarmé received a flying visit from Catulle Mendès, his wife and Villiers who, because of the recent outbreak of hostilities, had been forced to cut short their visit to Germany. He was therefore able to read them a completed chapter of *Igitur*, but the convoluted style and somewhat Gothic Poesque atmosphere of the work did not impress anyone.[32]

Delayed by the outbreak of war, the long-awaited decision from the authorities finally arrived in November. Thanks largely on this occasion to the efforts of a friend of Mistral's who, as private secretary to the Minister of Education himself, intervened on Mallarmé's behalf, he was granted an extension of his leave of absence for a further year on the same generous financial terms as before.

Preoccupied as he was with his own work, Mallarmé was not unaffected by the war. His uncle, General Magritte, was wounded at the infamous rout of the battle of the Sedan and died a week later. As the siege of Paris approached he sent newspaper accounts of the fighting to his stepmother in Sens, who had been cut off by the invading Prussian army. Worse still, in February 1871 Mallarmé read in the newspaper that the painter Henri Regnault, with whom he had gone on that memorable picnic in the forest of Fontainebleau so many years earlier, had been killed in the fighting.

By this time, however, Mallarmé had problems of his own to consider. Marie was expecting their second child. In the light of this development and the virtual certainty that he would not be granted a further extension to his leave of absence, which expired at the end of September, he began to think seriously about securing some form of employment which would allow him to return to Paris. In the capital itself, Mendès, Cazalis and their friends all began investigating possibilities on his behalf. The main difficulty, however, was that Mallarmé did not want to return to schoolteaching and ideally wanted only part-time employment, so that he would have plenty of time to devote to his own work. Ignoring Mendès' earlier warnings not to try to live off his writing, he initially imagined that he might be able to earn enough by writing weekly articles for a national newspaper and producing a series of translations into French, at the rate of one volume per year, of the most important recent works of English fiction. Other possibilities seriously entertained by Mallarmé himself or by his friends included part-time posts as a librarian or museum-keeper, both of which would allow him to pursue his own research in optimum conditions.

For the rest of the spring, while Mallarmé worked on various theatrical projects which probably owed more than a little to the recent enthusiastic discussions of Wagner's work which he had had with Mendès and Villiers,[33] his friends and family all continued to seek some form of employment for him. Despite their lack of success, which was quite understandable given the rapidly deteriorating situation in Paris, where the Commune had rapidly turned into a bloodbath, at the end of May, borrowing money from his stepmother in order to pay off his debts and cover their travel expenses, he left Avignon with his wife and daughter and travelled up to Sens. He left Marie and Geneviève at his stepmother's house, where they would await the arrival of the new child, and moved in as the guest of Mendès and his wife in Paris.

As the weeks wore on with no immediate prospects in sight, the summer turned into a nightmare. Mallarmé felt increasingly guilty that he was forced to be separated from his wife at such a time and that he was abusing the hospitality of Mendès and his wife. The final stages of her pregnancy were particularly troublesome for Marie, who found it difficult to get to sleep in the intense heat and who grew more and more anxious about their situation. Mallarmé was unable to be with her in Sens when their son Anatole was eventually born on 16 July, and only managed a brief visit to see his wife and the new child several days later before a hurried departure to London where, thanks to the efforts of Mendès and other friends, he had been offered the chance by some French newspapers of filing some reports on the Great Exhibition.

Even this well intentioned initiative proved a disaster. The

Exhibition, which had opened in May, was in its closing stages when Mallarmé arrived, and in the event two of the three newspapers which had commissioned his articles refused to publish them, finding them either not topical enough or too long. Mallarmé used his brief visit to London to meet the poet and Wagner enthusiast John Payne and to seek permission from Longmans to translate George Cox's *Mythology*, which he intended to offer to a French publisher. While he was in London, he received a letter from Geneviève Breton, the former fiancée of Henri Regnault and the granddaughter of Louis Hachette, the founder of the publishing house of that name. As a school inspector herself, she had taken an interest in Mallarmé's plight and had managed to use her influence and that of her grandfather, who had friends in the Admiralty, to obtain for him the post of French teacher on the British training ship HMS *Trafalgar*.

Mallarmé decided to decline this offer because it would have meant long spells away from his family. It was becoming clear, however, that he was going to have to reconcile himself to remaining in the teaching profession, for which at least he was qualified. Returning to Paris, and this time staying with Cazalis so as not to burden Mendès and his wife, Mallarmé began to explore the possibility of teaching posts in or near Paris. Officially, he asked the Ministry either to extend his leave of absence for a further year or to transfer him to a post in Sens. In the meantime, unknown to Mallarmé, his son Anatole had become desperately ill. Marie, who understandably did not want to alarm him when he was already so preoccupied with money worries and was desperately seeking employment, did not inform Mallarmé of this fact until the child was eventually out of danger.

By the end of summer, as the new school year approached, nothing had been settled. Mallarmé and his wife, who against Anne Mallarmé's advice had already brought all their furniture to Paris with them, now faced the expense of having to return it to Avignon. Their worst fears were realized when, around the middle of October, Geneviève Breton informed them that, as a great favour to herself and her father, the Minister of Education Jules Simon was prepared to offer Mallarmé his old job back in Avignon. Faced with this horrendous prospect, Mallarmé went in person to the Ministry, where to his great relief he learned that there were to be additional posts created in Modern Languages. On 20 October 1871, after further pressure from Geneviève Breton and her father, Mlle Breton informed him that he was to receive one of these new posts. Five days later Mallarmé received official confirmation that he had been appointed to the Lycée Condorcet. A week later he had taken up his duties. Within a fortnight he had found rented accommodation for himself, his wife and their two children, not in the prestigious and expensive Tuileries as he had at one point quite unrealistically suggested, but in a new residential quarter around the Gare St-Lazare.

All in all, it was hardly the triumphal return which Mallarmé had dreamt of all those years earlier. Nonetheless, he was at long last where he genuinely wanted to be. Furthermore, the years he had spent in the provinces, and which at times had seemed so desperately frustrating, had not in fact been wasted. Far removed from the hustle and bustle of the capital with its incessant distractions, he had undergone a unique and quite extraordinary experience in the course of which he had confronted and come to terms with himself as an individual and as a writer. Just before the family moved to Paris Mallarmé had confidently announced to Cazalis:

> Purely and simply, I have become a writer again. My *oeuvre* is no longer mythical. (One volume of short stories, which I have thought about a lot. One volume of poetry, which I have glimpsed and can murmur already. One volume of criticism, or what was previously known as the universe considered from a strictly *literary* point of view.) In short, enough to fill my mornings for the next twenty years. I don't know whether it is the arrival of spring which leads me

to believe that provided I organize my life, I have these years ahead of me.[34]

It was, as far as his published work was concerned, a programme which for the greater part he would successfully respect. Alongside all that there still remained of course the long-term challenge of producing the great work which would express his personal and totally unsentimental vision of the world in terms which would be relevant to a modern secular age. An important and decisive chapter in his life had ended. A new and equally demanding one had just begun.

6

Paris: The Early Years

The Paris to which Mallarmé now returned bore little resemblance to the city it had been some thirty years earlier at the time of his birth in 1842. Until then it had retained much of its medieval character, with narrow congested streets, obscure alleyways, and cluttered vennels. The creation of the railway system (the first line between Paris and Saint-Germain was opened in 1837) and the lessons to be drawn from the Revolutions of 1830 and 1848 changed all that. In the wake of the 1848 Revolution and the coup d'état which brought him to power, Louis Napoleon realized the strategic advantage to be gained from replacing this labyrinth of narrow streets, which lent themselves to the use of barricades and favoured the mob rather than the forces of law and order, with wide boulevards suitable for artillery fire and cavalry charges. Other motives were less overtly political and more obviously practical. The old city could simply no longer absorb its expanding population, and drastic action was required to accommodate a rapidly growing railway system.

Above all, however, the new emperor sought prestige. He wanted to embellish Paris and to make it an industrial, commercial and financial centre the equal of London. Within a year of his coming to power the neighbouring Bois de Boulogne had been annexed and vast city works begun to clear areas on the Ile de la Cité and around the Louvre palace. With the appointment of Baron Haussmann as *Préfet de la Seine* in

1853 the transformation of Paris had quickly gathered pace. Under Haussmann's direction the Bois de Vincennes and other adjacent communities were annexed. With the inclusion of this outlying countryside within the city limits, the surface area of Paris virtually doubled. Twenty new *arrondissements* replaced the original twelve. Hundreds of miles of old streets were widened and connected to new ones. The city was opened up to light and air and provided with elegant squares, parks, bridges and fountains. Buildings were demolished along the Seine to provide new *quais* that opened up the riverbanks to pedestrian and commercial traffic. In an incredible building boom, the homes and streets around the cathedral of Notre-Dame were razed to make way for government and commercial buildings and expensive apartments for the rich. The indigenous working-class population were largely expelled from the centre of the city and deposited on the plains of La Villette and Belleville. (By Haussmann's own estimation some 350,000 people were displaced, 12,000 of them alone during the construction of the majestic rue de Rivoli and the market of Les Halles.)

This dramatic transformation of the old Paris into the elegant city we recognize today had been mostly completed by the time Mallarmé returned to it in 1871. Admittedly, the recent bombardments by the invading Prussians and the bloody street fighting of the Commune had caused extensive damage to some areas of the city, and the new opera house, intended to be a symbol of its new pre-eminence, was as yet unfinished. Nonetheless, Paris was already well on its way to becoming the cultural and commercial capital of Europe. It had long since begun to act as a magnet, drawing thousands of tourists from all over the world, lured by the sheer splendour of the transformed city itself and by the apparently limitless and diverse pleasures which it could provide. Four years earlier, the World Fair had attracted over 11 million visitors. The permanent population of the city had also grown, as thousands of people from all walks of life sought to exploit the various opportunities which it offered to those who were enterprising enough to seize them. From a base of just over half a million in 1801, the population of Paris had doubled to one million by 1836. It was now rapidly approaching two million.

Like most of these newcomers to the capital, Mallarmé could not afford to live in any of its more exclusive districts. He rented a flat in the rue de Moscou, a modest little street situated some distance behind the new opera house and the *grands boulevards* whose glittering theatres, shops, restaurants and cafés buzzed with cosmopolitan visitors. As the name of the street itself reminds us, the rue de Moscou was part of the district known as *le quartier de l'Europe*, a bustling mixed residential and commercial quarter which, in the building boom of the Haussmann era, had rapidly grown up around the Gare Saint-Lazare. Few houses in the entire *quartier* were more than ten years old when Mallarmé moved in, and the rue de Moscou itself had only been completed and given a name some four years earlier in 1867.[1]

Mallarmé had chosen to live in this area of Paris (which in fact he would never leave) partly because the rents there were fairly low but also because the rue de Moscou was within walking distance of both the Lycée Condorcet to which he had been appointed and the *grands boulevards* whose theatres in particular interested him. For the first year or so, however, he had little occasion to visit the latter. Quite simply, he could afford neither the time nor the money to do so. He had been appointed to the Lycée Condorcet in the neighbouring rue du Havre as an unpromoted teacher, and was now earning less than he had been when on his full salary in Avignon. To make ends meet, he was forced to take on extra classes. Unfortunately, these were not held in the Lycée Condorcet, but in the Lycée Saint-Louis, far away on the opposite side of the city at the top of the boulevard Saint-Michel opposite the Jardin du Luxembourg.

This made life extremely difficult for Mallarmé. As the first term ended and his first Christmas in the capital approached, he began to wonder if he had made the right move. 'I would like to come and see you tonight,' he wrote despondently refusing an invitation, 'but Wednesday is a bad day for me. I leave the house early in the morning only to reappear for lunch, then late in the evening for supper. If I manage to open a book or find a sheet of paper, I feel it is my duty as much as my reward to do some real work for an hour or so with what is left of the day. And I have so much to do, without talking about boring matters . . . I almost ask myself: why did I come to Paris?'[2]

Her husband's long periods of absence from their flat and their desperate financial position made life equally impossible for Marie Mallarmé, who on top of everything else had a home to run and two young children to contend with. Extremely worried by their desperate financial predicament and anxious to avoid anything which might upset their landlord, she was quite dismayed when Eugène Lefébure, who had been meeting Mallarmé regularly since his friend had returned to the capital, asked somewhat tactlessly if he could use their flat temporarily as a convenient place in which to meet and leave letters for a Parisian lady friend. It was a thoughtless and spontaneous request on Lefébure's part, but one he was soon to regret, for it had serious consequences. Informed by Mallarmé, at Marie's insistence, that such a proposal was quite unacceptable, Lefébure realized that he had placed his friends in an impossible position. A few days after that meeting he wrote to Mallarmé more in sorrow than in anger:

> Please excuse me if what I say causes you any pain. It causes me even more pain, I can assure you. I have thought a lot about what you said to me last Friday and about what was implied when you announced that my receiving someone whom I respect in a house of which you are merely the tenants would not be acceptable. I am not judging you or blaming you. But I have no choice. I cannot prevent myself

coming to the conclusion that diplomacy prevents me from seeing both parties at the same time. I shall therefore have to stop coming to your home as long as this relationship lasts.[3]

Once tempers had cooled, both men made efforts to smooth over their quarrel. Marie Mallarmé, usually so understanding, was unwilling to compromise on this occasion. She would not tolerate Lefébure in her house as long as he continued his illicit relationship with someone of whom she strongly disapproved. Thus an important and rewarding friendship which had lasted for almost ten years and had been of inestimable value to Mallarmé came to an abrupt end in the most pathetic of circumstances.[4]

The long-standing friendship with Lefébure was not the only casualty of those first difficult months in Paris. Mallarmé's own work suffered, and any attempt at serious writing was soon abandoned. After less than six months of daily commuting between his two lycées, he could sustain this crippling routine no longer and was forced to give up his post at the Lycée Saint-Louis. The financial implications of this decision were extremely serious. With the loss of his income from the second school, he was now earning a mere 1,700 francs per annum. It was half the sum which, two years earlier, Mendès had informed him was the absolute minimum required to survive in Paris. François Coppée, who worked part-time in the Senate Library, tried to secure a similar position for Mallarmé in the Palais du Luxembourg. When this proved unsuccessful, in desperation Mallarmé resorted once more to private lessons, printing a prospectus offering courses in modern and classical literature on Tuesday and Saturday afternoons.[5] No doubt too few takers materialized, for a month later, at the beginning of June 1872, he found himself with no alternative other than to make good some of the income he had lost by taking on two extra hours at the Lycée Condorcet.

The 250 additional francs which these classes generated brought little relief. Marie was being hard pressed by the tradesmen and shopkeepers to whom they owed money, and part of their rent had had to be used to pay off debts. As the school year drew to its close, Mallarmé wrote to Charles Seignobos to explain his desperate plight. Seignobos, a family friend ever since their days in Tournon, had always taken an interest in Mallarmé's career. Fortunately for Mallarmé he had recently been elected to the Chamber of Deputies and was quite prepared to put his political clout at his old friend's disposal. Accordingly, he wrote directly to the Minister of Education, Jules Simon, requesting that Mallarmé be promoted.

For his part, Simon was quite sympathetic. He initiated an enquiry and was informed by the headmaster of the Lycée Condorcet himself that the salary Mallarmé was then earning was 'inadequate to support a family in Paris'. Thanks to the influence of Seignobos, in July of that year Mallarmé found himself promoted to section head, which meant that he only taught the senior classes. More importantly still, as a consequence his salary was doubled to 3,300 francs a year with immediate effect. But this was not all. After the summer holidays, Seignobos returned to champion Mallarmé's cause, arguing that a similarly qualified colleague at the same school was earning 500 francs more. Initially, believing that Mallarmé was seeking further promotion, Simon refused to increase his salary, but, after further investigation, not to mention additional pressure from Seignobos and Geneviève Breton and her father, he conceded. By January 1873 Mallarmé's salary had been increased by a further 500 francs to 3,800 francs per annum.

If, against this background of constant financial worry, he found little time during that first year to produce anything more than the occasional newspaper article and work on some of his translations,[6] it would be wrong to assume that Mallarmé led little or no social life. On the contrary, one of the main reasons why he had returned to the capital had been to escape from the sense of isolation which had been his lot in the provinces. Above all, he wanted to meet other writers and artists and keep abreast of the latest developments. He therefore employed such free time as he could muster to good effect, reacquainting himself with old friends and making many new ones.

Through Cazalis, he was introduced to the stunningly beautiful musician and singer, Augusta Holmès, of whom he had heard so much already. For her part, she had been greatly impressed with the scene from the *Hérodiade* project which he had offered as his contribution to the second *Parnasse contemporain*. Both quickly warmed to each other, and Mallarmé soon became a regular attender at her Friday evening musical soirées. The main focus of his attention, however, apart from the ubiquitous Catulle Mendès and the slightly more elusive Villiers de l'Isle-Adam, was the group of writers which congregated around Alphonse Lemerre, the publisher of the *Parnasse contemporain*. Mallarmé knew some of these people already: he had met Leconte de Lisle, François Coppée and José-Maria de Heredia during his earlier visits to Paris. Now he was able to meet Paul Verlaine, with whom he had only ever corresponded before. Verlaine soon invited him to the informal Wednesday evening gatherings he was starting at the rue Nicolet.[7]

It was once again through his friendship with Mendès that Mallarmé made the acquaintance of Jean Marras, the dramatist and ardent socialist whose political convictions forced him to flee for a while to Spain until an amnesty for communards could be arranged. Marras and his wife Nelly would become lifetime friends of Mallarmé and his wife. More importantly, it was through Mendès that Mallarmé became involved with Alphonse Lemerre himself, whose bookshop, run by his wife and himself in the narrow Passage Choiseul just behind the Bibliothèque Nationale, had become the meeting place for much of the literary avant-garde. Writers, critics and fellow publishers gathered regularly in Lemerre's premises on Saturdays. Here Mallarmé encountered Emile Blémont, founder and director of *La Renaissance littéraire et artistique*, to which he and many of his new friends all became regular contributors.[8] It was in this review, founded in April of that year, 1872, that he published a flattering article on the collected poems of another new friend, Léon Dierx, whom he likewise met at Lemerre's shop.[9]

It was almost certainly at Lemerre's that Mallarmé came across Philippe Burty. Twelve years older than Mallarmé, he had started his career as an ornamental painter at the Gobelins factory and in 1859 had switched to journalism, becoming the editor of the *curiosités* section of the *Gazette des Beaux-Arts*. A prominent and respected critic, who was later to write with some authority on the Impressionists, many of whom were personal friends, he was also a printmaker and etcher. What seems most to have attracted Mallarmé was that Burty was a very keen collector of Japanese artefacts of all sorts. He was even a founder-member of the secret *Société du Jing-lar*, whose members did much to promote enthusiasm for things Japanese.[10] One of the first people in Paris to be interested in the art of Japan, which he had first discovered in the curiosity shops of the rue de Rivoli in the early 1860s, by the time Mallarmé met him in the late spring of 1872 he had already amassed a remarkable private collection of Japanese books, prints and curios. Their friendship soon blossomed and quickly extended to their families. Mallarmé was one of the first people to whom Philippe Burty wrote a few months later when his young daughter Renée, who had become a friend of Geneviève, tragically died.[11]

Mallarmé's own growing interest in painting and the decorative arts is apparent from the three long articles he had published the previous year (to which he had since added a fourth) on the London International Exhibition.[12] It also helps to explain the notion he seriously entertained in April 1872 of launching an expensive monthly magazine to be called *L'Art décoratif*. He had actually gone as far as having the official letterheads printed and had arranged for a frontispiece from the engraver Claudius Popelin when, accepting the advice of Burty and his friends, who argued forcibly against the move, he agreed to shelve the project.[13] Although abandoned for the moment (to be resurrected and successfully developed two years later), the ambitious nature of the enterprise illustrates Mallarmé's rising confidence in himself as he began to grow familiar with the literary and artistic circles of the capital. On that front at least, his first year in Paris had not been wasted.

Of this growing circle of friends whom Mallarmé met regularly either at Lemerre's bookshop or at the other numerous and varied meeting places which played such an important part in the cultural life of the time,[14] the two people who most immediately shaped his destiny were Lemerre himself and Philippe Burty. The first became, for a while at least, his publisher. The second initiated him into the art world of the capital, in which hc was to form some of his most enduring friendships and in whose important battles he himself was soon to find himself a participant.

When, upon the death of Théophile Gautier in the late autumn of 1872, Alphonse Lemerre agreed to publish a memorial volume, Mallarmé was naturally invited to take part. It was the first of many commissions which he would accept throughout his life, despite his earlier determination not to publish anything until he had completed the Great Work.[15] On this particular occasion, he was provided with an extremely detailed brief. It was agreed that the tribute would take the form of an imaginary banquet at which, after a prologue by Catulle Mendès explaining that these poets had gathered together to honour the memory of a great master, each contributor would address a toast directly to Gautier, high-lighting one of his distinctive qualities.

Mindful that Gautier had begun his career as a painter, Mallarmé chose to stress the sharpness of his artist's vision. He also decided to use the opportunity here afforded him to widen the scope of the poem: he would make a general statement about the place of the poet in the scheme of things which would enable him to justify the existence of all creative artists. He worked on the poem for part of the winter, but once the summer holidays arrived, feeling that only a dramatic clifftop view of the sea would provide the appropriate inspiration for such a solemn and grandiose theme, he waited until Marie and the children had left to spend the summer with her father at Camberg near Wiesbaden[16] before setting off for the Breton coast armed with a rail pass obtained from a newspaper in exchange for an article.[17]

On the recommendation of Heredia, he headed for Douarnenez on the Finistère coast, but was bitterly disappointed with what he found there. 'You cannot see the open sea,' he complained, 'but a placid lake caused by a bay with two arms which virtually meet.'[18] He tried to repair the situation by seeking permission to lodge in the local lighthouse, but when this was understandably refused, he spent ages looking for a suitable location. Eventually, after almost a fortnight, he at last found what he wanted, a house right on the edge of the sea. Writing to his wife and children, he described his farcical search in terms which are quite unflattering to himself, and all the more endearing:

Chapter III
In which Father becomes the Wandering Jew

Do you remember how I travelled the whole length of the coast after we had reached Bandol? The same kind of exploratory expedition began again in Brittany. Seeing that permission to stay in the Raz Lighthouse was refused 'O come now, father!' I left Douarnenez straight away and came via hundreds of coaches and trains to Le Conquet, a little port which according to the map is situated virtually on the edge of the sea. That is not quite correct, but I caught sight of an empty house on a promontory from which the view is outstanding.

It only took me a moment to write to the owner to ask how much the price would be. I received a telegram allowing me to set up home within these four walls and, I have every reason to believe, for absolutely nothing. I am delighted. A bed, a table a comfy chair and a chair will be brought by cart tomorrow. All I have to do is to find these basic furnishings. Two flower pots and two Japanese screens will take care of the rest.[19]

Mallarmé spent a month at Le Conquet. 'The ocean is sublime and quite captivating,' he wrote almost a week later. 'One of these days I shall have the spectacle of a really heavy sea if the wind continues.'[20] The wind kindly obliged. Indeed the weather remained awful for most of his stay, forcing him to remain indoors for days at a time. On one occasion when he did venture out, he was rewarded with an awesome sight which he just had to describe to his daughter:

If you just knew what a terrifying walk I had a short while ago, surprised by nightfall on the edge of rocks that are higher than our balcony and watching and listening to the white thundering foam far below, deep down at the bottom of hundreds of dark chasms. I said to myself: Oh! if little Geneviève (or even Villiers) were with me, how frightened they would be to have lost their way.

I am writing this straight away now that I am back in the big room of my house where the howling wind, which did not allow me to close my eyes last night, is going to do the same tonight. And with voices. Oh! those voices! I would love to make out what they are saying in their anger, at times quite sullen, at others quite furious.[21]

The month which Mallarmé spent in that abandoned house on the storm-tossed Breton coast, amid the rain, the mist and its howling winds, made a profound impression upon him and haunted his imagination for some time to come. The turbulent seascape reappears transformed into a cosmic setting in 'Toast funèbre' ('A Funeral Toast') in the highly orchestrated and dramatic central section of that unsentimental commemoration, where, in a deliberate reworking of the Judgement Day scenario in decidedly unchristian terms, an empty Eternity taunts the mere mortal who has just died by asking him to provide an explanation of the meaning of Life which, as an inarticulate being (i.e. non-poet), he is unable to do:

Vaste gouffre apporté dans l'amas de la brume
Par l'irascible vent des mots qu'il n'a pas dits,
Le néant à cet Homme aboli de jadis:
'Souvenirs d'horizons, qu'est-ce, ô toi, que la Terre?'
Hurle ce songe; et, voix dont la clarté s'altère,
L'espace a pour jouet le cri: 'Je ne sais pas!'

[Vast hole created in the mass of fog
By the irascible wind of the words he has not spoken,
The Void to this Man of yesteryear now reduced to nothing:
'Memory of horizons, O tell me what is the Earth?'
Howls out this nightmare question. And, voice of faltering clarity,
Space can amuse itself with the cry: 'I do not know!']

The memory of the same howling winds makes its way into a short sketch which some time later Mallarmé worked on as a theatrical development of the abandoned *Igitur* project. This reworking of the earlier short story into a dramatic dialogue was discussed a year or so later with George Moore, who has left us the following account of the conversations he had with Mallarmé:

'And how many acts does your play have?'
– 'Three.'
'And how many characters?'
– 'Two, myself and the wind.
'. . . A young man, the last of his race, is dreaming in a decrepit castle. What is he dreaming of? Of wars and duels and adventures in distant forests. He dreams up project after project and asks his ancestors to show him the way forward. But it is always the wind in the old tower which replies to him or seems to be trying to reply to him.
'And the young man listens to the wind . . . without ever being sure if what the wind means is "Yes".'
On many occasions Mallarmé spoke about his play and when I asked him where he wanted to put it on, in what theatre, he spoke of

travelling in a caravan and playing the part of his hero himself at all the Fairs in France. He was excited by the idea that the poet himself would be the performer.

The play was never written (at the most he made some notes for it) but he described it so well, standing in front of the stove, that I can still remember it, not to mention the backs of his legs which were roasting and his fine face.[22]

'Toast funèbre' was published by Lemerre at the end of October 1873. By that time, almost certainly through their mutual friend Philippe Burty, Mallarmé had made the acquaintances of someone whom, alongside Villiers de l'Isle-Adam and Catulle Mendès, he thought of as one of his closest and most valued friends.[23] We do not know exactly where or when Mallarmé met Edouard Manet for the first time, but he certainly knew him well enough by that same month of October to be able to invite John Payne, who was visiting Paris at the time, to accompany him to the painter's studio.

Edouard Manet was a full ten years older than Mallarmé. The son of a high-ranking official in the Justice Department who would finish his career as a judge, he had briefly flirted with the possibility of a career in the navy (as an alternative to the one in the judiciary which had been expected of him), before deciding, largely against his family's wishes, to become a painter. The first work which he submitted to the official State exhibition or Salon, in 1859, *The Absinthe Drinker*, had decidedly Baudelairean echoes and was unceremoniously rejected. From that moment on, despite his genuine desire to receive official recognition, his paintings were generally denied it. If his more traditional *The Spanish Singer* and *Parents of the Artist* were accepted in 1861, his now celebrated *Lunch on the Grass* was refused in 1863 and provoked a furore at the *Salon des refusés* where, in a gesture of liberality which was not to be repeated, the Emperor Napoleon III allowed artists to exhibit paintings rejected by the official jury.

Manet himself had been quite unhappy about the scandal which his paintings had caused, since his intention had not been to give offence. The painting was simply a reworking of well established themes, and the nude figure at the centre of it was far less sexually provocative or erotic than many of the paintings accepted by the Salon that year. He was equally displeased that the scandal had made him, quite against his will, the unofficially acknowledged leader of the anti-establishment faction in the art world. Two years later in 1865, although it was for once accepted by the Salon, his *Olympia*, which was fundamentally a translation into the contemporary idiom of the traditional and indeed clichéd theme of the recumbent Venus, again sparked a controversy. Three years after that, *The Execution of the Emperor Maximilian*, in which the firing squad was depicted wearing uniforms rather similar to that of the French army, did little to endear him to authorities who were quick to see the obvious political implications and banned the publication and distribution of any prints made from the painting.[24]

By the time Mallarmé met him in 1873, Manet's intelligence and wit, to say nothing of his growing notoriety, had already attracted around him a number of followers. A gregarious man by nature, at the end of a day's work he virtually held court either in his studio in the rue de Saint-Pétersbourg (now the rue Leningrad) or in the Café Guerbois in the rue des Batignolles (now the avenue de Clichy), where working people, prostitutes and potential models regularly rubbed shoulders with painters, writers and art critics. The novelist Armand Silvestre, himself a *habitué* of the Guerbois, has left the following description of Manet at around this time:

> [Manet] had the manners of a perfect gentleman. With his often gaudy trousers, his short jacket, his flat-brimmed hat set on the back of his head, always wearing immaculate suede gloves, Manet did not look like a Bohemian, and in fact had nothing of the Bohemian in him. He was a kind of dandy. Blond, with a sparse, narrow beard

which was forked at the end, he had in the extraordinary vivacity of his gaze, in the mocking expression on his lips – his mouth was narrow-lipped, his teeth irregular and uneven – a very strong dose of the Parisian street urchin. Although very generous, and very good-hearted, he was deliberately ironic in conversation, and often cruel. He had a marvellous command of the annihilating and devastating phrase.[25]

It is easy to see why, despite their age difference, Mallarmé was attracted to such a charming and obviously charismatic figure. Manet's wit alone, his ironic turn of phrase and lack of pretentiousness would have endeared him to the younger man. But there was more to the deep and lasting friendship which rapidly developed between the two than a mere affinity of temperament. They had in fact a remarkable amount in common. Both came from similiar upper-middle-class backgrounds which neither entirely shook off and to which they had reacted in the same way. Both had rebelled against careers in the civil service which had been pre-selected for them without consultation by their families. Both had likewise flouted convention by marrying, in quite remarkably similar circumstances, foreigners judged by their respective families to be of inferior social status.[26]

Artistically too they shared much common ground, as they soon discovered in the almost daily conversations which they had at Manet's studio, which was conveniently located near to Mallarmé's home in the rue de Moscou and which quickly became an obligatory stopping-point on his way home from the Lycée Condorcet. As trains rumbled by on their way to and from the neighbouring Gare Saint-Lazare, sending up clouds of smoke and causing the floor to tremble and shake 'like the deck of a fast-moving boat',[27] Mallarmé learned that Manet was keenly interested in literature and had been a friend and admirer of Baudelaire and Gautier. Furthermore, it soon became clear that they shared if not exactly identical visions, then at least a common goal. Although fiercely independent of spirit, they were innovators and experimenters rather than revolutionaries. Both sought not to abolish tradition but to improve upon its major achievements and incorporate them into a new artistic statement which was relevant to their own age.

Mallarmé's undisguised admiration for Manet, whether in the articles which he subsequently wrote defending him, or merely in private conversations,[28] is easily understood. In the latter's dogged determination to respect the integrity of his own vision in the face of mounting public outcry and derision, he clearly found an encouragement and an inspiration for sticking to his guns and pursuing his own long-term objective. Such apparently uncritical enthusiasm has led critics to infer that the friendship between the two men was largely one-sided, or that in any event, not being a painter himself, Mallarmé had little real understanding of what Manet was trying to achieve. Both of these statements are quite without foundation.

Admittedly and somewhat paradoxically, precisely because both men became such good friends, rather than exchanging letters they met and talked with each other almost daily, and as those tantalizing conversations have been lost to us for ever, the full extent of their relationship cannot be documented. Their surviving correspondence is consequently rather disappointing, being limited, for the greater part, to cursory notes setting up their meetings or rearranging their busy schedules. Most of the time these exchanges shed little light on what they actually talked about, or on what Manet actually thought of Mallarmé beyond an obvious gratitude and warmth. The following note, however (one of the few touching on matters of any substance), written some time later by Manet to Mallarmé when both were separated by illness, provides us with a rare glimpse of the banter which characterized their conversations and, more significantly, underlines the importance which Manet attached to Mallarmé's opinion:

23 June 1880
Wednesday

I was upset, my dear Mallarmé, when I got your letter yesterday. – What! while I envied you, imagining you rushing late as usual to the college, you were flat on your back in your bed! – Well at last you are now convalescing, but how the weather is ill suited to a recovery. I am desperate for some lasting sunshine.

Have you read Zola's articles in *Le Voltaire* entitled 'Naturalism at the Salon'? If so, give me your opinion on them. If you have not got them I shall send them to you and you shall describe to me the effect they have had upon you and the effect that they may have had on the general public.

Best wishes
E. Manet

My mother and my wife ask me to send their best wishes to Madame Mallarmé and to you all. Please add my name to theirs.[29]

It is clear from this letter and others of a similar nature that Manet valued Mallarmé's opinion just as much as his support, and there is no reason to believe that Suzanne Manet was recording anything other than the simple truth when, writing to Mallarmé after her husband's death to thank him for his continued support, she stated, 'You were truly his best friend and he loved you dearly.'[30]

As if to underline the friendship which was rapidly developing between them, the names of Manet and Mallarmé appeared together on the covers of a new magazine, appropriately called *La Revue du Monde Nouveau* (*The New World Review*), which was launched in February 1874. Manet contributed a portrait entitled *The Parisienne* (the model for which was none other than Nina de Villars herself) alongside a prose poem which Mallarmé had written several years earlier. 'La Pénultième' (later entitled 'Le Démon de l'Analogie', thus reminding us that the piece owed not a little to Edgar Allan Poe's short story 'The Imp of the Perverse') was a largely experimental piece which dated from Mallarmé's earliest interest in linguistics. As such it created quite a stir. In a highly critical review of the magazine, an anonymous critic of the conservative *Le Temps* interestingly singled out Manet and Mallarmé for his strongest sarcasm:

> Artists too have joined in the feast. *Le Monde nouveau* can thank Monsieur Manet for the portrait of a *Parisienne* which hides, behind this vague pseudonym, a rather well known name of that Bohemian literary set which teems between the rue des Martyrs and the Place Pigalle. So that the title of the new review should be fully justified, a curious poet, M. Stéphane Mallarmé, has made his contribution, a prose poem entitled *La Pénultième*, which introduces us indeed into an entirely new world. [A paragraph of the prose poem is quoted.] Take some words, throw them into a hat, take them out at random and then line them up on the page in the order or rather the disorder in which they come, and you can do just as well, if your aim is to mystify your neighbour.[31]

This dismissive article, typical of the hostility of the right-wing press to anything new or unconventional, did not go unnoticed by Mallarmé's family. Already worried about her stepson's future and alarmed at his increasing involvement in literature to the detriment of his school career, Anne Mallarmé felt that it was time to intervene. Having been unable to talk with him in Paris as she would have wished, she wrote to him from the family home in Sens in the bluntest of terms:

> What your sister did not inform you of was the misgivings I brought back with me from Paris for not having been able to have a serious chat with you about your present situation and your future. Such misgivings as I had were increased, if that is possible, by an article which I read concerning you in *Le Temps* of 26 February. The criticism is cleverly formulated and seems to be justified by the few lines quoted at random from *La Pénultième*. I do not pretend to be a censor, and even less, believe me, a critic. I shall restrict myself to my role as a mother and advise you to be careful. Are you not worried that you have taken the wrong road; that you have misdirected the gifts which God provided you, allowing yourself to be misled by your friends who all, I am prepared to accept that, are quite sincere? In short, I am afraid lest all the efforts you have made over so many years will bring you little reward from every point of view. What money have they brought your household, what glory have you

achieved? If you have the time, think about all that. I really would like to see your work considered seriously by an unbiased person who likes you enough to tell you frankly what they think and for you to have enough confidence in them to change direction if that is what they recommend. Is such a thing not possible? After all, it just cannot be that you are in the right. Just think of the consequences! Your household expenses will increase as your children grow older but how can your position in the lycée improve if you are not working for the *agrégation* as we all hoped? Even without working for that, which would ensure you a fixed income in perpetuity, you can align yourself with writers who are more easily understood by the public and who consequently are appreciated and read in greater numbers.

I did not dare ask Marie for a few *sols* for Monsieur Faye because I don't think she has any to spare and I regret that more than I can say. I also had to present your excuses to Monsieur Amy, to whom you are not paying back interest any more than you are to Monsieur Faye. It pains me to have to remind you of these borrowings which I cannot repay. Life is difficult for us too. Don't hold these comments against me. They stem from the affection I have for you all and my desire to see you happy and striving seriously to be so. Nobody gets more help than you do from your dear wife, who is so clever at making ends meet and such an intelligent mother. How much we all talked about you all, Geneviève, that darling Tolé [Mallarmé's son Anatole]. Embrace everyone for me and believe me to be

Your affectionate mother A[nne] M[allarmé].[32]

We do not know what reply Mallarmé gave to this salutary and pointed reminder of what his family thought of his situation. In the event, Anne Mallarmé's tactics had exactly the opposite effect to the one she had intended, for the bewilderment and incomprehension which his own work now engendered only served, if anything, to drive her stepson even more enthusiastically towards Manet and his circle. Within the next twelve months he met and became friendly with the art critic Théodore Duret and the engraver and printer Félix Bracquemond, both of whom, like Manet and himself, were keenly interested in Japanese art.[33] He also became acquainted with Manet's one-time pupil and now sister-in-law, Berthe Morisot, and his ally and, until then, principal defender in the press, Emile Zola.[34]

Berthe Morisot and Emile Zola would each have an important part to play in Mallarmé's life. But that was later. For the moment, Mallarmé's main focus of attention remained Manet himself. Already a respected and entertaining companion, the latter now became a collaborator as the disregard which both men had for commercial success, their refined tastes – Mallarmé loved expensive objects, Manet was wealthy enough to afford them – and finally their love of the rare and the exotic all found concrete expression in the illustrated editions upon which they now embarked.

It was Mallarmé who took the initiative here, asking Manet to provide drawings for a translation of Edgar Allan Poe's poem 'The Raven' which he had completed and persuaded Alphonse Lemerre to publish. 'Manet is delighted to become a member of the Passage Choiseul' (the address of Lemerre's bookshop) he cheerfully informed Lemerre around the middle of March, adding: 'He wants to see you and at the same time he wants you to see what he is finishing off for the exhibition. He is very rushed and is not leaving the studio as long as there is any daylight left. So pretend you want to twist the ear of our *bambino* and come and collect me tomorrow at the rue Caumartin [address of the Lycée Condorcet] when classes are over and we shall go and smoke a cigarette or just chat (because I know you do not smoke) in his studio which is close by.'[35]

The paintings to which Manet was then putting the finishing touches were *The Masked Ball at the Opera, Swallows*, and *The Railway*. When he submitted them to the Salon a few weeks later, only one, *The Railway*, was accepted. Mallarmé was outraged. Rising to Manet's defence, he ridiculed the decision in a caustic article which Emile Blémont kindly published in *La Renaissance littéraire et artistique* of 12 April 1874. Portraying Manet as a 'redoubtable outsider' victimized by the philistinism of the jury, he began with some ironic remarks which owed more than a little to the private reprimand and public criticism which he himself had recently suffered:

> Everyone whose curiosity is aroused by the approach of the Salon and those lovers of painting who are interested in what is going on in the newer studios have suddenly learned, in the last few days, that the painting jury has rejected two out of the three canvases submitted by M. Manet.
>
> Many people, including several members of the general public, are bitterly disappointed that they cannot examine this year the full expression of an exceptional talent. For their part, those who are the determined adversaries of any attempt to break new ground can only cry out: 'Why did they not reject the submission in its entirety?'
>
> Personally I share the sentiments of the former and can agree wholeheartedly with the latter.

The article was deliberately provocative and polemical in tone, allowing Mallarmé both to defend someone whom he genuinely admired and to poke fun at several inconsistencies in the decision of the authorities. It would be a mistake, however, to read it as nothing more than that. Mallarmé raises wider issues too, questioning whether the public or the Salon should be the final arbiter of taste and accusing the jury, themselves artists, of betraying a sacred trust placed in them by the people.

It is when he deals with the individual paintings themselves, however, that he is at his most interesting from a twentieth-century perspective. From certain of his comments, some of which may very well bear the stamp of recent conversations with Manet, it is obvious that he already had a definite understanding both of what Manet was trying to achieve and of what constituted his originality. He states for example – quite correctly, as any modern social historian would agree – that the apparently inoffensive painting *The Railway*, which the jury had accepted, might just prove to be, on closer inspection, much more subversive and disturbing than anyone might have imagined.[36] Likewise, he was not wrong to insist that Manet's modernity was a deliberate stance, stating with regard to *The Masked Ball at the Opera* that it was a 'noble attempt to encapsulate within the confines of the canvas, through the refinement of technique which true art demands, a total vision of the contemporary world.'

Finally, and most important of all, in defending Manet against the often repeated criticism that his paintings appeared unfinished and slapdash, Mallarmé insisted that Manet used his vision to analyse, simplify and then re-create reality in a manner which deliberately sought not to conceal its technique.[37] Here he was already focusing attention on the fundamental misunderstanding which, less than a fortnight later, would lead an obscure journalist to use the then wholly pejorative term 'Impressionist' as a convenient way of lumping together the paintings of a disparate group of artists and thus unwittingly create a label and an art movement which in a sense never really existed.

A mere three days after Mallarmé's article appeared, there opened in the former studio of the photographer Nadar on the boulevard des Capucines a group exhibition organized by the cooperative of artists whose main aim was not ideological but merely practical. In the face of the economic depression which had followed the short-lived postwar boom, they had decided that the best way to sell their work to the public was to organize a group exhibition where each exhibitor would donate one tenth of his sales to cover the administrative costs.[38] Ironically, Manet, who saw this as a largely peripheral event, had refused to participate. Ten days after the 'Exhibition of the Limited Company of Artists, Painters, Sculptors and Engravers' (to give it its accurate title) opened, it was scathingly reviewed by Louis Leroy for the magazine *Charivari* under the title 'Exhibition of the Impressionists' in which he made much play with the term 'Impressionist' borrowed from a painting of one of the exhibitors, Claude Monet. The word had been used before. Manet himself, in the catalogue of his one-man exhibition in 1867, had spoken of 'attempting to convey an impression', and Mallarmé in his recent article had used it twice,[39] but somehow the word captured the public imagination and stuck.

It is against the background of the noisy, furious and largely irrelevant debate which ensued in the press, that Manet's brief note of thanks to Mallarmé is best understood. Beneath his embossed motto '*Tout arrive*' ('*Anything can happen*'), printed in the top left-hand corner of the page, the minimal text read:

> My dear friend,
> Thanks. If I had a few people like yourself to defend me, I would not give a f. . . for the Jury.
> Yours Ed. Manet[40]

It was, in the circumstances, quite a compliment. The bluntness of the message conveyed Manet's genuine emotion. In it he was expressing thanks not just for the article itself but for the perceptiveness and understanding with which Mallarmé had written it.

Manet expressed his gratitude in other ways too. From his letters to Mallarmé it is clear that, along with Philippe Burty and Félix Bracquemond, he gave some useful advice about the engraver Mallarmé should use for his own magazine *La Dernière Mode* (*The Latest Fashions*) which he began to plan a month or so later and which absorbed so much of his time during that summer. Likewise, when, exhausted by his efforts, Mallarmé began to look for somewhere in the neighbouring countryside in which to spend a relaxing summer, Manet did what he could to help him, writing a letter of introduction to someone who might be able to point out likely properties in the Chevreuse valley area some twenty miles or so from Paris.[41]

Mallarmé took a trip out to the Chevreuse valley and found it very beautiful. But for some reason or other (perhaps the cost was too high) he did not end up renting any property there. Instead, he took the advice of Philippe Burty, who suggested that he try the little village of Valvins on the edge of the Forest of Fontainebleau where he himself had a summer house. Mallarmé's first attempt to reach Valvins was less than auspicious. At the Gare de Lyon, he missed his train by just a few minutes. Despite this minor setback, he found the small cluster of houses on the bank of the Seine quite enchanting and had no hesitation whatsoever in deciding to rent the first floor of one of these, an old country inn next to the stone bridge spanning the river where boatmen and bargees had broken their journey in earlier times. Close by stretched the magical Forest of Fontainebleau, which held such special memories for him. It was there that he had gone on that first memorable outing with Cazalis and his friend, and there too that he had taken Marie to ask her to go to London with him.

Above all, Valvins was off the beaten track and undiscovered by the majority of Parisians. It was an exceptionally quiet and peaceful place, an ideal antidote to the hustle and bustle of city life. Curiously enough, Mallarmé did not return there the following summer, but that was to prove an exception. That small house with its vine-clustered external stone staircase, tiny front garden filled by a few roses and trees, and large untended orchard to the rear, was destined to become his second home. From 1876 onwards, the summer months were always spent in 'Valvins-Spa', as it was affectionately known to the locals.

The peace and tranquillity afforded by Valvins, where he could alternatively work or rest or go for long walks in the forest, was especially precious to Mallarmé in the summer of 1874 after the weeks he had spent organizing virtually single-handed the launch of his new magazine. Announced to the public as a fortnightly 'Society and family Gazette published with the assistance of the greatest specialists in Paris', each number of *La Dernière Mode* provided an illustration of one of the latest dresses, a fashion article signed 'Marguerite de Ponty', a review of literary, theatrical and artistic events in

Paris (including news 'from the salons and the beaches') signed 'Ix', 'Le Carnet d'or' (literally 'Golden Notebook'), which gave cooking and other practical hints, a review of the salient cultural events in the capital in the following fortnight, plus literary contributions from a list of collaborators which included all of Mallarmé's current friends, including Emile Zola. In fact, the magazine editor, 'Marasin', 'Marguerite de Ponty', 'Ix' and the other anonymous contributors were none other than Mallarmé himself. It was an extraordinary undertaking. 'I am leaving Paris distraught and exhausted as soon as the cover of my review is printed,' Mallarmé wrote to Alphonse Lemerre as the school term ended and the summer holidays at last began. The respite was no less welcome to Marie Mallarmé, who, after months of financial worry, was suffering from stomach cramps, nausea and loss of appetite.[42]

Mallarmé and his family spent a well earned month at Valvins that year. The first number of *La Dernière Mode* appeared on 6 September, and Mallarmé remained wholly preoccupied with it until, after eight editions, it was forced to fold at the beginning of January 1875 because the subscribers, although theoretically more than enough to support the magazine, did not in practice pay up in sufficient numbers to keep the creditors at bay.

Not surprisingly, Mallarmé soon found himself in serious financial difficulty. In March, in order to generate some income, he tried but failed to interest an English newspaper in a weekly column on the current literary and artistic scene in Paris, stating – quite fairly – that through his contacts he 'lived precisely in the desired milieu, for nothing important or unusual to escape his attention.'[43]

Worse, however, was yet to come. By now Manet had finished his drawings for *The Raven* and the completed text and illustrations had been submitted to Lemerre. To Mallarmé's utter astonishment, the latter refused to publish the work, claiming that some academic acquaintances of his had advised him not to print a translation which, in their opinion, would seriously damage his reputation as a respected publisher. 'I had not read your translation,' he informed Mallarmé quite unceremoniously, 'but I now find that it is totally obscure and cannot be published by your servant.'[44] A similarly curt letter was dispatched to Manet.

In the face of this setback, Manet, quite undaunted, set about finding another publisher. After one or two approaches, he managed to interest Richard Lesclide in the project. Things now moved very quickly and *Le Corbeau* was published at the beginning of June. The finished book was certainly very expensive at 25 francs, but it had been expensively produced and was published in a limited edition of 240 copies. The inside cover plates were tied together with two white silk ribbons and contained the famous black ink drawing of a raven by Manet. The title page had been printed in contrasting black and red inks, and on the reverse side the number of each copy had been carefully inscribed in black ink in Mallarmé's hand, just above the autograph signatures of himself (black ink) and Manet (dark brown ink). In addition to the head of a raven for the cover, Manet had produced an *ex-libris* depicting a raven with its wings unfolded and four other separate illustrations.[45]

This luxurious edition, intended primarily for bibliophiles,[46] was confidently described as the first of a series of collaborative efforts between the translator and the artist. The reverse inside cover proudly proclaimed that Poe's *City under the Sea* would shortly receive similar treatment, and Mallarmé's projected popular edition of Poe's poems was announced, optimistically, as 'forthcoming'.

This all sounded very promising, but by the time the first reviews of his edition of *The Raven* began to appear towards the end of June, Mallarmé was already engaged on two quite different projects. He had still not recovered financially from the collapse of his magazine earlier in the year, and in order to subsidize a brief trip for himself to London that summer and to ensure that Marie and the children could visit her father in Germany, he had already signed a contract with the educational publisher Truchy for a philological study of modern English, and was desperately trying to persuade Alphonse Labitte, the stationer and printer to the National Library, to undertake a re-edition of Beckford's *Vathek*.

In the middle of all this, Mallarmé learned that Alphonse Lemerre was planning a third *Parnasse contemporain*. When Lemerre himself informed him that he still had time to submit something, Mallarmé quickly copied out the most recent state of his earlier *Faun* project, now entitled *Improvisation d'un Faune*, and sent it to him at the beginning of July. This third volume of the *Parnasse* proved extremely controversial. Bickering broke out between several of the contributors and the three members of the selection panel comprised Anatole France, Théodore de Banville and François Coppée. Verlaine's contribution was rejected, and it was proposed that Leconte de Lisle's should suffer the same fate. Mallarmé, Mendès, Dierx and Marras all vigorously defended Leconte de Lisle, whose poem was finally accepted after much heated discussion. Informed of this verbally by Lemerre, Mallarmé learned at the same time that his own contribution had likewise been rejected, being judged somewhat obscure by two members of the jury. At first Mallarmé imagined that this was a joke, but when he realized that it was not, the news did little to improve his dealings with Lemerre. These had been considerably soured by the latter's refusal to publish the Poe poem, and Lemerre himself was smarting at the favourable publicity which had been given to the luxurious Lesclide edition.[47]

A final decision was put off until the end of the summer. In the meantime, exhausted and depressed, Mallarmé stayed on in Paris after Marie and the children had left for Camberg, in order to attend the school prizegiving and to work on his English textbook. On 16 August, the day after Marie's Saint's Day, he sent a dejected letter to his wife:

My dear child,

    I really would have loved you to have a letter for your *fête*. On the evening you were due to leave, kitten [Geneviève] and myself were supposed to go and buy you a flower. Alas, nothing ever comes of the projects which one makes. I have only now, late in the evening, interrupted my constant work to scribble this note, both because I was waiting to get a letter from you first and because of my dreadful unwillingness to write.

    The flat is almost big with you all gone, and if I did not miss you at every moment, I would say that it is not unpleasant to live in amid such peace. I spend my time gazing, motionless, at the paper. If I finish tomorrow night, which is Tuesday, I shall be off on Thursday. I shall need two days to arrange the travel pass and obtain 100 francs. There is no movement on that front. Apart from the 60 francs that were brought yesterday for the private lessons and which will cover minor expenses, I had to borrow 100 sous from Dierx. As for the gas and the rent etc, I shall put them all off until things improve.[48]

Not surprisingly, his work was not going well. 'Apart from all that,' he added with a hint of humour, 'the house being built in the distance is being finished quicker than my book, and the jar with the cherries in brandy is visibly emptying, that being, along with my cigarettes, my only distraction.' A week later, although the book remained unfinished, he eventually persuaded Truchy to advance him 100 francs. With the money he retrieved his watch from the pawn-shop and set off, armed with railway passes to Boulogne and London.

Mallarmé had been invited to London by one of the earliest of his English acquaintances, John Payne, whom he had first met four years earlier. Payne now introduced him to the little group of writers who were all employees of the British Museum, including the critic Edmund Gosse and the poet Arthur O'Shaughnessy. Mallarmé couldn't help comparing the way he was received on this occasion with his experience on his first visit with Marie. 'What a difference!' he wrote to her. 'Unknown then, I return now fêted or at least made welcome.'[49] He had at last received his salary, and sent presents for everyone: some Dakin's tea for Marie, a mechanical mouse for Geneviève, and rubber figures – an unruly boy being whipped by his aunt – for Anatole. All in all, the visit was a great success. It provided Mallarmé with a much needed tonic after what had been an exhausting year, and above all it allowed him a welcome, if temporary, respite from his constant financial difficulties.

Inevitably, these worries returned as the holiday period drew to its close. During the trip to London Mallarmé had arranged with O'Shaughnessy to generate some additional income by sending a regular bulletin on the Paris literary and artistic scene which the latter would translate and publish in *The Athenaeum*. After the first of these 'Gossips'[50] had appeared, from Equihen on the Normandy coast, where he had broken his return journey in order to spend the remainder of his holiday by the sea, Mallarmé proposed a similar arrangement, but this time on the London literary scene, to the Parisian newspaper *Le Gaulois*. In the meantime some potentially good news arrived when Manet wrote to announce that the New York publisher and owner of the Poe copyright, Mr Middleton, had expressed interest in a special edition of *The Raven*.

However, when *Le Gaulois* refused his proposition and a decision on the Middleton project was delayed, at the end of September, as he was preparing to return to Paris, Mallarmé found himself obliged to ask Marie and the children to stay on in Germany a little longer than they had planned until he could raise the money for their return fares – this despite the fact that Marie was already trying to save money by travelling third class and by lying about Anatole's age so that she would not have to pay for him. Even at such dire moments, Mallarmé's humour did not desert him. '*Saint Corbeau [Holy Crow]*, pray for us!' he wrote to Marie, announcing that the decision on an American edition of *The Raven* had been put off until the middle of October.[51]

When he returned to Paris in the first week of October,

Mallarmé completed his English philology textbook *Les Mots anglais*, which a month later was listed in Truchy's catalogue for 1876. He also learned that three of his friends, Mendès, Dierx and Léon Cladel, had all threatened to withdraw their poems from the *Parnasse contemporain* unless he was accepted. It was a significant gesture on their part which brought considerable pressure to bear on Lemerre. After some delay, the latter proposed a compromise: he would agree to the inclusion of Mallarmé's poem provided that he could insert a note pointing out that it had been refused by the selection panel and only reinstated after protests. Not surprisingly, this solution was quite unacceptable to Mallarmé, who from that moment on sensed that no future relationship with Lemerre was possible. In the following weeks, therefore, he began to look not only for another publisher for his poem but also for a means of replacing Lemerre and his *Parnasse contemporain* as the main vehicle for new young talent.

Within less than a month, he found the answer to both of these quests in the person of Alphonse Derenne, a printer who had specialized till then in medical texts but who was interested in trying his hand at other sorts of publishing. By the end of November, a note was dispatched to O'Shaughnessy for *The Athenaeum* announcing that a de luxe edition of *L'Après-midi d'un Faune* (*The Faun's Afternoon*), illustrated by Manet, was in preparation for Derenne and that the first issue of a new literary magazine called *La République des lettres*, also to be published by Derenne, would appear in the middle of December. Catulle Mendès was named as the editor of the new review, but the main driving force behind it was Mallarmé himself. It was through his contacts in London that it could claim, as one of its distinctive features, to count several contemporary English writers, including Algernon Swinburne, among its first contributors.[52]

★

Those months which followed Mallarmé's return to Paris in October 1875 were truly hectic. He was trying to finish his preface for the *Vathek* re-edition, coping with all sorts of technical difficulties with the printing of the *Faun*, and closely involved with the detailed preparations for the launching of *La République des lettres*. On top of all this, he was dispatching regular 'Gossips' to O'Shaughnessy for *The Athenaeum*, teaching at the lycée, and trying to put together his book of Poe translations. Understandably in such circumstances, it proved impossible to adhere to strict deadlines. Initially scheduled for the Christmas period, *Vathek* and *L'Après-midi d'un Faune* were put off again and again, then suffered further delays at the printers and binders.

Eventually, by the end of April 1876, *L'Après-midi d'un Faune* was ready for publication. Dedicated to Cladel, Dierx and Mendès, all three of whom had supported Mallarmé against Lemerre, and published in a limited edition of 195 copies, its title was printed in gilt lettering on a white felt cover, and its cover plates tied by pink and black silk tassels. The text was set in specially designed Elzevir type on hand-produced imported Japanese paper, and the illustrations by Manet, in black and in pink, which had been hand-tinted by the artist himself in a desperate effort to reduce the costs of the enterprise, were a deliberate attempt to imitate Japanese techniques 'not hitherto attempted in Europe' according to the note which Mallarmé had published in *The Athenaeum* of 11 December 1875.[53]

Mallarmé's numerous literary activities during this time inevitably had a detrimental effect upon his school work. During the annual inspection the previous year, he had already received a poor report and had been criticized for his deteriorating command of English. Less than a fortnight after the publication of *L'Après-midi d'un Faune* the same team of inspectors returned to the Lycée Condorcet. A fortnight after that Mallarmé received a friendly piece of advice from his former headmaster, Monsieur Clément, who had just been visited by the same team in Besançon. His comments were hardly reassuring:

> Last year, when I asked Mr Lerambert who had inspected you how you were getting on, I was saddened to see that he had a poor opinion of your teaching and that you ran the risk of being returned to the provinces. I therefore recommended you to him as best I could. At that time, he seemed quite prepared to accept my recommendation. Well M. L[erambert] has inspected you again this year. He has been with us since this morning and one of the first things he said when he entered my office was that he regretted not being able to give me any better news of my former pupil, that his teaching still left a lot to be desired and that he was not giving his classes enough attention. Now look, my dear Stéphane, I can see the possibility of such serious consequences for you that I feel obliged to write to you for your own good. I would point out that M. Lerambert does not bear you any personal ill will and that as he left me a short while ago, he promised that once again he would act kindly towards you. But he does seem convinced that one of these days you could be transferred.[54]

Mallarmé's own headmaster took a much less charitable view. The report he filed in July 1876 was scathing:

> According to the Inspectorate it appears that M. Mallarmé is not very strong in English and that despite the friendly warning he received last year, he has done absolutely nothing to acquire what is required for him to be equal to his duties. This teacher spends his time on other things rather than his teaching and his pupils. He is trying to make a name, and no doubt some extra money, for himself with *outrageous publications* in prose and in verse which have nothing whatsoever to do with his functions at the Lycée Fontanes. Those who read such strange mystifications must be astonished to learn that he has a position at the Lycée Fontanes.[55]

In the light of such damning comments, Mallarmé was fortunate indeed only to receive an official warning from the Vice-Rector of the Paris Academy.

It was amid these developments – which, in his precarious financial situation, provided serious food for thought – that Mallarmé received an approach from an English magazine,

The Art Monthly, for an article on Manet and the French Impressionists. The request was not totally surprising. Ever since he had begun to send his regular contributions to *The Athenaeum*, Mallarmé had been doing what he could to promote Manet's interests and defend him in the English press. As early as November 1875, shortly after the painting was newly finished, he had sent a note on *Le Linge* (*The Linen*) emphasizing the absolute modernity of Manet's open-air technique. Unfortunately on that occasion the piece was not published, but part of it was incorporated into a second piece which Mallarmé sent O'Shaughnessy in March when the same painting was submitted to the Salon of 1876. As translated by the latter, it read as follows in the edition of Saturday 1 April:

> M. Edouard Manet, who is well known as the head, or more properly the pioneer, of a very advanced realistic movement in French painting, and whose habit of executing outdoor subjects strictly in the open air has already produced striking results, apparent in his last contribution to the *Salon*, 'Les Canotiers', soon to be exhibited by the Society of French Artists, sends this year to the *Salon* a still more remarkable example of his style – a picture entitled 'Le Linge'. It represents at about life-size, and in a blue dress, a lady washing linen in a very Parisian garden, the background being of foliage and blue atmosphere, with white clothes drying in the air; a child issuing from a mass of flowers looks on. The figure of the lady is bathed by, and, as it were, absorbed into, the sunny light which fills the picture, realising an aspect at once solid and vaporous, in accordance with open air conditions. The painting of the flesh in particular shows the fruits of most original studies of effects of light and atmosphere. The work will probably be looked on as one of the most valuable illustrations of a new idiosyncratic development of Art.[56]

By the time the original French text of this note reached London, *Le Linge*, along with its companion piece, had already been refused by the jury of the Salon. Outraged that such an important work had been dismissed, but unwilling to participate in the second exhibition of the 'Intransigeants' (as the group was now known) which was due to open in the gallery of Durand-Ruel, Manet cocked a snook at everyone by holding a one-man exhibition in his own studio in the rue de Saint-Pétersbourg.

All of these developments had been carefully reported in the English press and had caused quite a stir. In its edition of 29 February, *The Art Monthly*, run by George T. Robinson, had announced that an exhibition by members of the 'ultra-realist school in France' was to be held in April, and in the course of that month, reviewing the exhibition in the most scathing terms and dismissing the contributors as 'attention-seekers', the Paris correspondent of the same magazine agreed with the decision of the Salon jury whilst regretting that 'its very severity deprives visitors to the *Palais de L'Industrie* of the possibility of some innocent amusement.'

Given the interest in events across the Channel and the obviously informed comment of Mallarmé as demonstrated in the columns of *The Athenaeum*,[57] it was quite natural that George Robinson should enquire of O'Shaughnessy whether Mallarmé would be interested in providing a major article on Manet and his contemporaries. Robinson's letter, written in halting French, reached Mallarmé in the second half of July:

> Notre ami mutuel Mr Arthur O'Shaughnessy m'a dit que vous aura [*sic*] la bonté de m'écrire un article sur les vues et les aims des impressionistes et surtout les vues de Manet. Je vous donnera [*sic*] deux ou trois pages de deux colonnes . . . Exprimez votre opinion et votre récit ou critique toute [*sic*] franchement, je vous prie. Parlez au publique [*sic*] comme vous parlerez [*sic*] aux amis – nettement, pas trop discussion mais non trop court [*sic*].[58]

Mallarmé was not one to let such an opportunity pass. He was only too delighted to be able to explain Manet and his friends to the English public whilst receiving a fee for doing so. Within three weeks George Robinson had received the article and had translated it into English. 'M. Robinson has been charming in every way,' Mallarmé wrote to O'Shaughnessy. 'Apart from one or two minor misunderstandings which can easily be put right (this is strictly confidential!) his excellent translation respects my prose and makes the whole piece acceptable. I have received generous and prompt payment, but I don't need to tell you that.'[59]

Although it contains the occasional awkwardness of phrase alluded to in the letter to O'Shaughnessy, the article as published in *The Art Monthly* is a truly remarkable document in which Mallarmé demonstrates a familiarity with and understanding of Manet's aims and objectives which were the direct result of his almost daily conversations with the painter. When he goes on to discuss the relationship to Manet of Monet, Pissarro, Degas, Morisot and Renoir, it is equally clear that he has been a frequent visitor to the exhibitions of their work.

In what, with hindsight, can now be seen to constitute one of the earliest and most enlightened attempts to define and explain the history of modern painting, Mallarmé begins by briefly tracing its origins to the pioneering work of Courbet. Commending Manet's tenacity in clinging to his own ideas with the support first of Baudelaire, then later of Zola, he describes the gradual evolution of Manet's own style, and goes on to praise his willingness to modernize old subjects whilst learning from the example of earlier European traditions such as Velazquez and the Flemish school and the recently discovered and totally contrasting Japanese culture, from which Manet has borrowed a different definition of perspective and unusual angles and framing devices. Turning next to Manet's most recent work, *Le Linge*, which is defined as a significant moment in the history of all painting, Mallarmé makes his central point: that the originality of Manet and his fellow painters lies in their new, refined sort of realism whereby they seek neither to idealize nor to represent reality but rather to make it seem new and strange by depriving it of its apparent solidity and conveying instead the blurred mirage effect of each momentary perception.

There is an extraordinarily dense and lyrical passage at the end of the article which reveals to what extent Mallarmé had discovered and appreciated in the paintings of Manet a confirmation of the view of reality as a perpetually unstable, constantly changing continuum hovering between being and non-being which one day he himself hoped to express in some literary form. Here he quotes Manet, or rather expresses his definition of his art, in terms which presuppose a view of the world which is remarkably similar to his own:

> that which I preserve through the power of Impressionism is not the material portion which already exists, superior to any mere representation of it, but the delight of having re-created Nature touch by touch. I leave the massive and tangible solidity to its fitter exponent, sculpture. I content myself with reflecting on the clear and durable mirror of painting that which perpetually lives yet dies every moment, which only exists by the will of Idea, yet constitutes in my domain the only authentic and certain merit of nature – the Aspect. It is through her [i.e. this] that when rudely thrown at the close of an epoch of dreams [Romanticism] in front of reality, I have taken from it only that which properly belongs to my art, an original and exact perception which distinguishes for itself the things it perceives with the steadfast gaze of a vision restored to its simplest perfection.

In other words, and this takes us to the intellectual revolution as the heart of modern painting, Mallarmé sees Manet's objective as being to fragment, analyse, simplify and reassemble in order to more truthfully, more realistically, represent the world around him. It is this attempt to express the perpetual metamorphosis of life itself which, according to Mallarmé, explains the recent obsession of Manet and the other painters with open-air painting and their attempts to capture through the use of colour and brush technique the effect of objects bathed in air:

> The search after truth, peculiar to modern artists, which enables them to see nature and reproduce her, such as she appears to just and pure eyes, must lead them to adopt air almost exclusively as their medium, or at all events to habituate themselves to work in it freely and without restraint . . . As no artist has on his palette a transparent and neutral colour answering [corresponding] to open air, the desired

effect can only be obtained by lightness or heaviness of touch, or by the regulation of tone.

The other major point upon which Mallarmé seizes, and in this he is anticipating the reassessment of the Impressionists which has only really taken place in the last two decades of our own century, is the political implication of their paintings. The revolution in perception achieved by such painters is described as being in harmony with, if not indeed a forerunner of, the social revolution gradually overtaking nineteenth-century France:

> At a time when the Romantic tradition of the first half of the century only lingers among a few surviving masters of that time, the transition from the old imaginative artist and dreamer to the energetic modern worker is found in Impressionism.
>
> The participation of a hitherto ignored people in the political life of France is a social fact that will honour the close of the nineteenth century. A parallel is found in artistic matters, the way being prepared by an evolution which the public with rare prescience dubbed, from its first appearance, Intransigeant, which in political language means radical and democratic.
>
> The noble visionaries of other times, whose works are the semblance of worldly things seen by unworldly eyes . . . appear as kings and gods in the far dream ages of mankind; recluses to whom was given the genius of a dominion over an ignorant multitude. But today the multitude demands to see with its own eyes; and if our latter-day art is less glorious, intense, and rich, it is not without the compensation of truth, simplicity and child-like charm.

In the lines which immediately follow these remarks, Mallarmé proceeds to make a moving plea to all modern artists to have the courage of their revolutionary convictions and to remain steadfast to their ideals:

> At this critical hour for the human race when Nature desires to work for herself, she requires certain lovers of hers – new and impersonal men placed directly in communion with the sentiment of their time – to loose the restraint of education, to let hand and eye do what they will, and thus through them, reveal herself.

One of the key 'new and impersonal' artists in tune with his revolutionary age is deliberately not named here. Present nonetheless by implication, he was, of course, Mallarmé himself.

Manet's answer to this impassioned and well informed introduction to his work was quite fitting. He did the only thing he could. He painted the delightful little portrait of Mallarmé, thoughtfully seated on a sofa dreaming of brave new worlds, which so long adorned the latter's modest flat in the rue de Rome but which now hangs in the Musée d'Orsay.[60]

Mallarmé recaptured the passion and at times almost evangelical fervour with which he had written of Manet in *The Art Monthly* in the sonnet which he sent to America in October 1876 as his contribution to the volume being prepared by Sara Sigourney Rice and Sarah Whitman to commemorate the somewhat belated erection of a statue to Edgar Allan Poe in Baltimore. It was a commission which Mallarmé had agreed to in April, and one which, despite his exhaustion from a frantic year, he completed out of his respect for Poe during a month's welcome break at Valvins in September. Intended primarily to celebrate Poe, whose penchant for alcohol and morbid fascination with death are referred to in the poem, the sonnet has wider implications too, evoking the fate of all artists misunderstood and maligned by their contemporaries. (The examples of Manet and himself were obviously in Mallarmé's mind as he wrote the poem.) There are other echoes of the recent *Art Monthly* article with its emphasis on the artist as a prophet working for, but reviled by, the masses. Mallarmé's recent most unpleasant communication from the education authorities gives added meaning to the key theme of the avenging angel and the carping voices which, merciless in life, are silent and impotent against the solidity of the double monument (the tomb and the work) evoked in the final line:

> Tel qu'en Lui-même enfin l'éternité le change,
> Le Poète suscite avec un glaive nu

Son siècle épouvanté de n'avoir pas connu
Que la mort triomphait dans cette voix étrange!

Eux, comme un vil sursaut d'hydre oyant jadis l'ange
Donner un sens plus pur aux mots de la tribu
Proclamèrent très haut le sortilège bu
Dans le flot sans honneur de quelque noir mélange.

Du sol et de la nue hostiles, ô grief!
Si notre idée avec ne sculpte un bas-relief
Dont la tombe de Poe éblouissante s'orne,

Calme bloc ici-bas chu d'un désastre obscur
Que ce granit du moins montre à jamais sa borne
Aux noirs vols du Blasphème épars dans le futur.

[Such as into himself at last Eternity changes him,
The Poet arouses with a naked sword
His century horrified not to have realized
That death triumphed in that strange voice.

They, a vile writhing hydra hearing the angel
Give a purer meaning to the words of the tribe
Proclaimed loudly that his magic was drunk
In the honourless flow of some dark beverage.

O struggle between warring earth and sky
If I cannot with that notion carve a bas-relief
To adorn Poe's dazzling tomb,

Calm block fallen earthwards from an obscure disaster
Then may this granite monument for ever mark a limit
To the hideous flights of Blasphemy scattered in the future.]

This sonnet was the last poem of Mallarmé's to appear in print for a considerable number of years.[61] Only too aware of the seriousness of the reprimand which he had received from the authorities, in whose eyes he was now a marked man, he was reluctant to jeopardize the security and well-being of his wife and family, especially as, during the month which he had spent with them at Valvins that September, Marie had suffered a worrying recurrence of the stomach cramps and nausea which, during moments of stress, had plagued her earlier. Apart from a handful of Poe translations completing the series inaugurated in *La République des lettres* earlier that year, in the following three years Mallarmé only published two things, neither of which could cause offence to his superiors. Both were in fact educational texts aimed at secondary schoolteachers and their pupils. Both had been in progress for many years. In December 1877 Truchy at last published *Les Mots anglais*. In December of the following year, J. Rothschild published under the title of *Les Dieux antiques* (*The Ancient Gods*) Mallarmé's free adaptation of Cox's mythology.

The ambitious project which had brought Mallarmé to Paris in the first place was none the less never far from his thoughts. Both his *Art Monthly* article and the defiant tone of the Poe commemoration sonnet are clear signals that since his return to Paris and his close association with Manet and his friends, Mallarmé's resolve to produce a truly original work which would express his artistic vision had, if anything, been strengthened. Thus if, as his stepmother Anne Mallarmé rightly suspected, he had abandoned any pretence of working for a university degree, he had not ceased to pursue the basic research which he knew his goal demanded.

In fact, although it might not at first appear to be the case, each one of the various projects upon which he had been engaged had, in its own way, made some contribution to that overall objective. The expensive editions of *Vathek* and *L'Après-midi d'un Faune*, and the little treaty of philology, *Les Mots anglais*, had all provided Mallarmé with ways of experimenting with the visual layout of the text and the use of an Elzevir typeface which would eventually lead to the visual and typographical experiments of *Un coup de dés*. In its own way, *Les Mots anglais* had allowed him to continue his linguistic studies and to examine, in another language and culture, the complex relationship between the sound, the shape and the meaning of words. *Les Dieux antiques* had provided a useful introduction to the processes at work in the formulation of myths, rituals and religions, which constituted an important aspect of the proposed masterwork. Likewise his position as editor and main contributor to *La Dernière Mode* had permitted him free access to theatres, concert halls and opera houses. As his regular contributions to *The Athenaeum* demonstrate, he had continued to keep abreast of the latest literary and artistic events of the capital. All in all, with an economy of effort that we can only admire, ever since his return to Paris four years earlier almost everything that Mallarmé had done or written had been in some way or other related to his greater goal.

Mallarmé had long since come to the conclusion that the appropriate vehicle for his work was the theatre. Only the theatre, along with the concert hall, could provide the setting that was required for the collective experience which he now envisaged as an important aspect of the work. Both had continued to grow in popularity as the reading public declined. In the aftermath of the Franco-Prussian invasion and the Commune, the theatres of Paris had begun to flourish as the capital returned to its pleasure-orientated culture. Several, like the Théâtre de la Porte Saint-Martin and the Théâtre de la Renaissance, which had closed during the hostilities, had reopened their doors. As the theatre column and gazetteer section of *La Dernière Mode* remind us, a bewildering choice of spectacle now faced the theatregoer. As a regular among these, Mallarmé had been bitterly disappointed to see what an opportunity had been missed, 'What treachery there is,' he wrote in the opening editorial of *La Dernière Mode*, 'when an evening of our life is wasted in that dark hole filled with plasterboard, painted canvas, or with genius, that theatre is! if there is nothing going on there worthy of our interest.' 'The dramatic art of our time,' he had concluded, 'vast, sublime and almost religious, remains to be invented.'

Such thoughts, of course, were not unconnected with the achievements of Richard Wagner in Bayreuth. Mallarmé had first come across the name of Wagner in Baudelaire's articles on the furore provoked by the first performance of *Tannhäuser* in Paris in 1861. Since 1870, however, through Villiers de l'Isle-Adam and, more especially, Catulle Mendès and his wife Judith Gautier, who were both friends of the German composer and visited him regularly, Mallarmé had been kept abreast of the various stages of the Bayreuth Festival theatre project. Regretting somewhat pointedly in the seventh issue of *La Dernière Mode* that 'for lack of an exceptional French work which would subjugate the whole of Europe' a foreign work might have to be used for the inaugural performance in the newly completed Paris Opera House in January 1875, Mallarmé had conceded that he would have proposed *Tannhäuser* itself had the recent war with Prussia not rendered such a choice impossible.

It was certainly no coincidence, therefore, that from January 1876, as the opening performance at the Bayreuth Festival House approached,[62] Mallarmé began to work feverishly on his own theatrical project. Theoretical notes dating from around this period have survived,[63] but these are rather fragmentary. Additional information is provided by Mallarmé's correspondence during this period, and from these twin sources it is possible to surmise what he was working on.

In 1876 the project was mentioned in the vaguest of terms. Mallarmé informed Swinburne, Sarah Whitman and O'Shaughnessy that he was working on a 'vast popular melodrama' which, along with his Poe translations, was totally absorbing his rare moments of free time. From the notes published by Jacques Schérer, it is clear that what Mallarmé had in mind was a kind of modern mystery play, that is to say a mixed-genre spectacle, incorporating music, text, mime and dance. In May 1876, like Wagner himself and for similar reasons, he was evidently having difficulty in solving the problem of blending together the scenic, verbal and musical elements of the work.[64] In January 1877, in response to Wagner's project, he was clearly thinking in terms of an annual festival production. 'My Poe translations,' he informed Sig-ourney Rice, 'or at least their publication, have been delayed by a major piece of work – a play which will be performed at a fixed period of the year.'[65] In May, pressed for more details by Sarah Whitman, he provided the following description of the project:

> You ask me how the theatrical project is coming along. Well, at least I feel that I am making progress, but this huge attempt in which I am involved to produce a totally new sort of theatre will take me several years before I have anything visible to show for it. It is perhaps too ambitious because I am concerned not with a single genre but with all those which I consider to belong to theatrical performance: magical, popular and lyrical drama. It is only when I have completed this triple work that I shall have it performed more or less simultaneously, like Nero setting fire to three corners of Paris. There are such a number of theoretical and practical aspects to be considered.[66]

The three-part spectacle described here had obviously been conceived as a response on behalf of the French nation to Wagner's four-part *Ring* cycle, a fact which is underlined by a revealing comment made in a letter to Arthur O'Shaughnessy in December 1877. Apologizing for his long silence, Mallarmé excused himself on the grounds that he was 'studying every-where the various parts of a new kind of theatre being prepared in France' and to which he was making his modest contribution.[67]

In fact the technical difficulties which he encountered soon forced Mallarmé to delay the project for another year or two. But this was not the only reason for the postponement. By the summer of 1877, he was yet again in serious financial trouble. 'We are leaving for the outskirts of Fontainebleau in the most dire conditions,' he informed O'Shaughnessy in July 1877.[68] Much of his free time during the following year was taken up with a whole series of contracts which, out of necessity, he signed with the educational publisher Truchy, now that he had published *Les Mots anglais*. Advances on an abridged version of this, *Ce que c'est que l'Anglais* (*What English Is*), and an anthology of English poetry brought momentary relief in April 1878, but, as France prepared to celebrate its recovery from the war and its reinstatement as leading player on the world scene with a spectacular opening to its World Fair,[69] Mallarmé had little to celebrate. In June he was forced to sign yet another contract for a mere 600 francs for a voluminous and time-consuming translation of *The New English Mercantile Correspondence*.[70]

In June 1878 Mallarmé was once again obliged to appeal to his old friend Charles Seignobos to see what could be done to obtain an increase in his salary. Having made some approaches to the Ministry, Seignobos reported back in mid-June that he had encountered some opposition, primarily from an official named Mounier:

> He made several objections: 'You lack method; your pupils are not making progress – you spend your time in class on other things – your mind seems to be elsewhere – they even think that you are writing poetry there!!! – You seem only to give to teaching any time which you have left over from other things – You would make more money from private lessons than from writing books, etc., etc.' I am reporting all this accurately in the hope that it may be of some use to you. However, in the end, he accepted that you had a case. He took notes during the interview and I considered what he told me at the end of it to be a formal promise. 'You will not forget?' I added. 'I attach great importance to this.' He replied with the most formal and positive affirmations.
>
> He reminded me that in 72 I had supported you on the grounds that you would present yourself for the *agrégation*. – I retorted that the vicissitudes of life etc.
>
> In short, apart from a letter to remind him a little later (you will remind me of this) things are going well.[71]

In the event, this letter proved rather optimistic. At the end of July Mallarmé was informed that he had been granted a modest increase of 400 francs with effect from October. At the same time, he was reminded that his teaching had to improve. Fortunately, a fortnight earlier he had obtained an advance from Rothschild for *Les Dieux antiques*. Even so, when, at the end of the summer, Lesclide, who in the course of a stock-taking exercise had found a large number of unsold copies of Mallarmé's translation of Poe's *Raven*, asked Manet and Mallarmé to buy them back, the latter was in no position to do so.

After a depressing and exhausting winter which left him little time for his own work – he may well have been obliged to take on extra private pupils – Mallarmé spent the Easter holidays of 1879 at Valvins with his daughter Geneviève. Marie had been forced to remain behind with Anatole, who had suddenly experienced a dramatic recurrence of the rheumatic condition which had so nearly proved fatal in his infancy.

Upon Mallarmé's return to the capital, Manet, who had been one of the few people with whom he had kept in regular contact during the previous eighteen months, asked him to see whether Rothschild would be interested in the edition of Poe's poems which they had postponed earlier. 'Judging by the place that I have been allocated at the Salon this year,' he wrote, 'I think that I am going to be broke as before, and I need some money.'[72]

More than sympathetic to his friend's plight, Mallarmé obliged, and three drawings by Manet were executed and submitted to Rothschild by the end of the summer. The latter was informed by his printers, however, that there was no way that these could be reproduced, and so the ill-fated edition of the Poe poems was postponed yet again.

In the meantime, through the offices of Seignobos and of Henri Roujon, with whom he had become friendly at the time of *La République des lettres* and who was now private secretary to the new Education Minister, Jules Ferry, Mallarmé had once more been trying to have his salary improved. The efforts of both men were being strongly resisted, however, by the new Director of Secondary Education, Charles Zevort. The situation was all the more desperate for Mallarmé because Anatole's condition had worsened and now required regular and expensive medical care. He sought some temporary relief by signing yet another contract with Truchy, this time for a set of grammar exercises, but this on its own was not enough.

The difficulty was that Mallarmé was not only in extremely bad odour with the inspectorate, but his situation was already quite irregular in that he held a post normally reserved for people who had already obtained the *agrégation*. In order to avoid the establishment of an official committee, which almost certainly would have been to Mallarmé's disadvantage, it was agreed to ask the headmaster to request a special hardship payment which only required the Minister's signature. At first, the headmaster objected strongly to this procedure, but under pressure from Seignobos he agreed in principle that, provided the same concession could be made for another colleague in the English Department, he would contemplate such a recommendation in Mallarmé's case.

In August, as the summer holidays arrived, the whole family moved out to Valvins as soon as Anatole's condition allowed him to travel. They took with them the brilliantly coloured yellow canary in a gilded cage which Robert de Montesquiou, who was later to be immortalized as the character Charlus in Proust's *Swann's Way* and who had recently become friends with Mallarmé, had generously bought for Anatole to cheer him up.

As the boy's health began to deteriorate rapidly, Mallarmé grew desperate. The Director of Education was blocking a salary increase and, despite his promises, the headmaster had done nothing. He was however informed that, in view of his son's condition, the Ministry was prepared to agree to the one-off payment of 300 francs. Worried that this might prejudice any hope of a permanent increase, Mallarmé found himself in a total dilemma, all the more so in that technical difficulties had delayed the publication of *Les Dieux antiques*. By now it was clear that Anatole's condition was extremely serious. It was beginning to affect the vital organs. Cazalis advised Mallarmé and his wife to consult a specialist, Professor Peter, who lived in the rue de Rome. In fact, Anatole was suffering from a rheumatic condition, streptoccal endocarditis, which affected the valves of his heart and for which, at the time, little could be done. The only hope offered by modern medicine, cardiac valve replacement, had yet to be invented.

By the beginning of October, when Anatole was well enough to return to Paris, an alarming cough had developed. In the meantime, Mallarmé had received a sincere but remarkably insensitive letter from his cousin, Georges Chéron, who was a Catholic priest:

My dear Stéphane,
  I have just been truly pained to learn that the condition of your dear child is still causing you some anxiety. I sympathize with your pain, believe me, and believe that if I could provide a solution, I would be delighted to do so. But, alas! I have no more control over Nature than anyone else. Let us therefore confidently place ourselves in the hands of He who has determined these laws and who can modify and channel them at his whim, as his wisdom and goodness allow. We must never forget that ever-powerful Doctor. Where others are powerless, he can effortlessly achieve anything as he has frequently shown.
  Would you allow me, my dear cousin, in the name of our former and still genuine friendship, to entreat you to touch the heart of our divine and infinitely good Master by some prayer, by some pleasing gesture which he is waiting for from you. Is he surely not, by this trial which he has sent you, offering you some fatherly advice? And if you were to follow this fatherly advice, would there not result a whole series of graces and favours of which the first would be the good health of our beloved little Anatole? That is what I wonder.
  And so, in the name of our long friendship, I have two questions to ask you: Firstly, are you absolutely sure that at the age of 8 an intelligent child has never experienced a few minutes of momentary lapse such as when, away from the paternal home, he found himself in the care of a careless teacher and in the company of ill-educated companions? Consult on this subject any experienced priest!
  Secondly, have you acquired the experience with the afflicted which

shows absolutely that, with the grace of God, what ought to move them and drive them to despair, calms them and frequently returns them to good health without any holy intervention? You need to have seen this to believe it.[73]

This remarkable assemblage of clichés and platitudes, so typical of the time, had little effect upon Mallarmé, who had long since given up on the Catholic Church. He placed his limited faith in the specialists who, in the event, were power-less against the disease. Despite all their efforts, Anatole died on 8 October just as Mallarmé had gone out to post the latest bulletin on his health to Montesquiou. 'I do not wish you to learn of our misfortune by an official acknowledgement,' he wrote to the latter the same day. 'Our adored child was very fond of you.'[74]

The winter of 1879 was the coldest in living memory in Paris. The Seine froze over, people skated on the river, barges were frozen into canals and braziers appeared on the streets. In the little flat in the rue de Rome, that Christmas was devoid of good cheer. The loss of Anatole was all the more grievous for Mallarmé because, in his own mind, he had already seen his son as his successor, carrying on the work that might prove too much for a single lifetime. 'You can imagine our pain, knowing how much a family man I am,' he had written to John Payne the day before Anatole died. 'Besides, that charm-ing, exquisite child had captivated me to the point where I still include him in all my future projects and my dearest dreams.'[75]

7

Growing Celebrity

The impact of Anatole's death upon Mallarmé and his wife was profound and long-lasting. From now on, Marie Mallarmé became almost continually unwell, suffering from stomach cramps either real or imagined and from nervous dyspepsia. She never really fully recovered.[1] As for Mallarmé himself, he was quite simply devastated. Apart from a short review of John Payne's *New Poems* and a translation of C. W. Elphinstone's *Star of the Fairies* for the publisher Charpentier, undertaken at Banville's kindly suggestion as a means of earning extra income, he wrote nothing during the year which followed his son's death. He became very ill himself with articular rheumatism which forced him to take to his bed during the months of May and June 1880. In July his condition was serious enough for his doctor to prescribe a month's sick leave from the lycée and to advise him to seek fresh air and rest in Valvins, where he remained until October.

By the beginning of the following year, however, life slowly began to return to normal. Mallarmé gradually re-established the practice of entertaining friends in his home on Tuesday evenings after dinner, as he had begun to do shortly before Anatole's death. 'I still exist on Tuesday evenings,' he reminded Verlaine in January.[2] The Tuesday evening crowd, or *Mardistes* as they came to be known, which would later swell to include virtually every major figure from the literary world of Paris and beyond, was restricted at this point to old and trusted friends such as Verlaine, Cazalis, Mendès, Villiers, Marras and Roujon. After dinner, the small dining-room was made ready. The old Louis XVI dining table was folded away to create some space, and an old Chinese bowl filled with tobacco and placed upon it, along with cigarette papers for the guests who began to arrive from nine o'clock onwards. Mallarmé or his daughter Geneviève would answer the door as the cat Lilith looked on, bemused, from an old sideboard, and people were led into a gently lit room where Japanese crêpe paper had been strategically placed over the light fittings.[3]

Mallarmé soon began to feel the need to work once again. 'The old demon of the past few years has unexpectedly pounced once more on your servant Stéphane Mallarmé,' he confided, with some relief, that same month to Robert de Montesquiou.[4] Just as he had sought a cure from his earlier crisis over the death of his grandmother in the composition of *Igitur*, he now tried to exorcize his grief over Anatole by incorporating the child's death and his reaction to it into his theatrical projects. He thus began to scribble a series of pencilled notes which marked the beginning of a dramatic scenario upon which he worked for the next year or so.[5]

Galvanized into activity by the news that others, including his old friend Emile Blémont, were about to publish their own translations of the poems of Edgar Allan Poe, he also began to seek a publisher for his own illustrated edition which had earlier come to nothing. In the hope that a foreign publisher might prove more amenable, he approached Henry Kistemaeckers in Brussels, offering him at the same time an edition of his own collected prose poems. Kistemaeckers, who admitted that he was not fond of Poe's work, was equally unconvinced of the commercial viability of either proposition, and rejected them both. Mallarmé persevered and when at last he found an enthusiastic taker in André Rouveyre, at the end of July he entreated Manet, as a matter of some urgency, to come up with some illustrations.

By now, however, Manet himself was beginning to manifest serious symptoms of the debilitating circulatory disease, *locomotor ataxia*, which had forced him to undertake treatment first at Bellevue and then at Versailles. During Mallarmé's convalescence in the previous year, he had been unable to visit because his own doctor had forbidden him to climb stairs. He had likewise been unable to attend any of the *mardis*, the Tuesday gatherings. From Versailles, therefore, where he was once again undergoing treatment, he sent his excuses:

> My dear captain,
> You know full well how much I enjoy embarking with you on any piece of work, but at the moment such a thing is beyond my strength. I do not feel capable of doing properly what you ask of me. I have no models and above all no imagination. I would produce nothing of any value, so accept my apologies.
> I am not at all satisfied with my health since I arrived in Versailles. I don't know whether it is the change of air or the variation in temperatures, but I feel much less well than I did in Paris.[6]

Mallarmé managed to stall Rouveyre for a month, by which time, feeling rather guilty about his rather summary earlier refusal, Manet had written to him again:

> My dear friend,
> I am full of remorse and am afraid that you might bear me a grudge. The more I think of it, it was pure selfishness on my part not to have accepted the work which you offered me. But some of the things which you suggested seemed to me quite impossible to achieve. Among other things the drawing of a woman in her bed seen through a window. You poets are amazing and it is often impossible to see what you are getting at. Besides I was not well and I was worried that I might not be able to produce anything in time. If we can retrieve the whole affair when I get back to Paris, I shall try to be worthy of the poet and the translator. Besides I shall have you by my side to inspire me.[7]

It was clear from this letter that Manet had little heart for the project. Nonetheless, out of consideration for an old friend, he set to work and completed some drawings which, although he considered them 'dreadful',[8] were sent to Mallarmé by mid-September. Mallarmé, Rouveyre and Manet met at the latter's studio in October. The project was still very much alive in November when suddenly, for reasons which are not clear, it foundered at the very last moment.

Those abortive discussions with Rouveyre in the winter of 1881 were to prove the last attempt at collaboration between Mallarmé and Manet. During term-time Mallarmé continued to visit his friend when he was able to work in his studio, but Manet was now terminally ill and spending more and more time in the country. Mallarmé himself was doing the same, and the visits between the two men became less and less frequent. The last letter Mallarmé sent to Manet in September 1882 consisted of the obligatory enquiry about his health. 'You are very fortunate, my dear friend, to be feeling well,' Manet replied.[9] Within six months, at the beginning of April 1883, he had been confined to his bed. On 18 April, a desperate attempt was made to save his life by amputating his left leg, which had become gangrenous. On 30 April a telegram was dispatched to Valvins announcing that Manet was in a very serious state of health. By the time it reached Mallarmé next day, Manet was dead. Two days later Mallarmé followed Manet's funeral cortège as it left from his home in the rue Saint-Pétersbourg.

For years after Manet's death Mallarmé remained in regular touch with his widow, Suzanne Manet, and cared about her welfare. He never missed an occasion to defend his old friend or thank others who did so. In May 1884, when Théodore Duret published a collection of art criticism under the title *Critique d'Avant-garde*, dedicated to the memory of Manet, Mallarmé specifically wrote to thank him. He was a frequent visitor to the posthumous exhibition opened at the Ecole des Beaux-Arts in January 1884, and likewise attended the commemorative banquet held at the fashionable Père Lathuille restaurant in the boulevard Clichy in January 1885. It was also partly out of respect for his old friend that he began to attend some 'Impressionist dinners' held on the first Thursday of the month in the Café Riche as of 1886.

None of this, however, could replace Manet himself. The death of the artist in whose studio he had found a welcome haven for over a decade from a largely uncomprehending and indifferent world left a considerable gap in Mallarmé's life. This space was, in part at least, taken over by Méry Laurent, to whom, significantly, he had been introduced by Manet. The daughter of an obscure laundress, born in 1849 as plain Anne-Rose Louviot, Méry Laurent was always known by the stage-name she had adopted during her brief and largely unsuccessful career as an actress. Renowned for her stately good looks, her statuesque and buxom features, luxuriant blonde hair and a perfect complexion, she had become the mistress of a rich American, Dr Thomas Evans, who was a pillar of Parisian society and private dentist to the imperial family. Thanks to Evans she occupied in the winter a luxurious flat in the rue de Rome (just across the landing from Evans' surgery) and in the summer a villa in the boulevard Lannes, overlooking the old city fortifications on the edge of the Bois de Boulogne.

A *mondaine* who liked to surround herself with writers and artists, Méry had first met Manet when she visited his private exhibition in his studio in April 1876. She soon became his model and posed for several paintings by him. It was commonly believed at the time that she also became his mistress, but this has never been substantiated. What is beyond doubt is that a close friendship developed between the two. Manet gave her one of his versions of *The Execution of the Emperor Maximilian*, and for her part she was extremely kind and attentive to him. When he was ill, she visited him regularly or sent her maid to enquire about his health. In March 1883 the maid arrived in Manet's studio with flowers and was asked to sit for a pastel portrait. It was found unfinished on his easel, after his death. Every year, on the anniversary of Manet's death, Méry Laurent would place the first lilac of the season on his grave.

Mallarmé had thus known Méry for several years. It was only after Manet's death, however, that their friendship blossomed. We do not know exactly when he began to visit her regularly after school, as he had done with Manet, but it was sometime between Manet's death in April 1883 and the beginning of 1884. One of Mallarmé's visiting cards from this period contains some gallant verses on Méry's golden hair, announcing his visit for five o'clock.[10] By the following summer, Mallarmé could introduce Méry to the photographer Nadar as 'one of my excellent and dearest friends'.[11] Henceforth, when he was in Paris he would visit her virtually every day either at 51 rue de Rome, a few doors away from his own house, or, during the summer months, at her villa 'Les Talus' in the boulevard Lannes. He likewise wrote to her assiduously when he was away from the capital.

Because much of this voluminous correspondence will not be accessible until after the year 2000, it is impossible to make categorical statements about the precise nature of the relationship between Mallarmé and Méry Laurent. From what evidence is already available, it is clear that at some point, in or after 1888 onwards it developed briefly into a full physical relationship. Equally clearly, their complex relationship did not involve just Méry and Mallarmé themselves, but impinged on others as well. Coquettish and flirtatious by nature, Méry had many admirers and lovers, several of whom simultaneously competed for her favours. Evans himself could arrive unexpectedly, and although aware of his mistress's additional conquests, he liked to preserve appearances. At least one private telegram from Mallarmé to Méry fell into the wrong hands.[12]

For their part, Marie Mallarmé and Geneviève were very hurt by Mallarmé's association with 'Madame Laurent'. Writing from Valvins to her father, who was back at school in

Paris, Geneviève, now a young woman of twenty herself, pointedly observed: 'We think and talk about you a lot, especially during your hours of prison. Afterwards . . . oh well, we know that you are enjoying yourself and mother sulks at such times.'[13]

On the face of it, Stéphane Mallarmé and Méry Laurent had little in common. Physically, Méry was tall, about five feet ten, and very powerfully built, while Mallarmé himself was a little under five feet six, and frail-looking. In public, as Henri de Régnier, who spent much time in their company, points out, they looked an ill-assorted couple.[14] Intellectually, as Mallarmé himself recognized, they were hardly on the same plane.[15] But Méry liked to surround herself with creative people. Her salon was frequented by Coppée, the playwright Henri Becque and the society painter Gervex. She was flattered by Mallarmé's attentions and by his reputation. For his part, Mallarmé found her sensuality, her coquettishness and at times her vulgarity irresistible. Some, like the aristocratic and rather strait-laced Henri de Régnier, found her rather common,[16] but in Mallarmé's eyes she represented someone with whom he could pursue ordinary pleasures and in whose company – as in Manet's before her – he could unwind and relax both from the rigours of teaching and from the complexities of his literary life. A brief extract from Henri de Régnier's diaries casts some light on the atmosphere in Méry's drawing-room when Mallarmé and others were present:

At Méry Laurent's the other day, there were Champsaur and Mallarmé and [Augusta] Holmès, looking beautiful despite being forty. Champsaur must certainly be sleeping with Méry.

In the middle of the drawing-room towered an orchid . . . out of its metallic grey bespeckled leaves soared a single red flower, and Mallarmé who loves to provide explanations of things said: 'It is just like the skin of a snake, I bet it is venomous. And the red flower, well that is the breast feather from a canary.' When Méry says that when it is mature the red flower will bloom, he adds with that extraordinary conviction which is the source of his charm: Oh in that case it is a firework![17]

Above all, Méry Laurent represented for Mallarmé real, honest and full-blooded womanhood which was not afraid to use its power over men. As such she both fascinated and frightened him. His admiration, tenderness and love for her are expressed in some of the great erotic sonnets and other verse[18] which she inspired, as well as the charming and frivolous quatrains with which he embellished her fans and other possessions. Some of his other, much more ambiguous feelings about her are beautifully summed up in the following outline for a short story which he described to Henri de Régnier one summer evening as they walked back through the city after an evening spent in her company:

We are walking down the long avenue which is shimmering all the way down to the Arc de Triomphe . . . and I talk to him about the beauty of all these carriages whose progress you can follow for ages thanks to the gaily coloured summer parasols on display. 'Oh! a carriage, I have always wanted to write a story about that, I have been turning the idea over in my head, and this is how I see it; up front the two jet-black fast horses driven by silent coachmen, and in the open carriage, the woman . . . that is one of my openings . . . a chance to say what I want to say and it will be terrible, women won't like me after that. Woman, through whom we die, bears a wound. She bleeds every month but knows how to hide her wound from us. It is that wound which I want to make her feel – there is a pamphlet to be written on that – I want the book to fall from her hands once she has read it as she says, "Yes" that is what it is like . . . You see, Régnier, our Soul is a woman like that who wants to be kept expensively but who gives us nothing on which to live . . .

'The Poet is defeated, he withdraws and sits down at the roadside. He is just about to look away when a lady drives past in her coach. And he wonders: why should she with her insulting riches come in the midst of all this solitude to witness my suffering . . . So he approaches her and says: Fine I accept everything and allow you to enjoy your work, but do not be haughty with me. I don't want you to strut around with that warlike hair, and he undoes her hair and tells her everything . . . Suddenly out of the carriage, from the beautiful lady's lap, where she held it hidden, there jumps a little dog and it is the dog whom I address, saying to him what I could not say to her, her for whom he is adequate and of whom he unjustly deprives me.

'Oh it will be cruel and terrible. I shall say it all.'[19]

Finally, and this was not the least of the attractions which she held for Mallarmé, Méry Laurent constituted a direct link with someone they both had loved, Edouard Manet. This alone added a special and unique quality to their relationship and guaranteed its durability.

Méry Laurent was not the only person who arrived to fill the void left by Manet. There were others too who entered Mallarmé's life, attracted by the celebrity which in the next year or so he suddenly acquired. This unexpected and in a sense unwelcome celebrity was the result of the actions of two men in particular, J.-K. Huysmans and Paul Verlaine.

At the start of the winter in which Manet died, Mallarmé received a letter from Huysmans, a bureaucrat and art critic who had been a contributor to La République des lettres, in which he requested some information for a novel upon which he was currently engaged:

My dear colleague,
    I am busy producing a curious short story of which the following is the general outline: the very last member of a mighty race retreats into a total solitude because he is disgusted with the American way of life and because he has nothing but contempt for the aristocracy of wealth which has permeated everything. He is a cultivated man, a refined man of the most exquisite tastes . . . He loves Poe and Baudelaire. Among modern poets, he naturally adores Théodore Hanon, Corbière, Paul Verlaine . . . Could you find me a copy of La Mort de l'anti-pénultième which appeared in a revue whose title I cannot remember and Hérodiade which I have a great need of, because in his home my hero shall possess the admirable painting by Gustave Moreau as well as the stupendous imaginings of Odilon Redon. I will reproduce your Hérodiade at the same time as I shall attempt to

describe the miraculous work of Moreau. I would also like, if that would be possible, some more verses of *The Faun*.[20]

Although Huysmans had misquoted the title of the prose poem which had so outraged the critics when it had appeared, the echoes of *Igitur* and the proposed subject of the novel were so in tune with Mallarmé's own thinking that he replied most enthusiastically, promising a copy of *L'Après-midi d'un Faune* and inviting Huysmans to his Tuesday gatherings. 'Such a book ought to be written before our epoch is over,' he exclaimed. 'It could not be understood at any other time and you are the one who ought to write it.'[21]

It is clear that Mallarmé and Huysmans discussed the latter's book on several occasions during the following winter, and at the beginning of the summer, as he was congratulating Huysmans on the publication of a collection of essays on the various art exhibitions in Paris during the previous four years, Mallarmé enquired what had become of 'that noble gentleman among his books and his flowers of whom I often think?'[22]

Later that same summer, while he was at Valvins recuperating from another year at the lycée, Mallarmé received from his old friend Verlaine a totally unexpected letter requesting a photograph to accompany a three-part series of articles to be entitled 'Les Poètes maudits' ('Damned Poets') and dealing with Tristan Corbière, Arthur Rimbaud and Mallarmé himself. The articles were to be published in the little review *Lutèce*, founded by Léo Trezenik. Mallarmé was taken aback by this proposal from someone whom he had not seen for some considerable time, especially because he himself had written nothing new for ages, being still preoccupied by his great theatrical project. Furthermore, he was in no position to supply a photograph, since he had deliberately taken the decision not to have himself photographed until he 'emerged safe and sound from the current literary project' as he rather coyly described it.[23] The only solution he could propose was to have Manet's oil portrait of him photographed instead.

Busy for the rest of the summer with his own work, Mallarmé did nothing about getting Manet's painting photographed until he returned to Paris at the beginning of October. Verlaine now reminded him that time was pressing. He also requested some unpublished poems for the article. As the deadline approached, Mallarmé apologized for the delay in providing the photograph. 'I've so little time,' he complained. 'As soon as I get a free minute, I disappear into my vast project. Every evening in October I meant to write to you, but I have my year's classes to prepare, as well as my own work (not forgetting the occasional escape to observe the fleeting beauties of the autumn, our joint passion).'[24] What really embarrassed him, however, was the fact that he had no new poems to offer. 'I would need ten minutes to explain to you that I have no new poems despite one of the most exhausting literary labours ever attempted, because as long as I have such little free time, I am working on the foundation of my work which is in prose. We have all been so far behind, as far as thought is concerned, that I have spent no less than ten years developing my own.'

Verlaine's study of Mallarmé appeared in three separate numbers of *Lutèce* during November and December 1883, accompanied by a reproduction of Manet's portrait. The articles contained some examples of Mallarmé's poetry, the most recent the already published sonnet to the memory of Edgar Allan Poe, written in 1877.[25] At the end of his third article Verlaine made a vague but intriguing reference to Mallarmé's great project, stating that he was engaged on 'a book whose profundity will astonish people no less than its splendour will dazzle all, save the blind.'

Although distributed only to a small and very specialized readership, the *Lutèce* articles had an immediate effect. In the months which followed their publication, Mallarmé began to receive letters from young poets and writers such as Jean Moréas and Léo d'Orfer, eager to be admitted to his Tuesday evening gatherings. What started as a trickle in the first few months of 1884 quickly gathered momentum once the Verlaine articles were published in book form by Léon Vanier in April. Almost simultaneously, in May, Huysmans' novel *A Rebours* (*Against Nature*) was published naming Mallarmé, along with Rimbaud, as one of the most exquisite poets of the age.

From the summer of 1884 a pattern began to emerge which was to continue unbroken until Mallarmé's death. New or prospective members of the Tuesday evening gatherings would contact Mallarmé or occasionally be contacted by him if their work or reputation had caught his attention. They would be asked to attend on a Tuesday evening slightly earlier than the others, before 10 pm, or at another convenient point in the week so that Mallarmé could talk to them on their own at least once. The hour of 10 pm had now been agreed as a starting-point to allow those who came from the other side of the capital time to make the journey. These Tuesday evening gatherings on the fourth floor of the little flat at what was now number 89 in the rue de Rome – which, in an interesting aside, Mallarmé once referred to as 'the small house of Socrates'[26] – became all the more precious to him after the summer of 1884 when, as a condition of his promotion to division leader, he was appointed to the Lycée Janson de Sailly in Passy, which caused him great inconvenience and reduced even further his small amount of free time.

It was in that autumn of 1884 that what Edouard Dujardin later called the 'heroic period' of the *mardis* began.[27] In November Félix Fénéon, the founder and editor in chief of the important *Revue indépendante*, joined the growing band of *Mardistes*. In January 1885 it was the turn of Edouard Dujardin himself, fresh from the Conservatory of Music and about to launch his own magazine, *La Revue wagnérienne*. March brought René Ghil, future inventor of 'Instrumentation', a poetic theory assimilating language and music. In April Gustave Kahn became a regular. Later the same year Odilon

Redon, a painter friend of Huysmans who would eventually collaborate on Mallarmé's highly experimental *Un coup de dés*, Maurice Barrès, a young novelist and future founder of the review *Taches d'encre*, Henri de Régnier and a young American established in Paris, Francis Vielé-Griffin, all joined the ranks of a whole new generation of young men who now entered Mallarmé's life.

But what were these gatherings like? Mallarmé's daughter later recalled that the younger guests, somewhat overawed by her father's reputation, refused to speak no matter how much he tried to make them do so.[28] Later *Mardistes* such as Camille Mauclair[29] have left the impression that much of the evening consisted of a monologue, with Mallarmé lecturing virtually uninterrupted to his captive audience. Edouard Dujardin, however, felt that such a description was totally unfair. 'Let us not imagine an austere *magister*,' he protested. 'It was a continuous change of subject from the sublime to the ridiculous during which jokes were fired off in all directions, no matter how serious the conversation became.'[30]

Dujardin's own correspondence with Mallarmé would tend to confirm his version of the facts, which in any case accords with Mallarmé's own highly ironic but sociable nature. One particular Tuesday evening, excited by something Mallarmé had said, he launched into a passionate speech. The next morning, racked with guilt, he apologized for the interruption. Mallarmé's reply makes it quite clear that what he wanted from his guests was a reaction, not subservience. 'You must be joking, my dear Dujardin,' he retorted. 'On the contrary I thought that you were fine last Tuesday. Still, it was the source of one of your really nice letters which I shall keep for those rather frequent times when one is feeling discouraged.'[31]

New and remarkably detailed evidence from the unpublished diary which Henri de Régnier kept from the beginning of 1887 provides a valuable insight into what the *mardis* were really like. His evidence, which totally vindicates Dujardin's recollections, shows that the topics of conversation were by no means always limited to high-minded literary concerns. Take for example the following account of the evening of Tuesday 18 January 1887:

> At Mallarmé's with Vielé [-Griffin]. Ghil was there along with Beaumanoir, Dujardin and Duret – about fifty, turning grey. They begin to discuss Manet. I suspect that Manet was such a charming man that he fascinated his friends to the point of inspiring in them admiration for his paintings, and now, through the large number of conversations about him here I see that he was an indecisive painter, full of doubt and preoccupied with success, waiting for a Rothschild to turn up.
>
> . . . some amusing details on [Philippe] Burty. Had tremendous flair. A passionate collector to the point of depriving himself to get *objets d'art* for the women he loved. But unreliable with regard to his writing. Sneaky. He has all the vices, the Goncourt brothers said, but that is why we like him.
>
> Then the conversation turns to the Eiffel Tower. Mallarmé says: When you see the whole of Paris you realize the buildings cover a surface that is too great for their height. He later adds: and where the Jardin des Tuileries currently is, on that space miraculously protected against buildings by trees, they will build some sublime palace, the monument to the coming age. It will be bristling with iron girders and have a gigantic glass dome; to crown its total frippery, some triumphal chariot totally out of proportion will rise in the air, bearing the Hero of the hour, his eyes fixed on a flame above him simulated by an electric flame so tall that its width will be concealed and the palace which is a theatre at night will be during the day an indoor garden and surrounded by the glass decorated caves as my brain like a gigantic crab applauds itself with its own claws, I can just imagine the delight of the children.[32]

Another extract reveals not only that these gatherings were quite relaxed, but also that other women in addition to Geneviève and her mother were frequently present:

13 December 1887:

> At Mallarmé's on Tuesday. Old [Tola] Dorian was flirting in a corner with annoying airs of false naïvety. She has Stéphane roll her cigarettes while he comments ironically on the silly things she says

and highlights 5 or 6 of them quite crudely. Nothing much new. A few pieces of gossip about this person and that person. About Villiers who thinks he only looks fine with his hair curled. Totally, hideously curled . . . Mallarmé says that Villiers did not want his portrait painted for the reason that he was afraid that the painters would not find him handsome the way he likes himself, namely with his hair absolutely, horribly, curled. For important occasions he can spend 7 hours at the hairdresser's.[33]

Other extracts show that at other times Mallarmé talked seriously about his heroes, Baudelaire and Hugo and Manet, about the work of others and about his own cherished project. The wide-ranging and spontaneous conversation was determined by several factors: who was present and more especially who was not; the topic of the day; Mallarmé's own mood on any particular evening and that of his guests. In other words, and this certainly explains how the *mardis* lasted so long and continued to attract so many people, they provided a friendly setting in which to relax in good company. Régnier himself summed them up very well when he concluded in his diary for December 1890: 'In short, nothing could replace these evenings at Mallarmé's where, in addition to the exquisitely perfect presence of the host, you have the good fortune to encounter an intelligent group of people.'[34]

The celebrity which Verlaine and Huysmans had more or less thrust upon him affected Mallarmé in several different ways. Encouraged, flattered even, by the admiration which he now appeared to inspire in a whole new generation of eager and enthusiastic supporters, he began to write and publish once again in response to invitations from the various literary magazines in which they were frequently involved. His most ambitious poem to date, provocatively entitled 'Prose' and dedicated to Des Esseintes, the fictitious hero of Huysmans' *A Rebours*, appeared in the January 1885 number of *La Revue indépendante*, edited by Félix Fénéon.[35]

Two sonnets, both dating from earlier periods, but no doubt reworked, 'Quelle soie aux baumes de temps . . .' (inspired

11. Drawing of Mallarmé and a raven
by Paul Gauguin, 1891

12. Mallarmé's study at Valvins,
decorated by himself in the Japanese style

Tu changes d'an comme de robe
Et ta toilette met la main
Ce quatre vingt . seize dont l'aube
N'est pas celle d'un lendemain

13. Méry Laurent photographed by Nadar
and a quatrain addressed to her by Mallarmé
on New Year's Day 1896

14. Mallarmé in the garden at Valvins
with his wife and daughter
and one of their friends, Mme Normant

15. Mallarmé *c.* 1890 standing in front
of his portrait by Manet in the tiny dining-room
of his flat in the rue de Rome

16. Mallarmé and Auguste Renoir in the home of
Berthe Morisot some time in the early 1890s. The
shadowy figures of Degas, who took this photograph,
and Geneviève and Marie Mallarmé, who are
observing from a settee, are just visible in the mirror.

17. Early draft of the preface written to accompany
the publication of *Un coup de dés*
in the magazine *Cosmopolis*

18. Mallarmé towards the end of his life

originally by Marie Mallarmé but now bearing the imprint of Méry Laurent) and 'Le Vierge, le vivace et le bel aujourd'hui . . .', followed in the same review two months later.

The sonnet 'Quelle soie . . .' had in fact originally been offered not to Fénéon but to Edouard Dujardin, who, during his first *mardi* had spoken enthusiastically of the new magazine he was launching. With the financial help of Houston Chamberlain and Agénor Boissier (who alone subsidized the project to the tune of 3,000 francs per annum) he had decided to create a magazine devoted to introducing the work and ideas of Wagner into France. A musical student himself, Dujardin had been made aware of Wagner's ideas by a book, *Le Drame musical*, published in 1876 by Edouard Schuré, who along with Mendès and his wife and Villiers was the main devotee of Wagner in France. Dujardin had persuaded Mendès, Schuré and Villiers to contribute to the *Revue wagnérienne*, which was distributed for the first time at the Lamoureux concerts in February 1885. This first number appeared however without Mallarmé's sonnet, because, according to strict principles enforced by the owners of the magazine to whom Dujardin was responsible, only contributions directly related to Wagner were acceptable.

In order to make amends for the rebuff and for the highly embarrassing position it created, Dujardin invited Mallarmé to accompany Huysmans and himself to one of Charles Lamoureux's popular concerts. Mallarmé attended for the first time on Good Friday of that year, thus inaugurating what would become the habit of a lifetime. Later on that summer, Dujardin also invited Mallarmé to contribute an article on Wagner for the *Revue wagnérienne*.

Flattering as they were, these commissions were in one sense quite unwelcome, because inevitably they diverted Mallarmé's energy and free time away from his own theatrical project, upon which he continued to work and which he increasingly mentioned to the *Mardistes*. Such free time as he did have was in any event limited because of the additional travelling involved in commuting to the Lycée Janson de Sailly in Passy. 'I am spewed out of the house into that hell-hole from around six o'clock in the morning until six o'clock in the evening,' he complained to Verlaine.[36]

Six months of such exhausting commuting took its toll on Mallarmé's health. After the annual inspection in February 1885, in the course of which a slight improvement in his teaching was noted, he requested three months' sick leave, supported by his doctor, Dr Hutinel, who reminded the authorities that Mallarmé had suffered a serious rheumatic attack four years earlier and reported that he was now suffering from inflammation of the spine and constant insomnia which required absolute rest. The headmaster was not prepared to grant Mallarmé's request except on the condition that he drew only half of his salary during his absence. After much wrangling, thanks to the intervention of Henri Roujon and yet another friendly deputy, Madier de Montjau, Mallarmé was eventually granted three months' leave of absence, on full pay, until the end of May. For much of this sick-leave, however, because Marie's own poor health kept her chairbound and unable to climb the stairs, Mallarmé was unable to spend much time in Valvins, where he could find the peace and quiet he needed. When Marie improved enough to travel, there was only a fortnight of his leave left.

By the time he returned to Paris to take up his duties the city was sweltering in exceptionally hot weather. 'This wretched lycée which is so far away,' he cursed when he had been back less than three days, 'is even more tiring in the summer, apart from the mornings, because of the intense heat. I am sick of it and feel like throwing up into the petals of the rhododendrons which are ironically in flower in its courtyard. And what magnificent weather!'[37] The insomnia persisted, and after three weeks of 'the daily mad dash' from the rue de Rome to Passy, Mallarmé became depressed and listless. He could not work because he was hardly sleeping at all and also because, fundamentally, he simply did not enjoy living on his own. He consequently spent most of his time at the lycée devising ways of extending his weekends, naïvely thinking that the authorities were unconcerned by his increasing absences. In fact, unknown to Mallarmé, the headmaster had already lodged an official complaint. When he became aware of this and realized that things could not continue as they had been, Mallarmé appealed to Montjau and Roujon to have him transferred to a school nearer his home address.

It was while these delicate negotiations with the Ministry were going on that Dujardin asked Mallarmé to write something on Wagner. The timing, he informed Dujardin, could not be worse. 'I am ill,' he replied, 'I am more than ever tied up with school, I have never seen anything by Wagner and above all I want to say something that is both original and correct and above all, not off the subject. I need time!'[38]

The subject, nonetheless, was one which fascinated him. With an as yet unidentified book on Wagner borrowed from Gustave Kahn, and the help of an article by Duret and what he knew from his discussions with Dujardin, Mendès and others, Mallarmé set to work producing what he had promised, an innovatory piece of writing halfway between an article of criticism proper and a prose poem. In this novel format, which he would use so successfully in times to come, he responded as a Frenchman and as a poet to the challenge from across the Rhine. Relieved to discover that the German composer had not produced anything similar to the great theatrical project upon which he himself was still working, Mallarmé praised Wagner for his undoubted achievements whilst suggesting that he had missed an opportunity and committed a tactical error in confining himself to Germanic legends. The confrontation and the challenge were implicit in the title of the piece, 'Richard Wagner, rêverie d'un poète français' ('Richard Wagner: Some Thoughts from a French Poet'), and in the final paragraph that hailed Wagner as a beginning, not an end. In private, Mallarmé was much more explicit. 'Perhaps from all my efforts,' he wrote later that summer to Maurice Barrès, 'there will emerge a fragment of the only drama worth attempting, which is the one dealing with Man and the Idea. In short, what was left unsaid in the Wagner article which you read so carefully.'[39]

It was one thing, however, to promise this brave new work, quite another to deliver it. For the past year or so Mallarmé had been dropping veiled hints about his mysterious project to his friends. In November and December 1884 he had mentioned a possible volume of sketches for ballets.[40] In December of that year he had optimistically informed Verlaine that like a tenacious dog who would not let go its bone he would one day 'howl sadly to the moon and take a few bites here and there.'[41] In January 1885 he had spoken of a four-volume work to Dujardin and others.[42] A month later, thanking Odilon Redon for a copy of his lithographs in homage to Goya, he had singled out the first of these as being particularly dear to his heart. 'My admiration,' he wrote, 'directs itself towards the great and inconsolable Mage, a determined searcher after a mystery which he knows does not exist and which he will pursue for ever for precisely that reason, from the dark sadness of his lucid despair, because *it would have been* the Truth! I do not know any drawing which communicates so much intellectual fear and terrible understanding as that grandiose face.'[43]

Mallarmé now realized that he had reached a crossroads partly of his own making. Having raised expectations, he had to produce something. Thus when Dujardin, delighted with the Wagner article, asked him to write a poem celebrating Wagner for the final number of *La Revue wagnérienne* and to agree to be a regular contributor to another magazine which he was currently setting up, Mallarmé felt he had no alternative but to decline. His reply to Dujardin, polite and courteous as ever, could not conceal the strain which the conflicting demands and pressures of the previous months had placed upon him. For the foreseeable future his plans did not include new poems:

> I have taken my time replying to you, because the torpor of my beloved September just swamps all my afternoons. In the mornings, I am busy working very hard on a task with which no writing paper can compete.
>
> On what? On studies for a Drama, as I imagine it. Because the best description is to show the finished product. I am drafting this and it will be the awesome work of my rare moments of freedom during the winter. At this critical moment in my life (when I have to sparkle definitively) you see how far removed I am from anything like a contribution even to the tempting journals you speak of. Apart from my project, and I can only make a supreme effort on my own in some corner or other, nothing else interests me. I have become therefore even less a collaborator of any review, even were it yours! A single quatrain drives me, ill and obsessed with what I have to do, for a fortnight from the straight and narrow path which I am climbing in my mind. But we shall talk of all this in the early days of October . . . and if, when you end your first Wagnerian year, I can see a space in which to write a poem, then you shall have it. But I can promise nothing, alas![44]

Thus when, in November of that year, Verlaine wrote again, asking for details about the great project so that he could describe it when introducing Mallarmé to the general public in a new popular series entitled *Les Hommes d'Aujourd'hui* (*Men of Today*) which he was publishing with Vanier, Mallarmé had an important decision to make. He could either make a public statement about his projected work or pass over it in silence. Confronted with the same dilemma by an Italian journalist friend of Dujardin's who requested similar details for a series of articles, Mallarmé was at first rather evasive, although, in fairness, we must add that when he replied to the enquiry from Vittorio Pica he was suffering from a severe bout of neuralgia. When it came to his old friend, however, he decided to comply. He carefully composed in pencil – deliberately chosen no doubt to remind himself that this was but a provisional statement – a biographical note which Verlaine merely had to transpose into the third person singular for the text of his introduction.

As we pointed out in Chapter 1, some of the biographical information supplied by Mallarmé in this letter is carefully doctored to comply with the image of himself which he wished to hand down to posterity. His comments on his ambitious project, *Le Livre*, the Book, as he now for the first time described it, are naturally rather cautious, but they constitute the most complete and coherent public statement he was prepared to make about his true goal. Casting a premature and somewhat exaggeratedly weary gaze backwards over his achievements so far and dismissing them as mere distractions from the main task in hand, he came at last to define this more clearly:

> Apart from my prose works, my early poems and those which followed in similar vein, published here and there, every time a new number of a literary review appeared, I have always dreamed about and attempted something else, with the patience of an alchemist, ready to sacrifice all my vanity and all my satisfaction just as in the olden days people burned their furniture and the beams of their roof to fuel the furnace of the Great Work. What am I talking about? It is very hard to explain. A book, quite simply, in many volumes, a book which is truly a book, structured and premeditated, and not a mere collection of random acts of inspiration, even if they were marvellous . . . I will go further. I will say: the Book, persuaded as I am that there only is one, which has been attempted whether they knew it or not by anybody who has ever written, including men of genius. The Orphic explanation of the Earth which is the sole task of the poet and the supreme literary game. For the rhythm of the book, which is impersonal yet alive, even down to its pagination, parallels the equations of this imaginative work or Ode.
>
> There, I have totally laid bare my private vice, my dear friend, which I have abandoned thousands of times, my spirits wearied and battered, but I am possessed by it and perhaps I shall succeed. Not in producing this work in its entirety (I do not know what you have to be to achieve that!) but in showing at least a fragment of it which has been completed and demonstrating by what is there its sparklingly glorious authenticity and suggesting the rest of it for which an entire life is not enough. Proving by the parts which have been written that

such a book exists and that I have knowledge of what I have not been able to accomplish.[45]

These remarks must surely have astonished Verlaine, and later not a few of his readers. They are a pretty accurate reflection nonetheless of what, from his conversations in the *mardis* and his surviving papers, we now know him to have been furiously working upon. Writing again a few months later to Vittorio Pica, Mallarmé enclosed further information about his great lyrical drama which he allowed the latter to publish in his study in the *Gazetta letteraria artistica e scientifica*:

I believe that Literature, rediscovering its origins which are a combination of Art and Science, will provide us with a Theatre whose performances will be the truly modern religious celebration. A Book which is an explanation of Man able to satisfy our greatest dreams. I believe that all of this is written in Nature in such a way that only those who are not interested in looking at things cannot see it. This work exists. Everyone has attempted it without realizing it. There is no genius or fool who has not discovered some part of it, albeit unknowingly. To demonstrate this and thus lift a corner of the veil of what just such a poem can be is, in my isolation, my joy and my torture.[46]

Although, for practical reasons, these statements would not be published for some time – the edition of *Les Hommes d'Aujourd'hui* would not appear until February 1887 – their very formulation represented an extremely important decision from Mallarmé's point of view. By writing them and agreeing to their publication, he had crossed his Rubicon. Within himself he now accepted his growing celebrity and the inevitable pressure which it imposed upon him. He had at last decided to enter the public arena.

The confident tone projected by these notes for Verlaine and for Pica was in part due to the fact that, thanks to the tireless efforts of Roujon and Montjau, at the start of the new school year in October 1885 Mallarmé had been transferred to the Collège Rollin in the avenue Trudaine.[47] This was not quite as near his home as the Lycée Condorcet (which in any event would not have him back), but it was within easy walking distance, thus saving him the tiresome and time-consuming commuting which for the past year had blighted his life.

Mallarmé had other reasons to feel optimistic. He had recently signed a contract with Verlaine's publisher, Léon Vanier, for an edition of the Poe translations, and was negotiating with the same publisher for a possible collected edition of his prose and poetry. In addition, complying with Dujardin's earlier request, he had found or made the time to produce a sonnet for the last issue of *La Revue wagnérienne*. A complex and over-elaborate piece, reflecting yet again his ambiguous feelings towards the German composer, it was not one of his most successful compositions, although in the circumstances this was not surprising. Writing to one of his uncles who had heard that a nephew had written an apparently incomprehensible poem about Richard Wagner, Mallarmé described it in the following terms:

> *L'Hommage* [à Wagner] is a bit grudging in spirit. It expresses, as you will see, the sadness of a poet watching the old poetic challenge flounder and the richness of language pale into insignificance compared to the splendid sunrise of contemporary music of which Wagner is the latest god.[48]

For once it would appear that Mallarmé's much-vaunted objectivity had failed him. What remained to be seen, however, was whether, in the name of poetry and in the name of France, he could rise to the challenge which Wagner had set him and which he had now publicly set himself.

8

The Banquet Years

In the course of the next few years, Mallarmé would find it increasingly difficult to cope with all the claims upon his time as his public and private life constantly competed for his attention. During his first year at the Collège Rollin, however, this problem was not as serious as it would become later on, largely due to the fact that for most of that year his health was very poor. In late November 1885, a month after the new school year had started, he contracted a bad head-cold which, with the onset of winter, developed into a severe and protracted attack of rheumatism which in turn triggered regular and debilitating bouts of insomnia. 'As for me,' he bitterly commented to John Payne in May 1886, 'I never sleep any more and that is how I imagine the state of eternal damnation.'[1]

As a consequence Mallarmé's social life during that first year at the Collège Rollin was severely curtailed. The *mardis* remained his principal and essential contact with the outside world. Otherwise, apart from his daily journey to the Collège, his main regular sorties were to visit Méry Laurent and to attend the Lamoureux concerts. His writing suffered too. Constantly pressed to supply material for the new literary reviews which began to spring up at an alarming rate, Mallarmé contented himself with authorizing the republication of old material. In fact, during the next three or four years he only produced three new poems, all three, significantly, written for and inspired by Méry Laurent.[2]

During the winter and spring of 1886, when his insomnia relented, Mallarmé busied himself with details over the Poe translations and a second edition of *L'Après-midi d'un Faune*, both of which were to be published by Léon Vanier. By the beginning of the summer, however, relations with Vanier were beginning to show signs of strain, primarily because of the latter's interminable delays, not only with Mallarmé's own projects, but also with *Les Hommes d'Aujourd'hui*, which was already six months behind schedule. Mallarmé's relations with his new headmaster at the Collège Rollin were hardly any better. In his first annual report, the latter noted that he lacked authority. 'His class is asleep,' he wrote. 'The pupils have no jotters and do not take any notes. The teacher does not return or mark homework. His classes are uninteresting and progress is slow.'[3]

It was in Valvins, where he had gone to recuperate from a fairly depressing year and to write the preface he had promised René Ghil for his *Traité du Verbe*, that Mallarmé heard from Edouard Dujardin in Bayreuth, where he had gone to attend the festival. Dujardin sent a copy of an article he had published the previous month in a Swiss review on the subject of contemporary French poetry and Richard Wagner, and in the course of which he had made a reference to Mallarmé's great theatrical project. The real motive of the letter, however, was to remind Mallarmé that he intended launching a new magazine to replace *La Revue wagnérienne* and that all contributions for the first issue, including the articles of drama criticism which Mallarmé had promised, should be ready by October. From Mallarmé's reply, it is obvious that the kind of references to his Great Work which Dujardin had made were becoming increasingly tiresome. 'Your study on Wagner is penetrating and definitive,' he began, 'but as for what you say about your humble servant, I would have preferred that to be tucked away in a little corner. Through your well intentioned friendship you are placing on my somewhat ageing shoulders the magnificent burden of a destiny which I may have dreamed of for someone, if not for myself. My life, my failing health (the same old problem at night), other increasing constraints (I shall not be returning to the Lycée Condorcet), all of that points to a depressing future.'[4]

Having thought about it over the summer, Mallarmé was also somewhat hesitant about committing himself to making regular contributions to any review. In the first place, apart from the obvious imposition upon his own time, he was somewhat alarmed by the number of partisan reviews which had begun to proliferate and did not want to become involved in the petty squabbles to which they were rather prone. When, for example, a month later Léo d'Orfer asked him to contribute something to *La Décadence*, which he was founding with René Ghil, Mallarmé commented quite pointedly that it was time to abandon such an infantile title, which was already out of date.[5] His major reservation, however, was that he did not wish to write a traditional theatre column and at the same time did not think that the public would be interested in what he would prefer, namely a series of discursive articles analysing the theatre in general without necessarily restricting himself to reviewing current productions.

So he replied that he would consider becoming the theatre critic of the magazine provided certain strict conditions were adhered to: he would have the same privileges and rights as a professional critic, namely free entry to the theatres of his choosing; he would make the final decision on the choice of play to discuss and should be allowed to decide whether he need attend a performance or merely read the text; lastly, he would be allowed on occasion to devote a considerable portion of his articles to expressing his own views on the theatre without any reference to current productions with which they had, as he stressed, 'absolutely nothing in common.'[6]

In the end, Mallarmé overcame his hesitations and agreed to contribute a monthly drama column to *La Revue indépendante*.

This was in part because Dujardin agreed to all of his conditions, but there were other reasons. After further discussions, Mallarmé realized that what Dujardin wanted to create was a serious magazine which expressed a moderate, i.e. slightly left of centre, philosophy. He was equally pleased to learn that other regular contributors were to include two of his closest friends, Huysmans and Villiers, and that the editor-in-chief was to be one of his *Mardistes*, Félix Fénéon.[7]

Finally, and not least of all, there was the respect which Mallarmé genuinely had for Dujardin himself, who had quickly become one of his favourites among the young regular visitors to the rue de Rome. Mallarmé already considered him, in some respects, as a potential substitute for the son he had tragically lost.[8] Thanking Théodore Duret for agreeing, at his suggestion, to become a founder patron of the new review, he expressed great confidence in Dujardin's abilities. 'Thank you so much,' he wrote, 'it is in a good cause. I believe strongly in the future of this magazine in the hands of Dujardin. He is a delightful man full of energy and, despite my formal oaths not to write for any magazine, I enthusiastically give him my support as a contributor.'[9]

There was, of course, one additional advantage to writing for *La Revue indépendante* from Mallarmé's point of view. Having got Dujardin to agree to his terms, he was now in a position to pursue his own research into the whole theatrical scene of the capital at the latter's expense. Laying aside all his earlier reservations, he therefore threw himself wholeheartedly into the venture, persuading Eugène Manet, George Moore and several others to become founder-patrons. Furthermore, when the first edition of a new series of *La Revue indépendante* appeared on 1 November 1886, its inside back cover carried a note announcing that by a special agreement, all new works by Mallarmé would make their first appearance within its pages. This new and exclusive association was reinforced when, from the second edition onwards and in each of its subsequent issues, *La Revue indépendante* carried the rapidly evolving details of a special manuscript edition of Mallarmé's collected poems to be published separately by the review.

In actual fact, relations between Mallarmé and Dujardin were not always quite as idyllic as such announcements might tend to suggest. An unpublished note by Dujardin's widow recounts that when he received Mallarmé's first article, which was a review of *Hamlet, prince of Denmark* by Meurice and Dumas, her husband was horrified to see that Mallarmé had not written it in the accessible conversational style which he had promised. He therefore went to see Mallarmé to explain that certain parts of his text would be quite obscure to the average reader. 'Mallarmé would hear nothing of it,' she writes, 'replying to every comment "respectfully" made to him by his disciple: "But this is perfectly clear!"'[10] This anecdote is given considerable credence by an unpublished letter from Dujardin to Houston Chamberlain, former patron of *La Revue wagnérienne*, in which, referring to the first issue of his new review, he remarks: 'In a word (apart from the few pages which Mallarmé sent us!) you will find it difficult for you to find *La Revue indépendante* any more extreme or less acceptable than *La Revue contemporaine*, which had more or less the same contributors on its prospectus.'[11]

In the meantime, things were not at all going well between Mallarmé and his other main publisher at the time, Léon Vanier. Mallarmé had already been dissatisfied with the sets of proofs which Vanier had produced for the popular edition of the *Faun* and with his interminable delays with the Poe translations. In February 1887, as Vanier was at long last about to publish the even longer-delayed *Les Hommes d'Aujourd'hui*, Mallarmé went as far as threatening legal action if he published a portrait of himself which was not entirely acceptable to him.

In the event, Vanier ignored the threat and published without further consultation a rather tasteless print by Luque representing Mallarmé with pointed ears, disguised as a Faun, and clutching a lyre. To add insult to injury, the text of Mallarmé's prose poem, 'La Gloire', written to complement and indeed balance Verlaine's eulogistic article, for which he had received no proofs, was published with several typographical errors which totally disfigured it. Mallarmé was always very sensitive to such matters, and extremely anxious that his work should appear totally unblemished before the public. He reacted immediately. First of all, he had the prose poem reprinted immediately in the April edition of René Ghil's *Ecrits pour l'Art* with an accompanying note that it had been earlier reproduced inaccurately.[12] Second, and much more important, the March issue of *La Revue indépendante* carried a hurried announcement of a popular re-edition of the *Faun* which was to be published by the review in direct competition to Vanier's, and a hastily written article on this new edition by the review's literary critic, Théodore de Wyzewa.

From April until the middle of August that year Mallarmé was totally preoccupied with copying out and amending his collected poems for the Dujardin edition, for although announced in the May edition of *La Revue indépendante* as having been just published, the final text of these poems was not sent to Dujardin until 16 August.[13] The very next day, Mallarmé wrote to Vanier demanding to know whether or not he was going to publish the Poe translations. When Vanier did not reply to his letter, Mallarmé wrote to him at the end of the month claiming that he would soon have no alternative but to seek another publisher. After a two-month interval, at the end of the summer break in Valvins he returned to the attack. At the beginning of October, at the risk of stating the obvious, he pointed out to Vanier that he was utterly fed up with waiting for proofs. By the end of the month, he threatened a court action for breach of contract, which he was eventually obliged to activate in November. At the beginning of December, both sides, anxious to avoid expensive legal fees, agreed to settle their differences out of court. The whole sorry affair thus came to a temporary, if on the whole unsatisfactory truce.

By the time this unhappy episode ended, Mallarmé was already seriously contemplating another major publishing project which was the direct consequence of his renewed friendship with someone he had first met many years earlier. Mallarmé had originally encountered Berthe Morisot in Manet's studio in the late 1870s. After Edouard Manet's death in 1883, he had remained in contact with Berthe and her husband, Eugène Manet, Edouard's brother, and, as we have seen, had persuaded Eugène to become a founder-patron of *La Revue indépendante* in October 1886. It may well have been this renewed contact with Eugène which rekindled the relationship with his wife, for in any event it was in November 1886 that Mallarmé first attended one of Berthe Morisot's weekly Thursday evening dinners in her flat in the rue Villejuste (today rue Paul Valéry). He only became a regular attender a month or two later.[14] These dinners, for which he was usually accompanied by his daughter Geneviève (replacing her mother, who was too ill to attend), were primarily a social occasion. They nonetheless allowed Mallarmé to re-establish contact with a world which had never ceased to interest him, but with which he had become less involved since the death of his great friend Manet. Claude Monet and Auguste Renoir were close friends of Eugène Manet and his wife and regular attenders at these dinners. Degas too dropped in from time to time. Mallarmé had been on acquaintanceship terms with all of these men for several years, and was familiar with their work, as his earlier article for *Art Monthly* had shown, but it was through Berthe Morisot that he came to know them well.

It was at one of these dinners a year or so later, in October or November 1887, that he first expressed his desire to publish an illustrated edition of his collected prose which would match the expensive edition of his poems which Dujardin had just produced. He already had a working title for the volume, *Le Tiroir de laque* (*The Lacquer Drawer*), which was very much in keeping with the contemporary vogue for Japanese art. Renoir and Berthe Morisot both agreed to collaborate on the project, but not without some apprehension. 'Please, please come for dinner on Thursday,' Berthe wrote to Mallarmé at the beginning of December, 'Renoir and I are very anxious. You need to explain to us what you want for your illustrations. Don't think you have to reply in writing. No reply will mean that you accept and I am absolutely counting on that.'[15]

It was Mallarmé's intention that John Lewis Brown would provide the cover, that Renoir would illustrate the beautiful woman of his science fiction tale 'Le Phénomène futur', and that Monet would produce something appropriate for the autumnal setting of the prose poem 'La Gloire'. Berthe Morisot, who had already agreed to produce a sketch of the river scene backcloth to 'Le Nénuphar blanc', undertook to enlist Degas for the fourth and final illustration. By the middle of December, thanks to her charm, Degas agreed to join the venture.

At this early stage, Mallarmé was still looking for a publisher. He dare not approach Dujardin, who had just informed him that the photolithographic edition of the poems was not selling well and that he fully expected to make a loss. Mallarmé had therefore already approached another Parisian publisher, Dentu, when an ideal solution to his problem arrived from a totally unexpected quarter. A young Belgian poet, Emile Verhaeren, who had favourably reviewed the Dujardin edition of the poems when it appeared a few months earlier, now sent Mallarmé a copy of his own volume of verse. It had been elegantly produced in Brussels by Edmond Deman, who was now offering to publish whatever Mallarmé might send him. Delighted at this turn of events, which in particular allowed him to avoid further dealings with Vanier, Mallarmé immediately suggested the *Tiroir de laque* volume to Deman, reminding him at the same time that his Poe translations were as yet unpublished. Within a week of receiving Mallarmé's letter, Verhaeren wrote to inform him that Deman would be willing to publish both volumes.

Whilst preliminary discussions were still continuing over the precise format to be adopted for *Le Tiroir de laque*, Mallarmé initiated another publication which, in its own way, was also a direct result of his recent connection with Berthe Morisot and her circle. A mere fortnight or so before writing to Deman, at the beginning of the year, he had been invited to lunch at Claude Monet's studio. There he met the flamboyant American painter, James McNeill Whistler, who was paying one of his short visits to Paris. Mallarmé had been introduced to Whistler some years earlier by Théodore Duret, and he certainly knew of him from Edouard Manet, who had also been a close friend. During the lunch Mallarmé was greatly impressed by Whistler, whose ironic sense of humour and independent spirit struck a particular chord.[16] Furthermore, he subsequently so much enjoyed reading Whistler's celebrated 'Ten o'Clock' lecture on Art, to which a recently published study by Duret had drawn his attention, that he immediately decided to translate it into French. He had no difficulty in persuading Dujardin to accept the translation on behalf of *La Revue indépendante*, where it appeared in the issue of May 1888, thus cementing another relationship between Mallarmé and a painter which would grow in importance over the coming years.[17]

Meanwhile, the two projects which had been accepted by Deman had begun to take shape, especially the edition of the Poe translations. In March, learning that Vanier was at long last considering going to press with his own edition, Mallarmé had advised Deman to produce theirs as quickly as possible. He was therefore feverishly correcting proofs for Deman at the start of May when an ill-timed and premature announcement of the imminent publication of the volume enthusiastically inserted in that month's issue of *La Revue indépendante* by Dujardin unfortunately alerted Vanier to the existence of a rival edition. Anxious to avoid a repetition of what had happened in the case of the popular edition of *L'Après-midi d'un Faune*, Vanier retaliated by sending proofs of his edition, which Mallarmé then delayed returning as long as he could in order to give Deman time to bring out his edition. As the review copies of this were in their turn delayed, Mallarmé was forced to trick Vanier into putting off his publication until after September.

Eventually, the whole business reached farcical proportions when Mallarmé was forced to return to Paris from Valvins at the end of July to distribute review copies of the Deman edition to the press. In a last desperate move to block the rival edition, Vanier wrote to Deman informing him that the rights to Manet's illustration were exclusively his. Informed of this by Deman, Mallarmé reminded Vanier, on behalf of Suzanne Manet and himself, that this was not the case. Distribution of the Deman edition therefore started at the beginning of August.[18]

The very least that can be said of *Le Tiroir de laque* is that its publication did not proceed at the same feverish pace. Having given his team of illustrators the required format as early as the beginning of April, Mallarmé was still awaiting draft sketches from them in the third week of June. Berthe Morisot, Renoir and John Lewis Brown had some excuse in that they had all been busy preparing canvases for an important exhibition which opened in Durand-Ruel's gallery towards the end of May. Aware of this, Mallarmé extended his deadline to 14 July, but even by that date nothing was forthcoming. The day after the deadline, eager to extract the remainder of his advance in order to be able to afford a pony and cart for the summer holidays in Valvins, Mallarmé reported back to Deman in optimistic terms. 'As for the illustrations,' he wrote, 'it is going to be fantastic. One of the most beautiful people in Paris is posing for the cover, in which she will be depicted pulling the drawer slightly open. Oh! you have no idea how much running about I have had for the illustrations. Everybody is promising me nothing short of masterpieces!'[19]

The reality of the situation was quite different. Méry Laurent (for she it was who was 'one of the most beautiful people in Paris') had indeed agreed to pose for John Lewis Brown, but the latter only began his preliminary sketches at the end of August, when both he and Méry had returned from their summer holidays. By that time Berthe Morisot's drawing was ready, but John Lewis Brown still had to obtain a lacquer cabinet from the oriental specialist Bing before getting on with the final sketches. So when, during the first week in August, Mallarmé thanked Deman for his advance and informed him that, 'apart from Degas', all the illustrations were ready, he was being less than truthful. He did indeed write to Degas at the end of August pressing him for his contribution, but the latter merely put everything off until he returned to Paris in September. At the beginning of September Mallarmé duly visited Degas in person and received a formal assurance that the promised drawing of a dancer would be ready by the end of the month. Inevitably, at that date it was still not forthcoming.

By the end of the summer, Mallarmé was running into other difficulties. Having seen John Lewis Brown's finished sketches, he was no longer happy with the original title. At the outset, he informed Deman, he had had in mind a drawing of a large Japanese cabinet (primarily because of the rectangular shape which would divide the page) with a woman in a long flowing dress pulling open one of its drawers. Instead of this, Lewis Brown had come up with a drawing depicting a seated woman lifting the lid of a box placed on her lap. In the light of this, the original title, which had nothing to do with the content of the book but rather with the cover as he had imagined it, now had no justification. He had other reservations too. Upon reflection, he felt that the original title was pretentious and rather constricting, in that it associated the book too closely with the spirit of a particular period and its predilection for Japanese art. 'It is detestable, pure chic, and not at all me,' he wrote, proposing a much simpler title – either *Pages* or *Vol de Pages*.[20]

For his part, Deman admitted that he rather liked the earlier title, but after a furious exchange of letters he eventually deferred to Mallarmé's judgement, and the title *Pages* was adopted.

However, that still left the major problem of the illustrations, and in particular the contributions from Degas and Monet. In a last-ditch attempt to galvanize the former, Mallarmé enlisted the support of Mary Cassatt, who informed him at the end of January 1889 that she had spoken to Degas and he had absolutely assured her about his drawing of the ballerina.[21] Needless to say, it did not materialize. Resigning himself therefore to the fact that it now appeared likely that Degas would default, Mallarmé turned his attention to the other contributors. Unfortunately John Lewis Brown had not made much progress beyond his preliminary sketches, owing to the disruption caused by the sudden death of his stepdaughter. As for Monet, he had not even made a start on his drawing.

Part of the problem here was that Monet did not much feel at ease with the medium which had been agreed, namely crayons. He would have much preferred oils. Thus, despite his reassurance in February of that year that he had not forgotten his promise,[22] he kept on postponing it. When at last he did attempt something, at the end of the summer, the results were disappointing. He wrote to Mallarmé in October:

> I am really ashamed of my behaviour, and I deserve all your reproaches. It is not for lack of good intentions on my part as you might imagine. The honest truth is that I feel incapable of producing anything of value. I am perhaps being over-sensitive, but truly as soon as I try to do the slightest thing with crayons the result is absurd

and totally uninteresting, and therefore unworthy of accompanying
your exquisite poems (I was delighted with 'La Gloire' and I am
afraid I do not have the talent required to come up with something
good). Please do not imagine that I just gave up. Alas, everything I
write is true. So please excuse me, especially for having taken so long
before admitting all this. You are aware of the warmth and admiration
which I feel for you, so please let me prove it by offering you a
canvas in memory of our friendship.[23]

From this letter Mallarmé could clearly see that Monet had
genuinely tried to cope with a medium with which he was not
happy. He was obviously disappointed, but he understood the
scruples of a fellow artist whom he held in the highest regard
and whom, as someone who admired and defended Manet, he
greatly respected. 'If I had been able to get to Giverny,' he
replied sadly, 'I would have forced you to find your attempts
quite excellent, for I am sure they must be so, but from the
distance which separates us I respect your solitary diffidence as
I do everything which emanates from you.'[24]

Despite the failure of their collaborative effort on this
occasion, Monet and Mallarmé continued to remain good
friends. Monet kept his word with regard to the painting,
which Mallarmé collected the following summer and with
which he was absolutely delighted.[25] Along with Berthe Morisot, he continued to see Monet when the latter made the
occasional excursion to Paris, and he visited Monet on several
occasions in his country retreat in Giverny, where his photograph had a place of honour in the most important room in
the house, namely the kitchen. He also used his contacts in the
civil service to obtain extended leave for Monet's son when
the latter became ill during his military service.

By the time Monet eventually admitted defeat in October
1889, thus putting paid, between himself and Degas, to what
would have been a magnificent prospect, Mallarmé was much
preoccupied with other matters. Some three years earlier,
during a brief two-day visit to Valvins, his old companion
Villiers de l'Isle-Adam had complained of stomach pains and

had asked him to arrange an introduction to Dr Robin, Méry Laurent's personal physician. Over the next two years, despite the occasional respite, Villiers had continued to be unwell, and by December 1888, as the following extract from Henri de Régnier's diary for January 1889 shows, it was quite clear to Mallarmé how serious matters had become:

> He [Mallarmé] has spoken to me a lot recently about Villiers, who is very ill. He tells me how angry he is to see bed-ridden, poor and alone an inventor of miracles and a man of genius. Seeing him so wretched, he said to him: 'You know, my old friend, when they read your books in a hundred years, people will say, "what kind of swine did that man live among?"' He gets very upset as he tells me this and adds that to witness such a thing is a public scandal, that we are clearly punished for having meddled with certain things. Villiers is aware of this, he says, and at such times behind the curtains of his bed he had foreseen everything including dying of hunger.[26]

The extremely rare bitterness of Mallarmé's reported comments shows how strong his feelings were for Villiers. He was very fond of him not just because he was a friend of long standing (who, alone among the *Mardistes*, was allowed to bring his son to these gatherings), but because in his eyes he epitomized, as did Baudelaire before him, the supreme example of an artist who cared for little else other than his art and who had nothing but contempt for material needs.

In March 1889, alarmed at the speed with which the disease appeared to have taken hold, Mallarmé discussed Villiers' condition with Méry Laurent and François Coppée, both of whom were equally devoted to him. It was agreed that all their friends should be discreetly contacted and requested to contribute to a special fund which would provide money to ensure adequate medical attention for Villiers. Mallarmé, whose idea this principally was, was elected the secretary of a three-man committee (composed of Dierx, Huysmans and himself) which would administer the fund. Approached by Heredia and Alexandre Dumas, the Académie Française replied that it could do nothing for the moment, but the Playwrights Society (Commission des Auteurs Dramatiques) agreed to donate 500 francs immediately. With this, plus individual donations to the trust fund which were quickly forthcoming, it became possible to move Villiers to a residence in Nogent-sur-Marne on the outskirts of Paris. There he would find the fresh air and rest prescribed by another doctor friend of Méry Laurent's, Dr Edmond Fournier, whom Mallarmé had wanted consulted.

In May, thanks largely to the beneficial effect of country air and rest, after an alarming initial crisis brought on by the move, Villiers' condition seemed to improve. Towards the middle of the month, however, Mallarmé became extremely alarmed and visited Villiers in Nogent in the company of Dr Robin, who told him next day that Villiers had an incurable cancer of the stomach.

By a cruel irony, which, had he but realized the true gravity of his plight, Villiers would have been the first to appreciate, while this terrible news was being broken to Mallarmé, Paris was in the midst of the most extravagant celebrations. The Universal Fair of 1889 had just opened, celebrating not only the centenary of the 1789 Revolution but France's emergence as a great colonial and commercial power. No expense had been spared. Displays and exhibitions of all kinds occupied what was virtually a sprawling city on the Champ de Mars under the watchful eye of the newly completed Eiffel Tower. People flocked to gaze fascinated at the latest invention, electrical power, thanks to which, every evening at 11 pm, an extravaganza of gaily coloured fountains was switched on, to the astonishment and delight of the assembled multitude.

For his part, Mallarmé was in no mood to join in the festivities. Asked by a reporter to make a comment on the Eiffel Tower, he was only able to reply, with a superb and devastating irony that was probably wasted on his interlocutor: 'The Eiffel Tower surpasses my greatest expectations!'[27]

By mid-July, as Mallarmé had feared, Villiers' condition worsened. Thanks to Mallarmé's contacts with the ever-amenable Henri Roujon, funds were obtained from the Ministry of Education which enabled Villiers to be transferred to a hospice in Paris run by the Frères Saint-Jean-de-Dieu. At Villiers' request, his whereabouts were kept secret and revealed only to Mallarmé, Huysmans, Dierx and Méry Laurent. Mallarmé's initial concern was that Villiers might find out how ill he really was, so he got Dr Fournier to ask the physician at the hospice to conceal from Villiers the fact that he had cancer.

By the end of July, Dr Robin informed Mallarmé that he did not think that Villiers would survive another month. As he was then spending most of his time in Valvins, Mallarmé arranged that, in an emergency, Huysmans would contact him by telegram. Within a week, the emergency arose. Realizing that Villiers was now close to death, Huysmans contacted Mallarmé to see what could be done to safeguard the interests of the latter's illegitimate son, Totor, for whom the authorities would do nothing unless Villiers officially recognized him by marrying his mother. Mallarmé was given the unenviable task of broaching the subject with Villiers. He went to the hospice, but found him unwilling to contemplate marriage for the moment. Mallarmé did however obtain from him an agreement to request a medical certificate which would allow for a marriage *in extremis* should his condition deteriorate. The problem was that normally ten days' notice would be required for the posting of the banns, and it was doubtful if Villiers would last that long.

In the event, a marriage *in extremis* was held on 14 August. Mallarmé, Huysmans and Dierx were witnesses, along with a person replacing Coppée, who, at the last minute, declined to attend. Méry Laurent was not present but, showing the same kindness and sensitivity as during Edouard Manet's last illness, she provided not only the ring for the ceremony but a bottle of Veuve Clicquot with which to toast the bride and groom.

Four days later, at 11 pm in the evening of 18 August 1889, Villiers died. He was fifty-one years old. The telegram informing Mallarmé that he was dying reached Valvins too late. He dashed to Paris to be by his old friend's bedside only to find that he was already dead. When Villiers' will was found, it named Mallarmé, along with Huysmans, as his literary executor. This involved a considerable workload, as Villiers had left not only his papers but his entire estate in a terrible state of confusion. Mallarmé spent days in Valvins reading manuscripts to see what could be salvaged in order to provide some income for Villiers' wife and child. For the next six months he and Huysmans devoted most of their free time to ensuring that the latter were financially secure, successfully obtaining a pension for Totor from the Ministry of Education and negotiating as best they could with Villiers' numerous publishers. They also managed to put together a version of Villiers' play *Axel*, which was eventually published in mid-January 1890. By that time, Mallarmé, who was also administering the trust fund set up by Villiers' friends and keeping detailed accounts for Villiers' widow, had grown weary of the constant misunderstandings between himself and Marie Villiers. At the end of January, having settled her affairs to the best of his ability, he asked her not to contact him any more.

Mallarmé's final tribute to Villiers was the lecture tour he gave in Belgium a few months later. Given the admiration he felt for Villiers, he was bitterly disappointed by the meagre and niggardly way the latter's death was covered in the Paris press. A year or two earlier, he had been invited by Octave Maus to address the Literary and Artistic Circle in Brussels, but had had to refuse the offer on that occasion because he had no lecture ready. In November 1889 therefore, Mallarmé wrote to Maus suggesting that, for an acceptable fee, he could provide a lecture on Villiers early in the following year.

By the time Mallarmé left for Brussels on 10 February 1890, a whistle-stop tour of six venues had been arranged. The first

lecture was delivered at eight o'clock the following evening to
the Literary and Artistic Circle of Brussels. Next morning, on
his way to the second stop on the tour, Mallarmé sent a hurried
telegram to his wife and daughter: 'FIRST LECTURE LASTS TWO
AND A HALF HOURS. STUPEFACTION. MALLARMÉ.'[28] A fuller
account of the proceedings followed in a letter dispatched later
the same day. From this it would appear that he had still been
working on the text of his lecture when the carriage called to
take him to the auditorium. Dressing in less than five minutes,
he had mounted the rostrum with one of his shoe-laces
undone. 'I did not read the lecture, I bellowed it,' he wrote to
Marie and Geneviève. 'The hall was as enormous as the
Madeleine Church. The audience were as patient as angels but
they were not amused. They were subdued, the topic being a
sad one. I was given the obligatory bravos at the end.'[29]

In fact, the evening had gone much worse than Mallarmé
was here admitting. Written in his mature prose style, thus
something more akin to a prose poem than a straightforward
lecture, it was incomprehensible to most of his audience. A
fortnight later, the Brussels magazine *L'Art moderne* carried the
following article:

> After M. Mallarmé's lecture, the administrative committee of the
> Literary and Artistic Circle of Brussels held an emergency meeting
> last Sunday at 2 pm. The president and organizer were taken to task.
> In vain they pointed out that M. Mallarmé is an example of French
> Literature and a bold innovator who is universally admired. They
> were told that in that case all that would have been required was to
> put him on stage for fifteen minutes like a comic turn and to devote
> the rest of the evening to Messieurs Coquelin, Frédérix, Dreyfus or
> Mademoiselle Thénard. In short, apart from two abstentions, there
> was a unanimous vote that in future guest lecturers would be obliged
> not only to give a test performance in front of a selected committee,
> but to restrict themselves to subjects which could be understood by
> the usual audience.

For the rest of the tour, Mallarmé sensibly omitted large
sections of his original text, reducing the lecture to just over

an hour. Even so, despite the positive gloss which he attempted to put on it in his regular bulletins back to his wife and daughter, the remainder of the lecture tour was not a success. In Antwerp, an army colonel who was a billiards fanatic abandoned his cue for a few moments to listen to Mallarmé's opening remarks. Within minutes he left the auditorium noisily shouting: 'That man is either drunk or mad.' The *Ghent Journal* described the lecture as 'execrable'. 'There is no hiding the fact,' they remarked. 'M. Mallarmé was scarcely understood by anyone except for a few rare listeners used to such a complicated and convoluted style. Even they had to admit that it was not a decent sort of style to use for talking to the general public. There is an enormous difference between a book that you can read in relaxed circumstances and a speech which you have to digest instantaneously. Our poet forgot that.'

For his part, Mallarmé was not unaware of the effect he was having upon his audiences. When he copied out part of his lecture for *L'Art moderne*, he added a brief covering note in which, not without humour, he described the opening section as 'A Preamble (*Cave canem*) slightly exaggerating the serious tone of the rest, with a pause at the end to allow those who found themselves lost, time to gain the exit.'[30] The whole experience did little to counter Mallarmé's growing reputation for obscurity, and in the circumstances he wisely decided not to give a public reading of the lecture when he returned to Paris. Instead he delivered it to a small group of carefully chosen people in the home of Berthe Morisot at the end of February. Even here, certain members of his audience encountered some difficulties. The reaction of Degas was somewhat similar to that of the billiards-playing Belgian colonel. During the reading he constantly fidgeted, making no attempt to disguise his obvious boredom and total incomprehension.

The weeks which Mallarmé and Méry Laurent spent together as they tended to the needs of the ailing Villiers brought them to an important turning-point in their own relationship. Méry, it will be recalled, had briefly allowed Mallarmé to become her lover, before requesting that their relationship revert to what it had been before. Just a few days before Villiers died, Mallarmé wrote to Méry thanking her for her support and expressing his gratitude for all the kindness that she had shown both to himself and to his friend:

> Your gentle presence envelops me, more than ever before. You are a unique woman, Peacock, you produce such new, exquisite and tender feelings in me that it seems to me that I have never known you as I do now, after all the years, do you hear? Unless it is that every day your charm increases, which is quite possible. I have for you the finest feelings I can have for anyone. You really are very beautiful. Love M.[31]

Sensing that Mallarmé was dangerously close to requesting a resumption of their physical relationship, Méry invited him to visit her in September in Royat, where he had spent a fortnight the previous year with herself and Dr Evans. Mallarmé returned to Valvins two days later, and from the letter he then dispatched to Royat it is clear that Méry and he had had a full discussion about their future:

> I said nothing when, this winter, you broke off an enchantment which was taking me over body and soul. I guessed, knowing how kind you are, that you had a very serious reason and I respected the fact that you did not wish to explain it to me.
>   You can imagine that that is why I did not wish to come to Royat, not for anything. With my new feelings for you I began to think that I had made the right decision and that there was no sense in suffering for nothing. But how difficult it is to resist you! . . . I came and spent two days filled with silences, with no abandon, when every one of my advances was rebuffed by yourself contrary to your true feelings. What an atrocious two days!
>   I understand, my dearest, just how absurd all this is. My whole existence, bearing the fibres of my being through an excessive literary dream, means that I can only settle for either this heightened sensitivity or indifference. I have sometimes steeled myself to being indifferent, as you understood, gearing myself to lose you totally.

You welcome our good old friendship of the past. I think I have such a feeling and I think that I shall find for you who wanted it to bind us until we die, a way of showing that I have discovered it again without the excuse of sadness or illness. You know, perhaps your current contentment, and, I swear it, just to know at this very minute that you are happy makes me . . . No, it is so difficult to describe – let us say that silent congratulations, believe me, are transmitted from me to you. No man like me can do any more than withdraw. It is not so easy when we see each other every day and so, dearest, we shall have to see each other less.

What do you expect! In spite of everything you are simple and uncomplicated (and for me superb). It is yourself entirely that I adore. My heart, I do not know what that means. My mind, well I use that to understand my art and I have loved a few friends with it. Come now, we scarcely have a thought in common about anything but it is wonderful how your attraction for me as a woman survives all that. Such a miraculous occurrence is what is frequently called love. Apart from that, what is there? Oh yes true devotion. You shall have that.

You are right. Too many things separate our lives for them to be brought together without us having to be what we are not. Let us see each other less and never again in that intimacy which, if it cannot remain total between two privileged people, is a source of unease.

A strong friendship, one which is free of such things, can bear that and that will be our test. Have no doubts. Whenever you call, I shall be there . . .

In the end you were right to have spoken to me as you did, like a true friend, or you would be forever constrained, ending up as you did being nothing but on the defensive around me, always ready to repel any act of tenderness which nonetheless you were provoking. What torture it was for me! Why did we ever meet!

I have tried (without your lightness of touch) to reply in the same calm, friendly tone in which you will discover some bitterness. I have avoided any regrets which, if expressed, sound like a form of reproach. I have nothing but gratitude, Méry. Thank you.

The only conclusion that you can come to is that the way I looked at you was unreasonable. Well you caused me to look that way. Offer me your forehead and, you know, a source of joy for me at this moment just before I kiss it, is the knowledge that I have been able to tell you the truth.

> Goodnight, Peacock.
> Your Stéphane.[32]

The death of Villiers de l'Isle-Adam greatly affected Mallarmé. Henri de Régnier, who visited him one evening towards the end of January 1890 as he was working on notes for the lecture he was about to give in Brussels, was quite shocked by the change he could see in his old friend. Although still only forty-eight, Mallarmé suddenly seemed to have aged:

> I found Mallarmé alone – the table was strewn with Villiers' books lying open amid preparatory notes for the Belgian lecture – he was more irritated than ever with his lack of time and with 'these twin diseases, insomnia and the college'. He has never seemed more ravaged and more ageing, rather than old, than he did in the semi-darkness of that long evening when we worked together. The flame of his deep, beautiful eyes expressed an indescribable sadness and, amid the virtual destruction of the man with his grave, deep and gentle voice, the power of his intelligence was truly impressive.[33]

The departure from Paris a few months later of Berthe Morisot and her husband only added to Mallarmé's gloom and despondency, as did the news, in June of that year, that his old friend Philippe Burty had died. Mallarmé published hardly anything that year. Apart from the text of his lecture on Villiers, the only thing to appear was a piece of light occasional verse which Whistler had requested for the English magazine *The Whirlwind*. In fact, ever since the Deman edition of his Poe translations two years earlier, Mallarmé had published very little. The only new work, undertaken primarily for the welcome additional revenue which it generated, was a series of amusing verses to accompany drawings of typical Parisian street scenes by J.-F. Raffaeli.

Needless to say, during this time Mallarmé had continued to work on his personal project of the Book. He had even talked about it in quite positive terms on occasion to friends. One Tuesday evening in January 1888, for example, he described to Henri de Régnier how he envisaged readings of the Book taking place: 'At Mallarmé's. He spoke to me about the project of a lecture in which he would explain his book to

24 people, 12 men and 12 women. He arrives on stage just like a passer-by, expressing astonishment that there is no piano available, and takes out the book . . .'[34] A week later, thanking Verhaeren for introducing him to the publisher Deman, Mallarmé again made a reference to these lectures, describing what he called his 'grand project for the year' – which, he wrote, was 'to appear in public around October, you hear that, and to juggle with the contents of a book'.[35] By June of that same year, however, these special lectures, conceived as a form of advance publicity for the Book, had been rescheduled for the following winter.[36] Mallarmé mentioned them again once or twice to Régnier at the beginning of the following year, and some ideas for a ballet discussed with the *Mardistes* in March 1889 show that his theatrical project was still very much on his mind.[37] By that time, however, Villiers de l'Isle-Adam had become very seriously ill, causing Mallarmé, yet again, to postpone his own plans.

As the school holidays ended in the late summer of 1890 and everyone busied themselves with the annual ritual of closing down the house in Valvins, for the first time in his life Mallarmé felt little inclination to return to the capital. Writing to Berthe Morisot, he revealed that he had been trying hard not to remember what the date was so as to delude himself into believing that the sudden spell of decent weather meant that the summer holidays were really only just beginning. How he wished, he told her, that he could be like the young model she had mentioned in her letters who was posing naked under a sheepskin cover. 'I am sorry not to be of an age to be able to wear such a costume myself,' he added wearily, 'so that I might have an excuse for never, never returning to the city. . . . I have spent a whole month feeling unwell and exhausted, the best that my mind could rise to was fishing.'[38] He struck a similar despondent note a week later in a letter to Octave Mirbeau: 'The winter is about to return with its obligations and with absolutely no possibility of escaping from them, even for a moment.'[39]

The Paris to which Mallarmé returned with such reluctance in the autumn of 1890 was about to enter one of its more flamboyant and self-indulgent periods. This was the beginning of the banquet years when any and every event, no matter how great or small, provided an excuse for large numbers of people to gather together in a hotel or restaurant and consume vast quantities of food, wine and cigars (for, needless to say, these banquets were an exclusively male preserve).

One of the most famous of these public banquets, and the one which, to a large extent, established the vogue for the others which followed, was the so-called Symbolist Banquet organized by Henri de Régnier and Maurice Barrès at the request of Jean Moréas to celebrate and promote the publication of Moréas' book of poems, *Le Pèlerin passionné*. Régnier and Barrès had originally intended to invite Paul Verlaine to preside over the festivities. As the author of *Les Poètes maudits* and co-originator, along with Léon Vanier, of *Les Hommes d'Aujourd'hui*, Verlaine was the obvious choice, especially as Vanier, the publisher of Moréas' volume of poetry, was also Verlaine's publisher. Verlaine however was still recovering from one of his periodic and lengthy stays in hospital. Mallarmé therefore was approached in December by Régnier and agreed to read a toast to Moréas on Verlaine's behalf.

Over eighty people attended the banquet, which was held in the Hôtel des Sociétés Savantes in the first week of February 1891. Octave Mirbeau, Odilon Redon and Charles Morice sat next to Mallarmé and opposite Jean Moréas and Anatole France. After what was reportedly an indifferent meal during which Mallarmé studiously spoke to Mirbeau and Moréas sat twiddling his moustache, Mallarmé rose and delivered the following, somewhat ironic toast, given that by then Verlaine and Moréas were not on speaking terms: 'To Jean Moréas, the first person ever to make a meal the outcome of a book of verse, and who has brought together to celebrate *Le Pèlerin passionné* promising newcomers and their ancestors, in the name of our dear absent Verlaine, other comrades in Arts and several journalists as well as of myself, I willingly propose this toast.'

The main significance of the banquet from Mallarmé's point of view was that overnight he was transformed into a celebrity. The banquet was widely reported in the popular press and created such a stir that a week later *Le Figaro* published an article introducing its president to the general public. Mallarmé's reputation among his peers had reached a similar high point, confirmed by the findings of an enquiry undertaken a month later by Jules Huret for the *Echo de Paris* into recent developments in literature. Mallarmé was one of the first to be interviewed, and in a poll taken among the sixty-four contributors, he received the largest number of votes, more in fact than Victor Hugo himself.

This was probably the high point of Mallarmé's celebrity, attracting to his door foreign visitors to the capital such as Oscar Wilde and Stefan George. It was from this time onwards also that the *mardis* became the focal point of the Parisian literary and artistic scene. A whole new generation of young writers joined those who regularly made the journey up the narrow staircase to Mallarmé's modest flat in the rue de Rome. This last and arguably most prestigious generation of *Mardistes* was led by Pierre Louÿs, who originally came to seek Mallarmé's approval for the review *La Conque* which he was about to launch but who subsequently introduced the older poet to his young friends André Gide, Paul Valéry and Camille Mauclair. Claude Debussy, who was to befriend all of the latter, had already become a *Mardiste* by this time.

Many of these young men, especially Pierre Louÿs and Paul Valéry, would come to occupy a special place in Mallarmé's affections. For the moment, however, it was someone else upon whom his attention focused. At the beginning of that same year, 1891, Charles Morice, whose friendship with Mallarmé stretched back to the time when Verlaine had asked him to call and collect the photograph of Manet's portrait which was required for *Les Hommes d'Aujourd'hui*, mentioned the difficulties facing one of his painter acquaintances, Paul Gauguin, who needed to raise some money in order to be able to go and live for a while in Tahiti, where he was convinced he would be able to produce the kind of work he found impossible to achieve in France. Mallarmé was both sympathetic to Gauguin's situation and impressed by the concern of Morice, for whom he had the greatest respect (interviewed by Huret a month later, he would name Morice as one of the rising young writers of his generation). It was agreed therefore that some publicity was required to boost the sales at an auction of Gauguin's paintings designed to raise the capital upon which he would survive for the next few years.

Mallarmé, who as yet knew Gauguin only by reputation, wrote to Octave Mirbeau:

> One of my young colleagues who is a talented and kind fellow and who is a friend of the ceramic artist, painter and sculptor, Gauguin, you know who he is! has begged me to put to you the following request, as the only person in Paris capable of achieving anything. That rare artist, who, I believe, is spared few mercies in Paris, feels the need to be able to concentrate in isolation and virtual savagery. He wants to set off for Tahiti, to build a hut and live amongst what he has left of himself over there, to work afresh and become truly himself. He needs 6,000 francs for a few years until he returns. The successful sale of his current works can provide him with that sum. Except that what is required is an article, not on the sale itself, we are not talking about anything commercial. Just something to draw attention to the strange case of this refugee from civilization.[40]

Mallarmé had not chosen Mirbeau by chance. Although he moved in avant-garde circles, the latter was well known and accepted in establishment newspapers with large circulations such as *Le Figaro*. Mallarmé also realized, however, that to insert such an article might prove difficult, as he told Morice and Gauguin when he met them some ten days later. 'Let's hope that *Le Figaro* will not sabotage our project!' he wrote to Mirbeau the same day.[41] His fears proved justified. François Magnard, editor of *Le Figaro*, objected to space being devoted to someone with a reputation like Gauguin's, and Mirbeau was forced to seek hospitality for his article elsewhere, publishing it in *L'Echo de Paris* a week before the sale of the thirty paintings, which took place in the Hotel Drouot on 23 February. Mallarmé attended the auction. Present too were Méry Laurent and Degas, both of whom bought some paintings. All in all, the sale raised some 9,800 francs, much more than Gauguin had estimated he needed. 'I have just come out of the auction room,' Mallarmé wrote excitedly to Mirbeau. 'It all went terribly well.'[42]

Exactly one month later, a celebration banquet was held in the Café Voltaire to bid farewell to the painter. Forty guests were assembled, many of whom were either *Mardistes* or Mallarmé's friends. At the end of the meal, Mallarmé was asked to give a farewell toast. 'Gentlemen,' he began, 'in order to speed up the proceedings, let us drink to the return of Paul Gauguin, but not before we express our admiration for his superb conscience, which, at the height of his talent, summons him to exile, so that he may re-immerse himself in those distant lands and in himself.' Toasts followed to Mirbeau and Roger Marx, another young art-critic friend of Mallarmé's, both of whom had written favourably in the press. Mallarmé's sonnet in honour of Edgar Allan Poe was read out as a fitting tribute to all misunderstood artists. Gauguin at last rose and spoke: 'I love you all,' he said, 'and I am very moved. I therefore cannot say much or even speak well. Several among us have produced the great works that are known to everybody. I drink to these works as I drink to all future works.' By the time the proceedings broke up, it was well past midnight.[43]

Two days after he attended the Gauguin banquet, Mallarmé applied for three months' leave of absence from the Collège Rollin. His request was granted, once again thanks to the strenuous efforts of Charles Seignobos. Although his intention in applying for the leave had been to rest and, if possible, to get on with his own work, he soon found himself caught up once more in the activities of his younger associates. In fact, at the end of the Gauguin banquet, the dinner guests were informed of a coming event with which he was already closely involved. It was announced that the following month, the Théâtre d'Art, run by Paul Fort, would be putting on a special matinée performance to raise money for Paul Verlaine and Paul Gauguin.

Mallarmé had for some time taken a keen interest in Paul Fort's career, ever since the day when, some eighteen months earlier, Fort had asked him to lend his name to the honorary committee of the new Théâtre Mixte, which he was founding as an experimental theatre similar in aims to the earlier Théâtre Libre created by Antoine. Mallarmé was a great admirer of Antoine's work. He had been a regular spectator at the Théâtre Libre, having in fact attended the inaugural performance in 1887 and written about it in *La Revue indépendante*. He had readily agreed therefore to offer Paul Fort his patronage. Invited a few months later to contribute something to the repertoire of the new company, he had suggested a theatrical version of the *Faun*. Writing to Deman in late November 1890, he mentioned that he was currently working on a definitive version of the poem which would be accompanied by some general remarks on the theatre and precise instructions for a stage performance of the work with a musical introduction.[44] The project contained the first germs of an idea which Debussy would later translate into his celebrated *Prélude à l'après-midi d'un Faune*. However, it was never completed, and although announced in the press, it had to be replaced at the last minute by a reading of a much earlier poem, 'Le Guignon'.

By the time this reading took place in March 1891, the Théâtre Mixte had changed its name to Théâtre d'Art, and Mallarmé had agreed to be its honorary director.

For the benefit performance in aid of Verlaine and Gauguin, he was asked to produce a short introduction to Poe and a translation of *The Raven* which would be accompanied by some of Manet's drawings. Paul Fort's objective in this gala concert, namely to bring together in a single performance the work of poets, playwrights and painters, was one which immediately won Mallarmé's approval as well as arousing his curiosity. He eagerly followed the preparations, travelling in from Valvins to attend rehearsals, including the final dress rehearsal and press review performance on 20 May.

A luxurious 24-page souvenir programme had been produced in which Mallarmé's translation was preceded by the text of his commemorative sonnet to Poe and illustrated by reproductions of two of Manet's drawings which had been used for the luxury edition of *The Raven* produced by Lesclide. It was altogether a delightful and elegantly produced brochure, with which Mallarmé was greatly impressed. He was much less so, however, by what he witnessed at the dress rehearsal. Much to his annoyance, Paul Fort had paid little attention to the precise instructions he had been given, with the result that the atmosphere which Mallarmé had specifically wanted to create was totally destroyed. Bitterly disappointed and angry at the lack of respect shown, not to himself, but to the work of Poe, he decided to boycott the actual performance and returned to Valvins in a rare fit of rage. From there, in a remarkably sharp letter to Paul Fort, he explained precisely why he no longer wanted to be associated with the Théâtre d'Art.

The row which Paul Fort's benefit performance had produced was not an isolated incident. The publication in *L'Echo de Paris* of Jules Huret's enquiry into the state of French literature gave rise to a whole series of arguments and misunderstandings which divided the literary community of Paris that summer. As he busied himself in the relative calm and seclusion of Valvins discussing with Deman the details of a new edition of his poems[45] and concentrating at last on his own work, Mallarmé received an urgent telegram from Catulle Mendès requesting that he intervene in a dispute which had arisen directly out of the publication of the Huret enquiry. He specifically wanted Mallarmé to state publicly that he, Mendès, was incapable of acting in the manner of which he had been accused by Vielé-Griffin, namely of having had Huret remove from the final version of his text some flattering remarks which Mallarmé had made about another young poet, Gustave Kahn. The whole episode was in fact the result of a genuine mistake which Mallarmé tried to rectify by allowing Mendès to publish a letter absolving him of any blame. Despite Mallarmé's efforts at conciliation, the whole affair culminated in an absurd duel in which Vielé-Griffin was slightly wounded.

So when Mallarmé contemplated the thought of returning to Paris later that same month, it is not surprising that his feelings were once again very mixed. He was still attracted by the Thursday evening dinners which Berthe Morisot had resumed, he told her, and by the prospect of attending the occasional concert on a Sunday afternoon. 'Otherwise,' he added, 'Paris doesn't mean much to me.'[46] As he reflected upon a year which had begun with a childish and public wrangle between Verlaine and Moréas and which had just led to a farcical sword fight between one of his oldest friends and one of his favourite *Mardistes*, Mallarmé was greatly saddened. Mindful of all this, and of his own less than glorious part in some of the year's more colourful events, he made an appeal to Henri de Régnier, who as joint organizer of the Moréas banquet was well placed to understand its origins:

I am on the eve of returning to Paris, somewhat refreshed and at the very least cleansed by river water and fresh air of anything that resembles flag-waving or squabbles over the names of literary groups.

No more banquets, eh! No more patronage. Let us all be good friends who do not always agree. The year which is ending will be called the year of blunders in our lives.[47]

'The world of literature is becoming very strange,' he ended sadly, 'and there is something almost indecent in appearing to be connected with it in any way whatsoever.' Clearly, as each year went by, Mallarmé was becoming more and more disenchanted with a world which, long ago, had seemed so incredibly attractive when distance kept him from it. Such disillusionment did not prevent him, however, from putting his recently acquired celebrity and considerable reputation at the disposal of his many friends.

Thanks to that growing reputation, and to his contacts in the art world, in particular his friendships with the art critic, museum inspector and enthusiastic young *Mardiste* Roger Marx, and with his old ally Henri Roujon, who happened to have just been appointed director of Fine Arts in the Ministry of Education and Culture, Mallarmé was especially well placed to help his various painter friends. The first of these to benefit was Whistler. Ever since the death of Villiers, he had become one of Mallarmé's most valued companions, with his wicked sense of humour and strange nervous laugh, which Henri de Régnier described as being quite independent of the joke he was telling but seeming to be added in an attempt to crown it like 'a fiery coloured feather stuck on a strange yet elegant felt hat'.[48]

Whistler provided Mallarmé with that curious blend of total irreverence and at the same time absolute commitment to art which he had found so irresistible in the persons of Villiers and Manet. When, for example, in November 1891 Whistler learned that his arch-rival and enemy Oscar Wilde was due to attend one of Mallarmé's *mardis*, he sent Mallarmé an amusing telegram warning him to beware of the Irishman's legendary and magpie-like capacity for stealing others' thoughts and *bons mots*: 'WARN DISCIPLES PRECAUTION FAMILIARITY FATAL KEEP

TIGHT GRIP ON PEARLS OF WISDOM GOOD EVENING WHISTLER.'[49]
'The evening was as dull as you would have wished,' Mallarmé replied:

> and probably would have been even without your telegram, which I kept thinking about and laughing at inwardly. Most of all, though, my dear friend, I missed you because, as I believed, in common with my two ladies, you were due to dine with us this evening. I had even gone to the trouble of catching some pike just beneath my window out in the country which we were obliged to serve up to ourselves alone. Out there in the country I was annoyed when I realized that I was spending the last two days of your current trip without seeing you, because, Whistler, your presence in Paris is one of my rare reasons for a celebration. Let us forget your masterpieces for the moment, you appeared in my life a few years ago (and I like to count each one) as the very personification of the artist and you have added to my joy by becoming a precious friend.[50]

When Whistler eventually settled in Paris a year or so later, his little one-storey house in the rue du Bac with its pale blue and white lacquered door and blue and white painted interior, spartanly furnished with the occasional Japanese screen and rug, counted – along with Méry Laurent's two residences – among Mallarmé's favourite haunts in Paris. He would go there, frequently accompanied by Henri de Régnier, after attending the Sunday afternoon concert.[51] Before that however, with the connivance of Gustave Geffroy, art critic of *Le Temps*, and the help of his own friends and trusty allies Roger Marx, Théodore Duret and Henri Roujon, Mallarmé was able to persuade the French government to acquire Whistler's *Portrait of My Mother* for the Luxembourg Museum, with the promise that it would later be transferred to the Louvre. The selling price was admittedly much less than Whistler had originally requested, but this was compensated for by the fact that he was offered the coveted ribbon of a *chevalier de la Légion d'honneur*, which Mallarmé handed over to him in person in February 1892.

Whistler expressed his gratitude by doing a pencil drawing

of Mallarmé which the latter used later that year as the frontispiece of his anthology *Vers et prose*, and which, incidentally, he considered to be by far the best portrait ever done of himself by any artist.[52] Whistler also put Mallarmé in touch with W. E. Henley, editor in chief of *The National Observer*, with the happy result that as of March 1892 eleven articles by Mallarmé began to appear somewhat unusually in their original French in that newspaper. Whistler also tried to interest first Heinemann and later Osgood & McIlvaine in publishing a selection of the amusing little quatrains with which Mallarmé frequently addressed his letters, but despite the fact that this project was discused in some detail and for quite some time, and although Mallarmé went to the trouble of preparing a manuscript, the project eventually fell through.

Mallarmé also successfully deployed his allies in the Ministry of Arts to persuade the State to buy Renoir's *Young Girls at the Piano* and a painting by Monet which was selected by the Minister of the Arts himself, Léon Bourgeois, during a visit he made to the artist's studio in Giverny in May of that year in the company of Mallarmé, Roger Marx and Henri Roujon. In recognition of Mallarmé's kindness, Renoir added his portrait to all the others which Mallarmé had gradually accumulated over the years.[53] Indeed, Camille Mauclair's description of Mallarmé's flat as he knew it at roughly around this time reads today like the catalogue of a prestigious art gallery:

It was Mallarmé himself who came and opened the door for me and, after we passed through an extremely narrow antechamber, he introduced us into a room which served both as a dining-room and a drawing-room. In one corner of the room there was a porcelain stove, a few pieces of walnut furniture and a lamp suspended over a central table on which lay a Chinese bowl filled with tobacco. There were several very beautiful things on the walls: a river scene by Claude Monet, a sketch by Manet representing Hamlet and the Ghost in front of Elsinore, the little portrait of Mallarmé by Manet which is now in the Louvre, a watercolour by Berthe Morisot, a pastel painting of flowers by Odilon Redon . . . On a sideboard, there was a plaster statue by Rodin depicting a naked nymph caught by a faun and an orange-wood log out of which Paul Gauguin had sculpted the profile of a Maori which Mallarmé, to tease me, said bore a remarkable resemblance to myself.[54]

Mallarmé was equally generous with his time in other ways, agreeing that year to join the Banville and Baudelaire memorial committees when they were formed, just as later he would agree to become president of the Verlaine memorial committee. Furthermore, despite his earlier comments to Régnier about patronage, he continued to follow with interest the careers of certain of his young friends and to help them in whatever way he could. When required by Camille Mauclair in March 1892 to lend his support to a group of young dramatists who wanted to put on an ambitious programme of new plays at the Odéon theatre, he gave the venture his wholehearted support. He likewise attended and promoted the first performance of the second two plays of Edouard Dujardin's *Antonia* trilogy, and wrote favourable reviews of them in his articles for the *National Observer*, despite the fact that the performance of the first of these two plays was exceptionally rowdy, forcing Dujardin to bring down the curtain and remind the audience that they were his guests!

Above all, however, Mallarmé did everything possible to promote the career of a young Belgian poet and playwright, Maurice Maeterlinck, to whom he had first been introduced in Ghent in February 1890 during his lecture tour. Greatly impressed by the two volumes of poetry which Maeterlinck had soon sent him, Mallarmé brought him to the attention of Octave Mirbeau, who in August of that year published an enthusiastic article on Maeterlinck's first play in *Le Figaro*, heralding him as a worthy successor to Shakespeare. 'I do not know anything about Maeterlinck,' Mirbeau wrote, 'I do not know where he comes from or what he is like. Whether he is rich or poor, young or old. The only thing I do know is that nobody is more unknown than he is, and I also know that he has produced a masterpiece which is good enough to immortalize his name and have it blessed by all those who are hungry for what is beautiful and great. Monsieur Maeterlinck has given us the most genial work of our time, the most extraordinary and the most naïve also and comparable – dare I say it – indeed more beautiful to all that is beautiful in Shakespeare. This work is called *Princess Maleine*.'[55] The article, which made Maeterlinck famous overnight, also unleashed a backlash of anti-Belgian sentiment in the press, so much so in fact that a few months later Mallarmé felt it advisable to write to Maeterlinck to calm his anxieties.

It was against this background of resentment and hostility that Camille Mauclair and Lugné-Poë decided to put on a performance of Maeterlinck's *Pelléas et Mélisande* which had originally been intended for Paul Fort's Théâtre d'Art. After much wrangling with Paul Fort and his co-directress, Tola Dorian, they obtained the right to perform the play and asked Mallarmé to offer his support by publicizing the performance among his friends and sending a letter of introduction to Octave Mirbeau. 'Well done, my dear friend,' Mallarmé replied to Mauclair, 'and how well you have done to clear a path among such wreckage and rebuild the whole enterprise. It goes without saying as far as the small number of people whom I see are concerned, namely our friends, that I shall be eloquent on this subject. As for the note for Mirbeau, for whom your initiative concerning a work by Maeterlinck would suffice, take it, whether you use it or not.'[56]

Hailed as a major event in the renaissance of the theatre in an article in *L'Echo de Paris* of 9 May 1893 bearing Mirbeau's name, but in all probability written by Mauclair himself, the performance took place a week later in the Théâtre des Bouffes Parisiennes. True to his word, Mallarmé was present at this historic occasion. He was accompanied by Théodore Duret, Henri de Régnier, Whistler and Claude Debussy, who would go on to write an opera based on the play. In addition,

Mallarmé published one of the few favourable reviews of the play, which appeared in *The National Observer* of 10 June 1893. When the article was reprinted in the Ghent magazine *Le Réveil* three months later, it attracted an interesting comment from Maeterlinck himself. 'It is a strange thing,' he informed Mallarmé, 'but ever since you wrote about *Pelléas*, he almost lives as a person for me – and he knows in which palace to take refuge on the days when I am on the point of denying his existence.'[57]

When Maeterlinck's letter of thanks eventually reached Mallarmé, it found him in a particularly buoyant mood. This was in part because he was then entertaining in Valvins an old friend, Berthe Morisot, who along with her daughter Julie Manet had come to paint, relax and rest and generally recover from the death of her husband earlier that spring.[58] As a consequence, boating trips, picnics, long walks in the forest and leisurely evening dinners in the open air had become the order of the day. The main reason why Mallarmé was in such good spirits, however, was that for the first time in his life he knew that at the end of that particular summer he would not be returning to Paris to face any more classes. At the start of the previous academic session, in October 1892, he had decided that he would retire at the end of the year. 'I have so much to do,' he admitted to a distant friend, 'and although I am old, my dreams have come to nothing, except for the occasional hint which I have dropped in conversations.'[59] At the time of the annual inspection in February 1893, he had therefore announced that he would like to retire as of the beginning of November, when he would complete the thirty years' service required to obtain a state pension.

That same month, Mallarmé had been the guest of honour at one of the series of literary (and frequently rowdy) banquets organized by the magazine *La Plume*. For the occasion, he had written a special sonnet thanking his young friends for their continued support and suggesting that, even though he was now giving way to a younger generation, he had never lost sight of his original goal. It is a deliciously ironic piece which amusingly exploits the visual similarity between the white tablecloth of the banquet hall and the sails of an imaginary boat. Yet from behind the humour and the wit, much of it directed against himself, as is always the case in Mallarmé's best poems, there emerges a serious statement about the heroic gesture of the solitary and determined artist. It is not surprising therefore that, when he later came to put together a popular edition of his collected verse, he placed it at the beginning of the collection as a provocative and defiant introduction to his work. It then had the title 'Salut', a deliberate pun on the greeting 'Hello there' and the noun 'Salvation', thus stressing the deliberate ambiguity of the poem:

> Rien, cette écume, vierge vers
> A ne désigner que la coupe;
> Telle loin se noie une troupe
> De sirènes mainte à l'envers.
>
> Nous naviguons, ô mes divers
> Amis, moi déjà sur la poupe
> Vous l'avant fastueux qui coupe
> Le flot de foudres et d'hivers.
>
> Une ivresse belle m'engage
> Sans craindre même son tangage
> De porter debout ce salut
>
> Solitude, récif étoile
> A n'importe ce qui valut
> Le blanc souci de notre toile.
>
> [Nothing, mere froth, virgin verse
> If I am referring to the cup;
> Just as in the distance a troop
> Of many sirens drowns upside-down.
>
> We are sailing, O my friends of many
> Kinds, myself already at the stern,
> You the glittering prow which cuts
> Through the waves of lightning and ice.

A heady drunkenness leads me
Without fear of keeling over
To stand up and make this toast

To solitude, rocks and star
To whatever it was which occasioned
The white care of our cloth.

Mallarmé's decision to retire was not unexpected. His own health, as well as his wife's, was beginning to cause him serious concern. In the months which followed his first reading of the above poem, he battled against a harrowing attack of influenza which totally undermined his already weakened constitution. Henri de Régnier, who visited him shortly after he had begun to recover, could not forget what he had looked like at the height of his illness:

> He has recovered from that terrible flu which, the last time I saw him, in his sunny bedroom, with a grey shawl over his shoulders, had as it were blackened his face and made his hair look tousled. It had aged him, destroying that way of walking which he has of making himself look taller than he is by standing up straight like a cockerel. He was walking painfully, staggering about, like someone who is injured or infirm.[60]

In July 1893, Mallarmé submitted his official request for retirement. François Coppée had advised him against it, fearing that he might be jeopardizing his pension rights. Mallarmé had been adamant. 'Our decision is not a sudden one,' he informed Coppée. 'It goes back eight or nine years, to the time when I began to be unable to sleep and the college became a brutal place for me. It would happen officially, one day or another. But my health has deteriorated or at least I am less able to cope somehow. So I want to take the initiative and secure a small sum of money which has been earned in such a hard way.'[61]

In view of Mallarmé's unsatisfactory record as a teacher, and a medical certificate confirming that he really was in no condition to continue, his headmaster made no objection. In fact, he was so keen to be rid of him sooner that he informed the Ministry of Education that the college would be prepared to award Mallarmé a whole month's paid sick-leave so that he need not return at the start of the new term. In the light of this, his retirement was confirmed by the Ministry on 8 August. 'The wretched college which devours all my time has done so more than ever this year, but for the last time,' he wrote somewhat ungraciously at the end of July. 'I am counting on not going back there, taking my retirement, and then really making a start as a writer,' he added confidently.[62]

9

A Throw of the Dice

Inevitably, given Mallarmé's previous history with the Ministry of Education, things did not go quite as he had planned. On closer examination, his dossier revealed that he would not officially complete thirty years' service until 23 December 1893. Thus, instead of savouring his retirement as he had imagined, he spent the first week of November in frantic last-minute negotiations with the authorities. With the help yet again of Henri Roujon and the complicity of the headmaster of the Collège Rollin, the matter was finally settled when the latter agreed to extend Mallarmé's sick-leave by a further seven weeks. On 8 November 1893 Méry Laurent received one of Mallarmé's small visiting cards signed 'Stéphane Mallarmé, retired.'[1]

Thanks to the determined efforts of Henri Roujon, Mallarmé was informed that he had been awarded a supplementary pension of 1,200 francs. When added to his annual state pension of 2,500 francs, this left him with a modest but regular income. It was hardly a king's ransom, and certainly insufficient for him to feel totally financially secure. Indeed, money worries continued to plague his existence right up until the day he died. Yet there was more than a little consolation in the knowledge that he would never again have to cross the threshold of any lycée and that, in theory at least, he was now free to devote himself entirely to his writing, and in particular to the Great Work which he had been promising for some years but which, so far, he had conspicuously failed to deliver.

First, though, Mallarmé had several outstanding commitments to honour, not the least of which was the completion of *Hérodiade* for the edition of his collected verse which he had promised to Deman almost three years earlier and for which he had received an advance. He had also agreed to give a guest lecture at the Taylorian Institution of Oxford University when invited to do so by Frederick York Powell, at the instigation of a local schoolteacher in Oxford, Charles Bonnier. Bonnier, who was a keen Wagnerian as well as a francophile, had begun a correspondence with Mallarmé after reading one of his articles in *The National Observer*. Originally, Powell had asked through Bonnier that Mallarmé give the lecture during Michaelmas term, in other words between the months of October and December. Mallarmé had stated his preference for the second term since, when he received the invitation, his uncertainties as to the eventual outcome of his retirement plans had led him to undertake some translation work which left him no time in which to prepare a lecture.

It was now agreed therefore that Mallarmé would give his lecture in Oxford at the beginning of March. In the meantime, through Charles Whibley, who was an editor on *The National Observer* and whose brother Leonard was a fellow of Pembroke College, Cambridge, he was also invited to lecture at the rival institution. Unfortunately for Mallarmé, January and February of that year were extremely cold months, and he suffered a severe attack of influenza which triggered his rheumatic condition. His badly swollen eyes prevented him from starting work on the lecture until the middle of February, so that it was still unfinished when he left for England on 24 February and was only completed during the weekend he spent in Haslemere in Sussex as the guest of Charles Whibley before travelling up to London on the way to Oxford. The drive through London filled Mallarmé with nostalgia for the time he had spent there with Marie so many years before. 'I have just travelled in London from one station to another, passing through very familiar parts of the city,' he wrote to his wife. 'I remembered them as if it were yesterday, when I saw them through the windows of the cab. I just caught a glimpse of some cakes. That ought to whet your appetite, mother. But I know where the best cake-shop is and I will soon be going there.'[2]

He was equally enthusiastic about Oxford, which he was visiting for the first time. He loved the setting of the university and the beauty and splendour of its ancient buildings. He dined in the Christ Church Hall, childishly stealing the dinner menu as a souvenir, and later spent part of the evening in the senior common room talking with some of the Fellows. Somewhat ironically, their extremely generous hospitality proved most upsetting to Mallarmé. Instead of beer, which was the only thing he could safely drink, they innocently plied him with wine, sherry and liqueurs, all of which merely aggravated his dyspepsia and prevented him from sleeping.

In contrast, the lecture itself was something of a disappointment for Mallarmé. Written in the same highly metaphorical style which he had adopted for his earlier article on Wagner, it must have been well nigh incomprehensible for his audience of around sixty people, very few of them Fellows or students, but for the most part ladies from the town who had come to listen to some French. 'The applause at the end was long and polite and a little mechanical,' Mallarmé wrote to Marie and Geneviève. 'But it was my fault. I gave them a dry piece on aesthetics when I should have spoken more or less without any preparation.'[3]

Although he had been specifically asked to talk on a different topic, Mallarmé repeated exactly the same lecture at Cambridge the following day. When he arrived there, he had not been optimistic. He was informed that ticket sales for his public lecture were poor as he was competing against a touring company who were appearing at the local theatre. His audience at Pembroke College that evening consisted of merely twenty people, but they were almost exclusively Fellows and listened 'religiously' as he later described it to his wife. 'If I have ever missed you both not being with me, it was last night,' he wrote to her next morning. 'No lecture has ever caused me or ever will cause me such rare and beautiful feelings. It just cannot be repeated.'[4] The reaction of his audience in Cambridge made such an impression on Mallarmé that he described it in glowing terms to his *Mardistes* the following week, as part of a highly romantic and idealized account of life in the two university towns. Henri de Régnier, who was present that Tuesday, has left us the following description of what Mallarmé said:

> Mallarmé, who has just returned from England, described his lecture in Cambridge in the hall of an old college, all plunged in shadow. On the table were two massive silver candelabra bristling with candles. Behind the speaker hung a sumptuous tapestry. It was a very select audience whose attention he could feel as he spoke, whose intellectual pulse he took. Those college cities are quite charming: a mixture of shady parks and palaces. It is a world of cloisters, study and sport where like peacocks adorning a garden, a select breed of men receive salaries just for being charming people. They elect each other and constitute, above the clergy, an academy of enthusiasts who live in old buildings which have been entrusted to them among beautiful books and refined thoughts, like superior pensioners. Democracies ought to create such cities for poets, Mallarmé said, and in my last lingering look before I left, he added, I imagined them as much in the future as I could in the past.[5]

The dreaming spires of Oxford and Cambridge which had so impressed Mallarmé during his brief visit must have seemed very different from the Paris which he had left behind and to which he now returned. For months now the capital had been rife with rumours of anarchist plots. Ever since Auguste Vaillant had thrown a bomb filled with nails from the visitors gallery into the Chamber of Deputies in December of the previous year, the authorities had mounted a vigorous public campaign against terrorism. It was a commonly held belief that several of the avant-garde literary set were in some way involved in such undemocratic behaviour, and whilst there was no truth in the accusation it was certainly a fact that many of Mallarmé's friends, and to a certain extent Mallarmé himself, at least sympathized with the grievances of the anarchist groups.

Octave Mirbeau, who was named by Vaillant during his trial, and who had written a preface to an anarchist publication, had already informed Mallarmé in his New Year's greeting that he suspected that he was being watched by the police. On the evening of the explosion at the Chamber of Deputies, Mallarmé, who had been attending one of the regular literary banquets of *La Plume*, was asked by a journalist to give his first reaction to the event. 'The only bomb of which I am aware,' he had replied rather sarcastically, 'is a book.' His young friend and occasional *Mardiste* Laurent Tailhade, who was also present, had given a less ambiguous reply: 'Who cares about the victims if the gesture is a beautiful one? What does the death of some anonymous person matter, if by that death, an individual can affirm his existence?'[6]

At the beginning of April 1894, within weeks of his intemperate remarks and not long after Mallarmé had returned to Paris from England, Tailhade became the latest victim of violence when a bomb placed in a flower-pot in the Foyot restaurant in which he had been dining exploded close to his table. In the course of the police investigation which followed another of Mallarmé's young friends was implicated. Whilst examining the correspondence of a suspected anarchist, the police found evidence suggesting that Félix Fénéon, an employee at the War Ministry who was also editor in chief of *La Revue blanche*, was part of a group of conspirators. At the end of April, all thirty supposed conspirators, including Fénéon, were arrested. Interviewed on the evening of the arrest by a reporter from *Le Soir*, Mallarmé protested Fénéon's innocence. 'I am very surprised, I can assure you, at the news you have brought me,' he declared. 'I knew M. Fénéon very well some time ago in the days of *La Revue indépendante*, and I still see him quite frequently . . . in short,' he concluded, 'the arrest of M. Fénéon is a mistake which will soon be remedied.' One cannot help wondering what, given the hysterical climate of the time, the readers of *Le Soir* would have made of the remarks made in private by Mallarmé to some of his *Mardistes* and recorded by Henri de Régnier. 'There is only one person who has the right to be an anarchist,' Mallarmé had said, 'and that is me, the poet, because I alone produce a product which society does not wish in exchange for which it does not provide me with enough to live on.'[7]

Sympathetic to the plight of his younger friends, who he felt were being victimized because they were writers, Mallarmé gave public support to both Tailhade and Fénéon. The following month he wrote a deliciously ironic preface for a book on Tailhade which Frédéric Cazals published later in that year in which, referring to the incident which had in the end cost Tailhade the loss of an eye, he accused the newspapers of disfiguring him more than the unfortunate bomb had done. 'My friend will come out of all this obligingly marked for those myopic people who never noticed that he always had been,' Mallarmé wrote.

The mass trial of the alleged conspirators was scheduled to open at the beginning of August. Three days before that, Fénéon's mother and his lawyer Maître Demange, who would later defend Captain Dreyfus, asked Mallarmé to appear as a character witness for their son and client. Mallarmé agreed. The trial itself became something of a farce when the prosecution failed to produce any significant evidence. At its height, the prosecuting counsel unwisely opened a mysterious package which had been sent to him under the belief that it contained some explosives. Instead it contained human excrement. When he requested a recess to wash his hands, Fénéon reportedly exclaimed rather loudly: 'Never since Pontius Pilate has a magistrate washed his hands with such ostentation.' Mallarmé's contribution to the trial, on the other hand, was a typically simple yet dignified statement. He gave the draft to Fénéon as a souvenir. It reads as follows:

> I am acquainted with Félix Fénéon. He is liked by everybody. I have offered him my friendship because he is a gentle and honest man and has a fine mind. We meet at my home on those evenings when I assemble my friends for conversation. I have never heard, nor has any other of my guests ever heard Fénéon discuss anything which is not concerned with art. I know that he is above using anything whatsoever, other than literature, to express his thoughts. I have responded to this summons, less out of my personal feelings for him which are strong, than in the interest of the truth.[8]

Fénéon, and all the others, were acquitted.

Given that public emotions were running extremely high in the months preceding the trial, Mallarmé wisely decided to absent himself from Paris. In July he joined Marie and Geneviève, who were then staying with the Ponsot family at Honfleur on the Normandy coast, where Geneviève had also spent the previous summer. Marguerite Ponsot's son Willy had been one of Mallarmé's favourite pupils, and her daughter Eve was one of Geneviève's best friends. Mallarmé himself had spent part of the summer of 1892 with this family and enjoyed their relaxed and undemanding company. Above all, he loved being near the sea again. 'Honfleur is a marvellous place,' he wrote to Whistler when he first visited it. 'I have never seen so much greenery next to the sea which, without being the open sea, is enchanting.'[9]

It was shortly after he arrived at Honfleur that Mallarmé received a letter from Deman in Brussels. Apologizing for all the previous delays, he now expressed his desire to start publishing the first volume of Mallarmé's collected verse by the end of the year. Somewhat embarrassed by the reminder of this outstanding commitment, especially since he had as yet made no attempt to complete *Hérodiade*, Mallarmé offered the convenient excuse that he could do nothing for a month until he returned to Paris. A month later, however, he was not in Paris but in Valvins, repeating the same excuse and using arguments about the choice of typeface as a means of procrastinating. The simple fact was that Mallarmé was extremely weary. He merely wished to relax and enjoy his freedom. 'For the first time in years, I am just allowing myself to exist,' he wrote to Berthe Morisot. 'I'm doing nothing, influenced as I am by the first radiant signs of the beginning of autumn.'[10]

As the weeks went by, Marie and Geneviève began to grow impatient to return to Paris. Mallarmé, however, wanted to linger on as long as possible. He was glad of the excuse which the promise of a late visit by Henri de Régnier and Francis Vielé-Griffin provided. 'The forest is changing colour,' he informed Régnier. 'The river, which [Vielé-] Griffin saw laid waste and looking terrible, is now filled out to its banks. Both will welcome you, as you know, with the greatest pleasure. Because you too shall go on the river. The unusual weather which we are currently having means that I am not thinking about coming back until at least a week into October. I know fine that the womenfolk are plotting, but your arrival will decide them to stay on a little longer.'[11]

What they saw during that visit prompted both Régnier and Vielé-Griffin to harbour doubts for the first time about Mallarmé's ability to produce the great work of which he had so long dreamed. Upon his return to Paris, Régnier made a very interesting entry in his diary:

> We thought about Mallarmé tonight and his work and I pointed out the contradiction between the writer that he is and the poet he would like to be. This cosmic dreamer is the most meticulous of writers. This man who has dreamt up another Bible is a producer of wondrous madrigals, and as for the frescoes he imagines, you could say that

they result in delightful snuffboxes. He has followed a thousand different paths leading to some mysterious grotto and yet he is caught in the labyrinth of his own complexity. Is he only going to be an astonishing precursor? Has he never occasionally thought of bequeathing to new forces the imperceptible and precious mass of material which will be his monument? His is the most astonishing literary adventure of the century. The very opposite of Hugo, where the infantile nature of his thought is compensated for by a prodigious verbal capacity, whereas in Mallarmé the hyperbolic imagination does not carry with it the weight of its own rocket.[12]

Eventually, around the third week of October, after spending a few days thanking people for the books which they continued to send him in increasingly large numbers and some time working on the project of the Book which he had by no means abandoned,[13] Mallarmé closed up Valvins, lured back to the capital largely by the thought of returning to Méry Laurent and to his beloved concerts. Addressing his letter rather pointedly as 'Paris (eventually and alas)', Mallarmé informed Deman that he had at last begun to work on the manuscript of his collected poems. Three weeks later it was dispatched to Brussels, almost a year exactly to the day since he had begun his retirement.

'I am working and preparing the coming year, my first full year of freedom, more or less,' Mallarmé had commented optimistically to Henri de Régnier a month earlier.[14] The reservation expressed at the end of this sentence, added almost as an afterthought, would be only too fully justified in the course of the next few years. During this period, although in theory Mallarmé's time was entirely his own, in practice it was constantly disrupted and fragmented, taken up with diversions and distractions of all kinds. To some of these, at first, he lent himself most willingly. Contrary to the rather austere picture which has conventionally been painted of him, Mallarmé was by nature an extremely affable and gregarious person. He needed the company of others. When, two years later, he disappeared off to Valvins on the pretext that he needed peace and solitude in which to work, but then let slip to Marie and Geneviève that he had spent the first evening dining with Dujardin and his wife who lived nearby, Geneviève made an illuminating comment. 'Blast the Dujardins,' she wrote. 'What, you had no sooner arrived than you felt the need to rub shoulders with someone. I recognize you there, father, and you know that I am quite right. You are not really a solitary monk, no, not at all.'[15]

As a consequence, his social life, particularly when he remained in Paris, was extremely full. In addition to his own *mardis* and the weekly dinners at the home of Berthe Morisot and Méry Laurent, his interest in music and the theatre led him to regularly attend a variety of concerts and a great number of first-night performances to which, because of his celebrity and his wide circle of dramatist friends, he was frequently invited. Because of his celebrity he was also invited to numerous official banquets, not all of which he agreed to attend. He did nonetheless appear as the guest of honour at his old school the Collège Rollin, for which occasion he wrote a poem in honour of the Rector of the Academy. He was also increasingly called upon to join official committees of all sorts. Furthermore, when his notoriety did not involve him in such distractions, it led to him receiving countless requests for toasts, speeches, prefaces, articles and contributions to all sorts of reviews and journals. For the most part he resisted these, although he did become a regular contributor to *La Revue blanche*, run by Thadée Natanson and Félix Fénéon, publishing a series of ten articles under the general title 'Variations on a Subject' to which we shall return later.

He also found himself asked to participate in the frequent celebrity interviews or *enquêtes* which were such a feature of the time. The subject matter of these, to which, out of politeness, he nearly always replied, ranged from the completely serious to the utterly trivial. In the course of the next few years Mallarmé gave his opinion, most frequently expressed in ironic terms which usually escaped the attention of the reporter, on a whole range of topics. Among others these included his views on Zionism, Franco-German relations, dreams, the significance of the top-hat and of handwriting, the effect of tobacco and the spring weather, the correct dress for female cyclists, not forgetting his opinion of Voltaire, Tolstoy and the theatre of Ibsen.

Not surprisingly, the frenetic pace at which he now lived in Paris had a serious impact upon Mallarmé's health. From this point on, his letters increasingly describe frequent and recurring bouts of flu and rheumatism, neither of which were much helped by the large numbers of cigarettes and cigars which he continued to smoke. He was now living in a virtually permanent state of insomnia. For weeks he would hardly sleep at all and would only be capable of a maximum of three to four hours' work during the day.[16] He admitted to Henri de Régnier that these attacks left him suffering from extreme nervous tension. It was a terrible situation for a writer, all the more frustrating in that his mind remained as active as ever. Before attempting to put pen to paper he now needed to lie down for half an hour with his eyes closed in order to artificially create a sensation of darkness in his head.[17] In February 1895, that is to say only two months into his first year of 'real freedom', Mallarmé was beginning to tire of Paris and the incessant demands it made on him. 'This winter I have often thought about the wisdom of your resolve,' he told Gauguin, when yet another incipient bout of flu prevented him from attending a second (and in fact quite disastrous) auction sale of Gauguin's paintings.[18]

Furthermore, within the space of the next twelve months, the capital lost two of its greatest attractions for Mallarmé. Barely two weeks after he had written to Gauguin, he found himself unexpectedly at the bedside of Berthe Morisot, who died the next morning from congestion of the lungs as a result of the flu which had developed after catching her daughter's head-cold. Then, in January 1896, Mallarmé was a pall-bearer at the funeral of Paul Verlaine.

Upon Verlaine's death, in a competition which caused him much displeasure and distaste, Mallarmé was elected to replace him as 'Prince of poets'. The whole event gave rise to the kind of publicity he intensely disliked. Interviewed the following day, he could only express his dismay that the profession of poet was being turned into a side-show. 'Decidedly,' he replied, 'people are talking far too much about someone like myself who is determined to live away from the public gaze. A poet is someone who makes marks on paper in his own private corner and who only seeks, in truth, the approval of a few people who are his friends. I am not and do not want to be the Master, nor have I ever sought to pass for any such thing. I am merely an older comrade of Henri de Régnier, Vielé-Griffin and a few other excellent poets . . . Really, there is too much talk about me, and I could end up despising myself for such trumpet-blowing for which I am not responsible. All literary homage should be expressed silently, without noise, and in no way can the situation of a poet become a matter of public interest or of topicality.'[19]

The remark he made in private to Henri de Régnier was briefer but no less eloquent. 'What,' he said with a familiar gesture of despair, 'they have even managed to think of that for me.'[20]

Such publicity was particularly unwelcome from Mallarmé's point of view because it led to a spate of disapproval in the press about the alleged obscurity of his writing. Several comments of this nature had already been made just over a year earlier when he had published the text of his Oxford and Cambridge lecture. In *Le Journal des Débats* an anonymous journalist had ironically called for the editor of *La Revue blanche* to provide a French translation of Mallarmé's article. A concerted campaign was mounted in the popular press. The following attack by Henri Fouquier in *L'Echo de Paris* provides a good example of the abuse to which he was more and more subjected:

> Undoubtedly amongst ourselves Mallarmé holds the record for obscurity. I can recommend to enthusiasts the little prose poem which he has entitled: *The death of the Antipenultimate*. Now I imagine that it is to this outrageous piece of work and to his excessive determination in persisting to the point of absurdity in pursuing a particular viewpoint that M. Mallarmé owes the laureate's sceptre which has been placed in his hands. To boldly go further, always further, even if it is beyond the very bounds of common sense, such is the character of the younger generation.[21]

Mallarmé replied to this senseless attack, and to the others which followed (all of which clearly upset him), in a scathing and ironic article entitled 'Mystery and Literature' ('Le Mystère et les Lettres') which appeared in *La Revue blanche* later that summer. In it he turned on his critics and reminded them that they should not expect to read a poem in the same cursory and casual way in which they read a newspaper.

By the time the article appeared, Mallarmé had already decided to distance himself from a world which was becoming increasingly distasteful to him. 'What a miserable farce is going on all around me, it makes me very angry,' he told Léopold Dauphin.[22] He remained in the capital until March for the opening of the Berthe Morisot retrospective exhibition which he had spent a considerable time helping Julie Manet to organize and for which he wrote a catalogue containing an important introduction to her mother's work. After attending the final day of the exhibition along with Julie Manet, Monet, Renoir and Degas, all of whom had a nostalgic meal together that same evening, Mallarmé concentrated his attention on Valvins.

At the beginning of May 1896 he organized alterations to the house in Valvins with a view to making the place a more comfortable and more permanent base. The kitchen was brightened up and enlarged. The whole house was repainted and some additional furniture shipped from Paris. Mallarmé also had his visiting cards reprinted. These henceforth announced that he would be in Valvins from May until the end of October every year. The familiar routine of the *mardis* was also altered. More and more frequently people were invited to visit Mallarmé in Valvins. When he was in Paris, however, the Tuesday evening gatherings took place much less frequently, and in addition they were rescheduled from their original time of nine o'clock in the evening onwards, to the new and much more restrictive time of four o'clock in the afternoon until around seven o'clock in the early evening.

As if to emphasize his decision to move his centre of operations away from the capital, Mallarmé returned there later than ever that summer, a full month after Marie and Geneviève. Apart from a brief sortie to visit Méry Laurent and attend a wedding, he spent the whole of November on his own in Valvins. Another reason why he stayed on longer was that he genuinely needed the peace and quiet in which to work. In April of that year, he had promised Deman that he would make a definite attempt to add a prelude and a finale to *Hérodiade* – a promise he had repeated again in July and in November. In addition, at around about the same time, that is to say in April 1896, he had agreed, no doubt for financial reasons, to publish with Fasquelle a new edition of his collected prose works which would include reworked versions of the *National Observer* and *Revue blanche* articles.

The second of these undertakings, which required a considerable amount of revision, fully occupied Mallarmé's time right up to and beyond Christmas of that year and delayed the *Hérodiade* project accordingly. His annoyance at the amount of time thus consumed, and his dissatisfaction at publishing texts which he felt still fell far short of his real objectives, explain in part the dismissive title *Divagations* (*Some Musings*) which he eventually gave the collection and the deliberately negative tone struck in the cursory three paragraphs which he now felt it necessary to add as some form of introduction.[23] On the other hand, the lengthy and detailed bibliographical notes which, despite a horrendous bout of insomnia, he insisted on writing for this collection make it equally clear that he saw some of these texts, especially the revised *Revue blanche* articles, as important experimental pieces in their own right and the collection as a whole as an opportunity to at least make some form of interim statement to his public. Indeed, given the hostility which now generally greeted his work, he composed a heavily ironic covering note which he only withdrew at the last moment, although by that time some versions of it had managed to make their way into a few newspapers. Presented as a publisher's note, it takes to task all those who had accused him of deliberate obscurity and reads as follows:

> Under this perhaps ironic title *Divagations*, M. Stéphane Mallarmé has brought together . . . passages made famous by the outrage which they engendered. They were accused of being incoherent and incomprehensible. For the reading public it will be something of a curiosity peculiar to our time to observe to what extent a perspicacious and direct writer acquired a notoriety totally at odds with his qualities, for having simply removed clichés and found a mould that was appropriate for every one of his sentences, thus practising absolute purism.

By the time the book appeared in January 1897, Mallarmé was already busy with another project. He had been in the middle of revising his texts for *Divagations* when, towards the end of October, André Lichtenberger, the Paris secretary of the international magazine *Cosmopolis*, wrote asking if he would be prepared to contribute something, as they had been accused of neglecting contemporary French poetry.[24] Normally, Mallarmé would have rejected such a request out of hand, especially as at the time he was suffering from persistent insomnia. On this occasion, however, he did not do so. This was in part because, as his letters to his wife and daughter for this period show, he was in some financial difficulty and therefore welcomed any source of additional income. But there was another reason. Despite the fact that he was genuinely reluctant to expose himself to further ridicule by offering an already hostile public something even more daring than the more experimental pieces in *Divagations*, there was also a part of him which was prepared to take the risk, out of simple curiosity. This inner conflict, which had been the hypothetical subject of the first of his 'Variations sur un sujet', was quickly resolved in practice in the course of a conversation during his brief trip to Paris in mid-November, when Lichtenberger informed him of the prospective fee and gave him, somewhat rashly, an assurance that the magazine would publish whatever he submitted to them. Less than a week later, Mallarmé told Geneviève that he was going to accept the offer.[25]

In the most adventurous and innovative texts produced for *Divagations*, Mallarmé had created a new hybrid prose form situated somewhere between the traditional prose poem and the review article. It was something with which he had first experimented in the even earlier Richard Wagner article and which, in the detailed bibliographical notes which he provided for *Divagations*, he called 'Le Poème critique' ('critical prose poem'). For some time now, he had been toying with the idea of attempting a similar experiment, combining aspects of the prose poem and free verse to create a new kind of verse form with something akin to a symphonic structure which would be expressed in the novel layout of the text. In an article entitled 'Le Livre, instrument spirituel' ('The Book as Intellectual Tool'), first published in *La Revue blanche* some eighteen months earlier in June 1895, he had pondered out loud whether it would not be possible to experiment with an alternative visual layout for a poem, constructing it around a single principal sentence or idea which would be printed line by line in capital letters, at differing heights of the page over several pages, around which other lines in smaller print could gravitate like clusters or constellations in such a way that the reader's own enthusiasm would hold the piece together.

Since the publication of that article, Mallarmé had clearly worked on the concept for, in spite of his continuing insomnia, only a few weeks after finishing *Divagations* he was able to deliver to *Cosmopolis* a ten-page poem of precisely such a revolutionary form. Around a single sentence – 'Un coup de dés jamais n'abolira le hasard' ('A throw of the dice will never eliminate chance') – printed in bold capital letters as a leitmotif throughout the text to remind us that every statement must necessarily remain provisional, Mallarmé places various secondary clusters through which he provides a poetic account of the evolution of Man, following the stages in the development of civilization from the moment when Life first emerges from the sea (the opening double page) until the last representative of Mankind, the final Artist-Seafarer (the Master of the Poem), disappears back into the sea apparently leaving no trace whatsoever of his passage (the final pages). This dense and intricate text, which conjures up a kaleidoscope of images that make exceptional demands on the reader, is the outcome of a lifelong interest in the relationship between science and art, language and myth, ritual and religion. Without being the Great Work itself, it is related to it and constitutes Mallarmé's first really serious attempt to produce the lasting literary monument to the post-Christian era which, many years earlier, he had announced to his friends. He probably had this text (or something very much like it) in mind when, more recently still, he had informed his *Mardistes* that 'in four pages' he could 'explain the world.'[26]

When it was sent off to the printers, the novel form of the poem understandably caused some consternation. Not having actually shown the manuscript to his Paris director before dispatching it off to London, André Lichtenberger found himself in some embarrassment:

It would appear that the originality of the form of your poem provoked some objections from our English publisher. He is afraid that our public, which is a little conservative in artistic matters and for the most part totally uninitiated into the harmony and aesthetics of modern French poetry, might be somewhat disconcerted by your experiment. His anxiety has not been without effect upon my director and friend Mr Ortmans who, I hasten to add, has never seen your manuscript. I protested most strongly against such an attitude and argued in favour of the independence and eclecticism which our magazine ought to adopt. I pointed out to him how new and original your experiment was and how it ought to be judged as such even by those who would not support it, and what a special honour it was for *Cosmopolis* to be at the origin of such a truly new artistic creation. I think and I hope that my arguments had an effect and that Mr Ortmans will share my view. You will soon receive some proofs.[27]

For his part, Mallarmé was sympathetic to Lichtenberger's delicate situation. He was also extremely grateful for his support and told him so:

Dear Sir,

The proofs arrived almost at the same time as your letter. I find that taken as a whole they produce something which is so very interesting and so pretty, just to look at! I know that I have a vested interest in all this. But I am not the only one, seeing that you were kind enough to send me a charming and reassuring letter in which you say out loud what I dared not say. I am grateful to you for showing such intelligence. But really, has your English publisher sufficiently understood that in the first place these pages contain more than a mere whim? Secondly, a review is neutral ground as it were which neither informs nor approves the work which it publishes of any of its contributors. It is above all a no-man's-land when, like yours, it addresses what is published in it under his name. Apart from convention, I have broken no rules.

But I know that I do not have to tell you anything which you have not thought about, and better, already and I hope that you will convince Mr Ortmans as far as the French edition is concerned. The consequences would be so unfortunate.

I enclose the proofs. Only some trifling corrections. The printer has astonished me. I did not expect him to succeed at the first attempt and above all else, whatever the outcome of the whole affair, could you please transmit to him my fullest compliments.[28]

To their credit, and no doubt thanks to the efforts of Lichtenberger, the editorial board of *Cosmopolis* agreed to publish the poem in the form in which it had been submitted to them. The only condition they imposed was that they be allowed to add a note designed to allay the fears of the more conservative of their readers. In the event, it was Mallarmé himself who composed the 'Editor's Note' which, in addition to an introduction justifying the use of different typefaces, appeared with the text of the poem in the May 1897 edition of *Cosmopolis*.

Given that the note was written by Mallarmé himself it makes instructive reading, not only because it provides a simple guide to the poem itself but more especially because it shows just how proud Mallarmé actually felt about his achievement:

> Keen to be as eclectic in literature as it is in politics and to defend itself against the criticism which it has received for ignoring the new school of French poetry, the editors of *Cosmopolis* offer its readers an unpublished poem by Stéphane Mallarmé, the undisputed leader of French symbolist poetry. In this work which is of an entirely new kind, the poet has attempted to create music using words. A sort of general leitmotif running throughout the poem provides it with unity. Accessory themes are grouped around it. The nature of the letters employed and the position of the blank spaces are designed to replace musical notes and intervals. This experiment may have its detractors. No one will however dispute the unique artistic effort of its author nor fail to be interested by it.[29]

By the time *Cosmopolis* was on sale in the Paris bookshops, Mallarmé had already signed a contract with (and received an advance from) the picture dealer turned publisher Ambroise Vollard for a luxury edition of his experimental poem, to be illustrated by Odilon Redon.[30] '*Cosmopolis* was brave and delightful,' he wrote to André Gide, who had sent him a letter of congratulations from Italy, 'but I could only offer them half of what I had intended, it was already such a risk for them! The poem is currently being printed as I conceived it as far as the page layout is concerned, which is where all the effect is to be found . . . The constellation will, according to precise laws and as far as possible in a printed text, inevitably adopt the shape of a constellation. The boat will tilt from the top of one page to the bottom of another etc., for – and that is the whole idea which had to be omitted in a magazine – the rhythm of a phrase describing an action or an object has no meaning unless it imitates them, and, when printed on paper and thus retrieved by literature, it should render something of its original stamp.'[31]

As usual, Mallarmé was being something of an optimist here. Through no fault of his own, the project would remain unfinished at the time of his death, even though by that time the printers Firmin-Didot had provided over sixteen different sets of proofs and Odilon Redon had completed his four lithographs.

For the moment, the only thing which Mallarmé sought was rest. His recent burst of energy on *Divagations* and *Un coup de dés* had left him exhausted and jaded. As Marie and Geneviève watched the carnival celebrations with Méry Laurent from the balcony of the home of Dr Evans, alone in their flat Mallarmé struck a despondent note in a letter to a friend out in the country. 'It would appear that for the first few months of this year I have been bad-tempered and behaving like a wild beast, like a caged animal,' he wrote to Elémir Bourges, 'but now I have got rid of my fury and in the end one is always tamed. People are harassing me here. Nothing interests me so I stay at home and work in the worst possible conditions, getting no fresh air and not going out. My insomnia each night is followed by an empty day of fatigue which is of no use. Each day I descend a rung of the ladder into emptiness and disgust. There is also the unbearable awareness that what I am doing is absurd. Paris and your humble servant have no longer anything to offer each other.'[32]

There was more to Mallarmé's mood than the inevitable

anticlimax and depression which frequently follow a period of intense creativity. Paris really had lost its attraction for him. Since the death of his wife the previous year, Whistler was no longer a frequent visitor there. Hostility against Mallarmé in the press had continued and, if anything, increased. In February of that year André Gide had felt it necessary to publish an open letter in the *Mercure de France* defending him against his detractors. In private too, petty squabbles and rivalries were only too common. Mallarmé had been able to witness this at first hand when Paul Valéry had organized a special banquet in his honour to celebrate the Tuesday evening gatherings. Catulle Mendès, Octave Mirbeau and Dierx all received their invitations rather late and, convinced that the younger generation was deliberately snubbing them, boycotted the celebrations which took place at the Père Lathuille restaurant. Paul Valéry himself only attended the banquet under duress, and after receiving a telegram from Mallarmé ordering him to do so.

In the circumstances, Mallarmé withdrew a week early to Valvins in order to prepare it for the coming season, leaving Geneviève to fend off any enquiries. 'I am incapable of anything,' he wrote rather sadly a day or so later, 'and confused as much as exhausted. It is going to take me some time to find myself again.'[33] Abandoning any thought of creative work, he turned to manual activity, spending hours painting the windows, doors and garden gate of the house in Valvins. He also spent much of his time sailing and entertaining guests. Julie Manet and her cousin, Méry Laurent and later Paul Valéry all visited Mallarmé at Valvins that summer.

Mallarmé showed Valéry Gide's complimentary letter on the *Coup de dés*, but otherwise literature was not on the agenda. 'We had fried eggs, bacon and cream cheese for lunch, and for dinner a thin soup, steak and potatoes with asparagus, gruyère and jam. Not bad eh!' Mallarmé informed Geneviève by letter. 'My young friend brought some Nougatine, an exquisite cake and some fine cigars, the poor boy. We sailed on the river to a good northern breeze and strolled in the garden in what was left of the afternoon sun.'[34] Valéry's account of the proceedings was no less instructive. 'Mallarmé on his own is truly so simply Mallarmé that you end up being like him yourself,' he told Gide. 'In the evening, after some boating and some drinks (always too many), we had a rather interesting and serious but rather dirty conversation.'[35]

By the end of the summer, Mallarmé was still awaiting satisfactory proofs of the Didot edition of *Un coup de dés*. A head-cold had developed into flu which had weakened him considerably – such an attack had never so completely undermined his health, he admitted to a young friend, Maurice Gravollet.[36] Bad health persisted right up until October and beyond, preventing him from doing much work. When the cold weather came, he returned rather unwillingly to the capital, and within a month or two of arriving he began to miss the forest and the river. 'I have to admit that I have had my fill already of evening outings and anything which does not allow me to stay in quietly and work undisturbed,' he grumbled to Méry Laurent at the end of January 1898. 'In these conditions, Paris is of no use to me.'[37]

Nor did he seek to be of any service to it. When Charles Morice asked him to use his influence with the publisher Fasquelle to help him place Paul Gauguin's autobiographical novel *Noa, Noa*, Mallarmé pointed out that as sales of *Divagations* had been fairly poor, it was extremely unlikely that Fasquelle would listen to his advice. Moreover, he added, politely but forcefully, he was now deliberately jettisoning whatever remained of his so-called influence in the capital.[38] It was for this reason that he took no part in the public debate which the Dreyfus case had aroused. This did not mean that he had no interest in it. When Zola was fined and imprisoned for the energetic press campaign he had waged in defence of

Dreyfus, Mallarmé sent him a telegram expressing admiration for, and total solidarity with, his actions.

Mallarmé left for Valvins even earlier than usual that year. He began a routine of working for a few hours in the morning, taking the afternoons off to visit friends, many of whom had by now moved out to the neighbourhood, or just walking in the forest or by the river. Much of his time was spent in and on the garden, instructing a new gardener. When he did venture into his study, accompanied by his faithful cat Lilith, whose tail in the past had smudged many a manuscript, he tended to tidy his papers as a way of avoiding making a start on *Hérodiade*.

The problem was that he had not only promised Deman to make a determined effort to complete the poem that summer, but he had also offered it to Ambroise Vollard, who had been keen to publish something else in addition to the *Coup de dés*. In the second week of May, Mallarmé wrote to Vollard expressing satisfaction with the extended version of the poem which he claimed was now finished. This in fact was not the case. Once he had secured the advance which had been the real object of his letter, he admitted to Geneviève that things were not going well. 'A terrible cold wind has descended and the rain is going to return,' he wrote in one of his daily bulletins. 'It is damp and I am currently lighting the stove to have a burst of flame during the day. I would also like to kindle the poet in me, who is rather inert. In view of Moreno's reaction, don't tell anyone that I am particularly working on *Hérodiade*. That could get back to Vollard for whom the poem is already finished.'[39]

At the end of May Mallarmé made one brief excursion to Paris. He went to the annual Salon, dined with Méry Laurent and visited his ward, Julie Manet. He also commiserated with Rodin about the high-handed way in which his statue of Balzac had been refused by the very people who had commissioned it. He returned to Valvins as quickly as he could. 'I want to stay in Paris as short a time as possible and to see as few people as possible so as not to be drawn into any new projects,' he told Geneviève.[40]

Paul Valéry went to visit Mallarmé in Valvins and spent the 14 July celebrations with him. He noticed that Mallarmé looked very tired and extremely pale. He also found it significant that he had not been doing any sailing on the river. 'We went and chatted in his bedroom,' he wrote to Gide the following day. 'He showed me some drafts of *Hérodiade* which he was working on. He changed his shirt in front of me, gave me some water for my hands and poured some of his cologne over me himself. In the evening, with his daughter, he accompanied me to the station at Vulaines. The night sky, the peace and the conversation were all quite unforgettable.'[41]

During the month of August Mallarmé tried to work, devoting the afternoons to *Hérodiade* and the mornings to what, in a letter to Léopold Dauphin, he called 'jottings for the dream', in other words the project of the Book which he was still doggedly pursuing. But he was finding it more and more difficult to make any progress. 'It is all rather a waste of time living behind closed shutters,' he confided. 'A lethargy settles within me which can be felt materially in the pen itself.' 'Besides,' he added, 'it is so much easier and possible to think about a few absent friends.'[42] A few weeks after writing these lines, Mallarmé began to complain of a sore throat. This developed into tonsillitis, which the doctor assured him was not serious. Towards the end of that same week, he got up feeling much better. When the doctor arrived, Mallarmé told him that he was thinking of going out. He began joking, saying that he looked like an exotic cockerel, he was so red in the face with coughing. In the middle of his sentence, a coughing fit overcame him. He looked quickly over at his wife and daughter, then made a grab for the doctor and collapsed on top of him, asphyxiated by a sudden contraction of the glottis. He was fifty-six years old.

In the lecture on music and literature which he gave at the

universities of Oxford and Cambridge just after he retired, Mallarmé had proudly stated what he had only hinted at in his earlier short study of Wagner, namely that literature could and should rise to the challenge thrown down by contemporary music. When Geneviève and Marie Mallarmé came to tidy his study, they discovered a book on Beethoven and Wagner lying open at the page he had been reading. Among his scattered papers lay, unfinished but clearly recently worked on, drafts and fragments of a verse drama for which he had already found a title. It was to have been called *Les Noces d'Hérodiade: Mystère* (*Hérodiade's Wedding: A Mystery Play*). Conceived as a passion play for a modern post-Christian world, the *Mystère* as envisaged at the time of Mallarmé's death included a new 'Overture', a reworked version of the earlier 'Scene', a 'Song of John the Baptist' and various other parts.[43]

Mallarmé had died on Friday 8 September 1898. His funeral took place two days later. On a brilliantly hot Sunday afternoon, guests began to arrive. They passed his untended sailing boat bobbing up and down at its moorings and made their way down into the small garden where his coffin had been placed on a trestle in the garden path which he himself had recently sanded, in the shade of the chestnut tree which Geneviève had planted when she was a young girl. Famous writers and artists rubbed shoulders with local peasants who had come to bury the man they knew merely as 'Mossieu Mallarmé', a genial neighbour who used to sit and smoke his pipe down by the bridge over the river in which his pony had drowned in a tragic accident a year or two earlier. Once all the guests had assembled, the funeral cortège made its way first to the little church in the neighbouring village of Samoreau. Then, after a simple ceremony, Mallarmé was buried next to his son Anatole in the little cemetery close by, overlooking the Seine and the forest of Fontainebleau in which, in his later years, he had spent so much time. Henri Roujon made an emotional speech at the graveside on behalf of Mallarmé's older friends. Paul Valéry, who had been chosen to reply on behalf of the younger generation of Mallarmé's friends and admirers, was too upset to speak. After the brief ceremony, Méry Laurent climbed into her carriage stationed in front of the church and returned, alone, to Paris.

The day after the funeral, Geneviève Mallarmé found on her father's writing desk an envelope on the front of which, clearly fearing the worst, he had written: 'Instructions for dealing with my papers'. The envelope, however, was empty. A fortnight later, tidying the study, she came across a rapidly pencilled note which Mallarmé had wedged into the side of his pad of blotting paper. Paul Valéry was summoned to decipher its contents. Addressed to Marie and Geneviève, and written the night before Mallarmé died, it read as follows:

> Instructions for dealing with my papers. – The terrible fit of coughing which I have just suffered may return in the night and see me off. In that case, you will not be surprised that my thoughts turn to my semi-secular mountain of notes which will only cause you many difficulties, seeing that not a single one of those sheets of paper can serve any purpose. I alone could make sense out of what remains . . . I would have done so if I had not been betrayed by the last few years which I shall now not have. Burn everything, therefore. There is no literary heritage, my children. Do not even submit anything to the gaze of any other person. Refuse any action proposed out of curiosity or friendship. Say that there is nothing to be discovered in these papers, moreover that is the truth, and you, my poor prostrate creatures, the only people in the world capable of respecting to such an extent the whole life's work of a sincere artist, believe me when I say that it was all going to be so beautiful.
>
> And so I leave no papers unpublished except some printed fragments which you will find, then the *Coup de dés* and *Hérodiade* which will be finished if fate allows it . . . [44]

The finding of this note raised quite a problem. Was it left unfinished deliberately? Did Mallarmé think better of it the next morning when fate seemed to have given him the opportunity he sought to proceed with the *Hérodiade* project?

Was that why he removed it from the envelope and hid it in the blotting paper? Understandably, Geneviève Mallarmé had great difficulty in deciding whether or not to comply with her father's final wishes. A letter addressed to her at the beginning of October by Charles Morice which refers to 'the pious ashes'[45] suggests that she had in fact started to do so. Sympathizing with the anguish she must have felt at destroying a life's work, Morice urged her to continue to burn all the notes which Mallarmé had scrupulously stored in the lacquer drawers of a Japanese cabinet which he had installed in Valvins.

But did she? In view of the number of important documents which have come to light and been published since Mallarmé's death,[46] it is clear that Geneviève and her mother only partly respected his wishes, saving from the holocaust those batches of papers which they felt to be of the greatest importance. We shall now never know precisely what or indeed what volume of material was consigned to the flames.

Postscript

UN COUP DE DÉS JAMAIS N'ABOLIRA LE HASARD – A THROW OF THE DICE WILL NEVER DO AWAY WITH CHANCE – No one can ever really avoid the contingency of the world. This basic statement around which the text of *Un coup de dés* is, literally, configured was graphically illustrated by Mallarmé's unexpected death as he awaited the final proofs of the definitive version of that work. Viewed with hindsight, his life is equally instructive. Vilified by the popular press of his day as a remote and uncaring obfuscator, a master of obscurity, transformed by the understandable enthusiasm of some of his more fervent admirers into an equally unreal and saintly figure, hailed retrospectively by recent critics as one of the originators of Modernism, Mallarmé was in reality none of these things. Throughout his life he hated labels of all kinds, because he found them dangerously misleading and restricting. 'I absolutely detest "-isms" and anything like them,' he said with rare annoyance when Jules Huret suggested that he was commonly regarded as the leader of the modern movement. 'Such academic distinctions seem totally repugnant to me when applied to literature, which, on the contrary, remains a question of individual originality.'[1]

Mallarmé rightly saw himself neither as a Symbolist poet nor for that matter as an exclusively modern writer, but considered both of these descriptions equally compromising. He saw himself rather as belonging to the long tradition of

myth-makers and storytellers stretching back as far as civilization itself. The shipwreck image of the *Coup de dés* and the
later sonnets pays homage to that ancient and continuing
tradition. It points backwards in time through Baudelaire's
concluding poem of *Les Fleurs du mal*, 'The Voyage', via
Hamlet's 'sea of troubles', to the Odyssey of Homer and
beyond. It is no coincidence, for example, that James Joyce
possessed an edition of Mallarmé's *Un coup de dés* as he worked
on *Finnegans Wake*. Such echoes remind us of the great lyrical
tradition to which Mallarmé rightly felt he belonged and from
which he has become unjustly separated.

On the personal level, the man whom they buried next to
his son on that beautiful summer's day almost a century ago
was a supremely complex human being who had meant many
different things even to those who, at such short notice, were
able to attend his hastily arranged funeral. To the local people
of Valvins, who suddenly found themselves rubbing shoulders
with elegant ladies in fashionable dresses and gentlemen in
top-hats and frock-coats, he had been the affable and kindly
schoolmaster who had chosen to spend most of his summers
amongst them for the previous twenty-five years. To Marie
Mallarmé and to Geneviève he had been a devoted husband
and father. To Julie Manet he had been an acquaintance of her
uncle Edouard and her own father and mother who had
become a considerate and attentive guardian. To Méry Laurent
he had been the charming and entertaining guest who had
showered her with frivolous and amusing verse, who had
briefly been her lover and who had remained her friend. To
Auguste Rodin and those of his generation he had been an
admired and respected fellow artist. To younger men like
Edouard Dujardin and Paul Valéry he had quite simply been
'the master'.

In the course of his funeral oration in the cemetery of the
tiny church at Samoreau, Henri Roujon brought tears to the
eyes of many when he described how, at difficult times in their

lives, all sorts of people had turned to Mallarmé and had never found him wanting. 'He would offer you a friendly hand and at the same time lower his eyelids over those enormous childlike eyes.'[2] Edouard Manet, Villiers de l'Isle-Adam, Whistler, Emile Zola, Robert de Montesquiou, André Gide, Claude Debussy and countless others who, for whatever reason, could not be present, would have shared these sentiments. Amid the tropical heat of Tahiti, when Paul Gauguin heard of Mallarmé's death, he was quite upset by the news. 'The most beautiful part of his work was his life,' he wrote to a friend.[3]

For once, Gauguin's comment was more than a simple cliché. It takes us to the heart of the matter. In the final analysis, what remains so extraordinary about Mallarmé's life and his work is their fundamental unity. Initially, with the impatience and intolerance of youthful idealism, he had seen the claims which life placed upon him as an obstacle, as a tiresome distraction from his literary pursuits. As a result of the crucial years of provincial exile, during which he had painfully come to realize both the sublimity and the absurdity of the human condition, he had learnt that, even if he did not always succeed in doing so, it was important to try to balance the competing demands of writing and living. A few weeks before he died Mallarmé was asked by a journalist to provide some random thoughts for a survey which he was conducting. Mallarmé was offended by such a request. 'I am somewhat embarrassed,' he replied politely. 'I do not have thoughts of such a kind. Mine form part of an orchestrated whole, and if they are separated I have the impression that they lose their meaning and produce a false note.'[4]

Ever since he had returned to settle in Paris, Mallarmé's life and art had formed an organic whole. His various activities, like his new friendships, had been chosen with care. His translation work, his theoretical writings, his literary and art criticism, his experiments with prose and verse forms, his investigations into the mysteries of language, myth and ritual, his interest in philology and linguistics, his insatiable curiosity about the latest developments in the music, painting and theatre of his time, in other countries as well as in his own, can now all be seen as different facets of a unique quest, pursued throughout a lifetime with dogged determination and remarkable tenacity, for an art form which would accommodate and express his complex vision and produce for a fundamentally secular age a literary monument which could stand alongside the great achievements of the past.

Mallarmé died without fulfilling this ambitious dream. But is he to be judged a failure for that? Surely not. As a man, his life had been far from wasted. Those whose lives had been touched by his would testify to that. Did he fail as a writer? He may not have produced the Book or the Great Work which he had promised his friends, but he left behind in his published work some of the most exquisite poems in the French language, an experimental work which of its kind is yet to be equalled, and a body of critical writings which raise many of the key issues which writers and literary theorists are still discussing today. When he was asked, a mere three weeks before his death, whether, in his own opinion he had fulfilled the dreams which he had entertained as a young man of twenty, he replied, 'I have been sufficiently faithful to myself for my humble life to have retained some meaning.'[5] Who would dare contradict that statement? It is a fitting epitaph for someone for whom life and art were truly inseparable, and whose life and art need to be taken together and in the context of each other if either is to be properly understood.

His writing, especially the most successful of his poetry, constitutes an unparalleled attempt to capture, through that imperfect tool which he, more than any other, knew language to be, the quintessential, perpetually vanishing, haunting yet ultimately untranslatable quality of life itself – 'la qualité tout d'insaisissable finesse de la vie.'

Mallarmé knew full well that the ambitious task which he

had set himself might very well prove to be an impossible one. Yet until the very end, his life remained a triumph of hope over despair. At the darkest moment of *Un coup de dés*, when all seems lost, a constellation slowly begins to appear in the empty sky. Each star spins across the desolate blackness, coming miraculously to a halt. In perfect position, like a set of dice thrown by some expert hand. Given the kind of odds against which he knew himself to be playing, Mallarmé's achievement remains just such a heroic and defiant throw of the dice.

Notes

1 Beginnings

1 Letter from Mallarmé to Paul Verlaine of 10 November 1885, *Correspondance*, vol. II, ed. H. Mondor and L. J Austin, Paris, Gallimard, 1965, pp. 299–300 (henceforth abbreviated as *Corr.*). For detailed comments on this autobiographical letter the reader should consult Austin Gill (for the bibliographical reference see note 2), who makes it the starting-point for his exceptionally detailed survey of Mallarmé's first twenty years. Our indebtedness to his work and to that of Carl Barbier will become obvious in the pages which follow.

2 For a detailed study of Mallarmé's ancestry and early life see Carl Barbier's *Documents Stéphane Mallarmé*, 7 vols, Paris, Nizet, 1968–79 (henceforth abbreviated as *DSM*), and Austin Gill's 2-volume study *The Early Mallarmé*, Oxford, the Clarendon Press, 1979 and 1986 (henceforth abbreviated as Gill.)

3 In his autobiographical letter to Verlaine Mallarmé writes somewhat ironically (and again it is a deliberate inaccuracy): 'From the Revolution onwards both sides of my family produced an uninterrupted supply of civil servants in the Registry Administration. Although they nearly always held high office, I avoided that career to which I was destined from the cradle.' (Letter to Verlaine of 10 November 1885: *Corr.* II, 299.)

4 A final receipt for payment dated 17 October 1845 gives Numa's address as still being 12 rue Laferrière. See *DSM* V, 163.

5 See *DSM* V, 166.
6 Letter from Mme Desmolins to Mélanie Laurent of August/
   September 1847 (*DSM* V, 168).
7 Henri Mondor, *Mallarmé lycéen* Gallimard, 1954, p. 69.
8 Letter of 7 December 1864 (*Corr.* I, 142 note).
9 Unpublished letter from Fanny Desmolins to Stéphane
   Mallarmé of 10 December 1867 (Bonniot Collection).
10 This view is expressed by Léon Cellier, *Mallarmé et la morte qui
   parle*, Paris, 1959, p. 15.
11 Henri de Régnier, unpublished diary, *Annales psychiques et
   occulaires* in 7 vols. Manuscript collection of the Bibliothèque
   Nationale, Paris, Nouvelles acquisitions françaises (henceforth
   abbreviated as BN N.a.fr.) 14977 fol. 166.
12 Unpublished letter from Fanny Desmolins to Stéphane
   Mallarmé of 6 July 1868 (Bonniot Collection).
13 A minor incident is instructive here. When in June 1867 Marie
   Mallarmé and Geneviève went up to Paris for the Universal
   Exhibition, leaving Mallarmé on his own in Besançon, Mme
   Desmolins met her great granddaughter for the first time. Her
   manner clearly frightened Geneviève somewhat: indeed, in a
   later letter Mme Desmolins confesses rather sadly, that she has
   an offputting manner, and illustrates her effect on an animal
   introduced into the family: 'I would be a little jealous, I have to
   admit, if I thought the lady who was standing in for me was to
   make our Vève forget her great-grandmother whom she
   perhaps remembers as a sombre and brooding person. It is quite
   amazing, the depressing effect I have on people! It even affects
   animals. A sweet little white thing recently brought into the
   family took a dislike to me for that reason. It took lots of sugar
   and titbits to let it allow me to stroke it. I hope Geneviève hasn't
   got to that stage yet. I really would be upset.' (Letter to
   Mallarmé of 25 October 1867: Bonniot Collection.)
14 Letter of 2 November [1850] (*DSM* V, 196).
15 Such efforts proved vain. Stéphane's paternal grandfather would
   also die in August 1851, thus leaving Fanny Desmolins and her
   husband almost entirely free to exert their moral authority over
   Stéphane and his sister.
16 Letter from Fanny Desmolins to Mélanie Laurent of 24
   September 1850 (*DSM* V, 194–5).

17 For an amusing recollection about this school see the anecdote
Mallarmé recounted to Henri de Régnier around March or April
1898, recorded in Régnier's diary: 'Before he left for Valvins
Mallarmé came to see us and spoke about the boarding-school
in Auteuil where he was educated as a child. It was an
aristocratic boarding-school, full of the nobility. You were
either called Talleyrand-Périgord or Clermont-Tonnerre. And
so when he arrived and they heard that his name was Mallarmé
he was welcomed with a salvo of punches and threatening
behaviour. So he struck upon the idea of saying that he was also
called the marquis de Boulainvilliers (his father had a property
of that name in Passy), and that was the name he was known
by. That's the name that was used to summon him to the
parlour. To let the children in the garden know that their
parents had arrived they shouted out their names in a kind of
horn. Mallarmé always hung back a bit so that his old aunt
wouldn't associate him with the marquis de Boulainvilliers who
could be heard in the horn. It was the old aunt who had got him
put into the boarding-school. Unmarried, obsessed with the
aristocrats having lived for a long time with an old relative,
Monsieur de la Roche-Aymon, I think, she rediscovered in the
parlour lots of her acquaintances of the faubourg from which
the death of the old nobleman had separated her. She used the
parlour as her drawing room and spent many hours there.' (BN
N.a.fr. 14977 fol. 169, quoted in Gill I, p. 10.) Apart from
anything else, this anecdote illustrates that the memory of
Mallarmé's great-great uncle was not entirely forgotten in
certain circles!
18 Quoted in *DSM* V, 51, and Gill I, 43.
19 See *DSM* V, 52.
20 See *DSM* V, 52–3.
21 Letter of 30 October 1854 (*DSM* V, 229).
22 Letter of February–March 1855 (*DSM* V, 234–5).
23 Mallarmé to his sister Maria, July 1856 (*DSM* V, 262–3).
24 See *DSM* VI, 40.
25 Letter to Marie Mallarmé of 28 August 1873 (*Corr.* IV, 388–9).
26 Numa Mallarmé to André Desmolins, mid-April 1859 (*DSM* V,
322).
27 See Gill I, 79–80.

28 Letter of 11 August 1859 (*DSM* V, 324).

29 Cf. Mallarmé's recollection as recorded by Henri de Régnier:
'He wrote his first verses in admiration of Béranger, whom he
frequently saw at an old relation's house when he was very
young, around seven years old' (Diary of Henri de Régnier: BN
N.a.fr.14977 fol. 166). In fact Mallarmé had met Béranger at the
house of Fanny Dubois Davesnes possibly as early as 1849, as is
reported by Henri de Régnier, or, more probably, slightly later
in 1854 when Béranger came to pose for the bust of himself
executed by Fanny Dubois Davesnes, the daughter of the actor
Dubois Davesnes. Fanny was a good friend of Stéphane's
stepmother, whose amateur painting she actively encouraged. A
frequent visitor to the Davesnes' house with Anne Mallarmé
and his sister Maria from 1848 until the Mallarmé family moved
to Sens in 1853, Stéphane had been able to admire the bust of
Béranger on many occasions after its completion in May 1854.

30 Letter from Fanny Desmolins to Mélanie Laurent of 24 August
1859 (*DSM* V, 337–8).

31 Letter from Fanny Desmolins to Mélanie Laurent of 13
November 1860 (*DSM* V, 342–3).

32 Ibid.

33 One of the earliest poems of the collection entitled 'Verses
Written on a Copy of "Les Contemplations"' is a virulent
defence of the Master. For a detailed account of Mallarmé's
various 'borrowings' in *Entre quatre murs* see Gill II, *passim*.

34 *DSM* VII, 165. Interestingly, both these confidences are written
in English, no doubt to protect them from prying eyes.

35 The Smythes and the Sullivans were respectively American and
English families who lived in Passy and were friends of Fanny
and André Desmolins. Stéphane had become acquainted with
their daughters during his visits to his grandparents. Harriet
Smythe died of consumption in the summer of 1859. In August
of that year Fanny Desmolins wrote to her cousin pointing out
that she feared Stéphane would be bored in her company as 'the
English and American families had gone away for the summer'
(*DSM* V, 324). Stéphane himself mentions both of these families
in a letter to his grandmother of 5 February 1862: 'I have begun
my English studies with something which was a duty in every
sense of the term. I mean a letter to Mr Smyth[e], which will be

followed, *quite soon*, by a letter to Mr Sullivan which I shall send
to you.' (*DSM* V, 369.)
36 This stanza is incomplete. No doubt Mallarmé could not think
of a rhyme!
37 Diary of Henri de Régnier [November 1888] (BN N.a.fr. 14974
fol. 172).
38 These lines are scribbled in pencil on a sheet of paper glued on
to the inside back cover of the jotter. See *DSM* VII, 165.

2 Rebellion

1 See Chapter 1, note 32, letter of 13 November 1860 to Mélanie
Laurent.
2 Letter from Mallarmé to Henri Cazalis of 5 August 1862 (*DSM*
VI, 52). This is one of the few personal comments which
Mallarmé has left us concerning his year at the Registry. Indeed
we have precious little first-hand information about this period.
We can infer things of course (and have done so) from the
family correspondence exchanged between the Mallarmés and
the Desmolins as well as from some letters from Fanny
Desmolins to other people. Such fragmentary evidence tends to
support the picture of Mallarmé at this time as recalled by
Emmanuel des Essarts in an obituary article penned some ten
months after Mallarmé's death. See Emmanuel des Essarts,
'Souvenirs littéraires: Stéphane Mallarmé', in *Revue de France*, 15
July 1899, pp. 441–7.
3 In a letter to Fanny Desmolins of January 1862 (*DSM* V, 350)
Anne Mallarmé states that they are anxious about the outcome
'of another exam'. This would seem to indicate that at the first
set of Registry exams, which were traditionally held in June,
Mallarmé had not done well. It is also possible, however, that
what Anne Mallarmé is referring to is Stéphane's failure at his
first attempt at his baccalauréat examinations.
4 Letter from Fanny Desmolins to Mélanie Laurent of 19 April
1861 (*DSM* V, 347).
5 Des Essarts, art. cit., p. 442. Des Essarts' comment is probably
inspired by his own recollection of an early sonnet of
Mallarmé's, originally entitled 'Contre un poète parisien' ('I

Accuse a Parisian Poet'), in which he criticizes his friend's enthusiasm for the polka!

6 Maurice Dreyfous, *Ce que je tiens à dire*, Paris, 1912, quoted by Luc Badesco in *La Génération poétique de 1860*, Paris, Nizet, vol. II, p. 825. Mallarmé liked to refer to Emmanuel as Punch. The comparison results in much punning in Mallarmé's correspondence, with frequent play on the rhyme 'Emmanuel'/ 'Polichinelle' ('Polichinelle' is the French for 'Punch').

7 Letter to Henri Cazalis of October 1862 (*DSM* VI, 56).

8 In mid-July 1862 Charles Coligny wrote to Mallarmé: 'I am very pleased to learn that my friend Emmanuel des Essarts is by your side. He needed a generous and spirited companion. You are that person.' (Bibliothèque Littéraire Jacques Doucet, Paris, Valvins Collection, Ms MLV 411.)

9 *Le Papillon* published a review of Emmanuel des Essarts' book of poems *Poésies parisiennes* by Mallarmé on 10 January 1862. He would of course have been aware that the review was coming out well in advance of that date. Likewise, although the little sonnet 'Placet' only appeared in *Le Papillon* of 25 February 1862 and the poems 'Le Guignon' and 'Le Sonneur' in *L'Artiste* of 15 March, Mallarmé would have known of their acceptance much earlier. From what we know of the organization of these little reviews, it would seem likely that Des Essarts had acted as Mallarmé's agent on his trip to Paris during the Christmas break of 1861.

10 Without the intervention of Des Essarts it is difficult to understand why, faced with the temporary indisposition of their regular drama critic, the local newspaper should turn to someone as unknown and totally inexperienced as Mallarmé was at that time.

11 That Mallarmé really was the author of these pages was first suggested as early as 1959 by Marilyn Barthelème in her unpublished doctoral thesis for the Sorbonne entitled 'Formation et mise en oeuvre de la pensée de Mallarmé sur le théâtre'. She based her claim on a stylistic analysis of the texts. In fact, we now know that the actor and playwright Léon Marc, who was the object of much favourable comment in these articles, actually wrote to thank Mallarmé for his generosity. See *DSM* VII, 167–88.

12 Interestingly, 'Galanterie macabre' and another poem 'Haine du pauvre', written approximately around this time (or just a short time later), were both omitted from the first manuscript collection of his poems which Mallarmé began to circulate to his friends a couple of years later. Presumably he felt that they were too obviously 'political'.

13 Letter to Cazalis of 1 April 1863 (*DSM* VI, 144).

14 As is made clear in the final piece, the identity of the 'anonymous' author had fooled no one.

15 Significantly, Mallarmé felt confident enough about this poem to agree to its publication, with only minor modifications, some twenty years later when Paul Verlaine was seeking representative samples of his poetry for a special number of *Les Poètes maudits*. The complex nature of the poem which, as with all of Mallarmé's early poems, can only fully be understood in the context of the highly emotional state of mind of their author at the time, is exceptionally well analysed by Austin Gill: Gill II, pp. 186–206. His arguments concerning the implicit criticism of Baudelaire seem to me to be quite convincing.

16 Letter to André Desmolins of 17 January 1862 (*DSM* V, 348–9).

17 Letter from Anne Mallarmé to Fanny Desmolins of 21 January 1862 (*DSM* V, 250–1).

18 Letter from André Desmolins to Stéphane Mallarmé of 25 January 1862 (*DSM* V, 352–3).

19 Letter from Anne Mallarmé to Fanny Desmolins of 26 January 1862 (*DSM* V, 359).

20 Letter to André Desmolins of 31 January 1862 (*DSM* V, 367).

21 Letter from André Desmolins to Stéphane Mallarmé of around 8 February 1862 (*DSM* V, 373).

22 Letter to Fanny Desmolins of 10 February 1862 (*DSM* V, 374–5).

23 This collection of short stories was never completed. It is probable that a manuscript of a short story frequently and erroneously referred to by the title of its first part, 'Ce que disaient les trois cigognes . . .' 'the story the three storks told . . .'), and which is clearly a fair copy of an earlier schoolboy essay, belongs to this project (see Gill II, 118).

24 Henri Mondor, *Eugène Lefébure sa vie – ses lettres à Mallarmé*, Gallimard, 1951, p. 169 (henceforth abbreviated as *Lefébure*).

25 *Lefébure* 170.

26 *Lefébure* 173.

27 Mallarmé mentions Glatigny in his article on Léon Marc's play which appeared in *Le Sénonais* of 19 March 1862. In September of that year, along with Emile Deschamps, Albert Glatigny was one of the first to inscribe some verses in an album bought by Mallarmé and reserved for special friends. He corresponded intermittently with Mallarmé and visited him on several occasions until his sudden and early death from tuberculosis in April 1873.

28 Letter to Henri Cazalis of 5 May 1862 (*DSM* VI, 27–8).

29 This photograph is reproduced by Henri Mondor in his *Documents iconographiques*, Geneva, Cailler, 1947, plate III.

30 Letter to Cazalis of October 1862 (*DSM* VI, 60).

31 Letter to Cazalis of 24 May 1862 (*DSM* VI, 31).

32 Writing to Cazalis several years later from his exile in Avignon and trying to entice him to make a visit, Mallarmé makes the following revealing remark: 'Yes, old friend, we'll repeat that *Fontainebleau outing* [Mallarmé's italics]. It all began there . . .' Letter to Cazalis of 18 July 1868 (*DSM* VI, 374).

33 See Chapter 1, note 24, letter to Cazalis of 1 July 1862. (*DSM* VI, 40.)

34 Fanny Desmolins informed her cousin of the bad news on 21 June 1862 and did not resist the temptation to criticize her wayward grandson: 'So now that large family is reduced to living on a pension of 3,000 francs, which is quite a modest sum compared to what has been lost, and Stéphane is still in no position to fend for himself. We really do need God's help for our poor friends. Help us, my dear, to achieve that.' (*DSM* V, 379.) It is clear from the same letter that Numa Mallarmé had been asked to request voluntary retirement, thus making things easier for him than if he was simply suspended. Even so, he was in no condition to comprehend what was happening to him.

35 Letter to Cazalis of 4 June 1862 (*DSM* VI, 35).

36 Letter to Cazalis of 7 July 1862 (*DSM* VI, 47).

37 Letter to Cazalis of 24 May 1862 (*DSM* VI, 32).

38 Letter to Cazalis of 7 July 1862 (*DSM* VI, 46). The trick of simulating tears in this way probably owes something to Mallarmé's reading of Flaubert's *Madame Bovary*, where the

cunning seducer Rodolphe uses a similar technique. He had certainly read the book. Commenting on the fact that women were often poorly educated in artistic matters he wrote dismissively to Cazalis of 'the female artist who comes from a boarding-school or a Bovary-type artist with her head crammed full of silly novels'. (Letter to Cazalis of October 1862: *DSM* VI, 57.)

39 They are printed in full in *DSM* V, 380–5.

40 For a detailed account of the literary borrowings from Hugo, but not from Baudelaire, which are not commented upon, see Gill II, 39–43.

41 It was Marie Daubrun for whom Baudelaire wrote the poem 'L'Invitation au voyage' in which he plays on the themes of 'enfant', 'soeur' and 'douceur'. Mallarmé echoes this play in his letters to and about Marie Gerhard.

42 Letter to Cazalis of 5 August 1862 (*DSM* VI, 51).

43 Letter to Cazalis of 25 September 1862 (*DSM* VI, 55).

44 Marie Gerhard was in fact several years older than Mallarmé. She was born on 19 March 1835, seven years (almost to the day) before Mallarmé himself.

45 Letter to Cazalis, undated [October 1862] (*DSM* VI, 58–9).

46 Letter from Fanny Desmolins to Mélanie Laurent of 26 November 1862 (*DSM* V, 389).

47 'Until now he has found very few resources to defray his expenses, which are many,' she confided to Mélanie Laurent. 'And he hasn't enough sense to present himself to those people for whom we provided letters of introduction, either through laziness or sheer cussedness, both of which are unforgivable . . .' (Letter of 21 January 1863: *DSM* V, 393.)

48 Letter from Fanny Desmolins to Mélanie Laurent of 26 November 1862 (*DSM* V, 388).

49 Letter to Cazalis of 14 November 1862 (*DSM* VI, 67).

50 Mallarmé was always greatly influenced by the physical surroundings in which he found himself. He associated London with its enveloping blanket of fog, just as he would later associate Tournon with its incredibly clear blue skies. 'I hate London when there is no fog,' he wrote to Cazalis shortly before leaving it, 'in its mists it is a city without rival.' (Letter of 24 July 1863: *DSM* VI, 160.)

51 Letter to Cazalis, undated [November 1862] (*DSM* VI, 77).
52 Financially Mallarmé was quite well off in London, although he concealed the fact from Marie and, initially, from Cazalis as well. He later admitted to the latter that the annual interest on his inheritance amounted to between 3,600 and 4,000 francs. That was twice what he would earn in his first post as a schoolteacher the following year.
53 This was not very surprising. His family had bought his dispensation for the price of 1,000 francs.
54 Letter to Cazalis of 1 April 1863 (*DSM* VI, 143–4). Anne Mallarmé's attitude was quite remarkable given some of the wild rumours circulating in Sens. The following garbled account was passed on to Eugène Lefébure by someone who had heard it from a mutual friend called Courtois: 'Courtois sends his greetings. He has told me that Mallarmé is now back in Sens. . . . Apparently among the burghers of Sens there was a young English schoolteacher. Mallarmé fell in love with her. The burghers learnt of this and informed the young miss, who did not stop off very long in Sens and returned to Paris, where she found herself in a very precarious position. Mallarmé found out about this and sent her money, anonymously. Then, a short time later, went up to Paris and offered his love to the beautiful blonde daughter of Albion, spending two months with her in Paris. They both left for London, where the English bitch up and left him plunged into despair. Mallarmé then fell victim to a melancholy and took two or three months to recover.' (*Lefébure* 78–9).
55 Letter to Cazalis of 27 April 1863 (*DSM* VI, 148).
56 Upon his majority, in March 1863, Mallarmé inherited around a third of what was left of the estates of his dead mother and sister, the remainder falling due to him upon his father's death. In the event, he did not have long to wait. By August of that same year he had assets of around 20,000 francs at his disposal. That was ten times what he would earn in his first teaching post.
57 Letter to Cazalis of 27 April 1863 (*DSM* VI, 149).
58 Letter to Cazalis of 1 April 1863 (*DSM* VI, 144).
59 As a married man, Mallarmé felt that some of his male friends misunderstood the meaning of the word 'love': 'What has

always put me off that word, which causes me an unpleasant feeling when I write it, is the stupid way that half a dozen clowns, including Des Essarts, have become the advocates of that big chubby-faced youth who reminds me of a butcher's boy and whom they call Eros, contemplating each other ecstatically like martyrs every time they accomplish its facile rites, climbing on the women they had seduced as if they were climbing on the martyr's fire! In short, pretending that it is everything, whereas the truth is that Love is only one of the countless feelings which besiege our soul and ought to occupy no more place than fear, remorse, boredom, hate and sadness.' (Letter to Lefébure of 1865: *Lefébure* 343.)

Part of Mallarmé's 'coldness' can probably be explained by the impact which the early deaths of his mother and his sister had had upon him. But we must be careful not to exaggerate this. Nor must we forget that like many young men of his time (indeed of all time) Mallarmé was both attracted to and repulsed by sexuality. After two years of marriage, he gave the following advice to his friend Cazalis, who was contemplating with some distaste the physical side of marriage: 'Yes indeed I can understand your noble squeamishness which does not want the woman who remains after the virgin. But, even so, I think you would be happy! A serious marriage is too primitive, you are quite right, but why do you not consider it as a way of having a home, namely some peace and a 'tea-maker' as De Quincy says. You are too obsessed with a Kama Sutra view of marriage! It is true that the solitary life is fortifying, and very tempting too. I would prefer it, I think. But seeing that I am married, I prefer to stay so.' (Letter to Cazalis of 21 May 1866: *DSM* VI, 318–19.)

60 Letter to Cazalis of 3 June 1863 (*DSM* VI, 155).

61 The birth certificate which Marie Gerhard produced gave her age as twenty-three when she was in reality twenty-eight. Either Mallarmé wished her to appear younger than she was, or, and this seems more likely, she had entered France initially with a forged certificate that made her appear younger, in order to be more certain of obtaining employment as a governess.

62 Letter to Cazalis of 24 July 1863 (*DSM* VI, 161).

63 A charming eccentric, who had fled to England for political reasons after 1830 and had taken English nationality in 1848,

Chatelain was an acquaintance of Mallarmé's old friend Emile Deschamps. He was a prolific translator of English poetry. Mallarmé, who had a rather low opinion of his poetic talents, was very fond of him as a person. Financially Chatelain was very generous to Mallarmé and his wife. They received regular sums of money from him, and upon his death in 1881 he bequeathed Mallarmé £800, the equivalent of four to five years of the salary Mallarmé was then earning.

64 Anne Mallarmé expressed the hope that the Desmolins could find it in their hearts to forgive their grandson and welcome him again into their home: 'Oh, if I had to ask you this on bended knees I would not hesitate, so important is it to me that he receives your pardon! You will allow him to come won't you, and you will not reject him?' (Letter from Anne Mallarmé to Fanny Desmolins, undated but early November 1863: *DSM* V, 412.)

65 Catulle Mendès, *Le Mouvement poétique français de 1867 à nos jours*, 1903, pp. 135–6.

66 Alan Raitt, *Life of Villiers de l'Isle-Adam*, Oxford, 1981, p. 50.

3 Tournon

1 Letter to Cazalis of May 1864 (*DSM* VI, 210).

2 In 1888 Henri de Régnier noted in his diary the following conversation with Mallarmé: 'One evening Mallarmé spoke to me about his life in the provinces for the five years from 1865–1870 – a life of total and dispiriting isolation in Tournon and Avignon. "A life where you can lose your sanity," as he put it. So much so that one day after entire months without speaking to anyone, overwhelmed by his own imagination, he no longer felt like getting up. He felt he had lost the power of speech. Vaguely sensing that things had become critical, he knelt down on a chair and appealed to language itself, reciting prayers all day long. It is to that effort that he ascribes his survival.' (BN N.a.fr. 14974 fol. 177.)

3 Letter to Albert Collignon of 12 December 1863 (*Corr.* I, 98).

4 The reader will remember that in actual fact Mallarmé and his

family were not Parisians. As yet he had spent very little time in Paris.

5 Letter of Albert Glatigny to Mallarmé of 9 January 1864 (Bibliothèque Doucet, Mallarmé-Valvins Bequest MLV 1153).

6 Letter to Cazalis of 7 January 1864 (*DSM* VI, 176–7).

7 The London prose poems were 'La Pipe' ('The Pipe') and 'Orgue de Barbarie' ('The Barrel Organ'), later renamed 'Plainte d'automne' ('Autumn Lament'). The Tournon poem was entitled 'La Tête' ('The Head'), later changed to 'Pauvre enfant pâle' ('Poor Pale Child').

8 Letter to Cazalis of July 1864 (*DSM* VI, 221). On the other hand, Mallarmé made an exception of one Madame Seignobos, a refined lady and mother of one of his pupils, because he had noticed her one day stroking a cat! The Seignobos family, as we shall have frequent occasion to note, were to become extremely good friends to both Mallarmé and his wife.

9 Letter to Cazalis of [23 March] 1864 (*DSM* VI, 191–2).

10 Letter to Cazalis of 25 April 1864 (*DSM* VI, 204).

11 The beautiful daughter of Dalkeith Holmes, a retired English army officer, Augusta Holmès, who was Irish by birth and enjoyed something of a reputation in the avant-garde literary circles in which she moved, was to become first the mistress and then the wife of Catulle Mendès. Mallarmé would later become one of her circle when he settled in Paris.

12 Indeed, learning of his friend's posting, Mallarmé had automatically assumed that he would stop off on his way south to Avignon. His decision not to do so (quite understandable in the circumstances, particularly because his new headmaster was impatient for him to start work) so provoked the wrath of Mallarmé that their mutual friend and wiser counsel, Henri Cazalis, had to point out to him that he was reacting quite unfairly.

13 Interestingly enough, when in May of that year Cazalis was toying with the idea of abandoning the Law and possibly leaving Paris to take up another profession, Mallarmé could remark: 'Anyhow, since Emmanuel [des Essarts] and myself can live in the provinces, alas, you can accept this martyrdom too!' (Undated letter to Cazalis [but of May 1864]: *DSM* VI, 210.)

14 Baudelaire seems to have been less than overwhelmed when, at

the home of Valentine Lejosnes, Des Essarts read to him
'L'Azur' and 'Les Fenêtres'. Cazalis wrote to Mallarmé that the
master had listened to his poems 'with great attention', adding
that, following the tradition of the house, 'he said nothing'
(letter of April 1864, *DSM* V, 195). Seeking to console his
protégé, Emmanuel des Essarts put an optimistic gloss on
Baudelaire's reaction. He informed Mallarmé that the latter had
listened to the poems 'without disapproval', which he
interpreted as 'a very strong indication of approval' (letter of 7
April 1864, *DSM* V, 196). Although he must have been bitterly
disappointed by Baudelaire's apparent indifference to his verse,
Mallarmé continued to admire his work. The two men never
became friends, but after Baudelaire's death Mallarmé agreed to
become president of his memorial committee.

15 This information is given in Austin Gill, 'Mallarmé
fonctionnaire', in *Revue d'histoire littéraire de la France* (*RHLF*)
LXVIII, no. 1, January–February 1968, p. 8. One of Mallarmé's
inspectors was convinced that, with experience, he would
improve: 'He needs some training. He has the right qualities. I
gave him some advice as to how to deal with each of his classes.
He accepted this with deference and promised to heed my
advice. He shows promise of being a good English teacher.'
This was in fact the best confidential report Mallarmé would
ever receive.

16 Letter to Cazalis of 9 October 1864 (*DSM* VI, 236).

17 Letter from Fanny Desmolins to Mallarmé of 22 October 1864
(Bonniot Collection).

18 'What little inspiration I have had, I owe to that name, and I
believe that if my heroine had been called Salomé I would have
invented that dark word which is as red as an open
pomegranate. Anyhow I intend making her a purely imaginary
creature entirely independent of History.' (Letter to Lefébure,
late February 1865, see *Lefébure* 341.) It was only much, much
later when *Hérodiade* was developed into *Les Noces d'Hérodiade*
(*Hérodiade's Wedding*), that Mallarmé introduced the overtly
Biblical element with 'Le Cantique de Saint-Jean' ('Song of John
the Baptist').

19 Letter to Cazalis of late October 1864 (*DSM* VI, 238–9).

20 Commenting on Geneviève's arrival to her cousin Mélanie

Laurent, Fanny Desmolins pointed out that her grandson had hoped for a girl rather than a boy (letter of 7 December 1864: Bonniot Collection). This is a further indication of how insecure Mallarmé felt within himself at this time. A male child could have meant a potential rival.

21 Letter to Cazalis of 26 December 1864 (*DSM* VI, 245).
22 Letter to Cazalis of 15 January 1865 (*DSM* VI, 249).
23 Letter to Cazalis of 7 January 1864 (*DSM* VI, 176).
24 Letter to Lefébure of late February 1865 (*Corr.* I, 154).
25 Mallarmé's enthusiasm for *Elen* explains in part why he ventured into the metaphysical short story himself with his unfinished project *Igitur*, whose very title may owe something to Villiers' play, where students sing the celebrated *Gaudeamus igitur*. R. G. Cohn makes this point in his excellent study *Towards the Poems of Mallarmé*, Berkeley, 1980, p. 280.
26 Letter from Théodore de Banville to Mallarmé of 31 March 1865 (Bonniot Collection).
27 Letter to Cazalis of 26 December 1864 (*DMS* VI, 245).
28 Letter to Cazalis of 15 January 1865 (*DMS* VI, 248).
29 Letter to Théodore Aubanel [early May 1865] (*Corr.* I, 162–3). Mallarmé's genuine affection for his daughter certainly struck his grandmother when he visited her in September of that year. She commented on it in a letter of 7 October 1865 to her usual confidante, Mélanie Laurent: 'We had Stéphane with us two or three times last month. But the greater part of his holidays were spent in Paris, from which he had the utmost difficulty in dragging himself away, seeing that, according to him, that is where the centre of Art and literary things are, which take precedence over everything else in that poor boy, even over family affections. Furthermore, it is no bad thing that his stay in Versailles was not longer, as much for my husband as for him. The difference in tastes, in behaviour and in attitudes is so great that there is a kind of embarrassment in their relationship as each one avoids subjects which he knows will upset the other. Total openness which is what is delightful in close relationships becomes quite impossible in these circumstances and that is unfortunately the state of affairs between the poor boy and ourselves, whose outlook is so different to his. It is only when

he talks about his daughter that he appears to us as we should like him to be. He is mad about her.' (Bonniot Collection.)

30 Letter from Des Essarts to Mallarmé of around 17 March 1865 (Bonniot Collection).

31 Letter to Frédéric Mistral of 30 December 1864 (*DSM* VII, 361).

32 In March 1865 Mallarmé discovered that the doctor who had taken care of him and Marie in the rue des Saints-Pères when they returned from London and to whom he had sent a New Year greeting had interceded on his behalf at the Education Ministry. As a result he believed he was being offered a transfer after the summer holidays to a more civilized town. He even entertained the idea of asking for Versailles. In the event he discovered that he had not yet been employed long enough to merit any special treatment.

33 Letter to Cazalis of early April 1865 (*DSM* VI, 263–4).

34 Letter from Cazalis to Mallarmé [undated, but beginning of April 1865] (*DSM* VI, 268).

35 Letter from Emile Roquier to Mallarmé of 5 April 1865 (*DSM* VII, 204).

36 *Hérodiade* was to undergo many transformations but was to remain an unfinished work. Very little has survived of the early manuscript versions. Only one fragment of a scene between the Nurse and Hérodiade herself was ever printed in Mallarmé's lifetime. This appeared in the second series of the collective work *Le Parnasse contemporain*, which was published in 1871. By then however Mallarmé had completely revised the whole project, on which he was to work intermittently throughout his life. He was working on a version of *Hérodiade* at the time of his death.

37 Letter to Lefébure of July 1865 (Bibliothèque Doucet, Mondor Bequest MNR Ms 556).

38 As originally conceived the *Heroic Intermezzo* comprised three scenes: 'Le Monologue d'un Faune' ('The Monologue of a Faun'); 'Le Dialogue des Nymphes' ('The Nymphs' Dialogue') and 'Le Réveil du Faune' ('The Faun Awakes'). As in the case of *Hérodiade*, little remains of the manuscript state of the first version, merely a few fragments which survived among Mallarmé's papers. The *Intermezzo* was to become first

Improvisation d'un Faune some ten years later and then in 1876
L'Après-midi d'un Faune (The Faun's Afternoon).
39 Letter to Marie Mallarmé of 27 September 1865 (*Corr.* I, 172).
40 Letter from Fanny Desmolins to Mallarmé of 13 June 1865
(Bonniot Collection).

4 The Crossroads

1 Letter to Aubanel of 16 October 1865 (*Corr.* I, 173–4).
2 The musical allusion in the title *Ouverture d'Hérodiade* clearly
demonstrates that even at this early stage, Mallarmé believed
that poetry could rival some of the achievements of music. The
definitive title which Mallarmé gave to the *Faun*, *Prélude à
l'Après-midi d'un Faune (Prelude to the Afternoon of a Faun)*, makes
a similar point.
3 Letter to Marie Mallarmé of 27 September 1865 (*Corr.* I, 172).
4 The headmaster's report is quoted in full in Austin Gill,
'Mallarmé fonctionnaire', loc. cit., p. 9.
5 Letter to Cazalis of 5 December 1865 (*DSM* VI, 300). Letter to
Aubanel of 6 December 1865 with a postmark of 7 December
(*Corr.* I, 181).
6 Lefébure's wife had died of tuberculosis in July 1865 at the
tragically early age of nineteen. It was in part to recover from
his grief that he began to interest himself in Egyptology.
Having inherited some modest funds from his grandmother, he
was, for the time being at least, a man of relatively independent
means and had decided to settle for the next few years in
Cannes, where Mallarmé visited him.
7 Letter to Marie Mallarmé of 23 December 1865 (*Corr.* I, 186).
8 Letter to José-Maria de Heredia of 30 December 1865. This
letter, which has been omitted from the first volume of
Mallarmé's *Correspondance*, is quoted by Pierre-Olivier Walzer
in his *Essai sur Stéphane Mallarmé*, Paris, Seghers, 1963,
p. 121.
9 Letter to Cazalis of 21 or 28 April 1866 (*DSM* VI, 307).
10 Letter from Lefébure to Mallarmé of 9 May 1866 (*Léfébure*
216).
11 Letter to Cazalis of 28 April 1866 (*DSM* VI, 310).

12 Letter to Marie Mallarmé of 4 April 1866 (Bonniot Collection).
13 Letter to Lefébure of 3 May 1868 (*DSM* VI, 368).
14 Letter to Cazalis of July 1865 (*DSM* VI, 286).
15 This passage is taken from the chapter 'Crise de Vers', from the collection *Divagations*, 1896 (*Oeuvres complètes*, 364).
16 Letter to Cazalis of 28 April 1866 (*DSM* VI, 308).
17 Letter from Fanny Desmolins to Mallarmé of 5 May 1866 (Bonniot Collection).
18 Letter to Cazalis of 28 April 1866 (*DSM* VI, 308).
19 Letter from Lefébure to Mallarmé of 27 May 1867 (*Lefébure* 247).
20 Letter to Cazalis of 21 May 1866 (*DSM* VI, 316).
21 'Having discovered the void, I have discovered Beauty', Mallarmé wrote to Cazalis on 13 July 1866 (*DSM* VI, 321), and to the same correspondent, a year later: 'I have descended deep enough into the Void to be able to speak with certainty. There is only Beauty – and it has only one perfect means of expression, Poetry.' (Letter of 14 May 1867, *DSM* VI, 343.)
22 The expression is used by Mallarmé in one of his later articles of drama criticism, 'Notes sur le théâtre', in *La Revue indépendante*, January 1887, p. 58.
23 Letter to Cazalis of 28 April 1866 (*DSM* VI, 308).
24 Letter from Lefébure to Mallarmé of August 1866 (*Lefébure* 221).
25 The sonnets, which are untitled, were again grouped together under the general title *Tryptique* in the final edition of his poems which Mallarmé himself prepared for the Belgian publisher Deman in 1894. Known by their first lines, each sonnet takes as its starting point some object of an interior domestic setting: a table – 'Tout orgueil fume-t-il du soir . . .' ('Does the pride of all our evenings smoke . . .'); a vase – 'Surgi de la croupe et du bond . . .' ('Soaring out of the rounded back . . .'); and a lace bed-cover/curtain – 'Une dentelle s'abolit . . .' ('A lacework vanishes . . .'). Their common subject is the absence/presence paradox, expressing Being and Nothingness, which is so central to Mallarmé's thought.
26 Letter to Cazalis of 13 July 1866 (*DSM* IV, 321).
27 Letter to Aubanel of 16 July 1866 (*Corr.* I, 222).
28 Letter to Aubanel of 28 July 1866 (*Corr.* I, 224). The lacework

image employed here, which arises by analogy with the spider image, would tend to confirm that it was at this time that Mallarmé was working on an early version of his sonnet 'Une dentelle s'abolit . . .' which works a whole series of changes upon this image. See above note 25.

29 Letter to Aubanel of 23 August 1866 (*Corr.* I, 231). An amusing letter from Villiers de l'Isle-Adam to Mallarmé of 11 September 1866 confirms that Mallarmé had sought from him some advice on alchemistic and cabbalistic works: 'When will your *Traité des pierres précieuses* [*Treatise on Precious Stones*, Mallarmé's projected book of poems on Beauty] be published? I have more confidence in your alchemy than in that of Auriole Théophraste Bombaste known as the Divine Paracelsus. Nonetheless, I would suggest *Les Dogmes et rituel de haute magie (Dogma and Rituel of High Magic)* by Eliphas Lévy 2 vols in–8 (1850, Dentu, Paris) if they are in the library of your town. As for Hegel, I am really very pleased that you have paid some attention to that miraculous genius . . .' (Bonniot Collection). Villiers' comment on Hegel would suggest, if further evidence were required, that Mallarmé had resisted earlier recommendations to read him.

30 Quoted in Austin Gill, 'Mallarmé fonctionnaire', loc. cit., p. 9.

31 Letter from Fanny Desmolins to Mallarmé of August 1866 (Bonniot Collection).

32 Letter from Fanny Desmolins to Mallarmé of September 1866 (Bonniot Collection).

33 Quoted in Gill, loc. cit., p. 11.

34 Interestingly, Fanny Desmolins was quite relieved that her grandson had not been transferred to his home town of Sens, as she feared that there were those in his family who still had not forgiven him for his marriage to Marie. 'Many personal disappointments perhaps awaited you there,' she wrote pointedly on 17 October 1866 (Bonniot Collection). 'There are many in the family who would make life difficult for Marie,' she repeated some twelve days later, adding: 'Do not read this sentence to Marie.'

35 Letter from Lefébure to Mallarmé of 1 November 1866 (*Lefébure* 232).

5   Besançon and Avignon

1 Des Essarts quotes this comment back at Mallarmé in a letter to him of 22 December 1866 (Bonniot Collection).
2 Letter to François Coppée of 5 December 1866 (*Corr.* I, 233).
3 Quoted in Gill, 'Mallarmé fonctionnaire', p. 14.
4 Letter to Heredia of 7 March 1867 (*Corr.* III, 382).
5 Letter to Cazalis of 14 May 1867 (*DSM* VI, 340).
6 Letter to Léo d'Orfer of 27 June 1884 (*Corr.* II, 266). This definition of poetry was published by the latter two years later in the third number of *La Vogue*, 1886, 70–1.
7 Letter to Verlaine of 16 November 1885 (*Corr.* II, 301).
8 Letter to Villiers de l'Isle-Adam of 24 September 1867 (*Corr.* I, 259).
9 Mallarmé had recently read an article by Emile Montégut, 'La nouvelle Littérature française. Les romans de M. Victor Cherbuliez'. See *La Revue des Deux Mondes*, 15 May 1867, pp. 483–501.
10 Letter to Lefébure of 27 May 1867 (Bibliothèque Doucet, Mondor Bequest MNR Ms 558). We have quoted the manuscript of this letter, which in several parts is inaccurately transcribed in Mallarmé's *Correspondence*. The italics are Mallarmé's.
11 This is precisely the subject of 'Le Cantique de Saint-Jean' ('Song of John the Baptist'), the final part of the unfinished *Les Noces d'Hérodiade*.
12 Letter to Lefébure of 27 May 1867 (Bibliothèque Doucet, Mondor Bequest MNR Ms 558 bis). In his edition of the *Correspondance*, Henri Mondor reproduces the curious reading for the beginning of this passage: 'la nature *en* pensant', which makes little sense in French. The actual manuscript reads 'la nature *se* pensant' (my italics).
13 Is it necessary to point out that Mallarmé is at one and the same time both a sensuous and a cerebral poet and that his best writing fuses the two? Likewise it is precisely the relationship between absence and presence and not absence itself which interests him. For him, absence and death are only one part of the equation. (This point is made very forcibly in the sonnet commemorating Poe, 'Tel qu'en lui-même enfin . . .' 'Such as

into himself at last . . .'), where he asks that the perpetual and mutually dependent struggle between the earth and sky be the bas-relief added as a fitting monument to the American poet's tomb.) By placing too much emphasis upon the deaths of Mallarmé's mother and sister, critics unfairly and inaccurately stress the negative aspect of Mallarmé's work. To do so is both to deform and to profoundly misunderstand his thought.

14 Fanny Desmolins replied on 25 May 1867 saying she had written to M. Lebourgeois, who had been helpful the year before (Bonniot Collection).

15 Letter from Mallarmé to Aubanel of 7 October 1867 (*Corr.* I, 264).

16 Letter to Lefébure of 3 May 1868 (*DSM* VI, 369). Mallarmé would also make a point of being absent from Avignon during the poetry festival organized by Aubanel and the others that summer.

17 Letter of 1 April 1868 (Bonniot Collection). Clearly her recent visit had improved her relationship with her grandson. When Mallarmé's migraines persisted she advised him: 'Above all, my dear friend, take care of that poor head of yours, it is prematurely exhausted by your lack of prudence in the past. Those sleepless nights and your intellectual activity are beyond your physical strength.' (Letter of 9 April 1868: Bonniot Collection.)

18 Letter to Lefébure of 3 May 1868 (*DSM* VI, 368).

19 The collection *Sonnets et eaux-fortes (Sonnets and Watercolours)* was published later in the year by Alphonse Lemerre, without Mallarmé's contribution. By the time it arrived, there were too many poems and not enough artists! The collection had been organized by Philippe Burty and included among the painters one who, when he met him much later, was to become one of Mallarmé's closest friends, Edouard Manet.

20 Letter to Cazalis of 18 July 1868 (*DSM* VI, 375–6).

21 She replied warmly enough on 13 July 1868, but with her customary lack of diplomacy: 'My dear friend, I don't know why I did not congratulate you on the small *poetic* victory you mentioned in your last letter but one. I want to tell you straight away and before anything else that I am pleased to share it, in so far as it will stop you for some time from wanting to take up

again that occupation which should only be a distraction for the mind but which you quite wrongly used to exhaust your brain. So, until further orders, I want absolute rest on that front. You understand?' (Bonniot Collection.)

22 Once again, it is the final, much reworked version of the poem which is reproduced here. The 1868 version entitled 'Sonnet allégorique de lui-même ('A sonnet which is an allegory of itself') can be examined in *DSM* VI, 377.

23 Letter to Cazalis of 19 February 1869 (*DSM* VI, 420).

24 Letter from Fanny Desmolins to Mallarmé of 13 February 1869 (Bonniot Collection).

25 Letter to Fanny Desmolins of 27 April 1869 (Bonniot Collection).

26 Letter to the Minister of Education of 6 December 1869 (*Corr.* III, 385).

27 Letter to Lefébure of 20 March 1870 (*Corr.* I, 318). Some of Mallarmé's notes on language from this period have survived in fragmented form, principally because, forced to economize whenever possible, he used the reverse side of the sheets of paper for the drafts of other work undertaken at a later period (Private Collection). Fragmentary notes have likewise survived of a proposed thesis on comparative religions, *De Divinitate*. Lefébure greatly approved of Mallarmé's choice of Linguistics which, with remarkable foresight, he predicted was 'the coming science' (letter to Mallarmé of 25 March 1870, *Lefébure* 319).

28 Letter to Lefébure of 20 March 1870 (*Corr.* I, 318). It may well have been at this time that Mallarmé began 'Quand l'ombre menaça . . .' and even 'Le vierge, le vivace et le bel aujourd'hui . . .' but of course we cannot be sure of this.

29 Letter to Lefébure of 20 March 1870 (*Corr.* I, 318).

30 Letter from Catulle Mendès to Mallarmé of 25 May 1870 (Bonniot Collection).

31 Undated letter from Catulle Mendès to Mallarmé but of July 1870 (Bonniot Collection).

32 For an amusing account of this reading see Catulle Mendès, *Rapport sur le Mouvement poétique français de 1867 à 1900*, Paris, 1900, pp. 135 ff. At the time of Mendès' visit Mallarmé probably read to his friends the chapter entitled 'Le Minuit' ('Midnight'), which had by then undergone six or seven rewritings. Its

lugubrious and sinister atmosphere, compounded by much internal assonance, has more than a little in common with Poe's tale 'The Fall of the House of Usher'. The curious title *Igitur*, meaning 'therefore' in Latin, which has frequently baffled critics, probably owes something to Descartes' famous *cogito ergo sum* ('I think therefore I am') which Mallarmé had been studying. (But see also Chapter 3 note 25, above.) The manuscript or rather different manuscript versions of *Igitur* which were worked and reworked at many different times in Mallarmé's life, right up to and including his final years, are a much more complicated matter than the misleadingly simplistic text published by Mondor for the *Oeuvres complètes* would suggest.

33 As the riots of the Commune broke out in Paris, Mallarmé wrote to Cazalis: 'Just at the moment I am working on a Drama and a Vaudeville aimed at discrediting in the eyes of an attentive audience the old distinction between Art and Science. It can be done, I tell you.' (Letter of 23 April 1871, *DSM* VI, 467.) An extremely rough draft for a play containing similar ideas and annotations has survived. It was published by Jacques Schérer in *Le 'Livre' de Mallarmé*, Gallimard, 1957, pp. 16A to 26A.

34 Letter to Cazalis of 3 March 1871 (*DSM* VI, 454).

6 Paris: The Early Years

1 The whole area had still been uncultivated fields when a royal decree of 2 February 1826 allowed speculators to open up a whole series of roads bearing the names of European capitals which would meet in a circular square to be known as La Place d'Europe. In fact, building did not begin until the 1850s, when the Haussmanization of Paris gathered momentum. See *Paris-Atlas*, Larousse, Paris, 1900, p. 90. This fascinating book, a mine of information about the historic development of Paris, was fortunately reprinted by Larousse in 1989, with a foreword by Jacques Chirac.

2 Letter to Augusta Holmès of 20 December 1871 (*Corr.* V, 211).

3 Letter from Lefébure to Mallarmé of 21 December 1871 (*Lefébure* 333).

4 Cazalis intervened to calm matters, and as a result Lefébure and Mallarmé both wrote to each other in conciliatory terms after Christmas. A year or two later when their friendship might have taken up where it had left off, Lefébure was unfortunately posted to Lille, from where he moved on to Lyon and then Algiers.

5 The text of this prospectus, published by the printer of Alphonse Lemerre, is reproduced in *Oeuvres complètes*, Gallimard, 1961, p. 1607.

6 That first winter in Paris Mallarmé completed his abridged translation or rather 'free adaptation' of George Cox's *A Manual of Mythology in the Form of Question and Answer*, London, 1867. He also finished translations of several of the poems of Edgar Allan Poe. The first of these began to appear in *La Renaissance littéraire et artistique* at the end of June 1872. In July of that same year he contributed a short article on the London Exhibition to *L'Illustration* (20 July) and in November, a critical appraisal of Dierx's collected poems, again in *La Renaissance littéraire et artistique* (see note 9 below).

7 It was in June 1872 that through Verlaine, Mallarmé met Arthur Rimbaud at one of the monthly '*Dîners des Vilains Bonshommes*'.

8 Mallarmé published a whole series of his Poe translations in *La Renaissance littéraire et artistique*. The first of these appeared in the issue of 28 June 1872 and the last in that of 19 October.

9 'L'oeuvre poétique de Léon Dierx', in *La Renaissance littéraire et artistique*, 16 November 1872.

10 For an interesting discussion of this craze for things Japanese see the catalogue of an exhibition shown at the Cleveland Museum of Art, 9 July–31 August 1975, published under the title *Japonisme: Japanese Influence on French Art 1854–1910*, 1975. Burty's ornate membership card for the *Société du Jing-lar* is reproduced on p. 30.

11 Letter from Philippe Burty to Mallarmé of 31 August 1872 (*Corr.* IV 583).

12 Three reports on the London Exhibition appeared in *Le National* of 29 October, 14 November and 29 November 1872, not under Mallarmé's name but under the pseudonym of L. S. Price. Significantly, when he came to write the fourth article,

published by *L'Illustration* on 20 July 1872, Mallarmé used his own name.

13 His friends argued, quite correctly, first that he himself was not well known enough to attract sufficient subscriptions or collaborators, and second, that the timing was quite inappropriate given the depression that had followed the short-lived boom in the aftermath of the Franco-Prussian war.

14 In addition to public meeting places such as the numerous cafés, bars and restaurants of the time, various individuals held regular salons. Among Mallarmé's immediate circle, these were organized by Mendès and Verlaine on Wednesdays, by Augusta Holmès on Fridays and by Lemerre, Nina de Villars and Leconte de Lisle on Saturdays. Mallarmé's free time during any given week was thus easily accounted for. These gatherings varied considerably in nature. The salon of Nina de Villars, who was Manet's model for the painting *Lady with a Fan*, was renowned for its relaxed and Bohemian atmosphere. In his unpublished diaries Henri de Régnier recalls how one evening Villiers threw at people's heads a cage with a screaming monkey in it which had been rendered drunk with absinthe. (BN N.a.fr. 14974 fol. 32.)

15 Nearly everything Mallarmé published during his lifetime began in this way. In that sense his work largely consists of occasional pieces – *pièces de circonstance*.

16 As a consequence of the Franco-Prussian war in which Henri Regnault and members of his own family had been killed, Mallarmé resolutely refused to visit Germany, despite having a German wife.

17 Mallarmé completed the article but it was never published. See letter to Marie Mallarmé of 25 August 1873 (*Corr.* IV, 384).

18 Letter to Marie Mallarmé of 6 August 1873 (*Corr.* IV, 377).

19 Letter to Marie Mallarmé of 20 August 1873 (*Corr.* IV, 380). Interestingly, in a letter to Philippe Burty from Douarnenez, Mallarmé mentions having come across a museum there filled with Japanese things.

20 Letter to Marie Mallarmé of 25 August 1873 (*Corr.* IV, 384).

21 Letter to Geneviève Mallarmé of 28 August 1873 (*Corr.* IV, 387).

22 George Moore, 'Souvenir sur Mallarmé', in *Parsifal*, number 3,

1909, p. 263. A set of manuscript notes retained by Mallarmé in his *Igitur* dossier (Private Collection) correspond very closely to the scenario outlined by Moore.

23 Writing to Paul Verlaine in 1885, some two years after Manet's death, Mallarmé had no hesitation in naming the latter as one of his greatest friends: 'My great friendships have been with Villiers and Mendès and for ten years I saw every day my dear friend Manet whose absence now seems quite incredible.' (Letter to Verlaine of 16 November 1885, *Corr.* II, 300.)

24 In 1867 Maximilian had been imposed on the throne of Mexico by Napoleon III. When the United States put pressure on France, Napoleon abandoned Maximilian, who was overthrown and executed by the Mexican leader Benito Juarez. Manet painted the scene no less than four times. In the earliest version, the firing squad sported Mexican-style uniforms. He presented one of the later versions to one of his models, Méry Laurent, with whom Mallarmé himself would become extremely friendly from the middle 1880s after Manet's death.

25 Armand Silvestre, *Au Pays du souvenir*, 1892, as quoted by Bernard Denvir, *The Impressionists at First Hand*. Thames and Hudson, 1987, pp. 71–2.

26 While his father was alive, Manet had played the dutiful son, as required. But in October 1863, a few months after the latter's death, he had discreetly married in Holland a Dutch woman, Suzanne Leenhoff, whom he had first known as his piano teacher some twelve years earlier and with whom, a year or so after the start of this relationship, he had fathered a child.

27 E. Moreau-Nélaton, *Manet raconté par lui-même*, 2 vols, Paris, 1926, vol. II, p. 9.

28 It is clear from the unpublished diary of Henri de Régnier, who was a regular attender of the famous Tuesday evening gatherings in Mallarmé's home, that after Manet's death the latter remained a frequent subject of conversation. On such occasions, according to Régnier, Mallarmé spoke of Manet in almost reverential terms.

29 Bonniot Collection.

30 Letter from Suzanne Manet to Mallarmé of 21 October 1885 (*Corr.* IV, 499).

31 *Le Temps*, 26 February 1874.

32 Unpublished and undated letter from Anne Mallarmé to Mallarmé (Bonniot Collection).

33 President of the Winegrower's Society of Charente, owner of a cognac distillery, Théodore Duret was a close friend of Manet, who painted his portrait in 1868. An ardent republican, he supported Courbet's destruction of the Vendôme Column and diplomatically undertook a trip to the Far East when the Commune was defeated. It was from that time that he became a passionate collector of Japanese prints. A fine and perceptive critic, his *Peintres impressionistes* in 1878 was one of the first serious attempts to analyse the group. Félix Bracquemond was a printer and engraver. He was passionately interested in Japanese art. Like Burty a founder member of the Society of the Jing-lar, he owned numerous Japanese albums including a copy of Hokusai's *Manga*.

34 A friend of Cézanne, with whom he had been at school, and a frequenter of the Café Guerbois, Zola began to defend Manet and his friends as early as 1866. Mallarmé met him at Manet's studio. He admired Zola's novels and did his best to promote them to the English reading public.

35 Letter to Alphonse Lemerre of March 1874 (*Corr.* II, 44–5).

36 'I believe,' he writes teasingly 'that this canvas [*The Railway*], which has been protected from the scheming and plotting of the Salon organizers, has yet another surprise in store for them when what ought to be said about it is said by those who are interested in certain issues . . .'

   For an interesting analysis of the 'subversive' nature of this painting which Mallarmé describes as being 'rich in suggestions for those who like to look at things' and which challenges any complacent notions of progress and fulfilment in the anonymity of a modern industrialized city, see Robert L. Herbert, *Impressionism, Art, Leisure and Parisian Society*, Yale University Press, 1988, pp. 28–9.

37 Deriding the academic painters of the Salon for imagining that Manet's conception and execution somehow endangers their existence, Mallarmé praises in Manet 'the simplification brought to bear in such a positive manner by a visionary eye on certain techniques of painting (whose principal error consists in deliberately concealing that all art springs from oil and colour),

[which] can tempt foolish people into believing that they have in front of them something that smacks of facility'.

38 The cooperative was in fact wound up at a general meeting in Renoir's home on 17 December 1874 because of the financial liabilities which had been incurred.

39 Mallarmé describes *The Skylarks* as being 'an impression of the outdoors' and later he talks of 'the dose of impressions which are collected in every painting'.

40 Undated letter from Manet to Mallarmé (*Corr.* II, 44).

41 Letter from Manet to a M. Colliaux of 30 June (*Corr.* IV, 588), where the signatory of the letter is mistakenly identified as 'Ed Morin'. The manuscript state of the letter, which we have been able to consult, clearly bears Manet's signature.

42 Marie Mallarmé was, once again, desperately worried about their financial situation: 'Nothing new here', she wrote to Mallarmé while he was making his preliminary visit to Valvins. 'I do not know exactly what is the current position. I shall see Mme Seignobos tomorrow' (letter of 28 May 1874, *Corr.* IV, 399) – which would suggest that Mallarmé had asked Charles Seignobos to come once more to the rescue.

43 Letter to Richard Horne of 10 March 1875 (*Corr.* II, 58). Mallarmé had recently met Horne in Paris. He had been recommended by the Chevalier de Chatelain.

44 Letter from Lemerre to Mallarmé of 13 March 1875 (*Corr.* II, 59).

45 The four illustrations accompanying the text were: a figure at a table; a figure at an open window with the raven entering it; a figure contemplating the bust of Pallas upon which is perched the raven; the raven perched on a chair. The following note which Mallarmé managed to have placed in the London magazine *The Athenaeum* highlighted these drawings: 'The illustrations are of a very fantastic character, reminding us somewhat of the strange likenesses of Charles Baudelaire, done, we believe, by the same artist.' (*The Athenaeum*, Saturday 26 June 1875.)

46 Twenty-five francs was roughly the equivalent of one month's rent for the average working man of the time.

47 Mallarmé had done what he could to ensure the success of the book by using his now considerable contacts in the press. 'What

we need,' he wrote to Léon Cladel, who had a literary column in *Le Figaro*, 'is some early publicity which presents the book as terribly Parisian and terribly fashionable etc. A few lines like that, which could nonetheless give some praise to the translation and a lot to the drawings (because of the Lemerre affair), is so much more valuable from the point of view of sales than an arty or bibliographical article.' (Letter to Cladel of 4 June 1875: *Corr.* II, 59.)

48 Letter to Marie Mallarmé of 16 August (*Corr.* IV, 403). On 15 March of that year Mallarmé and his family had left their first flat for another one on the fourth floor of number 87 in the rue de Rome a mere few streets away and still in the same district.

49 Letter to Marie Mallarmé of 4 September 1875 (*Corr.* IV, 405).

50 The first of these 'Gossips' as Mallarmé called them appeared in *The Athenaeum* of 4 September 1875, the very day he left for France. It consisted of an announcement of his forthcoming preface to his re-edition of *Vathek* and a comment on the work of Gustave Flaubert.

51 Letter to Marie Mallarmé of 24 September 1875 (*Corr.* IV, 413).

52 Mallarmé had sent Swinburne a copy of *The Raven* at the time of its publication. A translation by Augusta Holmès of Swinburne's poem 'The Pilgrim' appeared in the first issue of *La République des lettres* on 15 December 1875. 'Nocturne', a poem written in French by Swinburne, was published in the third number of the same review on 20 January 1876. In the same issue Mallarmé published a review of Swinburne's *Erechtheus*. The other main English contributors to *La République des lettres* were Arthur O'Shaughnessy and John Payne.

53 Manet's oriental style for the woodcuts was quite deliberate. 'Manet will be pleased that you really appreciated his so unusual illustrations which mix in such a truly modern way the Japanese and the classical,' Mallarmé wrote to O'Shaughnessy on 25 May 1875 (*Corr.* II, 119). In fact the foliage motif produced by Manet as part of his illustrations was an exact copy of plants and flowers depicted in Hokusai's *Manga*, the first volume of which was published in 1814 and which Manet himself had been able to consult in a copy owned by Félix Bracquemond.

54 Letter from Clément to Mallarmé of 16 May 1876 (*Corr.* V, 354).

55 Quoted by Austin Gill in 'Mallarmé fonctionnaire' *RHLF LXVIII*, no. 2, March–April 1968, p. 263). The Lycée Condorcet had been renamed the Lycée Fontanes. It would later revert to its original name.

56 Mallarmé knew *Le Linge* very well, having followed its development closely. The garden used as a background in the painting was situated at number 58 rue de Rome, right across the street from his own flat.

57 Mallarmé's comments were not always carried in *The Athenaeum*. A note on a Meissonier painting contrasting its old-fashioned style with the new *plein air* style (December 1875) and an account of Manet's rejection by the Jury of 1876 and a prediction that his one-man exhibition would become 'the most popular meeting place in Paris for those who are thoughtful, thorough and critical' (10 April 1876) were both omitted.

58 Letter from G. T. Robinson to Mallarmé of 19 July 1876 (*DSM* I, 65).

59 Letter to O'Shaughnessy of 19 October 1876 (*Corr.* II, 129).

60 Manet continued to seek sources of extra income for Mallarmé. In November of that year, through his brother Eugène, he unsuccessfully tried to get Mallarmé appointed as the art critic of *La Révolution*.

61 The Poe memorial volume, edited by Sara Sigourney Rice, was published by Turnbull brothers and Co. in Baltimore in January 1877. It contained Mallarmé's poem but not the portrait of Poe by Manet which Mallarmé had sent along with his own contribution. It was not until 1883 that Mallarmé would authorize Paul Verlaine to publish some of his poems as part of a special number of the review *Lutèce*.

62 Wagner laid the foundation stone of the *Festspielhaus* on 22 May 1872, his 59th birthday. Stage rehearsals began in the summer of 1875. The dress-rehearsals took place on 6–9 August 1876. The first official performance (attended by Catulle Mendès) took place on 13 August 1876.

63 These notes, preserved among Mallarmé's papers, were published by Jacques Schérer. See *Le 'Livre' de Mallarmé*, Gallimard, 1957. The notes belonged to a dossier compiled by Mallarmé from around 1870 until the time of his death in 1898. He consulted and used them many times during that extensive

period, with the result that neither the original order of the notes nor their various dates of composition can be established with any exactitude.

64 See letter to Anatole France of 15 May 1876 (*Corr.* II, 116).

65 Letter to Sara Sigourney Rice of 12 January 1877 (*Corr.* II, 144).

66 Letter to Sarah Helen Whitman of May 1877 (*Corr.* II, 151).

67 Letter to O'Shaughnessy of 28 December 1877 (*Corr.* II, 159).

68 Letter to O'Shaughnessy of 4 July 1877 (*Corr.* II, 153).

69 The Exhibition opened on 1 May 1878 and continued until 10 November, attracting no less than 10 million visitors. The first electric street lamps in the world were switched on around the Etoile, and the Palais du Trocadéro, especially built for the occasion, was visited by Stanley, the finder of David Livingstone. Not one to overlook the financial opportunity afforded by the Exhibition, Mallarmé wrote a series of newspaper articles on it, but these seem not to have been published.

70 The completed manuscript of this translation exists. Mallarmé received an advance of 1,000 francs against a total of 1,500 for the anthology. He received 300 francs and 600 francs respectively for the abridged version of *Les Mots anglais* and the commercial correspondence. But, as he pointed out ruefully to a friend, much of that had been spent in advance (letter to Henri Roujon of 20 April 1878, *Corr.* II, 170).

71 Letter from Seignobos to Mallarmé of June 1878 (*Corr.* IV, 431–2).

72 Letter from Manet to Mallarmé of 8 May 1878 (Bonniot Collection).

73 Letter from Georges Chéron to Mallarmé of 26 September 1879 (Bonniot Collection).

74 Letter to Robert de Montesquiou of 8 October 1879 (*DSM* II, 58).

75 Letter to John Payne of 7 October 1879 (*Corr.* II, 201).

7 Growing Celebrity

1 'How is it that my wife's health, so robust in the past, has become such that when the slightest thing upsets her

monotonous illnesses, she is completely put out for several days!' Mallarmé lamented in a rare display of anger to Jean Marras (letter of November 1881: *Corr.* V, 253).

2 Letter to Verlaine of January 1881 (*Corr.* II, 221).

3 See Geneviève Mallarmé as quoted by H. Mondor in *Vie de Mallarmé*, Gallimard, 1942, p. 425.

4 Letter to Montesquiou of January 1881 (*Corr.* IV, 465).

5 The unfinished outline of this project, some 200 pages in total, which survived among Mallarmé's papers, was published with an important introduction by Jean-Pierre Richard: see *Pour un tombeau d'Anatole*, Editions du Seuil, 1961.

6 Letter from Manet to Mallarmé of 31 July 1881 (Bonniot Collection). Although it was not recognized as such at the time, the disease from which Manet was suffering was a possible manifestation of tertiary syphilis.

7 Letter from Manet to Mallarmé of September 1881 (Bonniot Collection).

8 Letter from Manet to Mallarmé of 16 or 18 September (the postmark on the envelope is unclear) 1881 (Bonniot Collection).

9 Letter from Manet to Mallarmé of 16 September 1882 (Bonniot Collection).

10 The manuscript quatrain (Collection André Rodocanachi), written on the visiting card in black ink and simply dated 'Tuesday', is unsigned. It reads:

> Avant que cinq heures ne sonne
> A la gaîne du corridor,
> On sera près de la personne
> Qui porte une coiffure d'or.

> [Before five o'clock chimes
> On the clock in the corridor
> We shall be close by the one
> Who wears golden hair.]

11 Letter to Nadar of June 1884 (*Corr.* IV, 475).

12 'I am rushing to post you this note,' Mallarmé wrote on 4 May 1895. 'I dare not use the telegraph system because of old memories.' (Published by André Rodocanachi in his important

article 'Stéphane Mallarmé et Méry Laurent' in *Bulletin du Bibliophile*, 1979, IV, 17.)

13 Letter from Geneviève Mallarmé to Mallarmé of 15 June 1885 (*DSM* IV, 397). A week later when her father mentions the same person, Geneviève retorts: 'What, Madame Laurent? Mother thought that you would be over her by now.' (Letter of 20 June 1885, ibid., 407.)

14 Henri de Régnier, 'Faces et Profils: Méry Laurent', in *Le Figaro* of 23 July 1932.

15 Letter to Méry Laurent of 11 September 1888 (*Corr.* III, 354).

16 Cf. this rather sharp and disapproving observation: 'The motives which led Méry Laurent to sleep with Manet, Bourget, Becque, Mallarmé and Champsaur – before they became really famous – are the same as those which drove Princess Mathilde to surround herself by the Goncourts, Taine and Gautier – they are both keen to be part of the epoch. Except that for the Princess to be successful, all she has to do is open up her drawing-room, the courtesan, however, has to open up her bed.' Diary of Henri de Régnier (BN. N.a.fr. 14974 fol. 154 [October 1888]).

17 Diary of Henri de Régnier (BN N.a.fr. 14974 fol. 137 [June 1888]).

18 Some of Mallarmé's earlier sonnets inspired by his wife were later reworked with Méry in mind. Others like 'La chevelure vol d'une flamme . . .' ('Hair streaking like a flame . . .') and 'M'introduire dans ton histoire . . .' ('Insinuating myself into your life . . .') were specifically written for her.

19 Diary of Henri de Régnier (BN N.a.fr. 14974 fol. 131–2 [June 1888]).

20 Letter from Huysmans to Mallarmé of 27 October 1882 (*Corr.* II, 235).

21 Letter to Huysmans of October 1882 (*Corr.* V, 356).

22 Letter to Huysmans of 12 May 1883 (*Corr.* II, 242).

23 Letter to Verlaine of 22 August 1883 (*Corr.* II, 245).

24 Letter to Verlaine of 3 November 1883 (*Corr.* II, 249).

25 The poems published by Verlaine were: 'Placet', 'Le Guignon', 'Apparition', 'Sainte', 'Don du poème', 'Cette nuit' ('Quand l'ombre menaça . . .') and 'Le tombeau d'Edgar Poe'.

26 The expression is used in a letter of 30 July 1888 to Léo d'Orfer

(*Corr.* III, 218). In a renumbering of houses, Mallarmé's address had officially changed from 87 to 89 rue de Rome at the end of March 1884.

27 Edouard Dujardin, *Mallarmé par un des siens*, Messein, 1936, p. 24.

28 See Geneviève Mallarmé as quoted by Mondor, *Vie de Mallarmé*, Gallimard, 1942, p. 78.

29 Camille Mauclair, *Mallarmé chez lui*, Grasset, 1935.

30 Dujardin, op. cit., p. 78.

31 Letter to Dujardin of 18 January 1887 (*Corr.* III, 84).

32 Diary of Henri de Régnier (BN N.a.fr. 14974 fol. 20). Given Mallarmé's derisive remarks about the glass domes of future fun palaces, one cannot help wondering what he would have made of the 'Pyramid' of the Louvre Museum erected for posterity in the name of François Mitterrand!

33 Diary of Henri de Régnier (BN N.a.fr. 14974 fol. 92).

34 Diary of Henri de Régnier (BN N.a.fr. 14974 fol. 95).

35 Dedicated to Des Esseintes as one of the exquisite pieces which he might well have included in his private anthology of rare literary gems, 'Prose', as we have said earlier, is fundamentally an account and a reaffirmation of Mallarmé's personal poetic vision. A slightly shorter version, minus the dedication to Huysmans' hero and without the last two 'Byzantine' stanzas, was first published by Henri Mondor in 1954 and republished by Carl Barbier alongside a copy of an intermediate version by Luigi Gualdo, a friend of Robert de Montesquiou. As is frequently the case, we do not know the exact date of composition of this important poem, but what Mallarmé seems to have done is to have submitted to Fénéon a reworked version of an earlier state dating some time from 1877–8 onwards.

36 Letter to Verlaine of 7 December 1884 (*Corr.* II, 274).

37 Letter to Geneviève Mallarmé of 3 June 1885 (*DSM* IV, 389).

38 Letter to Dujardin of 5 July 1885 (*Corr.* II, 290).

39 Letter to Maurice Barrès of 10 September 1885 (*Corr.* XI, 34–5).

40 See letter from Francis Poictevin to Mallarmé of 29 October 1884 (*DSM* IV, 352). Francis Poictevin (1854–1904) was a minor poet and friend of J. K. Huysmans.

41 Letter to Verlaine of 19 December 1884 (*Corr.* II, 277).
42 Letter from Huysmans to Mallarmé of 14 January 1885 (*Corr.* II, 263), and Dujardin, op. cit., pp. 70 ff.
43 Letter of 2 February 1885 to Odilon Redon (*Corr.* II, 280).
44 Letter to Dujardin of 10 September 1885 (*Corr.* II, 294).
45 Letter to Verlaine of 16 November 1885 (*Corr.* II, 301).
46 This statement was reproduced by Pica in the course of his article 'I Moderni Bizantini' in *Gazetta letteraria, artistica e scientifica*, 27 November 1886.
47 The Collège Rollin was built on what had been formerly the site of the slaughterhouse of the plains of Montmartre. The irony of this fact must surely not have been lost on Mallarmé.
48 Letter of 17 February 1886 (*Corr.* IX, 36).

8   The Banquet Years

1 Letter to John Payne of 24 May 1886 (*Corr.* III, 35).
2 Two of these poems were published. The first, 'M'introduire dans ton histoire . . .', appeared in the June 1886 issue of the newly founded *La Vogue* edited by Gustave Kahn. The second, 'La chevelure, vol d'une flamme . . .', was published as part of an extended prose poem, 'La déclaration foraine' ('An Announcement at the Fair') in the fashion magazine *L'Art et la Mode* in August 1887. 'Méry/Sans trop d'aurore', was sent to Méry Laurent as a New Year's greeting for 1888.
3 Quoted by Austin Gill in 'Mallarmé fonctionnaire', *RHLF* LXVIII, no. 2, p. 276.
4 Letter to Dujardin of 30 August 1886 (*Corr.* III, 54). As we see from this letter he had unsuccessfully tried to have himself transferred back to the Lycée Condorcet.
5 Letter to Léo d'Orfer of 23 September 1886 (*Corr.* III, 62). In the event, Mallarmé's kindness typically got the better of him. He authorized D'Orfer to publish a prose poem and a poem in verse both of which had already appeared elsewhere. A year later when René Ghil published a note in *Le Figaro* defending his 'Symbolico-Instrumentalist Group' which had been forced to take refuge in the Belgian review *La Wallonie* and sought to link Mallarmé's name to his decision, Mallarmé was outraged:

'Instrumentalist Symbolist! what doggerel! and how one gets implicated in such things without being aware of it!' (Letter to Dujardin of 30 August 1887: *Corr.* III, 134.)

6 Letter to Dujardin of 30 August 1886 (*Corr.* III, 55).

7 Félix Fénéon had been a co-founder of the original *Revue indépendante* in 1884. He had agreed to be Dujardin's editor for the new series with which the latter sought to replace the *Revue wagnérienne*, from whose patrons and financial controllers he wished to free himself.

8 When, three years later, Dujardin expressed an interest in marrying Mallarmé's daughter, it was Marie Mallarmé, not her husband, who objected. By that time the *Revue indépendante* had folded and Marie did not feel that Dujardin's financial prospects were very promising.

9 Letter to Théodore Duret of 10 November 1886 (*Corr.* III, 68). Recently posted to London, where he met Whistler again and had encouraged him to contact Mallarmé, Duret had written to the latter, full of nostalgia for *La République des lettres*: 'At last you and your friends are going to have a Review! I can just see you squaring your shoulders, starting fires everywhere, without any thought of attracting a large public or increasing your readership, hip, hip, hurray!' (Letter of early November, *Corr.* III, 68–9.) Duret of course was quite correct, it was the thought of having a platform again which in part had convinced Mallarmé to become involved.

10 Manuscript note belonging to a Private Collection.

11 Letter from Dujardin of 29 October 1886 (Private Collection). Dujardin also became impatient with the number of last-minute corrections which Mallarmé was making to his articles at the proof stage, thus adding to the expense of the exercise.

12 When he read the covering note, Verlaine wrote to Mallarmé expressing some concern. Mallarmé replied reassuring him that Vanier was the target of the note, not himself.

13 Once the photographically reduced manuscript copy of the text was ready, Mallarmé objected to the expression 'lithographically produced' which Dujardin proposed to include in the title. Eventually they agreed to refer to a 'photolithographical edition', which finally appeared, with a frontispiece by Félicien Rops, towards the end of October 1887.

14 On 11 December 1886 Mallarmé apologized for not being able to attend on the following Thursday as he had another engagement. Clearly, the dinners with Berthe Morisot had not yet become a regular fixture in his diary.

15 Letter from Berthe Morisot to Mallarmé of December 1887 (*Corr.* III, 151).

16 Reminding Duret that it was he who had originally introduced him to Whistler, Mallarmé stated that the latter had made 'an extraordinary impression' ('une très rare impression') upon him. (Letter to Duret of 2 March 1888: *Corr.* III, 174.)

17 When the translation appeared in *La Revue indépendante* and subsequently in a special private edition, Francis Vielé-Griffin, who had provided Mallarmé with considerable help, was understandably quite upset not to see his efforts duly acknowledged.

18 As Mallarmé in fact pointed out to Deman, the beginning of August was a notoriously bad month in which to publish anything. The timing, plus the relative expense of the edition (12 francs), ensured that very few copies were sold. When moving premises eight years later, Deman discovered 500 unsold copies out of the original run of 850.

19 Letter to Deman of 19 July 1888 (*Corr.* III, 226).

20 Letter to Deman of 21 November 1888 (*Corr.* XI, 43). Although this was not mentioned in his correspondence with Deman, one of the underlying reasons why Mallarmé preferred the title *Pages* was that it subtly hinted that the volume was not to be confused with the great project, the Book, but merely took some tentative steps towards it.

21 Letter from Mary Cassatt to Mallarmé of 22 January 1889 (*Corr.* III, 291). Mallarmé knew Mary Cassatt through Degas or Berthe Morisot and her husband.

22 Letter from Monet to Mallarmé of 15 February 1889 (*Corr.* III, 290).

23 Letter from Monet to Mallarmé of 12 October 1889 (*Corr.* III, 363).

24 Letter to Monet of 18 October 1889 (*Corr.* III, 364). By mid-July 1889, Duret, Monet and several others had already collected some 12,000 francs out of the 20,000 required to buy Manet's *Olympia* from his widow for the Louvre Museum. In his reply

to Monet of 18 October, Mallarmé enclosed a 25-franc donation.

25 Mallarmé collected the painting during a two-day visit to Giverny in July 1890 with Berthe Morisot and her husband. 'It is as expressive as the *Mona Lisa*'s smile,' he used to say. See Gustave Geffroy, *Claude Monet*, Crès, 1924, vol. II, p. 95. Writing to Régnier on 4 October 1890, Mallarmé commented: 'Come back quickly to Paris, a magnificent Monet is awaiting your visit, above the sofa we use for our Tuesday evening gatherings: so are we!' (*Corr.* IV, 137.)

26 Diary of Henri de Régnier (BN N.a.fr. 14974 fol. 183).

27 Mallarmé recounts this incident in a letter to Cazalis of 23 May 1889 in which he expresses great depression over the condition of Villiers. In fact, as the same letter makes clear, he was both fascinated and repulsed by the vulgarity of the Universal Exhibition. In the same letter he concludes: 'I am afraid that place might devour me; I'll go back there before returning to Valvins. But how all of that can do without us.' (*Corr.* IV, 542.) Mallarmé seems to have diverted Villiers with an account of the Exhibition, because during a period of remission he wrote to Mallarmé to inform him that he had thought of an amusing idea for a short story to be called 'The Ghost of the Eiffel Tower'.

28 Telegram to Marie and Geneviève Mallarmé of 12 February 1890 (*Corr.* IV, 51).

29 Letter to Marie and Geneviève Mallarmé of 12 February 1890 (*Corr.* IV, 53).

30 Manuscript sent to *L'Art moderne* (Private Collection).

31 Letter to Méry Laurent of 12 August 1889 (*Corr.* III, 340).

32 Letter to Méry Laurent of 11 September 1889 (*Corr.* III, 354).

33 Diary of Henri de Régnier (BN N.a.fr. 14975 fol. 39 [January 1890]).

34 Diary of Henri de Régnier (BN N.a.fr. 14975 fol. 100).

35 Letter to Verhaeren of 15 January 1888 (*Corr.* III, 162).

36 In June 1888 Mallarmé composed a biographical note on himself for some publication which subsequently never materialized. In it he described himself as 'someone who works in isolation preparing a work of art of an entirely personal nature for which the advance publicity, in ways which are equally original, will take place in the winter 1888–1889'. (*Corr.* III, 216.)

37 See Diary of Henri de Régnier (BN N.a.fr. 14974 fol. 1999
    [March 1889], and Jacques Schérer, *Le 'Livre' de Mallarmé*,
    Gallimard, 1957, pp. 16–26.
38 Letter to Berthe Morisot of 3 September 1890 (*Corr.* IV, 129).
39 Letter to Octave Mirbeau of 10 September 1890 (*Corr.* IV, 130).
40 Letter to Octave Mirbeau of 5 January 1891 (*Corr.* IV, 176).
41 Letter to Octave Mirbeau of 17 January 1891 (*Corr.* IV, 183).
42 Letter to Octave Mirbeau of 23 February 1891 (*Corr.* IV, 201).
43 As reported in *Le Mercure de France*, May 1891, p. 318.
44 Letter to Deman of 29 November 1890 (*Corr.* IV, 165).
45 Wishing to take advantage of his recent celebrity, Mallarmé had
    begun discussions on this with Deman as he awaited the
    publication of *Pages*, which eventually appeared, without
    illustrations, at the end of May 1891. By the end of August it
    had been agreed that Whistler would provide a portrait for this
    volume and that Deman would have special type designed and
    struck for the printing of the text.
46 Letter to Berthe Morisot of 29 September 1891 (*Corr.* IV, 313).
47 Letter to Henri de Régnier of 29 September 1891 (*Corr.* IV,
    315).
48 Diary of Henri de Régnier (BN N.a.fr. 14975 fol. 14 [May
    1892]).
49 Telegram from Whistler to Mallarmé of 2 November 1891
    (*Corr.* IV, 323).
50 Letter to Whistler of 3 November 1891 (*Corr.* IV, 323).
51 Henri de Régnier has left the following detailed description of
    Whistler's house in the rue du Bac: 'At the end of a long yard
    there was a little single-storey house with blue and white
    lacquered doors with glass panes in them. You step into a
    landing where an enormous Japanese basket made out of reeds
    woven into the shape of a water melon thrusts out its rounded
    belly. You go down a little stairway of five or six steps into a
    big empty hall with yellow Japanese embossed wallpaper. From
    there you step out into a large room. Its white lacquer panels are
    lifted by a suggestion of water and a shady river done in a
    delicate peacock blue. In a fireplace with a lacquered top and on
    whose lintel stand two fine Japanese cones in white porcelain on
    either side of a portrait of Whistler as a child, there burns a kind
    of bronze pot filled with holes and placed on a stack of wood. A

real cooking pot. The windows open out onto a garden, which links up with neighbouring gardens. On the floor, a bluey grey carpet, in a corner, in a yellow piece of pottery, between two large gladioli leaves rises a huge fan with orange flowers on it. In the middle of the room is a tiny writing table. There is a dining-room next door with the same blue and white décor, with lovely blue and white Chinese porcelain displayed on a black lacquer dresser. Tea is served and this house with no furniture is absolutely exquisite.' (BN N.a.fr. 14975 fol. 92).

52 Letter to Whistler of 5 November 1892 (*Corr.* V, 144). Henri de Régnier recounts how, whilst posing for this portrait, Mallarmé suffered great discomfort because he was asked to pose in front of a fire, which made it very difficult to stand still. When he later explained to Whistler just how uncomfortable an experience it had been, the latter exploded into his diabolical laughter. See *Nos Rencontres*, Mercure de France, 1931, pp. 213–14.

53 Although he had great affection for Renoir, Mallarmé was not at all pleased with this oil portrait, which he felt made him look like 'a stumpy financier' as he told the *Mardistes* in January 1893. See the comments of Edmond Bonniot, 'Notes sur les mardis', in *Les Marges*, 10 January 1936, LVII, number 224, p. 12.

54 C. Mauclair, *Mallarmé chez lui*, Grasset, 1935, pp. 18–19. Whistler's portrait and the portrait by Gauguin also need to be added to this list.

55 Octave Mirbeau, *Le Figaro*, 24 August 1890.

56 Letter to Mauclair of 18 April 1893 (*Corr.* VI, 79).

57 Letter from Maeterlinck to Mallarmé of 26 September 1893 (*Corr.* VI, 159).

58 Upon the death of Eugène Manet in April of that year, Mallarmé had officially become Julie Manet's guardian. It was a role he took extremely seriously, dutifully attending family councils and dealing with legal matters on behalf of his ward and her mother, to both of whom he was quite devoted. Julie Manet's diary (Klincksieck, 1979) contains several detailed and charming accounts of her visits to Valvins.

59 Letter to Jules Boissière of 24 November 1892 (*Corr.* V, 155).

60 Diary of Henri de Régnier (BN N.a.fr. 14975 fol. 100).

61 Letter to Coppée of 21 July 1893 (*Corr.*VI, 132).

62 Letter to Jules Boissière of 25 July 1893 (*Corr.* VI, 138).

9 A Throw of the Dice

1 Visiting card to Méry Laurent dated 8 November 1893 (*Corr.* VI, 186).
2 Letter to Marie and Geneviève Mallarmé of 27 February 1894 (*Corr.* VI, 228).
3 Letter to Marie and Geneviève Mallarmé of 28 February 1894 (*Corr.* VI, 232).
4 Letter to Marie and Geneviève Mallarmé of 3 March 1894 (*Corr.* VI, 236).
5 Diary of Henri de Régnier (BN N.a.fr. 14977 fol. 17).
6 Mallarmé's reply and that of Tailhade were both reproduced in a special supplement of *Le Journal* which appeared on 10 December 1893, entitled 'Dynamite at the Palais-Bourbon'.
7 Diary of Henri de Régnier (BN N.a.fr. 14977 fol. 28) . These remarks probably owe something to the manner in which intellectual activity seemed to be rewarded in the colleges of Oxford and Cambridge which Mallarmé had just visited. During the summer he raised in the French press the possibility of a tax on the reproduction of literary works which would ensure some revenue for writers and above all allow young writers to survive. This 'Literary Fund' aroused considerable interest but was not in the end pursued.
8 The manuscript notes were placed inside a first edition of *Divagations* given to Fénéon (Bibliothèque Doucet, Mondor Collection MNR Ms 1158).
9 Letter to Whistler of 7 August 1892 (*Corr.* V, 114). Madame Ponsot and her family were the recipients of many of Mallarmé's humorous and delightful occasional verses.
10 Letter to Berthe Morisot of 29 August 1894 (*Corr.* VII, 40).
11 Letter to Henri de Régnier of 7 September 1894 (*Corr.* VII, 47). In his letter Mallarmé is referring to the fact that the river had been deliberately dammed and rerouted earlier that month. This had prevented him from doing any sailing.
12 Diary of Henri de Régnier (BN N.a.fr. 14977 fol. 74).
13 Writing to Edouard Gravollet from Valvins that same month, Mallarmé described the autumnal landscape as being 'in harmony with some dreams which I have not abandoned' (letter of 7 October 1894: *Corr.* VII, 65). Lugné-Poë, who had visited

Mallarmé in Valvins towards the end of August, describes him as working away in his study on those famous 'little pieces of paper' upon which he jotted notes and ideas for the Book (see *Le Sot du tremplin*, Gallimard, 1931, pp. 231–2). The series of articles which Mallarmé was to write the following year for *La Revue blanche* contain frequent allusions to the project of the Book.

14 Letter to Henri de Régnier of 10 October 1894 (*Corr.* VII, 69).

15 Letter from Geneviève Mallarmé to Stéphane Mallarmé of 27 April 1897 (*Corr.* IX, 146).

16 Letter to Verhaeren of February 1895 (*Corr.* VII, 149).

17 Diary of Henri de Régnier (BN N.a.fr. 14977 fol. 125).

18 Letter to Gauguin of 18 February 1895 (*Corr.* VII, 161).

19 This interview, given to Georges Docquois in January 1895, was only published by Docquois after Mallarmé's death, in *La Critique* of 5 October 1898.

20 Diary of Henri de Régnier (BN N.a.fr. 14979 fol. 55).

21 *L'Echo de Paris* of 6 February 1896. These attacks reached their height in June of 1896 when *Le Gaulois* printed an interview with Leo Tolstoy in which the Russian writer referred to a Mallarmé poem as a typical example of the way in which French literature had become incomprehensible. When a brief and highly ironic retort from Mallarmé was printed in *Le Gaulois* of 22 June 1896, the editor could not resist adding his own comment: 'M. Stéphane Mallarmé is an exquisite writer and a distinguished poet, but why in the devil's name does he write in such a way that nobody can understand him?'

22 Letter to Léopold Dauphin of 25 February 1896 (*Corr.* III, 66). A musician and would-be poet, Dauphin had first met Mallarmé at Valvins in the late 1870s and had remained his friend ever since.

23 Up until this point, Mallarmé had remained convinced that prefaces were somewhat redundant, in so far as the work of art should speak for itself. He commented upon this rather humorously to Charles Guérin, who had invited him to preface one of his books. 'My dear friend', he replied, 'a true book requires no presentation, it creates its own *coup de foudre*, like a woman with her lover and without the aid of a third party or husband.' (Letter to Guérin of 24 December 1894: *Corr.* VII,

117.) It is symptomatic of how sensitive he now was to criticism that he felt the need to break this rule.

24 Letter from Lichtenberger to Mallarmé of 21 October 1896 (Private Collection).

25 'I am going to have to do some work for *La Revue blanche* and for *Cosmopolis* in order to repay my kind banker [i.e. his daughter Geneviève],' he wrote to Geneviève on 25 November 1896 (*DSM* II, 155). It is perhaps worth while to point out that Mallarmé agreed to publish a ten-page poem because the rates offered by *Cosmopolis* were 40 francs per page for verse and 20 francs for prose! (These rates were confirmed by Lichtenberger in a letter to Mallarmé of 15 December 1896: Private Collection.)

26 In March 1894 Henri de Régnier noted in his diary: 'Mallarmé often says "You can say everything in four pages; in four pages I could explain the world."' (BN N.a.fr. 14977 fol. 4.) The comment, as the *Coup de dés* demonstrates, was not made lightly.

27 Letter from Lichtenberger to Mallarmé of 4 March 1897 (Private Collection).

28 Manuscript copy of a letter to André Lichtenberger [undated, but March 1897] conserved among Mallarmé's papers (Private Collection).

29 The little note was placed at the foot of the opening page of the poem. The manuscript text, returned with the first proofs, now belongs to a private collection. When he gave Paul Valéry a set of these proofs Mallarmé apparently said to him, rather proudly: 'Do you not think I am mad? Do you not think that this is an act of folly?' (As recorded by Valéry on the envelope containing the proofs: Collection Paul Valéry.)

30 Vollard had approached Mallarmé through Odilon Redon as early as December 1896. Mallarmé was only too keen to work with Redon, whose work he had admired for a long time and whose career he had actively supported.

31 Letter to André Gide of 14 May 1897 (*Corr.* IX, 171).

32 Letter to Elémir Bourges of 1 March 1897 (*Corr.* IX, 92).

33 Letter to Geneviève Mallarmé of 27 April 1897 (*Corr.* IX, 145).

34 Letter to Geneviève Mallarmé of 23 May 1897 (*Corr.* IX, 196).

35 Letter from Paul Valéry to André Gide of 24 May 1897

(*Correspondance André Gide–Paul Valéry*, Gallimard, 1955, p. 297).

36 Letter to Gravollet of 28 September 1897 (*Corr.* IX, 280).

37 Letter to Méry Laurent of 24 January 1898 (*Corr.* X, 96).

38 Letter to Charles Morice of 4 February 1898 (*Corr.* X, 102).

39 Letter to Geneviève Mallarmé of 19 May 1898 (*Corr.* X, 196). Marguerite Moreno, the actress, who was staying close by with Marcel Schwob, had heard that the poem was finished and had expressed a desire to play the leading role. Two days after this letter Vollard brought a 200-franc advance to Mallarmé's flat in the rue de Rome.

40 Letter to Geneviève Mallarmé of 23 May 1898 (*Corr.* X, 202). A week earlier Mallarmé had written to Rodin: 'One of the punishments for living in isolation is that you can only shout your fury to the forest and the river. I am still angry. Who knows, perhaps after a shrug of your shoulders you may feel quite calm. After all, you have the glory of knowing that you are right.' (Letter to Rodin of 15 May 1898: *Corr.* X, 190.) Mallarmé had also congratulated Octave Mirbeau for stoutly defending Rodin against his critics.

41 Letter from Paul Valéry to André Gide of 12 September 1898 (*Correspondance André Gide–Paul Valéry*, Gallimard, 1955, p. 331).

42 Letter to Léopold Dauphin of August 1898 (*Corr.* X, 245).

43 All these documents were published for the first time in 1959. See Gardner Davies, *Les Noces d'Hérodiade: Mystère*, Gallimard, 1959.

44 Henri Mondor, *Autres précisions sur Mallarmé et inédits*, Gallimard, 1961, pp. 250–1.

45 Letter from Charles Morice to Geneviève Mallarmé of 4 October 1898 (*Corr.* X, 323).

46 The most important of these include: *Igitur*, published by Mallarmé's son-in-law Edmond Bonniot in 1925; *Le Livre*, published by Jacques Schérer in 1957; *Les Noces d'Hérodiade: Mystère*, published by Gardner Davies in 1959; and *Pour un tombeau d'Anatole*, published by Jean-Pierre Richard in 1961.

Postscript

1 Interview published in *L'Echo de Paris* of 13 March 1891.
2 From an account of the funeral given in the diary of Julie Manet (*DSM* IV, 514).
3 Quoted by Françoise Cachin in *Gauguin*, Flammarion, 1990, p. 217.
4 Letter published in *Le Figaro* of 29 August 1898.
5 Ibid.

Select Bibliography

Manuscript sources

In addition to the list of printed books which follows, two main manuscript sources have been frequently used. These are:

1 The as yet unpublished private diary of Henri de Régnier. This voluminous document, bearing the title *Annales psychiques et occulaires*, can be consulted in the Manuscript collection of the Bibliothèque Nationale, Paris, Mss Nouvelles acquisitions françaises 14974–77.

2 What survived of Mallarmé's own papers was originally and piously preserved by his daughter Geneviève and her husband, Edmond Bonniot. This collection eventually passed into the hands of Edmond Bonniot's second wife and her family. While the collection was still intact, it was extensively photographed and photocopied by Carl Barbier. In the last decade or two large parts of this collection have been dispersed among various libraries, museums and private collections. For the purpose of this book, we have used photocopies or photographs of documents where the originals are no longer accessible. For reasons of consistency we have consequently given the Bonniot Collection as the source of our documents.

Printed sources

(Unless otherwise indicated, the place of publication is Paris.)

Select Bibliography

Mallarmé works and documents

CORRESPONDENCE AND DOCUMENTS

Correspondance de Mallarmé vol. I (1862–71): recueillie, classée et annotée par Henri Mondor, avec la collaboration de Jean-Pierre Richard, Gallimard, 1956.
Correspondance de Mallarmé vols. II–XI (1872–98): recueillie, classée et annotée par Henri Mondor et Lloyd James Austin, 1965–84.
Documents Stéphane Mallarmé, présentés par Carl Paul Barbier, 7 vols, Nizet, 1968–79.

WORKS

Oeuvres complètes, édition établie par Henri Mondor et G. Jean-Aubry, Pléiade, Gallimard, 1961.
Oeuvres complètes I, *Poésies*, édition critique présentée par Carl Paul Barbier et Charles Gordon Millan, Flammarion, 1983.
Poésies, Préface d'Yves Bonnefoy. Edition de Bertrand Marchal, NRF Gallimard, 1992.

POSTHUMOUS PUBLICATIONS

Le 'Livre' de Mallarmé, présenté par Jacques Schérer, Gallimard, 1957.
Pour un tombeau d'Anatole, présenté par Jean-Pierre Richard, Editions du Seuil, 1961.
Les Noces d'Hérodiade: Mystère, texte présenté par Gardner Davies, Gallimard, 1959.

Principal works consulted

Austin, Lloyd James *Poetic Principles and Practice*, Cambridge University Press, 1987.
Badesco, Luc *La Génération poétique de 1860*, Nizet, 1971, 2 vols.
Edmond Bonniot 'Notes sur les mardis' in *Les Marges*, 10 January 1936, LVII, number 224, p. 12.
Bowie, Malcolm *Mallarmé and the Art of Being Difficult*, Cambridge University Press, 1978.
Cachin, Françoise *Gauguin*, Flammarion, 1990.
Cellier, Léon *Mallarmé et la morte qui parle*, Presses Universitaires de France, 1959.

Clark, T. J.   *The Painting of Modern Life*, London, Thames and Hudson, 1984.

Cleveland Museum of Art   Catalogue of an Exhibition 9 July–31 August 1975 published under the title *Japonisme: Japanese Influence on French Art 1854–1910*, 1975.

Cohn, Robert G.   *Towards the Poems of Mallarmé*, Berkeley, 1980.

Davies, Gardner   Mallarmé et la 'Couche suffisante d'intelligibilité', Corti, 1988.

Denvir, Bernard   *The Impressionists at First Hand*, London, Thames and Hudson, 1987.

Des Essarts, Emmanuel   'Souvenirs littéraires: Stéphane Mallarmé' in *Revue de France*, 15 July 1899, pp. 441–7.

Dreyfous, Maurice   *Ce que je tiens à dire*, publisher unknown, 1912.

Dujardin, Edouard   *Mallarmé par un des siens*, Messein, 1936.

Florence, P.   *Mallarmé, Manet and Redon*, Cambridge University Press, 1986.

Geffroy, Gustave   *Claude Monet*, Crès, 1924, 2 vols.

Gill, Austin   *The Early Mallarmé*, Oxford, the Clarendon Press, 2 vols, 1979, and 1986.

—— 'Mallarmé fonctionnaire' in *Revue d'histoire littéraire de la France*, LXVIII, no. 1, January–February 1968, pp. 6–37; no. 2, March–April 1968, pp. 254–86.

Hanson, A. C.   *Manet and the Modern Tradition*, Yale University Press, 1977.

Herbert, Robert L.   *Impressionism, Art, Leisure and Parisian Society*, Yale University Press, 1988.

Kearns, James   *Symbolist Landscapes: The Place of Painting in the Poetry and Criticism of Mallarmé and His Circle*, MHRA Texts and Dissertations, vol. 27, London, 1989.

Kristeva, Julia   *La Révolution du langage poétique*, Seuil, 1974.

Lugné-Poë, A.-F.   *Le Sot du tremplin*, Gallimard, 1931.

Mallet, Robert   *Correspondance André Gide–Paul Valéry*, Gallimard, 1955.

Mauclair, Camille   *Mallarmé chez lui*, Grasset, 1935.

Mondor, Henri   *Vie de Mallarmé*, Gallimard, 1942.

—— *Documents iconographiques*, Geneva, Cailler, 1947.

—— *Eugène Lefébure, sa vie – ses lettres à Mallarmé*, Gallimard, 1951.

—— *Mallarmé lycéen*, Gallimard, 1954.

—— *Autres précisions sur Mallarmé et inédits*, Gallimard, 1961.

Moore, George   'Souvenir sur Mallarmé' in *Parsifal*, number 3, 1909.

Moreau-Nélaton, E.   *Manet raconté par lui-même*, 2 vols, Paris, 1926.

Plessis, Alain   *The Rise and Fall of the Second Empire*, Cambridge University Press, 1985.

Raitt, Alan   *Life of Villiers de l'Isle-Adam*, Oxford, 1981.

Régnier, Henri de   'Faces et Profils: Méry Laurent' in *Le Figaro* of 23 July 1932.

—— *Nos Rencontres*, Mercure de France, 1931, pp. 213–14.

Rodocanachi, André   'Stéphane Mallarmé et Méry Laurent' in *Bulletin du Bibliophile*, 1979, vol. IV.

Sartre, Jean-Paul   *Situations*, Gallimard, vol. IX, 1972.

Walzer, Pierre-Olivier   *Essai sur Stéphane Mallarmé*, Seghers, 1963.

Index